Gordian III and Philip the Arab

Left: A coin of Gordian III
Right: A coin of Philip the Arab
Source: Cohen

A Legionary Horseman (first half of the 3rd century)
equipped with a *xyston*-spear, javelin holster with three javelins, *spatha*-sword (not shown), old-style *pugio*-dagger (a part of the handle visible), Newstead type *lorica segmentata* armour, round shield, and a hypothetical hybrid helmet mixing elements from Phrygian and Hedderheim helmets.

© Dr. Ilkka Syvänne 2020

Gordian III and Philip the Arab

The Roman Empire at a Crossroads

Dr. Ilkka Syvänne

'He [Gordian III] is a light-hearted lad, handsome, winning, agreeable to everyone, merry in his life, eminent in letters; in nothing, indeed, save his age was he unqualified for empire… all the people said Gordian was their darling. And, indeed Philip, after he had killed him, did not remove his portraits or throw down his statues or erase his name, but always called him divine.'

Julius Capitolinus, *Historia Augusta, Gordiani Tres* 31.4–7, tr. by Magie p.441.

'Next there will suddenly govern a purple-loving spearman shining forth from Syria, a terrible Ares, and with his son, a Caesar, he will ravage the whole earth.'

Oracula Sibyllina describing the beginning of the reign of
Philip the Arab, tr. by York, p.52

Pen & Sword
MILITARY

First published in Great Britain in 2021 by
Pen & Sword Military
An imprint of
Pen & Sword Books Ltd
Yorkshire – Philadelphia

Copyright © Dr. Ilkka Syvänne 2021

ISBN 978 1 52678 675 3

Printed and bound in the UK by TJ Books Ltd,
Padstow, Cornwall.

Pen & Sword Books Limited incorporates the imprints of Atlas, Archaeology,
Aviation, Discovery, Family History, Fiction, History, Maritime, Military,
Military Classics, Politics, Select, Transport, True Crime, Air World,
Frontline Publishing, Leo Cooper, Remember When, Seaforth Publishing,
The Praetorian Press, Wharncliffe Local History, Wharncliffe Transport,
Wharncliffe True Crime and White Owl.

For a complete list of Pen & Sword titles please contact

PEN & SWORD BOOKS LIMITED
47 Church Street, Barnsley, South Yorkshire, S70 2AS, England
E-mail: enquiries@pen-and-sword.co.uk
Website: www.pen-and-sword.co.uk

Or

PEN AND SWORD BOOKS
1950 Lawrence Rd, Havertown, PA 19083, USA
E-mail: Uspen-and-sword@casematepublishers.com
Website: www.penandswordbooks.com

Contents

Acknowledgements

First of all, I would like to thank the Commissioning Editor Philip Sidnell for accepting the book proposal. He also deserves a big thank you for his patience. Special thanks are also due to Matt Jones, Barnaby Blacker, marketing, and other staff at Pen & Sword for their stellar work and for the outstanding support they give the author. I would also like to thank my friends and family for their support and patience. Any mistakes are the sole responsibility of the author.

List of Plates

1. A coin of Julia Maesa. Source: Bernoulli.
2. A coin of Julia Mamaea. Source: Bernoulli.
3. Orbiana. Source: Bernoulli.
4–6. Alexander Severus depicted in three coins at different points in his life. Source: Bernoulli.
7–8. Maximinus Thrax depicted in two coins. Source: Bernoulli.
9. Maximinus Thrax and his son Maximus. Source: Bernoulli.
10. A coin of Gordian I. Source: Bernoulli.
11. A coin of Gordian II. Source: Bernoulli.
12. A coin of Balbinus. Source: Bernoulli.
13. A coin of Pupienus. Source: Bernoulli.
14. A coin of Furia Sabina Tranquillina, wife of Gordian III and daughter of Timesitheus. Source: Bernoulli.
15. A coin of Gordian III. Source: Bernoulli.
16. A coin of Philip the Arab. Source: Bernoulli.
17. A coin of Otacilia Severa, wife of Philip the Arab. Source: Bernoulli.
18–19. A coin of Alexander Severus. With the kind permission of ancientcointraders. com.
20. A coin of Alexander Severus. With the kind permission of ancientcointraders.com.
21. A coin of Philip the Arab Source: Bernoulli.
22–23. A coin of Jotapianus, usurper under Philip. Source: Delaroche.
24–25. A coin of Pacatianus, usurper under Philip. Source: Delaroche.
26–27. A coin of Philip Jr. Source: Delaroche.
28–29. A coin of Philip the Arab. Source: Delaroche.
30–31. A coin of Philip the Arab, Philip Jr. and Otacilia. Source: Delaroche.
32–33. Two sculptures depicting the emperor Alexander Severus. Source of the photos: Bernoulli.
34. A coin depicting Alexander Severus and Julia Mamaea. Source: Bernoulli.
35. A bust of Alexander Severus. Source: Bernoulli.
36–37. A bust of Julia Mamaea, mother of Alexander, Vatican. Source. Bernoulli.
38–39. A possible bust of Orbiana, wife of Alexander. Louvre. Source. Bernoulli.
40–41. A bust of Maximinus Thrax. Source: Bernoulli
42–43. A bust of Pupienus, Bracchio Nuovo. Source. Bernoulli.
44. A statue of Pupienus, Louvre. Source: Bernoulli
45. A bust of Balbinus, Vatican. Source: Bernoulli
46. A bust of Gordian III, Villa Albani. Source: Bernoulli.

List of Maps

Introduction

This book has been long in the making. It began as a project to understand the development of the Roman army and its cavalry forces of which the reign of Gallienus formed only a small part. Like the other books of mine dealing with the third century, the first version of the manuscript was ready in 2009. In this case it took until the fall of 2019 for it to be taken off the bookshelves.

When reading the following account, readers should keep in mind that the very poor survival of evidence for this era means that the material quite often allows many different interpretations. I will present all of these uncertainties in the following narrative together with the reasons why I have adopted a certain conclusion.

Timeline

The Likely Key Events of Gordian III's Reign (238–244)

238 Gordian III becomes the sole Augustus in June 238. The government is in the hands of his mother and her eunuch favourites until 241. The rebel Capelianus is crushed in North Africa in the fall of 238. Decius continues his revolt until 239 and surrenders. The invaders in the Balkans are crushed by Menophilus who keeps the area safe until he is sacked in 241.

239 The cashiering of the *legio III Augusta* in North Africa leads to endemic banditry. Ardashir I captures Dura Europos in 239, but then agrees to a truce. The ruler of Hatra raids Persian territory and breaks up the truce.

240 Sabinianus revolts in Carthage, but is defeated. Ardashir's son Sapor I besieges Hatra in 240 and captures it through treachery.

241–2 Sapor continues his invasion. An earthquake hits the Roman East, which helps the Persians to capture a number of cities which are defended by incompetent Roman commanders. The Persians capture Roman territory as far as Antioch and the Mediterranean Sea. The death of Ardashir gives the Romans a welcome break while Sapor secures the throne for himself. The Romans start to prepare a counterattack in 241. Gordian III removes his mother and her favourites from power. The barbarians invade the Balkans. The new de facto ruler is Praetorian Prefect Timesitheus. The Roman counterattack begins in 242. They defeat in succession the barbarian invaders in the Balkans and then the Persians.

243–4 Philip the Arab murders Timesitheus and succeeds him as Praetorian Prefect. The Romans are defeated at Mesikhe in early 244. Philip the Arab murders Gordian III in March 244.

The Likely Key Events of Philip's Reign (244–9)

244 Philip concludes peace with Persia in order to deal with two usurpations. He pays ransom for the captured soldiers and promises Mesopotamia and Armenia to Persia. After the usurpations were crushed, Philip betrays his promises to Sapor I. It is possible that Philip sent Decius to the Balkans to purge the army. Philip leaves his brother Priscus in charge of the East and goes to Rome.

245 Philip refuses to continue the payments to the Goths and provokes a war. Ostrogotha invades Moesia and Thrace. Philip marches to the Balkans and crushes the Gothic client tribes and arrives at Aquae in Dacia by 12 November 245. It is likely that operations against the Carpi were started at the same time. Philip dispatches Decius against the Goths. Decius is instructed to sack soldiers who then flee to Gothia. It is probable that these were purposefully infected with 'plague'. The soldiers incite Ostrogotha to invade again.

246–7 Philip instructs his brother Priscus to help the Armenians against the Persians in 246. The Romans and Armenians capture the Persian capital. Philip has now betrayed Sapor I twice. Ostrogotha assembles a massive army of 300,000 men under Argaithus and Gunthericus in 246. These invade Roman Moesia and besiege Marcianopolis. The Goths are unable to advance any further and settle on leaving in return for ransom. Philip engages the Carpi separately in a decisive battle at some point in time in 245–7. Philip incites the Gepids against the Goths in about 246 to divert them from Roman territory. The Goths, however, defeat the Gepids. The diversions and damage caused by fighting and germ warfare keep the Goths at bay until 250. Philip returns as a victor to the city of Rome by summer 247. Priscus is forced to abandon his Persian campaign and crush a revolt in Alexandria in late 247.

248 Millenary celebrations in Rome in April 248. The apogee of Philip's reign. Iotapianus usurps the power in the East during the summer, while Pacatianus usurps the power in the Balkans.

249 The fate of Priscus is unknown. Both usurpers are killed by their own men. Philip dispatches Decius to purge the army in the Balkans, which Decius exploits by usurping the power in his turn in April/May 249. Philip the Arab is killed in the battle of Verona or by assassins sent by Decius at Beroea in August/September 249.

Abbreviations

CAH	*Cambridge Ancient History*, several editors
HA	*Historia Augusta, Scriptores Historiae Augustae, Augustan History*
HA Alex.	*Historia Augusta, Alexander Severus*
HA Gord.	*Historia Augusta, Tres Gordiani, The Three Gordiani*
HA Max.	*Historia Augusta, Maximini Duo, The Two Maximini*
HA MB	*Historia Augusta, Maximus et Balbinus*
SKZ	*Res Gestae Divis Shapuris*

The principal legionary bases and headquarters in about 238

This map lists the known major bases of the legions in existence in 211, but it should be kept in mind that Alexander Severus raised new legionary forces for his eastern campaign. It is probable that these forces included also new legions and it has been suggested (e.g. by Parker, p.176) that Alexander raised *legio IV Italica* in 231, but which I would suggest was rather *legio IV Parthica*.

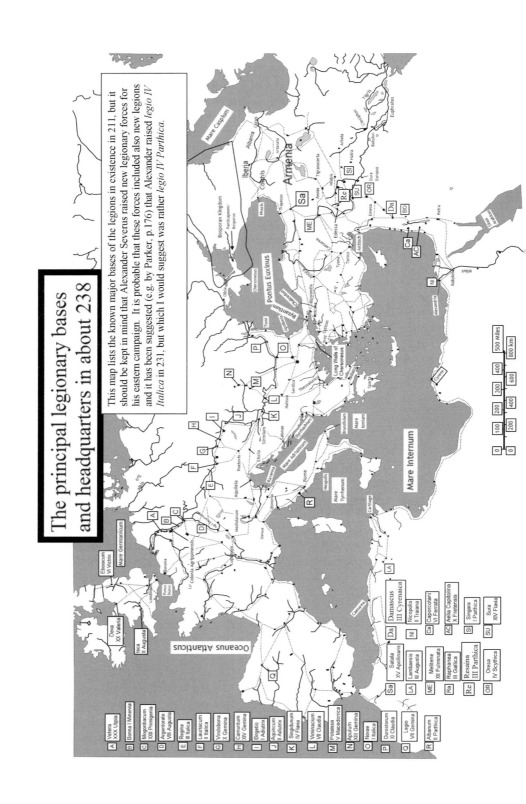

A	Vetera XXX Ulpia
B	Bonna I Minerva
C	Mogontiacum XXII Primigenia
D	Argentorate VIII Augusta
E	Regina III Italica
F	Lauriacum II Italica
G	Vindobona X Gemina
H	Carnuntum XIV Gemina
I	Brigeto I Adiutrix
J	Aquincum II Adiutrix
K	Singidunum IV Flavia
L	Viminacium VII Claudia
M	Potaissa V Macedonica
N	Apulum XIII Gemina
O	Novae I Italica
P	Durostorum XI Claudia
Q	Legio VII Gemina
R	Albanum II Parthica

Sa	Satala XV Apollinaris
LA	Lambaesis III Augusta
ME	Melitene XII Fulminata
Ra	Raphanea III Gallica
Re	Resaina III Parthica
OR	Onesa IV Scythica
Da	Damascus III Cyrenaica
NI	Nicopolis II Traiana
Ca	Caporcotani VI Ferrata
AC	Aelia Capitolina X Fretensis
SI	Singara I Parthica
SU	Sura XIV Flavia

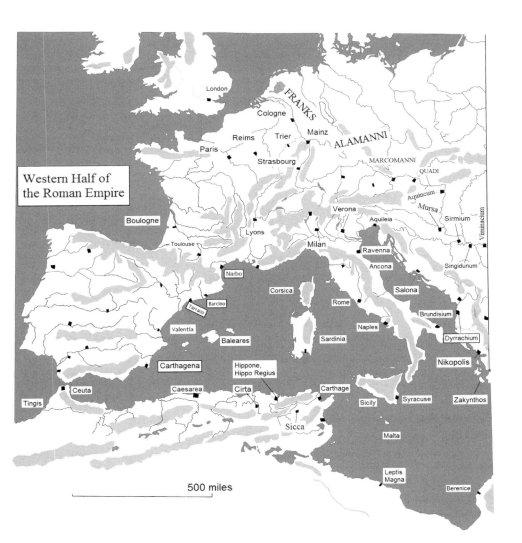

Western Half of
the Roman Empire

London
FRANKS
Cologne
Reims   Trier   Mainz   ALAMANNI
Paris   MARCOMANNI
Strasbourg   QUADI
                                    Aquincum
Boulogne   Verona   Mursa
Toulouse   Lyons   Aquileia   Sirmium
                         Milan   Ravenna   Singidunum
Narbo   Ancona
                    Corsica   Salona
Tarraco   Barcino   Rome   Brundisium
Valentia   Naples   Dyrrachium
         Baleares   Sardinia   Nikopolis
Carthagena   Hippone,   Carthage
Ceuta   Hippo Regius   Zakynthos
Tingis   Caesarea   Cirta   Syracuse
                         Sicca   Sicily
                         Sicca   Malta
                              Leptis
                              Magna   Berenice

500 miles

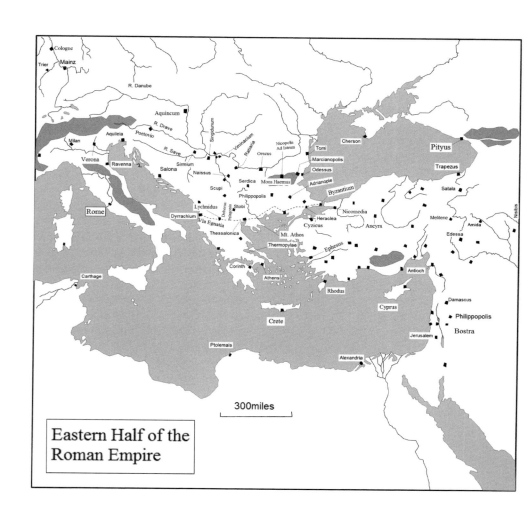

Eastern Half of the
Roman Empire

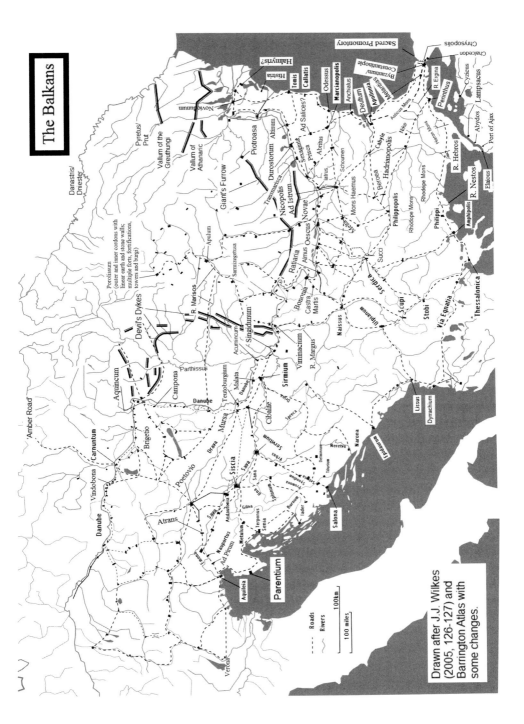

The Balkans

Drawn after J.J. Wilkes (2005, 126-127) and Barrington Atlas with some changes.

Roads
Rivers

100km
100 miles

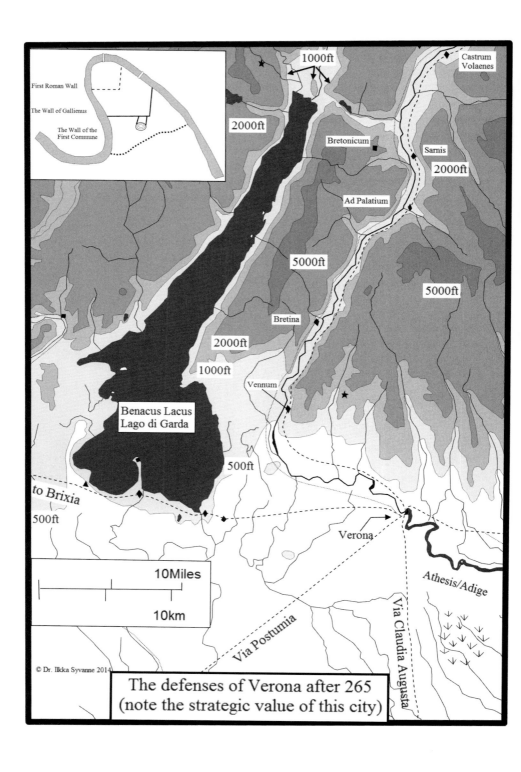

First Roman Wall

The Wall of Gallienus

The Wall of the
First Commune

1000ft

Castrum
Volaenes

2000ft

Bretonicum

Sarnis

2000ft

Ad Palatium

5000ft

5000ft

Bretina

2000ft

1000ft

Vennum

Benacus Lacus
Lago di Garda

500ft

to Brixia

500ft

Verona

Athesis/Adige

10Miles

10km

Via Postumia

Via Claudia Augusta

© Dr. Ilkka Syvänne 2014

The defenses of Verona after 265
(note the strategic value of this city)

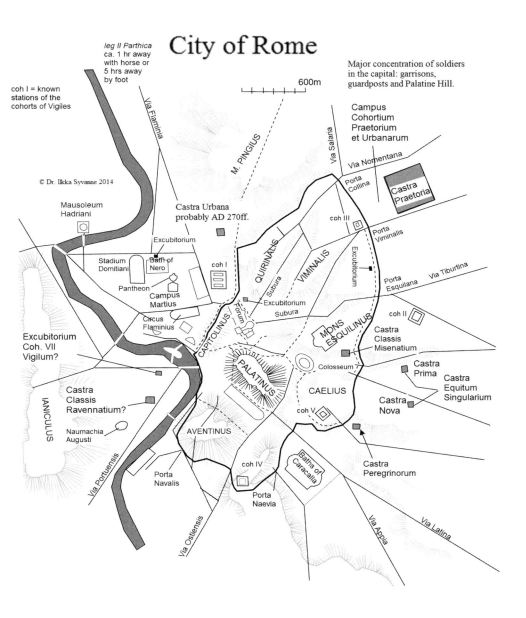

City of Rome

leg II Parthica ca. 1 hr away with horse or 5 hrs away by foot

coh I = known stations of the cohorts of Vigiles

600m

Major concentration of soldiers in the capital: garrisons, guardposts and Palatine Hill.

© Dr. Ilkka Syvänne 2014

Via Flaminia

M. PINGIUS

Via Salaria

Campus Cohortium Praetorium et Urbanarum

Via Nomentana

Porta Collina

Castra Praetoria

Mausoleum Hadriani

Castra Urbana probably AD 270ff.

coh III

Porta Viminalis

Excubitorium

QUIRINALIS

Stadium Domitiani

Bath of Nero

coh I

VIMINALIS

Excubitorium

Porta Esquilana

Via Tiburtina

Pantheon

Campus Martius

Subura

Via Portuensis

Porta Navalis

Circus Flaminius

CAPITOLINUS

Forum

Excubitorium

Subura

coh II

Castra Classis Misenatium

Excubitorium Coh. VII Vigilum?

MONS ESQUILINUS

Castra Prima

Castra Equitum Singularium

PALATINUS

Colosseum

CAELIUS

Castra Nova

Castra Classis Ravennatium?

IANICULUS

coh V

Naumachia Augusti

AVENTINUS

Castra Peregrinorum

coh IV

Baths of Caracalla

Porta Naevia

Via Ostiensis

Via Appia

Via Latina

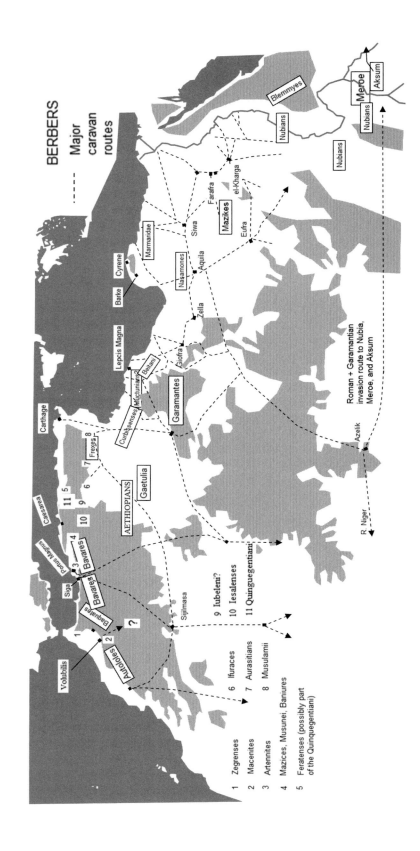

BERBERS

--- Major caravan routes

Berbers

Voltubilis
Caesarea
Carthage
Siga
Portus Magnus
Lepcis Magna
Cyrene
Barke
Marmaridae
Nasamones
Siwa
Farafra
el-Kharga
Blemmyes
Nubians
Nubians
Nubians
Meroe
Aksum
Maziikes
Aquila
Zella
Giofra
Eufra
Garamantes
Mictuniani?
Beltani?
Curubenses
Frexes
Gaetulia
AETHIOPIANS
Bavares
Bavares
Bavares
Baquates
Autololes
Sijilmasa
Azelik
R. Niger

Roman + Garamantian invasion route to Nubia, Meroe, and Aksum

1 Zegrenses
2 Macenites
3 Artennites
4 Mazices, Musunei, Baniures
5 Feratenses (possibly part of the Quinquegentiani)

6 Ifuraces
7 Aurasitians
8 Musulamii

9 Iubeleni?
10 Iesalenses
11 Quinquegentiani

11 5
9 6
10

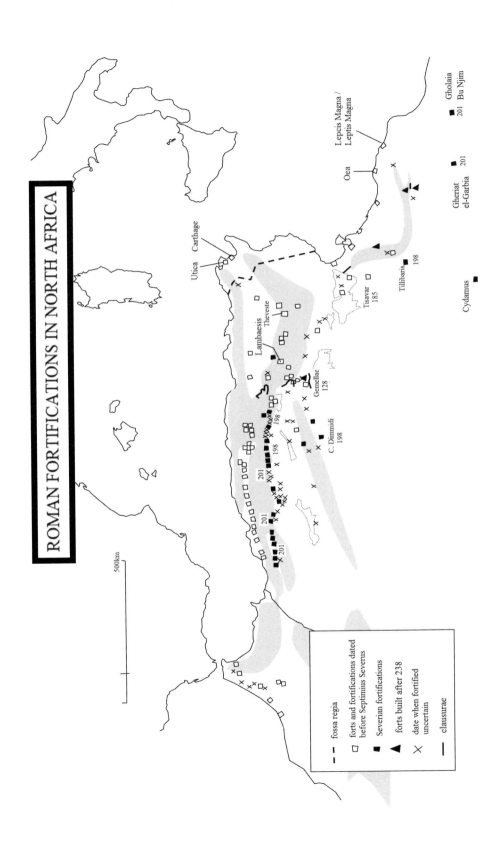

ROMAN FORTIFICATIONS IN NORTH AFRICA

500km

Utica
Carthage

Lambaesis
Theveste

Gemellae
128

C. Dimmidi
198

198

201

201

201

201

198

Oea

Lepcis Magna /
Leptis Magna

Tisavar
185

Tillibaris
198

Cydamus

Gheriat
el-Garbia

201

Gholaia
201 Bu Njim

fossa regia

forts and fortifications dated
before Septimius Severus

Severian fortifications

forts built after 238

date when fortified
uncertain

clausurae

BATTLE OF HARZHORN IN 235

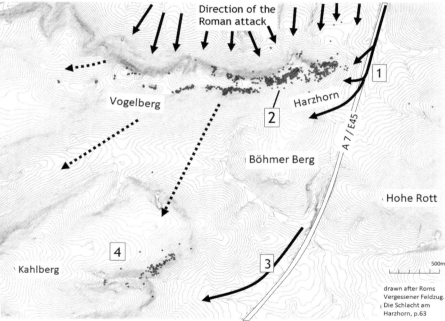

Direction of the Roman attack

Vogelberg

Harzhorn

1

2

A 7 / E45

Böhmer Berg

Hohe Rott

4

Kahlberg

3

500m

drawn after Roms
Vergessener Feldzug.
Die Schlacht am
Harzhorn, p.63

Archaeological finds.
Direction of the Roman attack.
Direction of the German flight.

BATTLE OF HARZHORN IN 235

1) Romans outflank the German right wing.
2) A Part of the German force was isolated and annihilated here while their left wing fled. This is proven by the direction of missile attacks from all directions.
3 Pursuing Roman cavalry cutting off the route of retreat.
4) Some of the fleeing Germans fled to Kahlberg where they were isolated and annihilated by pursuing Romans thanks to the effective pursuit shown in number 3 above.

Chapter One

The Sources and Analysis

1.1 The Sources

The principal literary sources for the reigns of Gordian III and Philip the Arab are: Herodian (early 3rd century), '*Res Gestae Divis Shapuris*' (3rd century), Anonymous *Eis Basilea* (3rd century), Eusebius of Caesarea with Jerome (4th–5th century), Orosius (375/80–417/8), Zosimus (early 6th century), Zonaras (beginning of the 12th century), *Synopsis Sathas/Synopsis Chronike* (1241), Cedrenus (11th–12th cent), *Historia Augusta* (turn of the 4th century and/or late 4th century also known as *Scriptores Historiae Augusta*), Sextus Aurelius Victor (c. 360 AD), *Epitome de Caesaribus* formerly wrongly also attributed to Aurelius Victor (turn of the 5th century), Eutropius' *Breviarium* (c.369 AD), Rufus Festus' *Breviarium* (c.370 AD), fragments of Herennius Dexippus (a period source from the 3rd century), fragments of Anonymous Continuator of Dio Cassius now attributed to Petrus Patricius/Peter the Patrician (6th century), Ammianus Marcellinus (4th century), Jordanes (6th century), Malalas (6th century), George Syncellus (early 9th century), fragments of John of Antioch (6–7th century), and other less important sources.[1]

The above list gives a misleading impression of the amount of evidence available for these reigns. In truth, there does not exist any detailed narrative of the reigns of these two emperors because we no longer possess the original period sources in their entirety – only the ones that have used them. The only detailed source is the period author Herodian, but his account stops at the death of Pupienus and Balbinus in 238. Thereafter the sources are far less detailed and reliable. It is because of this that there is a disproportionate amount of information available for the very beginning of the reign of Gordian III as *Caesar* in early 238, but there is far less available for his reign as *Augustus* from 238 until his death in 244. The situation is even worse for the reign of Philip the Arab. This results from the fact that the *Historia Augusta* has preserved a short biography of Gordian III but the reign of Philip the Arab is missing from the extant manuscripts. The end result of this is that we have more information for the beginning of Philip the Arab's reign in 244 because it is included in the biography of Gordian III, but we have very little evidence for the reign of Philip the Arab from 244 until his death in 249. In addition, much of this evidence is contradictory and unreliable. As a result, numismatics and analysis of inscriptions and legal codes have assumed extraordinary importance for the analysis of these reigns, especially for that of Philip the Arab. The inbalance in the evidence has also influenced the way in which I treat their reigns. As there is so much more information available for the period before August 238, it has taken a disproportionate amount of space in my biography of these emperors. However, it is impossible to understand the events after 238 without taking into account the events preceding it in 222–238.

The analysis of the extant narrative sources is also complicated by their biases. All of the extant narrative sources in the Greco-Roman tradition paint a favourable image of the reign of Gordian III while they paint the reign of Philip the Arab in the darkest possible terms. Most of these sources represented the viewpoint of the conservative faction within the Senate. These senators held a strong pagan bias against Christians and non-Romans such as Arabs, and when their views dominated the field among those who wrote histories, it was the view that was passed to the future generations. This strong and conservative senatorial block had been created under Septimius Severus and then strengthened under Alexander Severus, but it was internally divided in its attitude towards Christianity, hence the rise of two competing views towards it. I will therefore start my account of the reigns of Gordian III and Philip the Arab with a relatively long introduction of the reigns of Alexander Severus and Maximinus Thrax, which forms the background for the policies of the main narrative. On the basis of the fact that the emperor Licinius later claimed descent from the emperor Philip the Arab, it is clear that there existed at some point in time a version of history that was favourable towards him – Licinius would not have made that claim if it would have been harmful to him. This means that the rise of the Constantinian dynasty wiped clean that version of the history.[2]

The best narrative source for the era is the much maligned *Historia Augusta* and it is largely thanks to this text that we have better information for the reign of Gordian III than we have for the reign of Philip the Arab. A few words are in order to explain why this is so. The usual view among historians since the late nineteenth century has been that the *Historia Augusta* is a later fourth-century forgery by one person who pretended to be six different persons. This view can no longer be maintained. As discussed recently by Paul N. Pearson in his biography of *Maximinus Thrax* (Barnsley 2016, xxi ff.), the most recent research based on computer analysis has demonstrated that it is likelier that there were originally indeed six different authors as the book claims. The authors of the *Historia Augusta* claim that they wrote their texts at the turn of the fourth century and on the basis of their bias it is very likely that they did indeed do that. Uniform elements within these six texts are likely to be the result of the work of the person or persons who later united these six texts to form the *Historia Augusta* or merely from their similar cultural background. I will therefore call the authors of these books by their real names, but for clarity's sake I still use the traditional way of referencing so that I name the *Historia Augusta* as *HA* followed by the Book in question, for example as follows: *HA Gord.* (for Gordians) followed by the numbers. This approach to the sources removes the ridiculous situation in which historians use the *Historia Augusta* as a source but then make the cautious statement that it is not to be trusted. I do not deny that the *Historia Augusta* is highly unreliable – it is – but I am readier to accept its versions than is usually the case. In other words, I am inclined to accept its text when there are no strong reasons not to. The usual approach has been to accept its information only if it can be confirmed from other sources. As I have already shown in my previous books, the situation is sometimes the exact opposite: the other texts have to be confirmed against what is in the *Historia Augusta*. None of the sources named above are without their biases or falsifications, even if it is clear that a period source such as Dexippus is more reliable in general than the others. But unfortunately we possess only fragments of Dexippus's texts, some of which have been preserved only because the *Historia Augusta* used him. I take this same approach to the other sources too: I do not discard the evidence solely on the basis that it comes from an unreliable source. If one decides not to accept the evidence presented by the ancient source(s), one should always be able to explain why this is so, and the usual statement that it comes from an unreliable source will not do. This approach would result in the replacement of the only surviving evidence by our own subjective guess at what must have been.

The authors of the *Historia Augusta* that concern us here are:

Author:	Books
Aelius Lampridius	Antoninus Heliogabalus (Elagabalus), Alexander Severus
Julius Capitolinus	Maximini Duo, Maximus et Balbinus, Gordiani Tres
Trebellius Pollio	Tyranni Triginta
Flavius Vopiscus	Divus Aurelianus

To sum up my approach to the available sources of evidence I quote my biography of Gallienus: 'In short, there is one important difference between my approach to these sources and the traditional approach to the sources, which is that I put far more trust in the veracity of ancient sources than is usually done. History is a source-based art and when there are no strong reasons to suspect the information, it should be accepted as likely to be true or something which is as close to the truth as our defective sources would allow us to judge. If we decide to reject some piece of evidence presented in the sources, it should always be based on an analysis of the information known from other sources. The rejection of evidence solely on the basis of one's own subjective preconceived ideas is not real criticism. It is a travesty of our trade.'

Despite the above rather critical comments regarding the approach to the sources, my study has not been done in a vacuum. It still builds upon the work done by a number of great historians. In this study I have found most useful (in no particular order) the studies and translations (with perceptive comments) of the following: W. Ensslin, X. Loriot, E. Ketenhofen, T.M. Banchich, E.N. Lane, M.H. Dodgeon, S.N.C. Lieu, P. Southern, D.S. Potter, M. Christol, K. Herrmann, J.M. York, M.L. Meckler, C. Körner and Y. Zahran. I do not necessarily agree with their conclusions, but without their earlier groundbreaking research work this study would not be the same. As I noted in my biography of Gallienus: 'The surviving sources are so poor and contradictory that several alternative explanations and reconstructions are equally plausible. Therefore the reader is advised to read these previous studies to assess the probability of my reconstruction of the events. The following reconstruction is out of necessity quite speculative, but it has the advantage of being able to reconcile the other sources with the *Historia Augusta* – something that previous historians have not been able to do as they have not exploited the *Historia Augusta* to the same extent as I have.' The second of the reasons for the differing results of my studies is that I subject the sources to a new type of analysis.

1.2 My Analysis of Warfare and Battles

My approach to the analysis of warfare, combat and battles differs significantly from that typically followed by historians/classicists because those who have not specialized in military history fail to appreciate its intricacies. It is thanks to this that I believe that I have been able to use the military treatises and my knowledge of period military practices to fill in the blanks in the narrative sources. This means that I have used so-called 'military probability', which includes geography, rates of march, availability of information, logistical demands etc, and period military doctrine to shed additional light on the information provided by the sources.

As will be seen, it is clear that the extant narrative sources give us far too little information regarding period warfare. However, thanks to the fact that there exists some very specific information concerning methods of combat, battle formations and tactics in the period military treatise the *Kestoi* of Julius Africanus and in the sixth century *Strategikon* and in other ancient military treatises, it is possible to present some likely scenarios of what happened. Readers, however, are advised that these are speculative. Because of this I will always state when the reconstruction is based on an educated guess and include the thinking behind it. These sections are included for the purpose of giving readers a better sense of what is likely to have taken place and why I interpret the evidence the way I have. As I have noted in Gallienus, these sections of the text should be particularly useful for all those who are interested in the peculiarities of period warfare such as history buffs, military historians, wargamers, officers and officers in training.

I will provide a general overview of the Roman military and its combat methods in the introductory parts of this book, but since there exists better evidence for the reigns of Alexander Severus, Maximinus Thrax and Decius than there does for the reigns of Gordian III and Philip the Arab, I have decided to include longer discussions of combat methods based on the material from these reigns. I have already studied the reign of Decius in detail in my biography of Gallienus and have shown that it is an incontestable fact that he used large cavalry armies against the Gothic cavalry armies as described in the sixth-century *Strategikon*. Therefore I will not include discussion of his reign, but rather refer readers to this book. However, there are no detailed studies of the changes that took place in Roman armies under Alexander Severus and Maximinus Thrax and because of this I include relatively long discussions of these in two chapters preceding the rise of the Gordiani. It was the army of Alexander Severus and Maximinus Thrax that Gordian III inherited. This is the only way one can try to see what changes, if any, then took place under Gordian III and Philip the Arab.

Chapter Two

The Roman Military in the Third Century

2.1 The Background: Roman Society[1]

Roman society was a class society that was divided according to judicial and social hierarchies. The judicial hierarchy separated the populace into freemen, freedmen and slaves. The free populace consisted of those who had Roman citizenship and those who did not, but after the reign of Caracalla most of the free population were citizens. At the top of Roman society were the emperor and the imperial family. They were served by the imperial household with its staff that included freedmen, eunuchs and trusted slaves, while the emperor was advised and helped by his friends and advisors, including his official body of advisors called the *consilium*. The official social categories of the free citizens consisted of the senatorial order, equestrian order, and the plebs, but this division had become partly blurred because since the latter half of the second century there had existed a new form of class division which divided the people into *honestiores* and *humiliores*. The senators, equestrians, veterans, and decurions formed the *honestiores* class. They had legal privileges and exemptions from the harsher punishments to separate them from the *humiliores*. In addition there was a ranking system that added additional privileges. These included the following: the equestrian praetorian prefects had the rank of *viri eminentissimi*; the senators, the rank of *clarissimus*; and the officials of the court, the rank of *perfectissimi*. Despite these very real changes after the fall of the Roman Republic, the Senate and senators still expected to be treated with respect by the emperors. They still wielded very real informal power thanks to their great wealth and personal networks of connections. It was therefore important to court the opinions of these factions.

In theory the civilian and military offices still followed the so-called *cursus honorum*, which reserved certain posts for the members of the senatorial order and others for the members of the equestrian order in such a manner that the very highest posts were the prerogative of the former. However, the emperors could, if they so wished, bypass these requirements and appoint anyone they liked to any position they thought necessary, but obviously at the risk of alienating the senators. Furthermore, the importance of the posts reserved for the senators was illusionary because the most important military command(s) of the Empire, the post(s) of the Praetorian Prefect(s) was/were reserved for a member(s) of the equestrians order, but as already stated, the emperors could decide to bypass this requirement too. The prefectures of the legions in Egypt and of the Parthian legions were also officially reserved for the equestrians. The administrative system of the Empire reflected the special privileges of the emperor, senators, Italy and Rome so that there existed a special administration for Rome and Italy, while the provinces were divided into those governed by the Senate and into those (further divided into equestrian and senatorial provinces) governed by the Emperor.

The Roman economy was based on agriculture, but in contrast to most of its neighbours the Empire also had very significant artisan and merchant classes. This means that most tax income came from the peasants through the city councils for use by the imperial administration. This was problematic because the taxes obtained from the peasants varied from one year to another depending on the size of the harvest. Crops were vulnerable to foreign invasions and civil wars, as well as to the weather. So the emperors tapped also other sources of income to make up for the possible deficiencies. They taxed the produce of the imperial estates and mines, donatives, raised extraordinary taxes levied when needed, confiscated the property of the rich with various excuses like fake charges, conscripted soldiers (or threatened to do so to produce money), and raised tolls and customs (collected from internal and external trade). If the emperors did not want to anger the rich citizens they could also borrow money, debase coins or sell imperial property – the last of these was obviously a very dangerous practice if it included the selling of productive property such as mines or imperial farms because it was a one time fix that lowered income permanently. The customs duties collected from long distance trade with Arabia, Africa, India and China formed one of the most important sources of revenue for the emperor.

2.2 The Armed Forces and the Security Apparatus in ca. AD 222[2]

The Roman armed forces and security apparatus consisted of several different arms of service. The official part of the security apparatus consisted of the land forces (legions, auxiliaries, national *numeri*), navy, *vigiles* (firemen/policemen), *urbaniciani* (policemen, urban combat troops) and imperial bodyguard units (*praetoriani;* and *equites singularis augusti/germani; aulici/collegia/scholae/protectores;* and *evocati*). In addition, the Romans had treaty-bound allied forces (*foederati*) to bolster their armed strength, and land and naval forces provided by the paramilitary civilian citizen militias and policemen.

2.2.1 The Land Forces
Roman land forces consisted of: 1) the forces posted in or near the capital; 2) regular legions (citizens); 3) regular auxiliary forces (citizens); 4) national *numeri* (including citizens and non–citizens);[3] 5) veterans called for service; 6) urban and rural paramilitary militias; 7) and the allies.

Ever since the first century most of the regular forces (legions, auxiliaries, *numeri*) had been posted near the borders of the Empire to provide a zone of exclusive security for the provinces and the interior. These frontier forces may have obtained the nickname of the *limitanei* (*HA Pesc.* 7.7; *Alex. Sev.* 58.4) by the turn of the third century. The frontier forces and fortifications that housed them served four strategic purposes: 1) they acted as deterrence against would-be invaders; 2) the garrisons could be used to engage the enemy in the border region; 3) the garrisons could be used for surprise attacks and for major invasions/raids; 4) and they gathered intelligence.

In 222 there appear to have existed two different legionary organizations: the first created in the late first century and the second by Septimius Severus or by one of his immediate predecessors. The latter is described by Modestus and Vegetius[4]. The consensus among historians is that the standard legions consisted of about 5,120 heavy infantrymen plus recruits, servants, horsemen and specialists. The legion consisted of smaller units: 10 cohorts (nine quingenary cohorts with 480 men and one milliary cohort with 800 men), 32 maniples of 160 men, 64 centuria of 80 men, and 640 *contubernia* of eight men. Each *contubernium* (tent group/file in rank and file array) consisted of eight men, one green recruit and one servant so that it in truth consisted of ten men under a commander called the *decanus*. Severus's Parthian legions differed from the above in that they were always commanded by equestrians and had more infantry and horsemen. Regardless of type, all legionaries could vary their tactics. All were taught how to throw javelins, thrust with a spear or javelin, use swords and daggers, and how to throw stones and use slings, but only a third or quarter of the soldiers could fight as archers. In addition they were trained in martial arts skills and in the use of various tools as ersatz weapons.

The amount of armour worn by the legionaries and the type of shield and type of martial equipment depended on the mission and unit. Each of the legions had also a cavalry contingent consisting of 500 to 600 horsemen (but typically a 512 horseman *ala*) while the Parthian legions of Septimius Severus had 726 horsemen plus supernumeraries all of whom were taught how to use spears, javelins, swords, crossbow, shield and composite bow so they could be used for a great variety of missions. For additional details, see in particular Syvänne, *Aurelian and Probus*, Appendix 1. The inclusion of additional specialists like the artillerymen gave the legions great flexibility to perform all sorts of siege engineering projects and other engineering/building projects. The following lists, which are based on my earlier treatises,[5] give both legionary variants. In practice it was rare for the entire legion to march out into combat, so the campaigning forces typically consisted only of detachments of ca. 2,000–3,000 men.

STANDARD LEGION
Probable command structure of the regular legion c. AD 90–260

- 1 Legate (S) until the reign of Gallienus who abolished the office; or Prefect (E) for the Egyptian and Parthian legions. After Gallienus the commanders were prefects (E); commander of the legion.
- 1 Laticlavian tribune (S) changed by Gallienus into *tribunus maior* (E); in charge of one cohort and second-in-command of the legion.
- 1 *Praefectus Castrorum* (camp, medics, siege equipment etc) (E).
- 1 *Praefectus Fabrorum* (workmen, construction etc) (E).
- 5 tribunes (E) each in charge of one cohort 480 men.
- 1 *tribunus sexmenstris* (in charge of cav.?) (E).
- 5 centurions of the 1st Cohort (incl. *primus pilus* who could act as *praepositus* for the cohort).
- 54 centurions (called *centenarii* by the end of the third century):
  5 unattached centurions that could be detailed for variety of purposes; these could be used e.g. as acting *praepositi* (commanders for the cohorts (à 480 men).
  9 x 1 centurion each in charge of two centuries (2 x 80).
  9 x 4 centurions each in charge of one century (80 men).
  4 cavalry centurions of 128 horsemen.

- 64 infantry *decani* one of whom was optio/second-in-command to centurion (each *decanus* part of and in charge of their 8-man file/*contubernium*, in addition to which came a *tiro*/recruit and one servant used for the guarding of the camp).
- 16 cavalry decurions (each in charge of their 32 horsemen *turma*).
- 1st cohort 800 men (5 centuries à 160 men) plus 100 recruits and 100 servants.
- cohorts 2 to 10 = 9 x 420 men on foot (including the *decani* 480) plus 60 recruits and 60 servants per cohort.
- 496 horsemen (with the decurions 512; Vegetius may have been wrong in adding the decurions to the strength of the *turma*, because the Roman cavalry organization was based on the Greek one; however, if Vegetius is correct then these should be added to the total for a total of 512+16 decurions plus about 128 servants/squires.
- at least about 715 artillerymen in charge of the 55 *carroballistae* (cart-mounted bolt/arrow shooters) and 10 *onagri* (single-armed stone-throwers).
- 10 *speculatores* (formerly scouts), but now couriers, police officers, and executioners.
- *proculcatores* and *exploratores* scouted the roads. It is not known whether these counted as part of the cavalry or were separate from it. In practice the *mensores* could also act as scouts.
- unknown numbers of military police with the title of *stator*, and unknown numbers of guard dogs. Inside each camp there was also a police station called *statio* under a tribune. Some of the soldiers were also used as sentinels (*excubitores*) and there were other specific guards for various purposes.
- in addition there were unknown numbers of other specialists and bureaucrats consisting of surveyors, *campidoctor* (Chief Instructor), *haruspex* (read the entrails prepared by *victimarius*), *pullarius*, *actuarii*, *librarii* (*librarius a rationibus* worked also for the state post and could act as a spy), *notarii* (the notaries could serve simultaneously as the emperor's undercover spies whilst also serving as commander's notaries, diplomats and spies), *commentariensis* (archivist under head curator), heralds, standard-bearers, *draconarii*, cape-bearers, trumpeters, drummers, engineers, workmen, artisans, hunters, carters and cartwrights, doctors, medics etc.
- the legates/prefects were also guarded by a unit of *singulares* (both inf. and cav.), which consisted of detached auxiliaries. (Confusingly the staff officers in training could also be called *singulares*). These bodyguards were replaced by *protectores* detached by the emperor from his staff at the latest during the reign of Gallienus as a safety measure against usurpations.
- the legion also included beasts of burden (depending on the units could be horses, asses, mules, camels, oxen).

(S) = senatorial office; (E) = equestrian office

THE PARTHIAN LEGIONS CREATED BY SEPTIMIUS SEVERUS
The Ancient Legion of Modestus and Vegetius (2.6ff.) with additional comments in brackets.
- 1 *praefectus legionis* formerly *legatus*; commander of the legion.

- 1 *tribunus maior*; appointed by the emperor in charge of one cohort (probably the 1st; second-in-command of the legion).
- 1 *Praefectus Castrorum* (camp, medics, siege equipment etc).
- 1 *Praefectus Fabrorum* (workmen, construction etc).
- *tribuni minores* from the ranks (6 tribunes? put in charge of the cohorts and cavalry alongside with the *praepositi*).
- 5 centurions of the 1st Cohort (Vegetius' list differs from the other known lists of officers and is also 100 men short of the 1,100 men he gives for the 1st Cohort)
  primus pilus in charge of 4 centuries/400 men (this probably means that there were 440 men consisting of 4 centuries each with 110 men)
  primus hastatus 'now called *ducenarius*' in charge of two centuries/200 men (probably 220 men)
  princeps 1½ centuries/150 men (probably 165 men)
  secundus hastatus 1½ centuries/150 men (probably 165 men)
  triarius prior 100 men (probably 110 men)
- 5 centurions for the cavalry.
- 45 centurions of the 2nd to 10th COs each in charge of 100 men 'now' called *centenarii*.
- 1st Cohort: 1,105 men on foot (this probably means that there were 720 heavy infantry deployed 4 deep and 360 light infantry deployed by 2 deep + 10 optiones, 10 standard-bearers, and 5 centurions)
    132 horsemen (128 horsemen and 4 decurions; in truth the decurions may have been part of the 128 horsemen in addition to which came one centurion, 2 musicians and one standard-bearer; when trained to do so the 128 horsemen could form a rhombus so that at each apex stood one decurion).
- 2nd to 10th Cohorts: 9 x 555 men on foot ((this probably means that there were 360 heavy infantry deployed four deep and 180 light infantry deployed 2 deep + 5 optiones, 5 standard-bearers, 5 centurions)
    9 x 66 horsemen (64 horsemen and 2 decurions; as noted above the decurions should probably be included as part of the 64 horsemen; the 64 men could be formed either as a wedge or two rank-and-file oblongs).
- artillerymen (55 *carroballistae* each with 11 men and 10 *onagri* per legion), 'squires', servants and various kinds of standard-bearers and musicians and other specialists like clerks, medics, wood-workers, masons, carpenters, blacksmiths, painters, siege-equipment builders, armourers etc. (*aquiliferi, imaginarii/ imaginiferi, signiferi/draconarii, tesserarii, optiones, metatores, librarii, tubicines, cornicines, buccinators, mensores, lignarios, structores, ferrarios, carpentarios, pictores* etc.)

Regular auxiliary units, both infantry and cavalry, consisted of either quingenary or milliary units, but there also existed mixed infantry and cavalry units of these sizes. There were some specialist units of archers and javeliners, but most of the auxiliary units possessed similar flexibility as the legions in that they could be used either as line infantry/cavalry or as skirmishing forces. There was no uniformity in the size of the unit or type of unit among the so-called *numeri*. The allies (*foederati*) contributed whatever type of force they had available for Roman use so one cannot make any categorization of their types. These, like the *numeri*, came in various sizes and their equipment was equally varied. The following list (based on my earlier studies) gives an overall picture of the organization.

Approximate size and organization of auxiliary units:

Unit	Foot	Horse	Centuries	Turmae
Cohors Quingenaria Peditata	480		6	
Cohors Quingenaria Equitata	480	128	6	4
Cohors Milliaria Peditata	800		10	
Cohors Milliaria Equitata	800	256	10	8
Ala Quingenaria		512		16
Ala Milliaria		768 (campaign strength?)	24	
		1024 (paper strength?)	32	
Numeri (mercenaries)	varied	varied	varied	varied
Foederati (treaty based allies)	varied	varied	varied	varied

The forces posted in or near the capital formed the mobile reserve army at the disposal of the Emperor. The imperial bodyguards consisted of the *praetoriani* (10,240 foot 1,920 horse?); 300 cavalry *speculatores*; a *numerus* of *statores Augusti*; *equites singulares Augusti* (2,048 horsemen of barbarian origin); *frumentarii* (spies); *peregrini* (spies); *stablesiani* under *tribunus stabuli*; unknown numbers of *evocati Augusti* (veteran praetorians who had been recalled back to service); and unknown numbers of the *scholarii/aulici/candidati/collegia/ostensionales/protectores*. The capital also included the Urban Cohorts (*cohortes urbanae/urbaniciani*, 4,500 policemen also usable as a military force) and the *vigiles* (7,000 firemen and policemen) under *praefectus urbi*, and within marching distance there was the *legio II Parthica* located at Alba (Albanum). There were additional Urban Cohorts at least at Ostia, Puteoli, Lyon and Carthage, but it is probable that additional ones existed about which we know nothing. These units of *urbaniciani* operated throughout the Empire to secure supplies for the capital on behalf of the Urban Prefect. Rome had permanent detachments of marines/sailors drawn from the Praetorian Fleets of Ravenna and Misenum which accompanied the Emperor during important campaigns. Lastly there were always soldiers on leave in Rome to enjoy the many entertainments of that delightfully decadent city. In addition to this, the emperor could raise new legions out of Italians, but since this was highly unpopular it was not used often.

During this era the equipment of the legionary and regular auxiliary infantry was basically the same. The equipment of the bodyguard units differed from this only in that their gear was fancier with decorations etc added. The typical equipment of this era consisted of: 1) sword (the *spatha*-longsword used primarily for cuts, but could also be used for thrusts; short ring-pommel sword/*semispatha* primarily used against infantry)

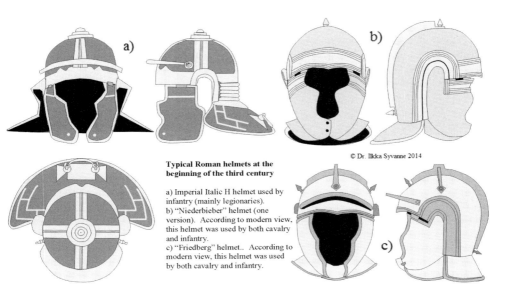

Typical Roman helmets at the beginning of the third century

a) Imperial Italic H helmet used by infantry (mainly legionaries).
b) "Niederbieber" helmet (one version). According to modern view, this helmet was used by both cavalry and infantry.
c) "Friedberg" helmet.. According to modern view, this helmet was used by both cavalry and infantry.

© Dr. Ilkka Syvänne 2014

and dagger (used in combat only in emergencies); 2) the shafted weapon (typically the traditional *pilum* heavy javelin or *hasta*-spear or *lancea* that had two variants: light javelin and thrusting spear); 3) flat or slightly curved shield (typically oblong or rectangular in shape, but also round, hexagonal and octagonal shields. Some of the rectangular shields retained their traditional heavily cylindrical curved shape); 4) armour (the traditional *lorica segmentata*, i.e. the segmented plate armour; the *lorica squamata* scale armour; *lorica hamata* mail armour; rigid and soft leather armour; muscle armour of bronze or rigid leather; *thoracomachus* or *subarmalis*, i.e. a padded coat of linen, leather, or felt) but when the situation demanded the soldiers could be ordered to fight un-armoured; 5) helmet (typically the so-called Imperial Italic H/Niedermörmter helmet or helmets like the so-called Niederbieber, Buch, Regensburg, Friedberg, Kalkar-Hönnepel, and Dura helmets; but older helmets, segmented, leather etc continued in use).

In about 233–4 Julius Africanus claimed that this type of equipment had some serious drawbacks.[6] The typical handle for the shield consisted of the single grip in the middle of the shield, which meant that it was not usable for pushing and shoving in a massed fight. This is true, but at the same time it is clear that the shield grip was quite well-suited to sword fighting. He also claimed that the typical period helmet which reached down to the shoulders made it difficult for the Roman soldiers to duck enemy missiles, and he also claimed that the helmet was too weak to resist slingshots and that it hindered the vision so badly that it was difficult for the soldiers to see missiles. This is only partially accurate. The helmets did indeed reach down to the shoulders, but it would have been easy enough for the men just to bend their knees or raise their shields for defence. He also claimed that the Roman spear was too short to stop enemy cavalry attacks. This was definitely true of the *pilum* and also of the standard size for the *hasta*, because it appears to have been only about 2.5 metres long. However, on the basis of archaeological finds the Romans also used a longer 3.74 metre cavalry spear (*kontarion*, *contus*), although it appears not to have

A lightly-equipped *lanciarius*. The *lanciarii* were javelin-armed legionaries who were used to fight in front of the battle line as *antesignani*.

Above middle: A typical archer
Above right: a drawing of a heavy armed soldier depicted on a painting in Dura Europos. Note the coif and six-sided shield.

there were several different types of pila some of which are shown here

there is no definite evidence for the use of these two types after late 2nd cent.

tanged pila

A legionary in typical period legionary equipment using the Imperial Italic H-helmet and the Newstead *lorica segmentata*. However, other types of helmet, armour, shield and spears were also used.

The archaeological finds from Harzhorn prove that the Roman heavy infantry used socketed *pila* at that battle.

Roman legionary
Legio II Parthica
- *hasta*, *spatha*, oval shield, Heddernheim helmet, greaves, *manica* arm-protection and *lorica hamata*.

(drawn partially after the reconstruction of A. Zimmermann in Gräf)

© Dr. Ilkka Syvänne 2014

the hasta was primarily used against cavalry, but could also be used against infantry

been standard issue for the infantry. This discussion, however, misses the most important point which is that it was quite possible for a well-drilled and motivated force to resist the charge of the enemy cavalry even with the shorter spears, the best evidence of which are the numerous instances in which the Roman legionaries resisted enemy cavalry when they were equipped only with the *pila*. As I have already pointed out, the above list of

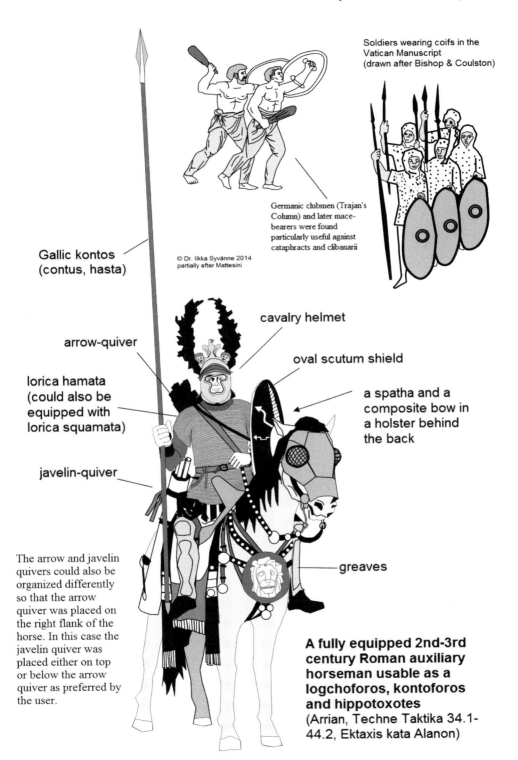

Soldiers wearing coifs in the Vatican Manuscript (drawn after Bishop & Coulston)

Germanic clubmen (Trajan's Column) and later mace-bearers were found particularly useful against cataphracts and clibanarii

© Dr. Ilkka Syvänne 2014
partially after Mattesini

Gallic kontos (contus, hasta)

cavalry helmet

arrow-quiver

oval scutum shield

lorica hamata (could also be equipped with lorica squamata)

a spatha and a composite bow in a holster behind the back

javelin-quiver

The arrow and javelin quivers could also be organized differently so that the arrow quiver was placed on the right flank of the horse. In this case the javelin quiver was placed either on top or below the arrow quiver as preferred by the user.

greaves

A fully equipped 2nd-3rd century Roman auxiliary horseman usable as a logchoforos, kontoforos and hippotoxotes
(Arrian, Techne Taktika 34.1-44.2, Ektaxis kata Alanon)

complaints come from commanders who excused their defeats on supposedly defective equipment. They also blamed defective tactics and tactical formation (the hollow square).[7] I will elaborate on this issue in the following narrative and will pinpoint the likely culprit behind these claims.

In addition, the Roman army included a number of other specialists: clubmen, archers, slingers, siege-engineers and artillerymen. A quarter to a third of the legionaries were trained as archers and all were trained to use slings and throw stones. This means that the so-called heavy infantry could be deployed in light gear in combat formation when necessary. Depending on the depth of the heavy infantry array, the archers and slingers usually formed ranks 5–6, 9–12 or 17–24 (these consisted of auxiliaries when possible), but the texts of Modestus and Vegetius show that when the heavy infantry was equipped with light gear they could be mixed in the ranks reserved for the 'heavy infantry' while true light infantry was still placed behind them (but they could advance in front to skirmish and back). When necessary the legionaries could use spades, axes, hatchets, pickaxes and so forth. The archery equipment used by the Romans consisted of recurved composite bows, wooden bows, crossbows with composite or metal construction (*arcuballista*) and of torsion-powered crossbows (*manuballista*). The slingers used either the traditional sling or the staff-sling. Artillerymen employed torsion or tension (steel or bronze springs) powered ballistae/catapults (dart, spear and stone throwers) and *onagri* of various calibres (stone thrower). The siege-engineers in their turn used various other kinds of siege engines.[8]

The regular legionary and auxiliary cavalry was equipped as the situation required because they had been trained as multipurpose troops able to fight at long distance and in mêlée. They used typically the four-horned cavalry saddle that gave the riders a secure platform for any kind of fighting, but they also used saddles without horns or mere blankets. The regular cavalry was equally usable as javelin throwers, lancers, swordsmen, archers and crossbowmen. Therefore the martial equipment used by the cavalry consisted of the various types of spears/lances (*lancea*, *xyston, hasta*, Gallic *contus/kontarion*), *spatha*-sword, *pugio*-dagger, sling, composite bow, and crossbow. The *lancea* and *xyston* were either thrown or used for thrusting (with underarm, overarm etc techniques). The *hasta* and Gallic *contus* (ca. 3.74 m long) were primarily used for thrusting, but could also be thrown if needed. Those units that used the Sarmatian *contus* did not carry shields because this lance required a two-handed grip. On horseback the *spatha* was primarily used for cuts but could also be used as a thrusting weapon. The type of armour and helmet depended in the unit and situation, as did the armour worn by horses; when needed the regular Roman cavalry used frontal armour and head protection for their mounts. Arrian's description of cavalry training and the composition of the legionary cavalry prove that the legionary cavalry could be used as line cavalry, and assault and skirmish troops as needed.

2.2.2 Combat on Land and Tactics

Roman military doctrine contained a number of expectations. Firstly, it expected that the generals would always possess first-rate intelligence of enemy activities and adequate supplies so that they could choose the time and place to engage the enemy in the most advantageous way, for example with surprise attacks or ambushes. Standard Roman combat doctrine continued to be based on the combined arms concept, but so that the Romans could use cavalry separately from their infantry. The use of the combined arms concept means that in most cases all of the Roman armies included light infantry, heavy infantry, light cavalry, heavy cavalry and/or multipurpose troops usable for combined and joint arms operations with the navy, siege engineers and allies.

The Standard Legionary Combat Formations in 275 according to Modestus

During this era the infantry forces could be deployed in cohorts (one to four lines) or as phalanxes so that the battle line was usually divided into left, centre and right. The infantry typically used rank and file formations in open, closed and tortoise orders (several different variants, each of which had a shield roof) as required. The irregular *droungos*-order was also used when needed. The standard ways to defeat the enemy were: 1) to push through the enemy line with deeper formations or with a wedge array; 2) to outflank the enemy on one flank; 3) to outflank the enemy on both flanks. There were several different grand tactical formations (e.g. oblique, forward–angled hollow square, rearward–angled hollow square, flanks sent forward separately) that could be used to achieve these. On the basis of Modestus and Vegetius the standard battle arrays of this era were the single line (*simplex acies*), double line (*duplex acies*), *acies quadratum* (hollow square/oblong) and *triangulum/cuneus* (triangle/wedge). However, this is contradicted by Julius Africanus who claims that the Romans employed only the hollow square as their principal combat formation. This contention receives support from the only extant details of period combat, but it is still clear that the soldiers were also taught how to fight in the other formations even if it is probable that the hollow square was indeed the principal formation in use. The double line/phalanx requires additional explanation. Its different lines could be formed in three different ways: 1) the units of the single phalanx could be divided in the middle so that the rear ranks marched back and formed the second phalanx; 2) the cohorts of the same larger division could be deployed one after another; 3) the larger units like legions could be deployed one after another. The single and double line formations and the hollow square usually had separate reserves of infantry and cavalry. The wedge array is likely to mean only the unit version rather than actual large scale combat array.

The principal cavalry combat formation consisted of two cavalry lines. The best description of this array and its details comes from a later military treatise called the *Strategikon*. However, it is probable that the third line (the 'rear guards') depicted in this treatise was added later by the Emperor Gallienus as a result of the lessons learned from the defeat of Decius at Abrittus in 251. In that battle the Goths used a double ambush, which removed the last Roman reserve, namely their second line from use so that they did not possess any reserves when the Goths launched their second ambush, hence the addition of the third line. The double cavalry line had three different variants: large cavalry army (10,000–50,000) with four larger units of reserves (in cavalry armies larger than this the extra units were deployed separately probably behind), medium sized force (5,000–15,000) with two reserve divisions and small cavalry army (5,000) with only one reserve division.

The standard tactical uses for all of these were: 1) the centre division was used to crush the enemy's centre if the Romans had fewer men; 2) the right wing was used to outflank the enemy's left wing if both had the same number of men; 3) the left wing was used to outflank the enemy's right, but this was used less often; 4) both flanks outflanked the enemy if the Romans had more men; 5) ambushers were used against the enemy flanks when possible; 6) the first line or its runners (*koursores* posted on the flanks of each division) were used for skirmishing to draw the enemy into a disorderly pursuit;

First line

Flank guards, 1-3 banda	Meros of Vexillations	Meros of Federates	Meros of Illyrikiani	Outflankers 1-2 banda

Second, or support line

Meros	Tagma	Meros of Optimates	Tagma	Meros	Tagma	Meros

Rearguard	Baggage train	Reserve horses 1		Rearguard

Reserve horses 2

⚇	Strategos (general)	ε	Merarch	†	Bandon of the koursores	T	Touldon
Φ	Hypostrategos (lieutenant general)	M	Moirarch	d	Deputatoi (medical corpsmen)	Ϟ	Bandon of the baggage train guard, if present
N	Taxiarch of the Optimates	♂	Bandon of the defensores	λ	Reserve horses, if present		

7) the entire frontline could charge on the double if it was advantageous to avoid for example showers of arrows; 8) if the enemy defeated any or all of the frontline divisions, the second line protected it; 9) the fill-up *banda* (and after their introduction the third line) could be used to defend the rear against outflanking; 10) the commander could use his own personal bodyguards (and the third line after its introduction) and fill-up *banda* as his emergency reserves. The combat unit orders were: 1) the close order with trot and canter for the defenders (*defensores* posted in the centre of each division to protect the *koursores*); 2) and the irregular *droungos*-order (throng) for the *koursores* and any unit that required speed to perform its duties.

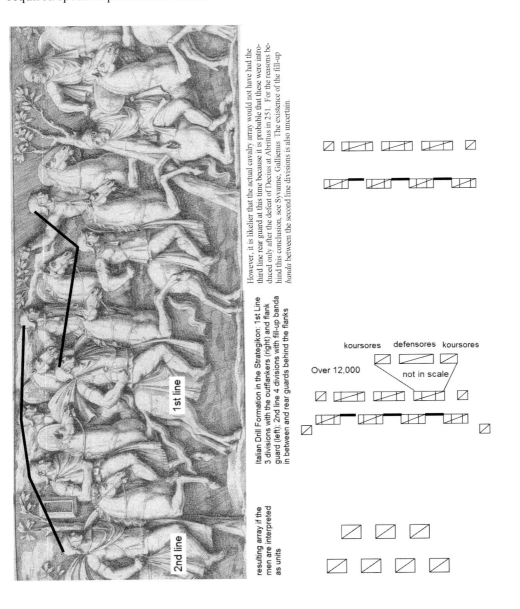

Italian Drill Formation in the Strategikon: 1st Line 3 divisions with the outflankers (right) and flank guard (left); 2nd line 4 divisions with fill-up banda in between and rear guards behind the flanks

However, it is likelier that the actual cavalry array would not have had the third line rear guard at this time because it is probable that these were introduced only after the defeat of Decius at Abritus in 251. For the reasons behind this conclusion, see Syvanne, Gallienus. The existence of the fill-up *banda* between the second line divisions is also uncertain.

resulting array if the men are interpreted as units

1st line

2nd line

koursores   defensores   koursores

Over 12,000

not in scale

The cavalry formations consisted of the divisions (*mere* 6,000–7,000 horsemen) each of which consisted of three *moirai* ('regiments', sing. *moira*, max. size 3,000 horsemen), and each of the *moirai* consisted of smaller *banda / tagmata / arithmoi* each of which had 200–400 horsemen. The *banda* etc in turn were divided into smaller units of approximately 100 men, which were apparently of no importance as battle units.

The diagram with Greek symbols on page 16 has been taken directly from the *Strategikon* and shows the standard battle array as envisaged by the Romans. It shows the diagram of the large cavalry array (the Italian Drill formation) in the *Strategikon*. The diagrams on page 17 of cavalry battle formations depicts my interpretation of one of the scenes in the Column of Trajan which shows the Romans using the same array.

© Dr. Ilkka Syvanne 2019

A Sarmatian or Alan cataphract shooting backwards at pursuers. However, on the basis of the Roman cavalry training, he could equally well be a member of, for example, the *Ala I Pannoniorum*. He is not a member of the *catafractarii* unit that would regularly wear the full panoply of armour, but he has been equipped as such in this image. Ever since the days of Hadrian (Arrian, *Ars Tactica* 44.1), officers could demand that Roman horsemen equip themselves like Parthian and Armenian horse archers and Sarmatian and Celtic *contus*-bearers, in other words, like Sarmatian cataphracts; in fact the Romans even had a unit called *Ala Gallorum et Pannoniorum Catafractaria / Catafractata*. The figure is based on Trajan's Column with the assumption that it is based on real life Sarmatian equipment. The assumption is that the legs of the horse could be armoured with scale armour in the same way as the legs and arms of men. It is quite possible or even probable that the well-known works of art from the east and the archaeological find of horse-armour from Dura Europos have preconditioned us to think that the artists of Trajan's Column must have made a mistake and that all finds of scale armour which appear to be intended for some limb are interpreted as intended for humans. Indeed, it is nowadays accepted that men could wear scale armour from head to foot, so why not horses? The scale armour could easily have been attached to the crupper and girth and other pieces of armour underneath the scales so it would not be visible to us from the Column, which, however, does show the division of armour for the horse's neck and for the midsection of the man. In other words, the artists show the divisions where those were visible. However, it is still clear that the use of scale armour in this manner for horses was abandoned at some point in time.

2.2.3 Roman Naval Combat[9]

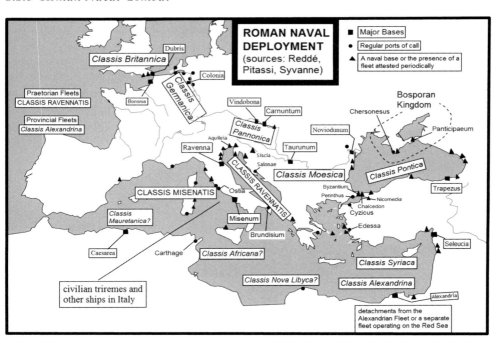

We do not possess much information about the Roman navy and its uses during this era so this account is based on information dating mostly from earlier and later sources. Therefore the following account follows my earlier studies very closely. On the basis of the evidence that we have the Roman Imperial Fleet consisted of two different types: 1) The Praetorian Fleets of Italy; 2) The Provincial Fleets posted in the provinces. The two Praetorian Fleets *classis praetoriae Misenatium/Misenatis* and *classis praetoriae Ravennatum/Ravennatis/Ravennas* were both based in Italy as the names imply. The Provincial Fleets consisted at least of the *classis Alexandrina, classis Syriaca, classis Nova Libyca, classis Germanica, classis Pannonica, classis Moesica, classis Britannica, classis Pontica, classis Mauretanica* (thirteen *liburnae*), *classis Nova Libyca*, and *classis Africana*. Each of the praetorian fleets had a single naval legion attached to them (Vegetius 4.31). We do not know whether the provincial fleets had legions as well, but it is clear that they had some sort of fighting contingents to man their ships.

The above map shows the naval deployment pattern at the first half of the third century. The praetorian fleets were used as strategic reserves while the day-to-day defence and protection of the sea lanes and rivers was left in the hands of the provincial fleets. All of the fleets were also used to support military operations and to ship men and supplies where needed.

The Roman coastal defence consisted of two separate systems: 1) passive/defensive measures (forts, towers, fortified cities and towns along the coasts and rivers); 2) active/ offensive measures undertaken by the fleets. The day to day defence (control of harbours, collection of tolls/taxes, prevention of smuggling and wrecking, guarding of the coasts against piratical attacks) was performed mainly by the civilian police/paramilitary forces, while active/offensive defence was mainly performed by the professional fleets with the possible help of corvéed civilian ships. During the third century, the Romans still expected civilians to contribute ships and men as part of their tax requirement whenever needed. The Romans were also in the habit of appointing special officers to protect their sections of the coast when there was a need for some unified command. Furthermore, as we shall see, if there was a need for large-scale naval command that unified all the available forces for example to suppress piracy, the Romans were prepared to place a special officer in charge of such activity.

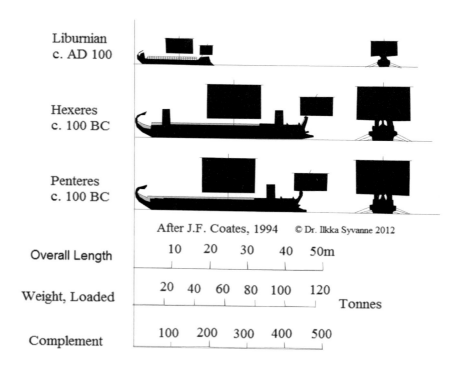

Liburnian
c. AD 100

Hexeres
c. 100 BC

Penteres
c. 100 BC

After J.F. Coates, 1994   © Dr. Ilkka Syvänne 2012

Overall Length   10   20   30   40   50m

Weight, Loaded   20   40   60   80   100   120   Tonnes

Complement   100   200   300   400   500

The workhorse of the third century fleets was the fast *liburna* (a fast galley) which formed the core of all fleets so that the trireme served as a flagship of each prefect of the provincial fleets. Only the praetorian fleets possessed larger ships (mostly triremes with fives and sixes serving as flagships) to make these superior in any possible naval battle with the provincial fleets that could be controlled by usurpers. In addition to this, the Romans used a great variety of ships, boats and rafts for all sorts of needs, which could be bolstered with corveed civilian transports or warships.

Naval Tactics
The naval warfare of this era followed the same principles as the Romans had always employed. They usually avoided sailing during the stormy winter season unless they particularly wanted to surprise the enemy. The basis of all naval tactics was a good

knowledge of the winds, tides, geography, and signs of weather to be exploited against enemies. Naval combat followed the same principles as on land in that it stressed the importance of spying, reconnoitring, ambushes and surprise attacks. Naval battles were usually fought in fair weather because of the limitations posed by galleys. Standard naval battle formations were: a) the crescent with the best ships and men posted on the flanks to outflank the enemy; b) the convex array in which the best ships and men were placed in the centre to break through the enemy array; c) a double convex array for greater safety; d) a line abreast with reserves behind; e) a double line abreast for maximum safety if there existed enough ships for that.; f) a defensive circle. These arrays meant the use of two basic tactics by ships: 1) penetration of the enemy formation with a *diekplous* manoeuvre in which one galley rushed forward into the interval between two enemy galleys which was then followed by other galleys so that the first sheared the oars and the second rammed the immobile ship; 2) the *periplous* manoeuvre in which the flank galleys extended their line to outflank the enemy line.

2.2.4 Siege Warfare[10]

One of the greatest advantages that the Romans had was their superiority in siege warfare over all other enemies except the Persians. This resulted primarily from the use of very sophisticated siege engines. Their siege equipment included various kinds of artillery pieces (e.g. ballistae, repeating ballista, onagri, and possibly also trebuchets), various kinds of siege towers, drills, borers, the *sambuca* (a hollow tube to land men on top of a wall), various kinds of battering rams (from simple rams all the way up to the city-taker *'helepolis'*), flails, 'fire hose' to spread liquids, mining equipment, various types of sheds, fire bombs, cranes, and so forth.

The siege warfare consisted of offensive and defensive techniques both of which followed some standard procedures. The typical features of offensive siege warfare were: 1) terms of surrender offered to the enemy at first to avoid a costly siege; 2) the use of surprise attacks if possible; 3) the use of a traitor to bring about the conquest of the city; 4) if the enemy refused to surrender, the use of assault in tortoise formation with ladders possibly with some sheds; 5) if the first assault failed, the building of siege engines and use of mounds and mines against the enemy; 6) if the place was considered too costly to take by other means the Romans could attempt to starve the defenders into surrender.

The standard defensive siege techniques were as follows: 1) the use of scorched earth to make the attack difficult if there was prior information of the enemy invasion; 2) the building of sophisticated fortifications with enough provisions placed inside to withstand a siege; 3) the exploitation of defensive features like walls and towers and the use of siege engines to negate the attack; 3) the sending of a relief army against the besiegers; 4) the use of a diversionary invasion; 5) the employment of guerrilla warfare against the besiegers to force them to leave; 6) if all failed, then the Romans offered terms of surrender.

2.2.5 Intelligence Gathering and Security[11]

At the heart of Roman intelligence gathering systems stood the needs of the Emperor. He wanted to ensure his own personal safety against internal and external threats. The personal safety of the Emperor was in the hands of his bodyguard units and other special units (*peregrini, frumentarii, urbaniciani*) headquartered at Rome that were usually commanded by one to three praetorian prefects. These units were not used only as bodyguards but also for intelligence gathering and other special missions like assassinations, arrests and interrogation. The *frumentarii* and *peregrini* formed the core of the intelligence gathering apparatus, but in practise the emperors could use anyone they trusted. The regular military units also performed internal and external security missions. Most of the intelligence gathered across the border was conducted by the units posted along the frontiers. Civilian paramilitary police forces and other civilians could also be used as sources of intelligence.

2.2.6 Strategy[12]

The general deployment pattern of the Roman forces was defensive. Thanks to the limitations posed by the means of travel at their disposal (feet, horses, wagons, and ships) it was impossible to transfer forces fast from one front to another to meet an emergency. Because of this the bulk of the forces were posted close to the border. Potential enemies were kept divided through a policy of divide and rule. This required a well-functioning intelligence gathering system to work. If intelligence gathering operations and diplomacy failed and the local frontier forces proved insufficient to meet the enemy invasion, then the Romans usually drew detachments from other legions and units (or entire legions and auxiliary units) from other fronts and dispatched them to the threatened sector. This had the drawback of weakening those sections of the frontier from which these reinforcements were drawn and could result in an invasion of that sector. In such major emergencies the emperors usually raised new legions and other units to meet the crisis. This is what happened under Alexander Severus, as we shall see. It should be remembered that the Romans changed this general deployment pattern when the emperors conducted offensive wars to increase their personal prestige. This gave the Romans the advantage of deciding when and where they fought.

The main weakness of the Roman defensive system was that it was always dangerous to trust large numbers of men to any general because they could try to usurp power. In fact, the greatest threats to the Roman Empire were the power–hungry generals and not the foreign powers. Because of this the emperors needed a well–functioning internal security apparatus, which would inform them of potential usurpations. The information could be used to eliminate these potential threats before they materialized.[13] Most crises, problems and invasions of Roman territory occurred either as a result of civil wars, or enemy invasions caused civil wars. The strategic goals of Roman foreign and military policies varied according to the personality of the Emperor and his political needs and the situation, but they were not always free to choose their own policies and were sometimes just forced to react to the events taking place around them.

Chapter Three

Alexander Severus (222–35)

Left: A bust of Alexander Severus. **Right:** A statue of Julia Mamea as Venus.
Source of images: Duruy.

3.1 The Early Reign of Alexander Severus and Julia Mamaea (222–30)[1]

Marcus Aurelius Severus Alexander became the sole Emperor of the Roman Empire on 13 March 222. He was a member of the Severan dynasty, but at the time of his accession he was young so he owed his position entirely to the imperial women, his grandmother Julia Maesa and mother Julia Mamaea. He was by nature a docile and kind person, obedient to his mother; he was a mama's boy. Julia Maesa was the sister of the late empress Julia Domna and this gave her enough prestige to be believed by the soldiers when she bribed them with money and promises. In 218 Julia Maesa had claimed that Antoninus Elagabalus was the illegitimate son of the great Caracalla (Antoninus Magnus) and this was believed by the soldiers with the result that they had raised Elagabalus on the throne. Elagabalus, however, had shown too much independence and upset the soldiers and the public morals. This had made him unpopular with Julia Maesa, the soldiers, senators and populace. So the two women overthrew Elagabalus and made Alexander Severus sole ruler. His position was legitimized by claiming that he too was an illegitimate son of Caracalla. The women did not use the name Antoninus, because this had been used by Elagabalus, but the name Severus to connect Alexander and his rule with the reign of Septimius Severus.

The first action that the new rulers Julia Maesa and Julia Mamaea took in the name of Alexander Severus was the removal of anyone sympathetic to Elagabalus from positions of power, followed by the purging of the Senate and equestrian order. After this the purge was extended to the 'tribes', army and the palace staff. The corrupt officers of the forces posted in the capital were dismissed and the central administration was put under closer scrutiny. Competent jurists, the most important of whom was Ulpian (he was appointed Praetorian Prefect), were tasked to go through all state business and law suits. Before being issued, all laws/edicts of Alexander were subjected to voting by twenty learned jurists and fifty skilled orators. This was a wise policy decision.

The position of Julia Maesa and Julia Mamaea was entirely dependent on the support they got from the soldiers and upper classes, so they wanted to involve as many members of the upper classes in their administration as possible. The idea that they came up with was to involve the Roman Senate in the decision making process by allowing them to appoint sixteen senators as councillors to Alexander Severus. The Senate had a say in the choice of his praetorian prefects. The imperial women assembled a separate military council which consisted of former military veterans and old men who had served with honour. In addition, Alexander used historians to learn what measures had been adopted by previous Roman or foreign rulers. This secured the support of the old Severan elite, both civilian and military, for the new regime. In practice, power was entirely in the hands of the imperial women, and then after the death of Julia Maesa in the hands of Julia Mamaea alone who was able to guide the actions of her son as she wished. However, she was wise enough to do this in such a manner that the senators felt that their opinions had been heard.

Aelius Lampridius (*HA Alexander* 23) makes it clear that Alexander and his mother did not trust that the above measures would be enough to secure their position. They were always prepared to listen to the accusations of the soldiers against their tribunes, and if found guilty they were duly punished. The most important security measure was the use of secret agents. The rulers had two principles which they followed when they sought information about any person. The first was that the agent had to be a person they trusted. The second was that they employed only such persons who were not known so that nobody could bribe them.

The libertarianism of Elagabalus had to make room for the return of conservative values. While the new regime respected the traditional Roman religions it still retained the religious tolerance that had marked the reigns of Caracalla and Elagabalus. This is not surprising in light of the fact that both Alexander Severus and his mother Julia Mamaea showed great interest in Christianity and its teachings. However, on the basis of Julius Africanus's *Kestoi*, the return of conservative values meant the return of the old traditional military equipment and tactics with the implication that Caracalla's experiments with Macedonian-style equipment and tactics were probably abandoned at this time.[2]

Left: A statue of Sallustia Barbia Orbiana as Venus. Source: Visconti.

Above right: A coin of Orbiana. Source: Cohen

The reign of Alexander was characterized by continuous military unrest and by attempts to restore discipline. The most obvious instances before the series of actual mutinies in 230–31 were the murder of the Praetorian Prefect Ulpian by the Praetorians in 228 and the flight of Cassius Dio from Italy in 229 because Alexander was unable to protect him against the praetorians. There were three main reasons for this behaviour: 1) The soldiers had become used to lax discipline under Elagabalus and all attempts to reinstall discipline resulted in resistance; 2) Alexander appears to have distributed only three donatives to the soldiers during his entire reign (*HA Alexander* 26.1.), which made him look miserly; 3) Alexander appeared as a mama's boy because he followed the wishes of his mother and because he was not conducting vigorous military campaigns in enemy lands in the manner of his supposed father Antoninus Magnus (Caracalla). As we shall see, the principal reason for the miserly behaviour was the avarice of Alexander's mother Julia Mamaea, but Aelius Lampridius (*HA Alexander* 22.9–23, 26, 29.3–10) notes that Alexander restored the grain supply for the Roman populace at his own expense, gave money to the populace three times, and started many other costly projects while he reduced the state taxes significantly.[3] It is obvious that if this is true, Alexander lacked money to bribe the soldiers in the manner they expected.

Alexander also faced troubles resulting from the meddling of his mother. In 225 Julia Mamaea decided that it was time to find a wife for her son. Her choice was Sallustia Barbia Orbiana, the daughter of the senator Seius Herennius Sallustius Barbius. It is possible that Sallustius was made *Caesar* at the same time, but this is not certain. The pair appears to have been happily married, but too much so for the liking of Julia Mamaea who appears to have started to fear for her own standing. Julia Mamaea started to abuse Orbiana and her father publicly with the result that the father started to plot against Julia Mamaea, or was claimed to have done so. When she learnt of this, Sallustius was executed and Orbiana was exiled. Alexander, the dutiful son, did nothing to protect his wife – perhaps it was clear that she was more loyal to her father than she was to her husband. We shall never know the truth, but it is quite clear that this incident again made Alexander look like mama's boy.

3.2 The Persians Invasion in about 229–30

Excluding some local unrests, some attempted usurpations and problems with military discipline, the reign of Alexander Severus was still largely trouble-free until Ardashir I ('Artaxerxes'), the founder of the Sassanian dynasty,[4] started his invasion of Roman territory in about 228/9 with the excuse of reconquering territories formerly belonging to the Achaemenid dynasty. Ardashir was a founder of a new dynasty. His claim for power was based on his claim of the restoration of Zoroastrian gods and the Persian Empire. To achieve this he needed military successes that brought booty and glory for his followers. Such successes would then prove that he was favoured by the gods. Ardashir had not yet defeated the Arsacids of Armenia. His first object of attack was the allied city of Hatra in 229, which had an Arsacid ruler. It is possible that it already had a Roman garrison, and if it did not, it acquired one immediately after this. The attack failed despite his forces managing to breach the wall. Ardashir continued his march north against Armenia where he was defeated by the Arsacid ruler of Armenia known as Khosrov the Great whose army included the sons of Artabanus V. This defeat did not deter Ardashir in the least. He marched his forces against Roman Mesopotamia and besieged Nisibis possibly also in 229.[5]

The Persian enemy[6]

At this time the Sassanian Empire of Ardashir/Artaxerxes I was still a new empire that had been built on the ruins of the Parthian Empire. The first Emperor to face this rising problem was Alexander Severus. The fact that the Sassanian Empire had overthrown the last major Parthian ruler as recently as 224 means that there were still rebels inside the Sassanian Empire that could be used as allies against their new overlord. The Romans did indeed attempt to do this in conjunction with another ruler who was opposed to the Sassanians. He was Khosrov the Great, the Arsacid king of Armenia, who obviously had a blood feud against Artaxerxes because he had killed his relative and benefactor Artaban/Artabanes V. In 230, the Georgians, Armenians, and Albanians were therefore allied with the Romans against the Sassanians.

My drawing below shows the principal players in the decisive battle of Hormzdagan on 18 April 224. It was in this battle that Ardashir/Artaxerxes I and his son Sapor/Shapur I defeated and overthrew the last important Arsacid ruler of Parthia, Artaban/Artabanes V. The sources claim that Ardashir killed Artaban in person.

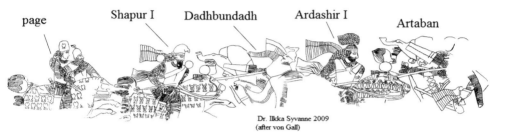

Dr. Ilkka Syvänne 2009
(after von Gall)

The Sassanian military, however, was far more threatening than the Parthian had been, for two reasons. Firstly, the new ruler Ardashir/Artaxerxes motivated his soldiers with fanatical Zoroastrian indoctrination. Secondly, he evoked the great past of Iran under the Achaemenids to instil a sense of nationalism to this force. The exact command structure of the army at this time is not known with certainty but it appears probable that right after the *shahanshah* (King of Kings) stood the crown prince Sapor/Shapur I and below him the supreme commander of Iran, the *Iran-spahbadh*, and under him four *vitaxae/spahbeds* (viceroys) in charge of the fourfold division of the Empire consisting of the East, West, North and South.

The Persian army (*spah*) consisted of the bodyguard units (the best known of these were the 10,000 Immortals cavalry), cataphracts provided by the Iranian and Parthian magnates loyal to Ardashir/Artaxerxes, light cavalry provided by mercenaries and tribal forces, elephants of the royal house, foot soldiers, navy, and the logistical services. The cataphract cavalry formed the vast majority and flower of the Sassanian army consisting of 20,000 elite bodyguard horsemen who served directly under the ruler. When the Sassanians were not threatened by several major powers simultaneously, they had the capacity to put to the field cavalry armies of about 70,000 to 120,000 horsemen, in addition to which came the infantry and servants.

The Persian and Armenian cataphracts were justifiably considered fearsome enemies to face. These knights were equally adept at long distance combat with bows and in mêlée with spears and swords, even if they preferred to weaken the enemy with arrows before engaging them at close quarters. Most of the Persian infantry consisted of spearmen and archers of dubious quality that were typically used only in sieges and as guards for the marching camps and as servants of the knights. However they did possess high quality infantry too. Most of these appear to have consisted of the descendants of the former

Roman soldiers who brought with them their legionary gear with rectangular shields so that they later became to be known as *murmillones*-style gladiators among their Roman enemies.

The Sassanians were the most sophisticated of the enemies the Romans faced. They produced works of military theory which combined ancient Indo-Persian military practices with Parthian nomadic cavalry tactics and Romano-Greek infantry tactics. Standard combat tactics was to use cavalry either in one or two lines each of which consisted of outer left, left, centre, right, and outer right. The cavalry employed two basic unit orders: oblong rank–and–file array, and the 128-horseman rhomboid. If infantry accompanied the army, it was usually placed behind these as a phalanx in front of a fortified marching camp. Standard combat tactics were: 1) to encircle the enemy with a crescent array; 2) to encircle the enemy on one flank; 3) to place the battle formation on high ground to put the enemy under constant archery bombardment. The Persians usually closed on the enemy only when it had been weakened enough with a prolonged archery barrage. The attack with the centre (convex array when the enemy outnumbered the Persians) and the defensive circle (cavalry dismounted or inside infantry circle) were used only in extreme emergencies. However, it was the superb siege skills of the Persians that made them the most fearsome enemies the Romans faced. Unlike their other enemies, the Persians could capture even the strongest Roman fortifications if they did not receive timely help in the form of a relief army.

The only serious weaknesses that the Sassanians had vis-à-vis Rome were that their economy was weaker, their infantry forces less, and their naval forces puny. The Persian dhows were too weak to withstand an encounter with the Roman nailed war galleys when they met in the Indian Ocean. It is therefore strange to note that Alexander Severus and his advisors did not post a fleet in the Red Sea and the Indian Ocean as the Romans had done earlier against the Parthians and were to do later during, for example, the reigns of Aurelian, Constantine the Great and Constantius II. However, there is a logical explanation, which is that Alexander Severus faced a serious piracy problem at this time and this appears to have required all his naval resources.

The beginning of the Persian war according to Cassius Dio:

'Many uprisings were made by many persons, some of which caused serious alarm, but they were all checked. But affairs in Mesopotamia were still more terrifying, and provoked in the hearts of all, not merely the men of Rome but the rest of mankind, a fear that had a truer foundation. Artaxerxes, a Persian, having conquered the Parthians in three battles and killed their king, Artabanus, made a campaign against Hatra, which he endeavoured to take as a base for attacking the Romans. He did make a breach in the wall but, as he lost a number of soldiers through an ambuscade [*this may mean that the Hatrans had built a new wall inside or that the attackers were ambushed in some streets*], he transferred his position into Media. Of this district, as also of Parthia, he acquired no small portion, partly by force and partly by intimidation, and then marched against Armenia. Here he suffered a reverse at the hands of the natives, some Medes, and the children of Artabanus, and either fled (as some say) or (as others assert) retired to prepare a larger expedition. He accordingly became a source of fear to us; for he was encamped with a large army so as to threaten not only Mesopotamia but Syria also and boasted that he would win back everything that the ancient Persians had once held, as far as the Grecian Sea. It was, he said, his rightful inheritance from his forefathers. He was of no particular account himself, but our military affairs are in such a condition that some joined his cause and other refused to defend themselves. The troops are so distinguished by wantonness, and arrogance, and freedom from reproof, that those in Mesopotamia dared to kill their commander, Flavius Heracleo. [*It is probable that the killing of Heracleo was followed by one of the usurpations mentioned by Dio and other sources. It is probable that this usurper was Taurinus/Taurinius*] and [*the following describes events preceding the Persian war, which I have included here to demonstrate the unruly behaviour of the soldiers of the time.*] The Praetorians found fault with me before Ulpianus because I ruled the soldiers in Pannonia with a strong hand; and they demanded my surrender, through fear that someone might compel them to submit to a regime similar to that of the Pannonian troops. Alexander, however, paid no attention to them, but promoted me in various ways, appointing me to be consul for the second time, as his colleague, and taking upon him personally the responsibility of meeting the expenditures of my office. As malcontents evinced displeasure at this, he became afraid that they might kill me if they saw me in the insignia of my office, and he bade me spend the period of my consulship in Italy somewhere outside Rome. Later, accordingly, I came both to Rome and to Campania to visit him. After spending a few days in his company, during which the soldiers saw me without offering to do me any harm, I started for home, being released on account of the trouble with my feet. Consequently, I expect to spend all the remainder of my life in my own country.' Dio 80.3, tr. by Foster, 108ff. with some changes and my comments inside parentheses.

Alexander Severus was upset by the news that Ardashir/Artaxerxes had invaded Mesopotamia and he assembled his council of senators to discuss the matter. Their reaction was to send an envoy who demanded that Ardashir stop his hostilities immediately. Ardashir paid no attention to this, which suggests that he saw it as a sign of weakness. Probably it only encouraged him. He overran most of Mesopotamia with infantry and cavalry, plundered Cappadocia and threatened Syria. Zonaras and Syncellus state that the Persians besieged at least Nisibis, but apparently unsuccessfully because Nisibis was still under siege when Alexander arrived in the east. As noted in Dio, Ardashir was successful largely because the Roman forces in the east were in a state of complete disorder: There were attempted usurpations; some soldiers refused to fight against the invaders; and there were even those who deserted to the Persian side. The Zoroastrian communities within Roman territory in Syria, Asia Minor and Cappadocia were also apparently cooperating with the Persians so evidently Ardashir's Zoroastrian and Achaemenid propaganda was working.[7]

The sources mention several usurpers for the reign of Alexander Severus one of whom was certainly the man who was raised on the throne by the soldiers who killed Heracleo in Mesopotamia. John S. McHugh lists these in his biography of Alexander Severus. The *Epitome de Caesaribus* names Taurinus, who drowned himself in the Euphrates when Alexander arrived in the East. Zosimus states that the soldiers attempted to force a man called Antoninus to become their Emperor, but he refused with the result that they raised Uranius in his stead. According to Syncellus, Uranius usurped power in Edessa, Oshroene. When Alexander reached the east, this man begged forgiveness from Alexander. There was also a similarly-named usurper L. or C. Julius Aurelius Sulpicius Uranius Antoninus of Emesa and Edessa in the east in 252/4 and it has been suggested that he was the same man and that Alexander forgave Uranius. However, there is the problem that Syncellus claims that Alexander had Uranius executed. Because of this some have claimed that there were two men with the name of Uranius Antoninus and that they were father and son. Whatever the truth, it is clear that the name of Antoninus Magnus (Caracalla) was so loved by the soldiers that they sought a new Antoninus to lead them when Alexander had proved himself unmanly by his inaction. It is therefore possible that these Antonines were distant relatives of Caracalla or claimed to be his descendants. The fifth century writer Polemius Silvius lists as usurpers Marcellus, Sallustius Uranius Seleucus and Taurinius. One may connect this Uranius with the above-mentioned Uranius of Emesa and Taurinius with the Taurinus of Mesopotamia. This suggests that there were at least two usurpations in the East at this time: one in Mesopotamia by Taurinus/Taurinius and another in Oshroene by Uranius. This leaves Marcellus unaccounted for.[8] It is possible that he usurped power in some unknown place in the East, but in my opinion we should identify him with the usurper mentioned by Aelius Lampridius in the context of the beginning of Alexander's march to the East (see below). Furthermore, it is clear that the other usurpers had also been successful in their defence of Roman territory against the Persians. Uranius in Oshroene had blocked the approach to Syria and it was because of this that he hoped for forgiveness. It is also clear that Taurinus had not been subdued by the Persians because he drowned himself in the Euphrates. It is very probable that he had defended the city of Nisibis.

The disorder among the soldiers in the East was not the only trouble facing Alexander and Julia Mamaea. There was an outbreak of piracy in the Mediterranean, possibly resulting from the same causes as the above troubles with the soldiers. And, according to Bohec (2005, 83), Q. Gargilius Martialis defeated the Faraxen (Fraxinenses) some time between 225 and 235. Unfortunately we cannot be more accurate with the year, but I will suggest a date later in the appropriate place in this study. In my opinion the principal reason for the troubles in the latter half of Alexander's reign was the long peace which had lowered the salaries of the soldiers because they had not received a succession of bribes in the form of donatives and booty.

The government's response to the piracy was vigorous. Alexander appointed a special officer, P. Sallustius Sempronius, to the task of destroying the pirates. It is probable that we should associate the severe famine in Rome under Alexander mentioned by Cedrenus (p.450) with this piracy – an energetic and swift response was certainly required. After initial hesitance the government responded with the same vigorousness to the crisis in the East. The attempted usurpations, the Persian invasion and the urgent pleas from the governors had finally brought home the need that the personal presence of the Emperor with a large army was needed. However, before the Romans could finally put into effect their plans, the Persians had already withdrawn from Roman territory, probably thanks to the threat posed by the Armenians against Ardashir's supply lines.[9]

3.3 The Preparations of Alexander for the Persian War

When Alexander Severus, Julia and their advisors learnt that the Persians had continued their campaign and significant portions of the armed forces were in the hands of usurpers, they began thorough preparations for the campaign worthy of the Emperor. In 231 the Romans started to levy recruits, troops were transferred and assembled, roads repaired or built, and magazines prepared. The coins and medallions minted in 232 were typical propaganda pieces which were meant to secure the loyalty of the soldiers with promises of victory. There was also an unusual series of *adluctio* coins, depicting a formal address of the troops by the Emperor on the eve of a campaign, which had the name of Julia Mamaea on one side, or Alexander and Julia facing one another. This propagated the importance of Julia Mamaea to the soldiers, but as noted by McHugh it was also poor propaganda because it made Alexander look like a mama's boy. The descriptions of these preparations in Herodian and *Augustan Histories* are well worth quoting at length because they show how the Roman armies were prepared and assembled for war. The account of Aelius Lampridius in the *Augustan Histories* is particularly important because it includes information about the composition and tactics of the Roman army during the reign of Alexander Severus which his successors also used.[10]

Herodian describes this process as follows:

'When he had reigned in this manner eight years [*emended from 14 years*]… letters arrived unexpectedly from the governors of Syria and Mesopotamia that Artaxerxes, king of the Persians, after totally overthrowing the Parthians, subverting their power in the East, and slaying their monarch Artabanus… had subjugated all the neighbouring barbarians, and loaded them with heavy tributes. That, not content with this, nor containing himself within the Tigris, but having passed the banks of the river, and the frontiers of the Roman territories, he was overrunning Mesopotamia and threatening the Syrians, claiming all that… bounded by the Aegean Sea and the Straits of Propontis as the possession of his ancestors… As Alexander had been brought up from his childhood in a long uninterrupted peace… he was struck with no little surprise… At first, a council of his friends being called, it was thought proper to send an embassy… However, the Persian… persisted in his purpose… He ran and rode [*Artaxerxes/Ardashir had both infantry and cavalry*] through all Mesopotamia, laying waste and plundering as he went; and besieged the Romans, who were encamped on the banks of the river to defend the boundaries of the Empire… while he was at Rome Alexander was informed of the bold invasion of the barbarian in the east. This was an insolence that he believed could not be tolerated, and the eastern governors demanded his presence. This was against his personal inclination, but he started preparations for an expedition. He levied forces from Italy and all the provinces, enlisting all who were physically fit and the right age. The entire Roman Empire was in a state of great commotion while they were collecting an army sufficient to withstand the multitude of barbarians… Alexander, having summoned together the Roman soldiers… makes an oration to the following effect: "…my fellow soldiers… At first I endeavoured by letters and admonitions to persuade this man [*Artaxerxes/Ardashir*] to curb his… madness and lusting after the properties of others. But the puffed up boasting barbarian will not contain himself [*this made the Roman cause just*]… Let us not therefore hesitate or delay, but let the elder among you remind themselves of those trophies which with [*Septimius*] Severus, and Antoninus [*Caracalla*] my father [*Alexander's claim on power was based on his claim to be son of the great Caracalla*] you have so often raised against the barbarians. [*For the victories of Caracalla, see my biography of him; and for the victories of Severus, see my forthcoming biography of him already completed at the time of the writing*] And let such as are in the flower of their youth be eager for fame and glory." As soon as Alexander had ended, the whole army … expressed their readiness to undertake the war. After distributing large sums of money among them [*these would be the Praetorians and others stationed in Rome or close by*], he gave orders to get everything ready for a speedy march. He went to the senate and announced his departure with a similar speech… On the appointed day, he first attended the usual sacrifices and then, attended by all the Senate and People, he set out from Rome… In a short time he arrived in Illyricum, where, going through the garrisons, he gathered together considerable reinforcements, and then put the army under march for Antioch. Here he stayed some time making preparations for war, exercising his soldiers and practising military drills [*The confusion among the army and the inclusion of new recruits made this necessary*].' Herodian 6.2.1ff., tr. by Hart 247ff. with changes, corrections and comments.

Aelius Lampridius gives us the following descriptions of the process of preparing the armies for the campaign:

'I come now to speak of his expeditions of war… I shall first observe what his custom was… he always maintained secrecy about the plan of his campaign, but announced openly the length of each day's march two months before in a public edict in these words: Upon such a day and such an hour I shall depart from this city and by the help of the gods I shall march the first day to such a place; and so he told his several stations and encampments in order; and marked the places where he was to receive provisions as far as the boundaries of the barbarians; from thence all things were kept secret and all marched without the barbarians being able to know the plans of the Roman army. *HA Alexander* 45.1ff. tr. by John Bernard 437–8 with some emendations, changes and corrections.

'During his campaigns, he disposed his armies so that they received their provisions at each halting place and were not required to carry with them subsistence for more than seventeen days; unless it was in the country of the enemy, and there he also assisted them by providing mules and camels, saying that he desired to look more after his men than himself because the safety of the state depended on them. He visited them when sick in their tents; even those of the lowest ranks; and had them carried in wagons and provided with all necessities; and if they were too sick to travel, he would leave them in the care of the good householders or virtuous women in the cities and villages to whom he paid their expenses.' *HA Alexander* 47.1ff. tr. by John Bernard p.440 with some emendations, changes and corrections.

'Ovinius Camillus [*this man is unknown, but it is possible that we should identify him with the usurper Marcellus of Polemius*], a senator of an ancient family, had once the vanity to think of revolting and setting himself up as emperor. This was reported and proved to Alexander who summoned him to the palace telling him that he gave him thanks that he was so willing to take upon him the care of the empire… So he took him with him to the Senate, and called him a colleague… When the war against the barbarians [*Persians*] was declared, he asked him if he would go to it … then Severus dismissed him and sent him under a guard to his country estate where he lived for a long time, but he was at last killed by the soldiers of the emperor.' *HA Alexander* 48.1ff. tr. by John Bernard p.440–1 with some emendations, changes and corrections.

The Composition of the Expeditionary Force

The above account shows Alexander Severus and his advisors at their best. The campaign was prepared with great attention to detail. The Emperor and his staff took everything into account, beginning with the expected behaviour of the Emperor: the soldiers expected their Emperor to be their comrade-in-arms and commander and Alexander put up a pretence to be so. It is also clear that Alexander levied new men to fill the ranks, but it is at the same time likely that Alexander also raised new legions and other units as emperors often did when they assembled a major army for a military campaign. It is probabe that it was then that Maximinus Thrax was made tribune of the *legio IV* formed out of recruits by Alexander Severus.[11] I would suggest that this legion was now taken to the East, and I would also suggest that it is probable that this legion was actually *legio IV Parthica* which has usually been considered a creation of Diocletian in about 300 – a date when it is attested at Circesium in the East. The principal reason for my speculation is that we do not know the exact dates when the late Roman legions were created thanks to the uneven survival of evidence, and the title *Parthica* would have been spot on for a member of the Severan dynasty because Septimius Severus had created the legions *I-III Parthica* for his eastern campaigns. Furthermore, the sources specifically note the raising of new units. As will be discussed below, it is possible that *Legio IV Parthica* was destroyed and recreated like some other legions. Marcus Aurelius, Septimius Severus and Caracalla had all raised new units and Alexander now followed their example. By announcing the planned route well in advance Alexander and his staff made certain that the senators and others who were required to contribute resources for the campaign did not have to spend money needlessly for security reasons as had been the case under Caracalla.[12] The preparations were also quite visible to the enemy and one can speculate that one of the reasons for such openness was psychological warfare against the Persians. Naturally Alexander and his staff kept the actual campaign plan a secret.

However, the above account makes it clear that Alexander faced serious problems as well. He, or rather his mother Julia Mamaea, had not spent enough money on the soldiers, and the fact that Alexander had not led the armies in person before this had made him look weak. It is therefore not surprising that there were usurpation attempts in the East and one even in Rome, the latter of which was exposed in time. The raising of the morale of the Praetorian Guard and others stationed in or near Rome was absolutely necessary in such circumstances. The making of speeches to the troops and the granting of a sizable sum of money before the launching of a military campaign were standard practices, but now especially necessary. The problem with the granting of money on this occasion was that it coincided with the decennial of Alexander, so it was expected. Alexander did not grant a double donative now, but only a regular one. This was not sufficient to remove the grievances the soldiers felt.

The above account makes it clear that Alexander gathered sizable reinforcements from Illyricum, but extant inscriptions and subsequent events prove that he also drew soldiers from the Rhine frontier, Egypt and North Africa for his eastern war[13]. The assembled army was then put through drills to make it combat ready. Subsequent events prove that this force was indeed in need of training.

It was also necessary to choose the commanders. They included many names that feature in our narrative later. The most important of these were Rutilius Pudens Crispinus and C. Furius Sabinus Aquila Timesitheus. Crispinus's career had benefited in particular from the patronage of Caracalla, with the result that his career stalled under Macrinus. Under Elagabalus he held some minor offices, but then under Alexander Severus his career started to prosper again. He became commander of *XV Apollinaris* and then governor of Lusitaniae, Thrace and Syria Phoenice followed by proconsular governorship of Achaia. The most important point here is that he was probably the governor of Syria Phoenice in 231–34, which would mean that he participated in the campaigns in the East. It is clear that he performed well because he received consulship after that. Timesitheus's career had also prospered thanks to Caracalla's, who had made him Procurator of *Rationis Privata*. Promotions continued under Elagabalus and Alexander Severus so that Alexander appointed him *Procurator provinciae Syriae Palestinae ibi Exactor Reliquorum Annonae* for his eastern campaign. This means Timesitheus was responsible for the collection of provisions in kind and other necessary resources for the campaign, or simply he was the man who was tasked to make certain that the logistical needs of the army were fulfilled.[14]

Before we deal with the problems with discipline among the soldiers we need to analyse what type of force Alexander led against the Persians. The key texts are quoted below.

'The emperor entered upon an expedition against Parthians which he conducted with such discipline that… wherever the legions marched, the tribunes, centurions, the soldiers were so quiet, so modest and so beloved for their discretion… and certainly the soldiers loved him as if he was their brother or son or as father because they were handsomely clothed and nobly armed and their cavalry well mounted and completely furnished with caparisons so that all saw the grandeur of the army of Alexander Severus… He particularly, with all his power, endeavoured to appear worthy of the name that he carried and, which is more, to surpass the Macedonian in fame; and last, that there ought to be a great difference between Alexander of Rome and Alexander of Macedon. He had companies in his army, as that Macedonian had, that were armed with shields of silver [*argyroaspides*] and with shields of gold [*chrysoaspides*]. He made a phalanx consisting of thirty thousand men, whom he called by the name of his *phalangiores* [*phalangarii*]; by whose means he did a great many noble exploits in Persia. This phalanx was composed of six legions, who were all equally well armed, and for their great services judged to be all at double pay after the end of the war of Persia… In all his campaigns and expeditions, he lunched and dined in the open tent and ate the soldiers' ordinary food in front of all and this pleased the soldiers greatly. And he made his round in every tent and quarter and suffered no one whatsoever to absent from his colours. If anyone turned aside during marching to take even the least thing from the inhabitants of the country, he was punished in the emperor's presence.' Aelius Lampridius, *HA Alexander* 50.1ff. tr. by John Bernard p.443–5 with some emendations, changes and corrections.

The key part of the above quote is the reference to the composition of the infantry forces (ed. by Magie with my comment added):

'fecerat denique sibi argyroaspidas et chrysoaspidas, [*the previous units are separated at this point from the 30,000 strong phalanx with the verb*] fecerat et phalangem triginta milium hominum, quos phalangarios vocari iusserat et cum quibus multum fecit in Perside; quae quidem erat ex sex legionibus similum armorum, stipendiorum vero post bellum Persicum maiorum.'

Magie (p.279–81) translated this more accurately than Bernard in the eighteenth century as follows:

'Finally, he provided himself with soldiers armed with silver shields and with golden, and also a phalanx of thirty thousand men, whom he ordered to be called *phalangarii*, and with these he won many victories in Persia. This phalanx, as a matter of fact, was formed from six legions, and was armed like the other troops, but after the Persian war received higher pay.'

Magie's translation has been generally accepted so that the 30,000 *phalangarii* have been thought to consist of the six legions each with about 5,000 men. This leaves out the *argyroaspides* and *chrysoaspides* and their strength. It is possible to think that the strength of the *argyroaspides* (*argyraspides*) is the same as under Alexander the Great so it would have been 3,000 men[15], on the basis of which one may assume that the *chrysoaspides* had the same strength. There is one problem though. It is possible to interpret the above Latin text so that *argyroaspides*, *chrysoaspides* and 30,000 *phalangarii* were all formed from six legions all of which were similarly armed. If we think that all of these men consisted of legionaries, then it is clear that they were all armed like the rest, but if we consider the *argyroaspides* and *chrysoaspides* separate from the *phalangarii*, then we should probably think that the *argyroaspides* and *chrysoaspides* were equipped like the phalangites/hypaspists of Alexander the Great, but unfortunately it is not certain that their strength would have been the same.

The description of the Roman army in the *Kestoi* (Amulets or Embroideries) of the Christian author Julius Africanus, which was written during the reign of Alexander Severus, is also unhelpful for solving of the above questions.[16] In this text Julius criticized Roman equipment and tactics in the strongest possible terms, and recommended the use of Hellenic gear. The Greeks of Julius were equipped with scale armour, hoplite-style concave bronze *aspis*-shields with two handles (usable for shoving), a double helmet, two greaves, a broad but not long sword, *akontion*-javelin, and *doru/dory*-spear identical to those used by the royal cavalry (this means the Roman imperial horse guard). The last mentioned *doru*-spear means the Roman cavalry *kontarion/contus*, which is confirmed by D11/F12, lines 1.75–6 (p.40.75–6). The later East Roman military manuals give us the length of this spear: 3.74 metres. The Greeks equipped like this were ideally suited for fighting in close order and also as individuals. They typically attacked the enemy archers head-on by running rapidly so that they got inside the trajectory of the missiles and thereby made them ineffectual. The shields, double helmets and scale armour also gave them ideal protection against missiles (both slingshots and arrows) and also in close quarters combat. The peltasts and slingers were posted behind these shield-bearers.

The Macedonians made minor changes to this so that they could face both the barbarians and one another. Julius notes in particular the adoption of the open Laconian helmet and the shaving of beards. The implication is that basic Macedonian equipment was the same as previously described, and as I have noted in my biography of Caracalla it bears close resemblance to the equipment that Caracalla adopted for his Macedonian and Greek forces. Caracalla's phalangites were equipped with helmets of raw ox-hide ('*kranos ômoboeion*'), a three-ply linen *thorax*-breastplate ('*thorax linous trimitos*'), a bronze shield ('*aspis chalkê*'), long spear ('*doru/dory makron*'), short spear ('*aichmê bracheia*'), high boots ('*krepides*') and sword ('*xifos*'). In this context it is also of note that the *argyroaspides* of Alexander the Great were actually the hypaspists (*hypaspistai*) and that their equipment varied in some unknown manner from that used by the phalangites that used the *sarissa*-pike. This makes it possible that we should actually equate the equipment used by the phalangites of Caracalla with the equipment of the *argyroaspides/hypaspistai* of Alexander the Great and the Greeks/Macedonians of Julius Africanus possibly also with the equipment of the *argyroaspides* and *chrysoaspides* of Alexander Severus. This can mean that the '*doru makron*' was actually the cavalry *contus* that was 3.74 metres long, but this is unfortunately inconclusive because the two emperors (Caracalla and Alexander) could have easily chosen to equip their men slightly differently.

In contrast, according to the *Kestoi*, Roman soldiers were equipped with helmets reaching down to the shoulders, chainmail breastplates, large single-grip *thureos*-shields, long *spatha*-swords, and short *doru*-spears (later equated with the *akontia*-javelins, which means the *pila*-javelins). According to Julius Africanus, the Roman helmets which reached down to the shoulders made it difficult to dodge and duck and and made the wearer vulnerable to slingshots. See the introduction. Furthermore, the Roman curved cylindrical *thureos*-shield with the single handle was unsuitable for the *synaspismos* formation (shields interlocked rim-to-boss in width). The Roman spears (*dorata*) were also shorter than those used by the Greeks and therefore unsuited to facing the Parthian/Persian cavalry charges. Only one in ten javelins thrown resulted in a kill. The Roman combat formation, the hollow square (*plinthion*), with pack animals placed inside, was also impotent because the Roman soldiers dropped to one knee and formed a shield roof against the Parthian missiles. This practice protected them against missiles, but it caused no harm to the enemy. As we shall see, this can be seen as scathing criticism of the tactic adopted by the Roman southern army during the subsequent Roman counterattack. Julius also claimed that Roman soldiers could not fight as individuals and duellists against a throng of enemy fighters.

Julius Africanus's answer to these problems was that Roman soldiers should adopt Greek equipment and combat tactics. He specified the adoption of Greek scale armour and helmet together with the *contus / kontos*-spear, and that soldiers should be taught how to throw spears (*doru*-type) more accurately. Julius does not mention the adoption of the hoplite shield, but one may guess that this is implied even if not stated. In other words, the treatise recommended the type of equipment used by the phalangites of Caracalla. It also recommended that soldiers make controlled short running assaults towards the enemy every time the enemy launched missiles so that they could get inside their trajectory. The recommendation of Julius Africanus was therefore the use of aggressive assaulting Marathon-style tactics as used by the Greeks and Macedonians in the past.[17]

Soldiers from the Ludovisi Sarcophagus (mid-third century)

© Dr. Ilkka Syvänne 2016

The way we should interpret the above evidence vis-à-vis the information provided by Aelius Lampridius depends on how we date the *Kestoi* of Julius Africanus. We know that it was written during the reign of Alexander Severus (222–235), but after 227 because he mentions the building of the bath and library of Alexander. Both J.R. Vieillefond and E.L. Wheeler have speculated that Julius Africanus wrote the *Kestoi* in the spring of 231 to serve as a guide to Alexander Severus who was about to depart to the East to fight against the Persians, while I have speculated in my biography of Caracalla that it could have been written after the war. What is clear is that most of its instructions do indeed concern the eastern theatre and its problems. Good examples of this are the instructions on how to fight against elephants ((D11/F12.18, p.88ff.) and on how to fight against chariots with slingers (D18, pp.108–109).

If one adopts the view that it was written before the campaign, then it is clear that Julius Africanus knew the relative merits of each side and that he recommended the right solutions to each. It is unfortunate that this is unhelpful for the solving of the above problems because we do not know if Alexander Severus adopted these solutions.

If the treatise was written after the war in about 233, there are two possibilities. Firstly, it is possible that it is a criticism of the Roman combat methods used during that campaign, which would mean that we should include the silver and golden shields among the six regularly equipped legions. Secondly, it is possible that the treatise was meant to praise the Emperor Alexander Severus for the solutions he had adopted during this war while it criticized the traditional equipment and tactics adopted by the traditionalist commanders of the southern column. In support of the second alternative one can point to 1) the praise showered on the Greek/Macedonian equipment and tactics which one would expect to have been used by the units named *argyroaspides* and *chrysoaspides*; 2) the praise afforded to a victorious king/Emperor who captured or killed elephants (see below); 3) Alexander Severus minted a series of coins that depict *Mars Ultor* (perhaps modelled after the *argyroaspides* and *chrysoaspides*) equipped with Greek gear on the reverse in 232 (see the plates for two examples); 4) The Ludovisi Sarcophagus (dated ca. 251/2), which depicts some men on foot equipped with scale armour and/or hoplite shield (see my reconstructions in the plates for examples) which suggests that similarly equipped forces remained in use throughout the era under investigation. Drawings of some of the soldiers depicted in the Sarcophagus are included here. The combined circumstantial evidence makes it likelier that the treatise was written after the Persian war as a praise of Alexander's performance in it. This would also mean that we should consider the *argyroaspides* and *chrysoaspides* to have been equipped in Greek/Macedonian manner and that we should not include these among the six legions.

This leaves the problem of who these *argyroaspides* and *chrysoaspides* were. Did these men consist of the Praetorians? The Praetorians are known to have been equipped with scale armour after the reign of Septimius Severus so that the change in equipment would not have been that radical. There were certainly enough Praetorians for this purpose: both units would have consisted of approximately 5,000 men. Or were these men the phalangites of Caracalla? Both are possible although one would expect that Alexander Severus, who claimed to be Caracalla's son and Roman Alexander, would have imitated Alexander the Great and Caracalla. This would mean that the overall strength of the silver and golden shields would have been 16,384 men, each having 8,192 men apiece.

This, however, is not conclusive because the emperors could easily have adopted different solutions when they created their Hellenic forces. And we should not forget that Caracalla's phalangites did not wear scale armour or double helmets or Laconian helmets, but linen armour and leather helmets. Therefore my educated guess is that it is likelier that Alexander actually re-equipped his Praetorians as Hellenic spearmen.

In sum, the above means that the 30,000 *phalangarii* consisted of regularly equipped legionaries and that these consisted of six legions, 5,000 men apiece. And who were these *phalangarii*? Herodian (6.5.1–2) notes that of the forces under Alexander's personal command, the Illyrian troops in particular, suffered from illness in 232. On the basis of this it would be easy to think that the *phalangarii* consisted of the six Illyrian legions (*X Gemina*, *XIV Gemina*, *I Adiutrix*, *II Adiutrix*, *IV Flavia*, *VII Claudia*), but this is uncertain. On the basis of tombstones John S. McHugh (pp. 190–1) notes the presence of soldiers in the Persian war that were drawn from the western legions as follows: *II Parthica* (Alba in Italy), *XIII Gemina* (Apulum in Dacia), *IV Flavia* (Moesia Superior), *VII Claudia* (Moesia Inferior), and *XIV Gemina* (Pannonia Superior). He also notes that the two Pannonian legions *II Adiutrix* (Aquincum, Pannonia Inferior) suffered the removal of the honorary epithet in 230 and so did *X Gemina* (Vindobona, Pannonia Superior) in 232, but that it was restored in 234. This makes it probable but not conclusive; at least *II Adiutrix* and *X Gemina* were not included in the six legions making up the *phalangarii*. However, one still cannot entirely preclude the possibility that both were included in the phalanx and that it is only the result of the incomplete survival of evidence that we do not have a similar restoration of the epithet among the extant inscriptions for *II Adiutrix* as we have for the *X Gemina*.

The Mutiny in Antioch
When Alexander reached Antioch he began to train and drill the soldiers in preparation for the war. Antioch was the traditional assembly point for the armies campaigning in the East because it was easily supplied from the sea via its port city Seleucia. Standard practice was to assemble the army here and then to march it to some forward base like Edessa or Hierapolis or Nisibis which was then meant to serve as base of operations.

The statement of Aelius Lampridius that Alexander Severus was a disciplinarian who dismissed several legions has usually been claimed as false because his text is considered as panegyric.[18] Those who do not accept this claim point out the instances in which Alexander was unable to protect his Praetorian Prefect Ulpian, Cassius Dio and the many military mutinies under Alexander. This fails to take into account the fact that the disciplining can easily have been one of the causes that led to these troubles as is claimed by Aelius Lampridius. In short, Alexander was a disciplinarian and tried to discipline his forces, but he often failed to achieve his aim in practice. It is worth quoting Aelius Lampridius's description of what happened in Antioch when Alexander drilled and prepared his army for combat. For a quote of the same incident by Herodian, see later.

'He [*Alexander*] paid careful attention to the *annona* of the soldiers, and executed tribunes who granted any privileges to the soldiers in return for their rations… He knew everything there was to know about his soldiers regardless of where the soldier was stationed. He had even in his bedchamber roster records detailing the number of soldiers and the length of each man's service [*This made it difficult for the officers to keep dead men in the records*]... In the company of friends belonging to the military forces, he followed the custom introduced by Trajan, which was to drink after dessert five goblets of [*wine or possibly mead, see 30.5*], but he gave his friends only one goblet per man to drink in honour of Alexander the Great [*It is probable that at least some of the officers disliked this lowering of their rations*]... he was an excellent wrestler and great in arms [*After the reign of Caracalla the soldiers expected this from their Emperor*]... Having been told once that a poor old woman had been outrageously injured by a soldier, he cashiered him and gave him to the woman as a slave... And when the soldiers complained of this, he persuaded them all to submit to his will and at the same time made them fear him... He was so stern to soldiers that he often discharged entire legions addressing the soldiers as citizens instead of soldiers [*This has been doubted, e.g. by Magie, because it resembles the speech of Julius Caesar preserved in Suetonius Julius 70. However, it is entirely plausible to think that Alexander imitated Julius Caesar just like his 'father' Caracalla had imitated many great historical leaders*], never fearing his army because he knew that they could say nothing against his character on the basis that he would have allowed his tribunes and *duces* to steal their pay from them. He thought that when a soldier is well clothed and armed, his belly full, and something in his purse, there is nothing to fear because it was poverty that reduced the soldier to despair [*It is quite probable that this statement is correct, but what Alexander and his mother failed to understand was that they should still have bribed the men regularly with sizable donatives because they expected this after the reigns of Caracalla and Elagabalus. Furthermore, the soldiers liked to buy exemptions from duties by bribing their officers*]... When he had arrived in the city of Antioch, he was told one day that some of the soldiers had put themselves into the baths with the women of pleasure. He ordered them all to be arrested and put into chains. [*This was a prudish and insensitive thing to do. A wiser commander would have allowed it as long as the soldiers performed their combat drills and duties as expected*] When this was made known to the legion unto which those soldiers belonged, they all immediately attempted to mutiny... the prisoners were brought before Alexander and he mounted the platform while all the other soldiers stood around him in their arms, and he spoke as follows [*this speech is obviously an invention, as noted by McHugh p.204, but it is possible that something like this was really said*]: "Shall Roman soldiers... drink, bath, whore and live in the soft luxurious ways of the Greeks?" With this the tumult increased and they shouted a war cry against him... "I disband you... lay down your arms." After these words, they all lay down their arms [*the mutinuous men were surrounded by other troops!*] ...his guards that had attended upon his person took up the standards that the others had laid down and carried them to the camp, and their arms were gathered up by the people and brought to the palace... However, this legion which he had thus cashiered in thirty days, afterwards... he restored again to the same rank... and it was largely thanks to their bravery that he gained the victory. [*This means that this mutinous legion was one of those that Alexander used as his phalangarii*] ... Nevertheless, he inflicted the death sentence on its tribunes because it was thanks to their negligence that the soldiers had debauched themselves at Daphne and because they had not taken sufficient care to prevent the mutiny.' Aelius Lampridius, *HA Alexander* 15.5, 21.5ff., 27.9–10, 39.1–2, 52.1ff. tr. by Bernard with changes, additions, corrections and comments.

Herodian (6.4.7, see the quote later) mentioned that the Egyptian *legio II Traina* and some of the Syrian troops mutinied. This revolt was quickly quelled and the culprits punished after which Alexander transferred some of the units to other countries. McHugh (203–4) identifies the Syrians as the *III Gallica* from Syria Phoenice and notes that *IV Scythica* was transferred from Syria Palestina to Egypt and that a *dux* was appointed in Egypt to make certain that the soldiers who had been left behind there would not revolt. The above mutiny may or may not have been a separate incident because Alexander did not transfer the troops elsewhere. What is certain is that Alexander and Julia Mamaea managed to anger large numbers of soldiers with their prudish attitude to whoring and drinking.[19] Instead of binge drinking with the soldiers like Caracalla and instead of drinking and whoring with soldiers like Gallienus was later to do, Alexander Severus chose to punish the soldiers for this behaviour.[20] This was not wise. Otherwise, he was acting like a good commander, but this was not enough.

This is even more surprising in light of the speech to the mutinuous troops that Lampridius puts into the mouth of Alexander and we have no compelling reasons to doubt that Alexander could indeed have modelled his speech on Julius Caesar's speech because he, like the other members of the upper classes, had been taught from old texts. Suetonius (*Julius* 65–7) notes that Julius Caesar was in the habit of allowing his soldiers to indulge themselves as they wished on all occasions except when the enemy was near. It was only then that he imposed the harshest military discipline on the soldiers. It was in this that Alexander and his staff erred. They expected their soldiers to be disciplined even when they were not near the enemy, but it was next to impossible to force the men who had become used to their privileges to behave differently all of sudden.

3.4 The Persian Campaign in 232–233

During the preparatory stage of the war Alexander Severus is claimed to have sent another embassy to the Persians in an effort to achieve peace through diplomacy, but to no avail. It is clear that this was not meant as an honest attempt at achieving peace through negotiations but rather a propaganda ploy with which Alexander once again demonstrated his moderation and enemy's hostility. The second of his aims would have been to obtain intelligence of enemy activities. It is very unlikely that Alexander would not have intended to use the massive force that he had assembled. Therefore it is not surprising that Ardashir refused to listen. Ardashir, however, then committed a horrible plunder. He sent 400 impressive looking nobles as his embassy to Alexander with the message that the Romans should evacuate the whole of Asia. Ardashir's aim was to frighten the Romans with the impressive appearance of these men. But Alexander violated the sanctity of the envoys and imprisoned them. He and his advisors had no intention of letting the enemy spies return to their ruler.[21]

The key text for understanding the Persian war is the following quote from Herodian. It is, however, marred by anti-Alexander bias as was noted by Aelius Lampridius

(HA Alexander 57.2–3) and Julius Capitolinus (*HA Maximini* 13.3–4), and it is because of this that Aelius Lampridius is quoted after Herodian. This is confirmed by the other sources which verify the success of Alexander in the east.[22]

'While matters were being transacted like this, and Alexander was preparing to pass the rivers and penetrate into the enemy's country [*This means that his plan was to cross the Tigris*], some of the forces which came from Egypt deserted; and several other seditions were raised in Syria against the Empire; But the rebels were soon taken, and brought to punishment [*see above*]. After which, Alexander sent several camps [*'stratopedôn' presumably means in this case camps/legions*] in these parts into the other countries, the better to hinder the barbarian raids [*this is likely to mean the transferral of mutinous forces away from the army*]. These dispositions being made, and a powerful army collected, judged sufficient to match the multitude of the barbarians, a council of war was held; the result of which was to divide the army into three separate bodies: one of which he ordered to march to the north through Armenia… and penetrate into the country of the Medes. The second was sent to the eastern marshes of barbarian territory, where they say the Tigris and the Euphrates join… The third and the bravest part he promised to lead himself, taking the middle route against the barbarians. His intent in thus dividing the army was that by different routes he might surprise the enemy off their guard, and that the Persians being separated into several parties, in order to oppose the frequent incursions of the Romans, should be weakened by these diversions and take the field with less order. For the barbarians do not have a paid army like the Romans, but the whole multitude of their men and sometimes their women assemble whenever the king commands… [*Despite the fact that the Sassanians like the Parthians before them had standing units, the vast majority of their forces consisted of feudal levies drawn from the Parthian magnates. The aim was to lure them away from the royal army back to their homes where their families were threatened by the Romans*] They use bows and horses not only in war as the Romans do [*the Romans had trained all of their horsemen as mounted archers after Hadrian. See Arrian, Techne Taktika 34.1–44.2*[23]], but they are brought up with them in their infancy… nor do they ever go on foot, or without quivers… [*As we shall see, the plan was to send the northern army in advance of the other two armies to divert the Persians and Parthians to Media and possibly also to Parthia proper. The other two armies advanced together, first to Palmyra, which is proven by the existence of an inscription that refers to a visit by Alexander. For this, see REF1, 22–23. Palmyra was located in the desert far inside Roman territory so the presence of this army was hidden from the enemy. After this the army apparently advanced together to Dura Europos where the southern division continued along the Euphrates to the marshes and Alexander advanced across the Tigris*].

But these measures of Alexander were not so fortunate as they appeared prudent; for the army that was sent through Armenia, having, with much labour and difficulty, passed the craggy and steep mountains in those parts (for as it was the height of summer, the season somewhat facilitated their passage) made descent upon the Medes, and having wasted their country, and burnt several villages, carried off the plunder. With the Persian king being informed, he fought back as well as he could, but could not drive the Romans out because the terrain was broken. This gave the infantry firm treading and easy marches, but the roughness of the mountainous ground greatly hindered the galloping of the barbarian horses so they were unable to make charges and attacks. [*The Armenian column was dispatched first to divert the Persian main force away from Mesopotamia. These forces consisted of the Romans and Armenians with their allies, and could therefore easily have consisted of about 100,000 men because the Armenians alone possessed military potential for about 120,000 knights. See also the discussion in Chapter 6.3.*]

At the same time news was brought to the Persian king that another army of the Romans had invaded eastern parts of Parthia and were scouring the plains. Fearing therefore that after overthrowing the Parthians, the Romans would invade Persia, he left what he thought a sufficient force for the defence of Media and hastened with the rest of his army to eastern parts. The Romans meeting no opposition marched in a careless disorderly manner supposing that Alexander with the third division of the forces [*If true, the commander and his officers, scouts and spies failed to perform their duty*], which was by far the greatest and most powerful, had by this time penetrated into the midst of the enemy's country and that the barbarians being constantly diverted to different places would render their march easy and unmolested. For it had been agreed that all three armies should break into enemy territory from different places and that a place was appointed where they were to meet once they had taken control of enemy territory. [*This is clearly incorrect for the initial stage of the conflict, because it is clear that the southern and northern wings were not advancing against some central point. However, it is probable that the intention was that the central and southern divisions would meet each other somewhere near Elymais so that the southern division advanced along the Euphrates while Alexander crossed the Tigris and then advanced along it in the same direction.*] But Alexander deceived them by not invading with his army. We cannot determine whether he did this through fear and unwillingness to hazard the safety of his own person for the defence of the Roman Empire, or whether his mother hindered him through womanish timorousness and excessive love for her son. [*This is propaganda put forth by Maximinus Thrax, which Herodian has believed. He seems to have blamed Alexander for his own defeat. See later.*] But this is certain, she always suppressed and dulled his manly spirit, persuading him that others ought to be exposed for him but that he himself should always keep aloof of danger [*This appears to be slander because Aelius Lampridius claims that Alexander exposed himself to danger. Then again, there is a germ of truth to it. Alexander obviously did not expose himself to danger in the same manner as the duelling Caracalla, and this seems to have been the expectation after the reign of Caracalla. Alexander clearly stayed behind his soldiers to direct the combat as traditional Roman combat doctrine expected commanders to behave.*]. This was the destruction of the Roman army that had entered the enemy's country. The Persian king attacked it unexpectedly with all his forces. [*The careless marching and this surprise mean that the Romans were not initially using the hollow square array for marching.*] He surrounded and trapped them in as if they were fish in a net; and, pouring volleys of arrows from every side destroyed the whole Roman army. The Romans were few in comparison with the enemy and could not stem the overwhelming odds and they were constantly forced to shield with arms those parts of their bodies that were exposed to arrows. They were content to adopt a defensive stance as a result of which they were all forced into a close body, and by the projection of their shields they formed a kind of wall, and fought like they were in a besieged city [*This means that the surviving Romans adopted the hollow square formation, which they used defensively. This is what Julius Africanus had criticized. The Romans should have adopted an aggressive stance even with the hollow square.*]. They were shot and wounded from every side, yet they made a brave and obstinate resistance until they were killed to the last man [*This statement seems to be an exaggeration because the information discussed at greater length below suggests that the southern division was led by Maximinus Thrax – he certainly survived. The likeliest reason for this discrepancy is that Maximinus and most of the cavalry forces under him fought their way out and left their infantry to be butchered*]. This great calamity was such a blow to Roman power as can hardly be paralleled in any of their former misfortunes, one in which a great army was destroyed, an army that in steadiness, strength and bravery was not a whit inferior to the best of the ancients. The victory swelled the Persians with hopes of greater achievements.

When the news was brought to Alexander, who lay dangerously sick... he fell into despair. And the rest of the army grew very angry with Alexander because he had deceived and betrayed their fellow soldiers because he had not performed his part of the agreement. Alexander was now unable to bear his illness and the stifling atmosphere. Sickness was raging among his whole army, especially among those who came from Illyricum... [*Alexander*] resolved to return to Antioch. Accordingly, he sent an order to the army in Media to return. The greatest part of this force perished in the mountains during their return trip, for the excessive cold of the winter mutilated their hands and feet. Alexander led his own division back to Antioch after losing great numbers to the illness. [*The withdrawal of the army as a result of the outbreak of illness was definitely the right thing to do, contrary to what Herodian states. The soldiers were clearly in no condition to fight.*] This inglorious expedition caused great discontent in the army and dishonour to Alexander... the greatest part of this army had been destroyed by disease, war and cold [*this is clearly a hostile falsification*]. He [*Alexander*] recovered his health... He likewise endeavoured to regain the soldiers' favour by distributing large sums of money [*This was necessary in the circumstances. It would have been the second time Alexander distributed money to his troops during this campaign. It was too little.*]. Herodian 6.5.1ff., tr. by Hart 253ff. with changes, corrections and comments.

'And so, having set out from there against the Persians with a great array, he [*Alexander*] defeated Artaxerxes, a most powerful king. In this battle he himself commanded the flanks [*This presumably means that Alexander commanded the argyroaspides and chrysoaspides and that the 30,000 phalangarii were placed between these wings. It was obviously impossible for Alexander to be in command of both wings simultaneously so we should rather take this to mean that Alexander's battle plan was to use both wings offensively at the right moment. I would therefore suggest that both wings and centre had their own commanders and that Alexander acted as overall commander who then commanded both wings to attack at the right moment*], urged on the soldiers, exposed himself constantly to missiles, performed many brave deeds with his own hand, and by his words encouraged individual soldiers to praiseworthy actions. At last he routed and put to flight this great king, who had come to the war with seven hundred elephants, eighteen hundred scythed chariots, and many thousand horsemen. Thereupon he immediately returned to Antioch and presented to his troops the booty taken from the Persians, commanding the tribunes and generals [*duces*] and even the soldiers to keep for themselves the plunder they had seized in the country. Then for the first time Romans had Persian slaves, but because the kings of the Persians deem it a disgrace that any of their subjects should serve anyone as slaves, ransoms were offered, and these Alexander accepted and then returned the men, either giving the ransom-money to those who had taken the slaves captive, or depositing it in the public treasury. After this, returning to Rome, he conducted a most splendid triumph and addressed the senate in the following speech: "There were 700 elephants provided with turrets and archers and great loads of arrows. Of these we captured 30, we have left 200 slain upon the field, and we have led 18 in triumph. Moreover, there were scythed chariots, 1,800 in number. Of these we could have presented to your eyes 200, of which the horses have been slain [*note the instruction to target the horses in the Kestoi*], but since they could easily be counterfeited we have refrained from so doing. 120,000 of their cavalry we have routed, 10,000 of their cataphracted horsemen, whom they call *clibanarii*, we have slain in battle, and with their armour we have equipped our own men. We have captured many of the Persians and have sold them into slavery, and we have reconquered the lands which lie between the rivers, those of Mesopotamia I mean, abandoned by that filthy monster Artaxerxes... we have routed and driven him from the field, so that the land of the Persians saw him in full flight." All this we have found both in the annals and in many writers. Some assert, however, that he was betrayed by one of his slaves and did not conquer the king at all [*This would be the commander who had caused the defeat of the southern army corps*], but on the contrary was forced to flee... But... this is contrary to the general belief. It is also stated that he lost his army through hunger, cold, and disease, and this is the version given by Herodian, but contrary to the belief of the majority. Aelius Lampridius, *HA Alexander* 55.1–523ff. tr. by Magie p.289–95 with some emendations, changes and corrections.

In short, we learn from Herodian that the Romans planned to use a three-pronged invasion for the campaign season of 232. It is also apparent that the goal was to conquer the Persian Empire as befitted a ruler named Alexander. The northern division invaded first through Armenia into Media with the intention of drawing the Persian main force to the north. In the meantime, the southern and central divisions advanced to Palmyra[24] and from there to Dura Europus (where a *Dux Ripae* is attested to have existed at this time). It was then at Dura Europos that the two forces separated so that the southern division advanced along the Euphrates to the point where it joined the Tigris and became a marsh, with the implication that it was to bypass Seleucia-Ctesiphon and invade the marshlands and possibly also Elymais. This makes it possible that there was a Parthian resistance movement against the Sassanians in the area south of Ctesiphon. The second of the divisions therefore threatened Fars/Persis. The third division, consisting of the cream of the army was under the personal command of Alexander Severus. Unfortunately we lack specific information about its intended invasion route beyond the fact that it was to invade Persian territory between the northern and southern divisions and it was meant to meet the southern division at some specific point. However, the reference to the plan of crossing the Euphrates and Tigris makes it probable that the intention was that Alexander would cross the Euphrates at Dura-Zaitha and then march through the desert to Hatra (allied with Rome at this time) after which he would then cross the Tigris and then march south along it. After this there are two possibilities regarding the Roman plans. Firstly, it is possible that the intention was to besiege Ctesiphon so that the southern army blocked any possible help from the south while Alexander's army besieged Ctesiphon and blocked any help from the north. Secondly, it is possible that the intention had been all along to make Ardashir march back and forth – first north against the northern division and then back south against the southern division. Then Alexander could intercept Ardashir's army en route, tired from the long march, and inflict a decisive defeat. Both are possible, but my educated guess is that the second is true for two reasons: Firstly because Alexander advanced through the desert to Hatra so his presence would have been hidden from the enemy as long as possible; and secondly because Herodian makes it clear that the southern division was not expecting the enemy attack.

The northern Roman army achieved considerable success thanks to the terrain, and it also distracted the Persian main army as planned with the result that the southern division was able to advance at its leisure just like Alexander Severus's division in the middle. However, when the Persian king learnt of the invasion of the southern division past Ctesiphon, he immediately realized that this threatened the heartland of his power, which was actually not in the Ctesiphon area but in Persis/Fars. Then, when he was en route to defend Persis, he suddenly came face to face with the Roman main army under Alexander, which had concealed its presence by marching through the deserts. The fact that Ardashir was forced to fight proves that the appearance of the Roman army came as a surprise to him. The Romans were clearly well aware of Persian movements, while Ardashir was not aware of Roman movements. The reason why the Romans knew the whereabouts of the Persian main army would be that it included Parthians who did not like to be ruled by a Persian.

We can attempt to reconstruct the battle by combining the information provided by Aelius Lampridius, Julius Africanus and the information regarding the size of the Roman cavalry army after the reign of Alexander Severus.[25] Readers, however, should keep in mind that most of what follows below is only my educated guesses or learned speculation based on the above sources. The resulting reconstruction is purely hypothetical.

Firstly, we have the problem of how large the infantry component of Alexander's force was and what was his battle formation. On the basis of Aelius Lampridius and Julius Africanus, it would appear unlikely that Alexander would have used the hollow square/ oblong formation. These imply the use of a phalanx. Taken together, they would rather suggest that Alexander used a frontline consisting of the 30,000 *phalangarii* posted in the middle and of the wings of *argyroaspides* and *chrysoaspides*. The strength of the latter two units is problematic as already discussed. If these consisted of the Praetorians re-equipped as Greeks/Macedonians, then both wings had about 5,000 men for a total of

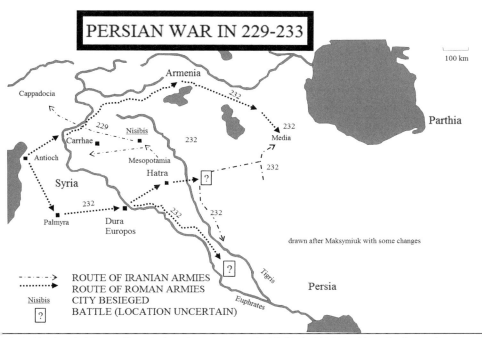

PERSIAN WAR IN 229-233

100 km

Armenia

Cappadocia

Parthia

229   Nisibis

Carrhae

232   Media

Antioch

232

Mesopotamia

Hatra   232

Syria

232

Palmyra   Dura
Europos

drawn after Maksymiuk with some changes

- - - - -> ROUTE OF IRANIAN ARMIES
.........> ROUTE OF ROMAN ARMIES
Nisibis   CITY BESIEGED
[?]   BATTLE (LOCATION UNCERTAIN)

Tigris

Persia

Euphrates

Ardashir I invaded Roman Cappadocia and attempted to seize Nisibis in 229-230. Alexander Severus's
response was to concentrate army at Antioch in 231 and then launch a three-pronged invasion of Persian
territory. The northern division advanced through the mountains of Armenia up to Media (Maksymiuk suggests
that it may have advanced as far as Parthia, but this is uncertain), the southern division marched together with
Alexander through the Syrian Desert up to Dura Europos and then towards the marshes of the Tigris and
Euphrates (this division was crushed by Ardashir after he had first engaged Alexander). The central division
under the emperor himself marched to Hatra and from there across the Tigris where Alexander defeated
Ardashir, but since he failed to pursue Ardashir, Ardashir was able to march to the south and defeat the Roman
southern division. The main sources for Alexander campaign are: Herodian 6.5-7; SHA Sev. Alex. 55-58, 61.
All sources are usefully summarized in REF1 16ff. and Maksymiuk pp.29-31.

40,000 heavy infantry for the entire frontline, but if these consisted of 8,192 men per
flank then the frontline had a total of about 46,000 heavy infantry. Both are possible,
but I have here adopted the former approach because it is next to impossible to find any
traces of the Macedonian phalanx after the reign of Caracalla so it is possible that it was
disbanded and the men transferred to other units under Macrinus. But at the same time it
should be kept in mind that we do not possess a complete record of the units in existence.

The next problem is the size of the light infantry force accompanying the frontline.
These would have been the peltasts and archers behind the men in Greek equipment.
The problem here is that the Romans trained all of their legionaries to fight like light
infantry with javelins and slings, and a quarter to a third of their legionaries to fight with
bows. It is also known that the Roman legions at this time had specialist lightly-equipped
javeliners called *lanciarii*. This means that they could have formed their light infantry
component entirely from the legionaries. But at the same time we know that they also
possessed specialized light infantry auxiliary units. I am here making the assumption that

the vast majority of the light infantry for the frontline was provided by their own units and that the auxiliary infantry provided only about 5,000 extra lightly-equipped men for the frontline so the entire frontline consisted of about 45,000 infantry.

The next problem is the size of the infantry reserve posted behind the frontline. Combat doctrine allowed two different solutions. If Alexander had built a marching camp from which he advanced far enough, he would have used the double phalanx formation for the protection of the rear with additional separate units under the commanders serving as small reserve forces. This would mean that he had about 90,000 men on foot if there were only small numbers of extra light infantry for the second phalanx. If he had taken with him the baggage train with its wagons and *carroballistae* to protect the rear or had the camp right behind him, then he had only smaller reserve forces posted in the flanks and middle with the implication that he would have had only about 55,000 men on foot plus the servants etc among the baggage train or camp. Both alternatives are possible because the later sources suggest that the cavalry contingent at this time consisted of about 30,000 horsemen or more,[26] and because professional Roman soldiers were in the habit of defeating numerically superior forces. However, Julius Africanus (*Kestoi* 18) states that the elephants always broke through the enemy ranks and overturned, smashed, destroyed, and snatched horses, men and chariots in their trunks. This piece of information suggests that Alexander had with him his baggage train so he had about 55,000 men on foot and 30,000 cavalry for a total of about 85,000 soldiers plus the servants etc among the baggage train. This would mean that about 85,000 Romans plus their servants etc faced about 120,000 Persians plus their servants etc on the battlefield.

On the basis of the composition of the forces and Julius Africanus's description, the battle appears have begun with the attack of the Persian elephants and scythed chariots. The Persians' battle doctrine allowed them to deploy their cavalry either as one line of rhomboids or as two lines, but in the following diagrams I have made the guess that they used two lines. The Romans appear to have effectively neutralized most of the scythed chariots with slingers (shots aimed at the exposed legs of the horses *Kestoi*, D18, pp.108–9) and some of the elephants by sending lightly equipped infantry javeliners and archers in front of the phalanx to target them or by scattering caltrops in their path [*Kestoi* 18]. It is probable that at least some of the caltrops were scattered by Roman cavalry when they apparently retreated behind the phalanx just as they did at the battle of Nisibis in 217.[27] It is probable that the Roman cavalry made a feigned attack first to lure the enemy forward, after which they scattered caltrops behind them and retreated behind the infantry. However, on the basis of the *Kestoi*, it is probable that some of the elephants still managed to penetrate through the phalanx so that they were able to wreak havoc among the Roman cavalry, baggage train and *carroballistae*.[28] One may assume that it was then that the *phalangarii* earned their pay rise and the legion that had mutinied at Antioch distinguished itself and either killed or captured the elephants and their drivers. It is quite possible that at least in some cases the Romans used the *antistomos difalangia* (facing double phalanx in which units wheeled backwards left and right to open a route for the enemy to penetrate) formation to allow the elephants to penetrate the formation without causing disorder so that they could then be killed by the lightly-equipped men posted behind. The fact that the Romans were able to kill 10,000 *clibanarii* in this battle suggests that at least some of the Persian cavalry posted behind the elephants (and probably also behind the scythed chariots) penetrated the Roman array at the same time, only to be killed when they entered the trap.

It would seem likely that the Romans started their counterattack once this immediate crisis caused by the scythed chariots and elephants was over and the Persians had retreated to their initial positions because the attack with the scythed chariots and elephants had failed.[29] However, before this the Romans would obviously have reorganized their ranks, files and formations. As noted above, Alexander cannot have been the commander of both flanks simultaneously because of the distance between them. It is clear that he was in the centre and as overall commander he ordered the flanks to perform the counterattack which decided the battle. The attack with the flanks would have been done either in a crescent (*menoeides*) or forward-angled half-square (*epikampios emprosthia*) formation.[30] Such an attack with the men in Greek gear would in all probability have been spearheaded by the cavalry wings which would have tied the enemy cavalry in place so that the elite *argyroaspides* and *chrysoaspides* could then slam into the enemy cavalry formation. This would have been the charge that limited the time that the Romans had to spend under the enemy arrows. The attack was a great success and the Persians were defeated. However, since the Persian force consisted of mounted men, the defeat did not prove decisive.

In sum, the Persians were defeated, but most of the Persians were able to flee with their ruler, on top of which the Romans failed to pursue them or warn the southern column of the approach of the enemy's main force. Alexander did not conduct any vigorous pursuit of the defeated enemy. The sources offer several different reasons for this. Some accused Alexander and his mother of cowardice, others claimed that it was because Alexander and his army, in particular the Illyrians, suffered from illness. In my opinion the likeliest reason for Alexander's failure to pursue to his advantage are that he and his forces had indeed contracted an illness and could not pursue the enemy. It is also probable that Alexander had fewer men than his enemy even after the victory so it would have been dangerous to pursue them. Therefore Ardashir was able to save most of his forces to lead them against the southern invasion force, which he then annihilated in its entirety with effective mounted archery when the Romans had assumed the defensive hollow square formation. When Alexander and his advisors learnt of the defeat, they ordered all Roman forces to withdraw from Persia. The northern division in particular suffered during their withdrawal through wintry Armenia highlands. The likeliest reason for the Roman failure to warn the southern column is that their couriers were unable to bypass the army of Ardashir/Artaxerxes which was now between the Roman armies.

In my opinion Maximinus Thrax[31] is likely to have been the commander of the defeated southern column and that it is also probable that Herodian has magnified the scale of the disaster while leaving out Maximinus's role in it. There are two reasons for my conclusion: the texts of Zonaras (12.16) and the *Synopsis Sathas* (35.8–15). As regards the latter, the latest editors and translators of Malalas think that it comes originally from Malalas. This text refers to the appointment of Maximinus Thrax as general by Alexander Severus during his Persian wars (tr. by Jeffreys, Jeffreys and Scott p.158 with my comments added): 'He [*Alexander Severus*] made an expedition with his mother against the Persians, and in Antioch appointed Maximinus as general [*strategos*]. The latter fought a battle against the Persians but was defeated, and the emperor grew angry with him. When the emperor learned from Rome that a war was being started by the

Alexander's Battle: The probable battle formations

Persian cavalry deployed in five divisions (outer left, left, centre, right, outer right) each consisting of two lines

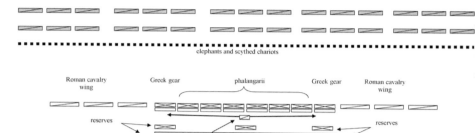

elephants and scythed chariots

Roman cavalry wing Greek gear phalangarii Greek gear Roman cavalry wing

reserves reserves

baggage train

Alexander moving back and forth behind his frontline to direct the combat.

Phase 1. The Persian attack.

The Persian scythed chariots and elephants attack the Romans with the support of their cavalry. If the Persians used two battle lines, they sent forward only their first cavalry line as depicted here. The Romans cavalry wings counter this attack with dropped caltrops and by using missiles, while the Roman infantry uses lightly-equipped men in front as a counter measure against the Persian attack. Some of the Persians manage to make their way through, but are still defeated by the Romans.

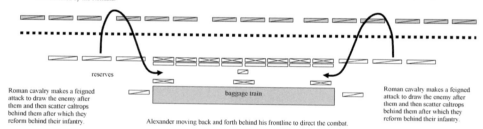

reserves

Roman cavalry makes a feigned attack to draw the enemy after them and then scatter caltrops behind them after which they reform behind their infantry.

baggage train

Roman cavalry makes a feigned attack to draw the enemy after them and then scatter caltrops behind them after which they reform behind their infantry.

Alexander moving back and forth behind his frontline to direct the combat.

Phase 2. The Roman counter-attack.

The Persians have redeployed their defeated first cavalry line behind their second line to form one united formation of 10 ranks while the surviving chariots and elephants reform behind the cavalry

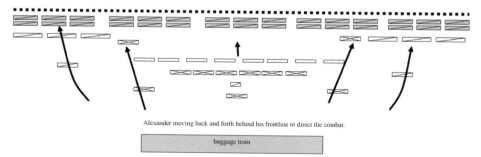

Alexander moving back and forth behind his frontline to direct the combat.

baggage train

The Roman counter-attack spearheaded by the cavalry and infantry wings. I have here made the educated guess that Alexander Severus would have used the *epikampios emprosthia* formation in the manner described by Vegetius (5th formation), namely by sending the lightly equipped footmen in advance of the phalanx to cover up the hole between the infantry wings and centre. The Persian wings are defeated with the result that the entire Persian force flees from the battlefield.

German people, he made peace with the Persians and marched against the Germans. Maximinus immediately rebelled behind him, was proclaimed emperor by the army, and set out for Italy. Alexander learnt of this, fought a battle with him, but was defeated [*on the basis of Herodian this appears inaccurate, but if one takes this figuratively then not necessarily so*].'

The same is confirmed by Zonaras (12.16). Zonaras states that Alexander Severus had appointed Maximinus Thrax as general, and that he then campaigned against the Persians but was shamefully defeated by the Persians with the result that he became the object of imperial anger. The latter means that Maximinus was demoted to the position of *praefectus tironum*, a mere trainer of recruits. It was then because of this that Maximinus felt such intense hatred towards Alexander and everything he represented. He hated the Christians too – Alexander honoured Christians and had many in his household.

Jordanes (*Getica* 83–8, esp.88) and Herodian have nothing to say about the defeats of Maximinus under Alexander, but my own educated guess is that there is more than a germ of truth in the version given by Zonaras and the *Synopsis Sathas* because it has now been recognized for a long time that Maximinus Thrax is the likeliest candidate for position of *dux ripae* headquartered at Dura Europos for this period. The title makes it clear that this was a special command in which several units were put under a single general. The reason for this conclusion is the artful speech put into the mouth of Maximinus Thrax by Herodian in which he spoke to the soldiers in 238 (7.8.4; tr. by Hart 289 with some changes and corrections): 'Even the Persians, who but lately were overrunning Mesopotamia, are now very quiet, and think themselves happy to enjoy their own possessions, being taught the danger of raising disturbances, by the renown of your arms, and the greatness of my actions when I was a commander of the camps on the banks of the river.'

If one reads the above text like a devil's advocate, it becomes obvious that the speech of Herodian Maximinus is actually not stating that he had been victorious when *dux ripae* at Dura Europos, but that he had fought bravely at the time and that it was this and the reputation of the Roman soldiers that kept the Persians at bay rather than the achievements of Alexander Severus. Jordanes' account is also clearly biased in favour of Maximinus and therefore unreliable (e.g. he claims that Maximinus had no role in the murder of Alexander), which is not surprising in light of the fact that Jordanes was himself a Goth and clearly considered the half-Goth Maximinus as his kinsman. When this is then connected with the subsequent appointment of Maximinus Thrax as trainer of the recruits it becomes obvious that he had been demoted from the larger command of troops to a position of inspector and trainer. In other words, he was no longer in charge of the veterans, but a trainer of mainly Pannonian recruits. It would appear probable that he had been put in charge of training a new set of recruits to replace those lost by him. If one then takes into account the probable survival of the *dux ripae* Maximinus Thrax and the numbers of casualties suffered by both sides in Herodian (both the Persians and Romans lost equal numbers) it becomes likely that at least some of the men belonging to the southern column managed to fight their way back to freedom under Maximinus himself, hence the reference to Maximinus's own actions and bravery of the soldiers in the speech. It is also very likely that it was Maximinus Thrax who excused his defeat by accusing Alexander Severus of cowardice and not sticking to the plan, and that it was this version that found its way into Herodian's text. On the basis of the narrative of Herodian and the above conclusions, it is probable that the southern division marched carelessly in column formations because they expected that Alexander's division would protect their rear, and then all of a sudden they were surrounded by Persians. Some of them, particularly cavalry, fought their way through the encircling forces under Maximinus; the rest formed the defensive hollow square formation, but were then eventually killed to the last man. If the *legio IV* (*Parthica?*) that Maximinus had formed and drilled accompanied him, it is probable that it was now destroyed in its entirety excepting those elements that may have been left behind to perform some administrative and logistical duties. If this was the case, it would also be likely that this *legio IV* was equipped and fought in the manner criticized by Julius Africanus.

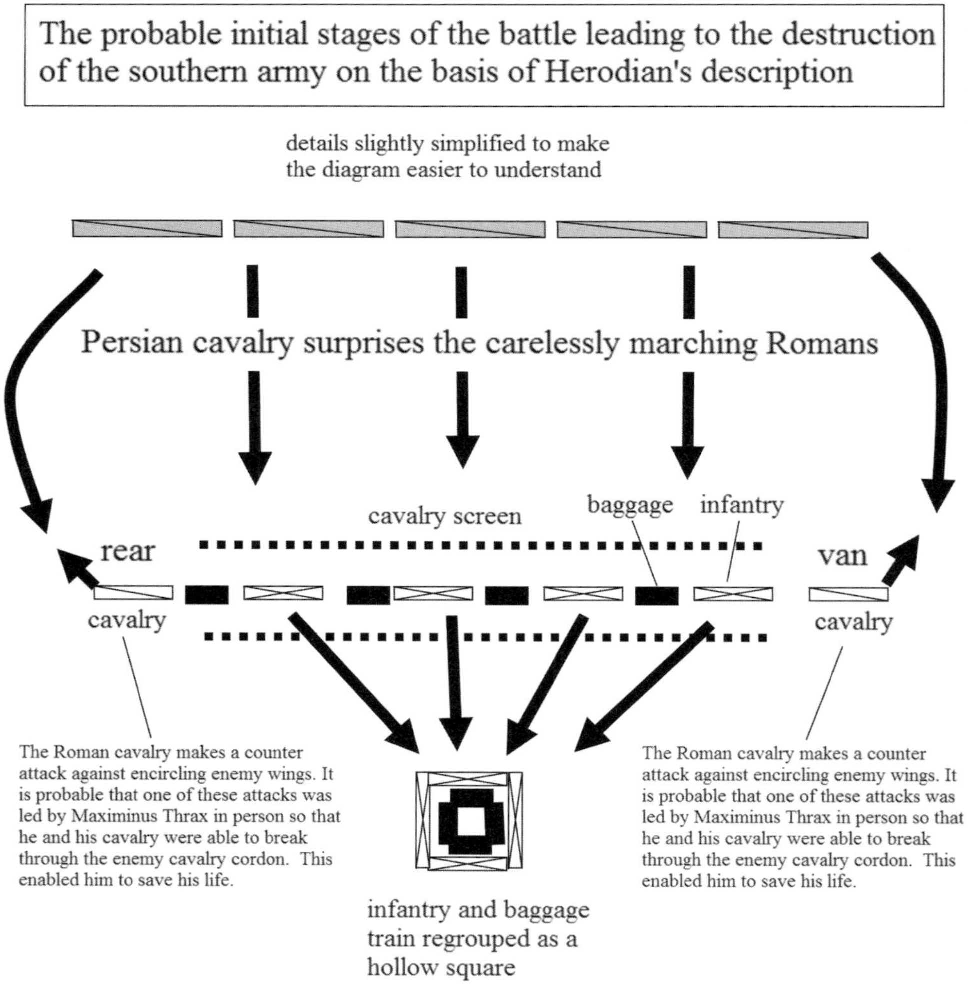

The probable initial stages of the battle leading to the destruction of the southern army on the basis of Herodian's description

details slightly simplified to make
the diagram easier to understand

Persian cavalry surprises the carelessly marching Romans

cavalry screen

baggage   infantry

rear

van

cavalry

cavalry

The Roman cavalry makes a counter attack against encircling enemy wings. It is probable that one of these attacks was led by Maximinus Thrax in person so that he and his cavalry were able to break through the enemy cavalry cordon. This enabled him to save his life.

The Roman cavalry makes a counter attack against encircling enemy wings. It is probable that one of these attacks was led by Maximinus Thrax in person so that he and his cavalry were able to break through the enemy cavalry cordon. This enabled him to save his life.

infantry and baggage
train regrouped as a
hollow square

As noted above, many soldiers accused both Alexander and Julia Mamaea of the destruction of the southern army. Because of their cowardice the enemies had managed to kill their comrades. It is probable that it was Maximinus Thrax and others who had accompanied him that accused Alexander to exculpate themselves from the blame of the defeat. They would also probably have blamed the equipment (spears too short to fight against Persian cavalry, cylindrical shields with a single grip preventing the use of the shields for shoving, and helmets reaching down to the shoulders making ducking difficult) and combat formation (hollow square in which men just stood in place when the enemy showered them with missiles) for their defeat, because it is these that are being blamed for the Roman defeats in the *Kestoi* of Julius Africanus. Regardless, the war had been relatively successful up to that point, so Alexander was able to mint coins celebrating his victory. The northern division had pillaged enemy territory far and wide, while the central division under Alexander had inflicted a defeat on the king of kings. Alexander's division had killed at least 10,000 *clibanarii* and their equipment was used to equip Roman cavalry. The equipment worn by the *clibanarii* is likely to have looked as depicted in the two accompanying illustrations drawn after the graffiti from Dura Europos, which date precisely from this period. They had also taken large numbers of captives and thirty elephants. The former, presumably deserters from Persia, were used to form new cavalry units which were called Parthians. The fact that Ardashir had overthrown the Parthians obviously made many Parthians quite willing to fight on the Roman side.

Dura Europus, cataphract
(drawn after von Gall)

Dura Europus, mounted
archer on armoured horse
(after fig. 17D James)

Alexander and his advisors were planning to continue the campaign because they knew that the Sassanian army would be difficult to collect once Ardashir had dispersed it back to their winter quarters. Once back home it would take a long time for him to be able to reassemble the feudal contingents serving under different Parthian nobles. An inscription from Egypt dated 232/3 suggests that Alexander was planning to visit

Egypt and preparations were made with this in mind.[32] My educated guess is that such a visit is to be connected with three things: the securing of supplies for the next campaign season, the securing of Egypt because its legion had been one of those that had mutinied, and the probable plan to use the Roman fleet and diplomacy in the Red Sea and Indian Ocean for the purpose of bypassing Persian traders.[33] However, this was not to be because the withdrawal of forces from the Danubian and Rhine frontiers had created a power vacuum which the barbarians across the rivers exploited by invading. Alexander and his mother had no other alternative but to lead their armies back. The Illyrian soldiers were particularly distressed by the news because they had suffered a double calamity. The Germans had invaded their homes while many of them had lost their lives to disease or were suffering from it. Alexander and Julia left a force behind which they thought sufficient and then began the march home. The victory, however, had enabled them to strengthen the army with sizable contingents of Parthian and Armenian mounted archers, both of which were very useful for wars against the Germans, Sarmatians and Dacians. This had been recognized since the days of Augustus.[34] They also took with them the Oshroenian mounted archers and Moors for the same reasons, and equipped some of the regular Roman cavalry forces with *clibanarii* equipment.

The Germans, Sarmatians, Alans, and Dacian Carpi as enemies
The Germanic peoples consisted of three major groupings: 1) the Scandinavian tribes (the tribes in the south of Denmark and north of Germany can also be considered to belong to this group); 2) The Western tribes and confederacies (Franks, Alamanni, Suevi/Suebi, Marcomanni, Thuringians, Lombards, western branch of the Heruls etc); 3) Eastern tribes and confederacies (Goths, eastern branch of the Heruls, Burgundi, Vandals, Gepidae, Quadi, Taifali, Rugi, Sciri, Bastarnae etc).

The Germanic foes included both tribes and tribal confederacies (Franks, Alamanni, Goths). Most of these were led by kings or high-kings, but during peacetime their rulers had only very limited authority over their subjects. The principal fighting forces of all the Germanic peoples consisted of the personal retinues of the king and nobles and they were naturally better equipped than all the rest because their employer's standing depended on his ability to bribe them with gifts. The Germanic peoples could field truly sizable armies because their entire free male population was required to serve in the tribal army when called to do so, but it was more typical for the Germans to use only their youth in wars because they were expected to prove their manhood before being allowed to marry. For example, the Goths with their allies could field armies of 100,000–300,000 men as we shall see, while the Franks could field armies of 100,000 men or even more.

The Romans considered all Germanic tribes to be fearless and brave warriors who preferred to fight in hand-to-hand combat. Most of the Germanic cavalry forces preferred to avoid complicated manoeuvres, because the Germanic armies were usually not drilled enough for this, but there were some notable exceptions to this rule – for example, under Cniva the Goth cavalry performed quite complicated manoeuvres. In practice the Germans often simply charged at a gallop straight at the enemy, which they sought to repeat by using spare horses if the enemy did not flee. The resulting wild and impetuous cavalry attack was a frightful sight and could scare the living daylights out of green recruits, even if veteran Roman infantry were usually able to withstand such attacks when in close order and in sufficient numbers. The use of such cavalry tactics was more typical for the East Germanic tribes. They often used wagon laagers as their place of refuge. When they were accompanied by a wagon laager, this usually meant that their infantry forces and possibly families were accompanying them. The East Germanic tribes had copied their mounted archery tactics from the Alans and Sarmatians, and in fact the Goths had incorporated entire tribes of both into their nation. The typical equipment of the East Germanic horseman consisted of a spear and/or javelin, sword, bow, and possibly a shield. The West Germanic horseman usually used a spear and/or javelin, sword and shield – only the elite wore armour and helmet. The Goths were an exception to the rule: they typically wore more armour than their compatriots as they had copied from the Alans and Sarmatians things they considered useful.

All of the Germanic tribes and confederacies were adept in the use of infantry phalanx/shield-wall, and knew how to form a wedge for attack and circle/hollow square in defence. At the unit level the Germans used the close order, tortoise, and open order to adapt their infantry forces to the terrain. In sum, the Germanic peoples were capable of using all of the principal combat formations and unit orders, and so were formidable foes. The use of infantry as the main striking force of the tribal army was more typical of the West Germanic tribes. They had three main infantry variants: the Franks typically used un-armoured infantry equipped with javelins and/or *francisca* throwing axe, shield and sword. The javelins and axes were first thrown like *pila* after which the men charged at the enemy. The second of the variants was that the men were equipped with thrusting spears, shields and swords. The third consisted of foot archers.

The principal weaknesses of the Germans were: 1) poorly organized logistical services; 2) poor siege skills; 3) tribal levies not as well trained as the Roman professionals; 4) with the exception of the Goths the missile arm was relatively weak; 5) the Germanic peoples wore in general less armour than the Romans. But there were exceptions.

The West Germanic tribes whose lands bordered the North Sea or Atlantic Ocean posed a naval threat to the Romans, but this took only the form of piracy because their ships were no match against the Roman war galleys. Their ships were far smaller Viking-style ships/boats with crews ranging from about 12 men to 60/70 men (at most perhaps 100–150 men), but during this period the vast majority of their naval vessels belonged to the smallest category of about 12 to 16 men per boat. Their principal tactic was to try to raid coastal areas without having to fight the Romans. The Romans countered this by using a combination of the following methods: 1) placing guard towers, forts and cavalry forces along the coasts; 2) engaging the enemy when they were withdrawing; 3) paying the raiders not to invade; 4) forming alliances with tribes that could be used against the raiders; 5) raiding their territories. The East Germanic tribes did not yet pose a naval threat, but this situation changed in the 250s when they managed to gain possession of the ships of the Bosporan kingdom. For this see my biography of Gallienus.

The Sarmatians and Alans were famed horsemen and it was in this capacity that they threatened the Romans. Typically they raided Roman territory and fled before the Romans could mount an effective response. The principal Roman responses to this were the increasing of the numbers of cavalry and the raiding of their lands. Both groupings were famous for their cavalry lancers and their ability to fight effectively at close quarters with their lances and swords. The lancers were known by two names: the *katafraktoi*

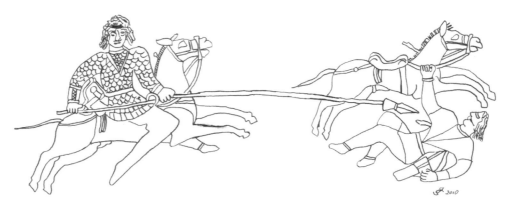

The so-called Kossika vase (Russia), first to third Century AD, (drawn after Brzezinski & Mielczarek, 15). It is usually thought that the men represent duelling Sarmato-Alans, but I would also suggest the possibility that the *contus*-bearer on the left could represent a Goth while the man on the right could represent a Sarmatian mounted archer. It is impossible to be certain, for both used the same tactical systems. Of note is the fact that the *contus*-bearer had shot at least two arrows before he charged. See also my drawing of the Sarmatian mounted archer in the first chapter.

(man and horse armoured) and *kontoforoi* (*kontos/contus*-bearer with less armour). They also possessed large numbers of mounted archers, who could be equipped as cataphracts or *kontoforoi*. The Romans faced Alans both separately and as subjects or allies of the Goths, while they faced Sarmatians mainly in the area between the Danube and Dacia. Their standard combat tactic was to use their '*koursores*-skirmishers' in advance of their '*defensores*-defenders' to disorder the enemy formation through archery and harassment and then engage the disordered enemy with their defenders equipped with the *kontos*-lances. Their battle line consisted of these so that every other 3,000-horseman *moira* consisted of either *koursores* or *defensores*. For additional details, see the diagram The Roman Alan Drill in Chapter 6.3.

We know very little about the combat methods of the Dacian Carpi. The only description of their tactics from this era dates from the reign of Philip the Arab (see Chapter 7.2) and it describes them using cavalry. When this is combined with the fact that all of their neighbours had been Sarmaticized or were Sarmatians and Alans and were using cavalry as their principal fighting force, it becomes probable that they too fought in the same manner as lancers and mounted archers. However, I would not preclude the possibility that they would have used infantry too because the Goths had infantry and so did the Slavs and Antae in the same area later.

3.5 Other Events in 232–34

'Victories were also won in the province of Mauritania Tingitana under Furius Celsus, in the province of Illyricum by Varius Macrinus, his [*Alexander's*] kinsman, and in Armenia by Junius Palmatus [*he is likely to have been the commander of the northern column*], and from all these places laurelled letters were sent to Alexander. These being publicly read to the Senate and the People on different occasions, and wished-for news had also arrived from Isauria, he found himself adorned and saluted by all of the titles/cognomina that these places carried... He gave the captives that he had made of divers nations amongst his friends, unless they were of royal blood or noble rank. Those were enrolled for warfare, but in no great posts [*most of these would presumably have consisted of Parthian and Persian deserters*]. The lands of the enemy which were conquered were given by his consent among the *limitanei* [*frontier*] officers and soldiers under the condition that their heirs after them should be obliged to take arms and that those lands should never come to persons of another condition [*this statement has been doubted quite needlessly because such an arrangement has usually been considered to belong to the late Roman period. One should rather see this as an instance of conditional land grant by the Emperor with the double intention of bribing the soldiers while ensuring that there were soldiers in the East receiving adequate subsistence from local sources. This arrangement actually bears some resemblance to the pronoiai of the later periods*] because he said that the men fought with greater zeal when they defended their own estates. He furnished them with cattle and servants necessary for the tillage [*the presence of servants enabled the soldiers to concentrate on training and fighting*] so that it would not happen that the lands bordering the barbarians would become uninhabited due to lack of inhabitants or old age of the owners.' Aelius Lampridius, *HA Severus* 58.1ff., tr. by John Bernard, 453–4 with some corrections taken from Magie and with some changes, corrections and comments of my own.

The above quote gives us important clues regarding the sequence of other wars that took place during the years 231–4. Since the laurelled letter of the victory of Furius Celsus over the Moors in Mauritania Tingitana was read in the Senate in about 233–4, it is clear that the war in Mauritania Tingitana took place in about 232–3. For a description of the Moors as enemies, see Chapter 6.1. My own educated guess is that the reason for the war was the transferral of Moorish cavalry units to the eastern theatre in 231 which created a power vacuum in the area which was then exploited by the local tribesmen. This makes it possible to date another war that took place in North Africa during the reign of Alexander Severus. This is the inscription that mentions the victory of Q. Gargilius Martialis against the Faraxen/Fraxinenses in Mauritania Caesarensis for the reign of Alexander. Since it is likely that the troubles with the Moors were roughly simultaneous in neighbouring areas, it is probable that we should date this war to have taken place roughly in about 232–34. It is also very likely that this war was also caused by the withdrawal of Moorish cavalry forces from the area to the army serving under Alexander.

The Romans were victorious in both cases. The Romans of the time were clearly able to operate in the desert and mountain terrains of North Africa, but we do not know exactly how the Romans achieved these victories. It would not be surprising if they defeated the Moors in pitched battles because the vast majority of the Moors were very lightly equipped by Roman standards. The typical equipment of the Moors consisted of a small shield and two javelins, which they used both on foot and mounted. They did use bows and other arms as well but their significance was small. The sources make it clear that the Romans habitually defeated the Moors even when outnumbered. It is therefore possible that the Moors made the mistake of facing the Romans in open conflict. Typically they tried to compensate for their light equipment by using superior numbers of men collected in the form of a confederacy of several tribes and by exploiting difficult terrain like mountains. In addition, they built palisaded camps to serve as bases of attack behind which there could be wooded mountains that hid an ambushing force. In emergencies they typically withdrew to the deserts or mountains. The typical Roman countermeasure was to isolate the Moors and force them to rely on their herds of animals for survival. This usually forced the Moors either to surrender or accept the challenge to fight a pitched battle.

The information regarding the war in Illyricum is particularly important because it was the gateway to Italy and Rome and after the transfer of forces to the East there existed a power vacuum in this area. It was because of this threat that Alexander was forced to abandon his eastern campaign and march back to the Europe. In light of this it is strange that we do not hear anything about a Roman counterattack led by Alexander Severus in person. However, we have an explanation for this. The above quote from Aelius Lampridius refers to a victory in Illyricum achieved by Varius Macrinus, Alexander's kinsman. The problem with this is that news of this victory was read in the Senate. This dates the victory in Illyricum either to the period 232–3, or late-233 until about mid-234. The latter dating is likelier. If Varius Macrinus had already defeated the enemy, Alexander and his advisors would not have feared for the fate of Italy as stated by Herodian (6.7.3–5). The text of Julius Capitolinus (*HA MB* 5.6–10, esp.5.9, tr. by Bernard p.80 with my changes, corrections and comment) explains what happened: 'He [*Marcus Clodius Pupienus Maximus better known as Pupienus*] was sent as a special legate into Illyricum where he crushed the Sarmatians. From thence he was transferred to the Rhine, where he conducted a campaign happily against the Germans. Then he was made *Prafectus Urbi* in which capacity he proved himself very practical, very able and very inflexible.'

We can date this series of events on the basis of Pupienus's nomination as consul and *Praefectus Urbi* in 234. This means that Pupienus had led some emergency forces to Illyricum in 233 with which he achieved a great victory against the Sarmatians, which enabled him to be transferred to the Rhine where he defeated the German invaders. Because of these achievements Pupienus was rewarded with the consulship and Urban Prefecture in 234, and it was because of these achievements that Alexander Severus did not have to campaign in person in Illyricum or in Gaul when he marched back to Europe. Alexander also flattered Pupienus with the appointment of his eldest son Tiberius Clodius Pupienus Pulcher Maximus as *consul suffectus* presumably in 235.

To sum up, the probable sequence of events in the Danubian and Rhine frontiers is that the Sarmatians (likely to have included at least the Germanic Quadi and possibly also the Marcomanni and others) invaded Illyricum in 233, and the Germans (presumably the Alamanni) invaded Gaul in 233 with the result that Alexander abandoned his plans to continue the campaign in the east. Alexander and his advisors then adopted the emergency measure of sending Pupienus to Illyricum against the invaders in 233. It is probable that he and his men (likely to have consisted mainly or solely of cavalry) acted as a vanguard force for the main army that Alexander led back to Europe. What is certain is that this army included significant numbers of horsemen because they were needed for the war against the swiftly moving Sarmatian cavalry. It would have been impossible to catch them without large numbers of horsemen. It is therefore possible that the father of the increased use of cavalry by the Romans after this was actually Pupienus. When Pupienus then achieved a victory over the invaders in Illyricum in 233, he was dispatched to the Rhine frontier where he was similarly victorious either in very late 233 or in early 234.

In the meantime, Alexander's main forces had reached the Balkans. There is an interesting reference to a victory achieved by Alexander against the Alans with the spreading of hellebore on the pasturages and fields in the *Kestoi* of Julius Africanus. All of the commentators, myself included, have thought that the Alexander in question is probably Alexander the Great.[35] However, this is not necessarily so. There were Alans in this area at this time both inside the Roman Empire (note the origin of Maximinus Thrax) and across the border as subjects of the Goths. If we identify this Alexander with Alexander Severus, then it becomes apparent that he destroyed the Alans in this area by spreading hellebore in their area of habitation. The Alans in question could have been the Alans who had been settled in Thrace and who would therefore have revolted, or the Alans east of Dacia and north of the Danube, in which case Alexander would have conducted an offensive campaign against a subject tribe of the Goths. If the latter is true, then this offensive pacified the Goths for the next three years because they did not invade Roman territory until 238. The reason for Alexander's attack would obviously be that the Alans had raided Roman territory, and it is not impossible to think that they had done that in conjunction with the Sarmatians and that Pupienus had also defeated them or that they had fled before he was able to do so. The spreading of hellebore on the fields would have made it difficult for the cavalry forces to pass through because there was no fodder. If either of these alternatives is true, then the destruction of the Alans would have given Maximinus Thrax yet another reason to hate Alexander.

After this, Alexander clearly marched to Illyricum and left some of his forces in the Balkans under his kinsman Varius Macrinus, and continued his journey to Rome where he celebrated his triumph over the Persians. In the meantime however, two things took place. Alexander is unlikely to have led his main army from Illyricum to Rome to celebrate the triumph. This means that these forces were marched straight from Illyricum to Gaul. Gaul, however, had already been pacified by Pupienus. The plan was therefore that Alexander would conduct in person an offensive campaign of punishment across the Rhine in 234–5. Alexander needed military successes because his achievements paled in comparison with those achieved by Pupienus. Pupienus was therefore promoted away from the soldiers and appointed as a City Prefect (*Praefectus Urbi*) in 234. The second of the things that took place is that Varius Macrinus achieved a victory in Illyricum either in very late 233 or early 234 either by mopping up the remaining invaders or by crushing yet another invasion so that Alexander was able to read the letter in the senate. However, the sending of the army to Gaul to await the arrival of Alexander led to trouble.

The above account also refers to a victory achieved in Armenia by Junius Palmatus. Since the same text clearly implies that the letters were sent at different points in time it is possible to think that there was some fighting in Armenia in 233 after Alexander left; but in light of the imprecise wording and the general untrustworthiness of the *Augustan Histories* it is likelier that this victory means the victory achieved by the northern column during the Persian war as has been suggested for example by Paul N. Pearson and others.[36] The latter option receives some support from the speech that Herodian (7.8.4) puts into the mouth of Maximinus Thrax, namely that Maximinus claimed that it was the bravery of the Roman soldiers and Maximinus's own actions that had kept the Persians in check after 233 with the implication that there was no fighting after early 233. This is unfortunately too imprecise, so both alternatives are possible. However, I would still think that the majority view is correct in this case. It is inherently likelier that Junius Palmatus had indeed been commander of the northern column during the Persian war. It is entirely possible to think that the victory was read to the senate and people roughly at the same time as Alexander reached Rome.

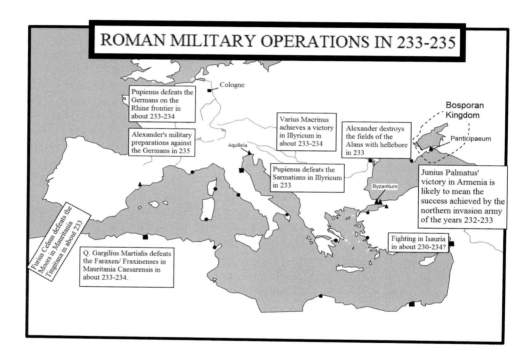

Aelius Lampridius refers also to a victory against the Isaurians, but there is no reference to the date or circumstances. It is possible that the Isaurians had revolted after Alexander had left; or that one of the usurpers already mentioned had been a usurper/rebel in Isauria and that it took until 232–4 for it to be crushed, or that there was an otherwise unknown revolt in Isauria in about 230–4.

Once again we lack details of this Isaurian conflict, but on the basis of the conflicts that took place in this area earlier and later it is easy to see that it followed the typical pattern in which the lightly-equipped Isaurians, typically armed with only shields, javelins and swords, descended from their mountain holdouts onto the plains and pillaged the area until the Romans brought enough soldiers to the scene that then forced the mountaineers to seek shelter in their mountain holdouts where they were then besieged until they surrendered.[37]

As noted above in the comments, the creation of the military lands for the soldiers by Alexander has quite needlessly been suspected as a fabrication. We do not know enough of the conditions prevailing in the third century to make this negative conclusion. It is entirely plausible that Alexander did this to obtain defenders and inhabitants for the areas in question while also saving money. The system adopted was quite similar to the one later adopted by Probus (see my double bio of him and Aurelian) in Isauria and it is probable that Alexander used it in Isauria. It is not that different from the system of providing supplies in kind (*annona*) for the men. The only real difference between *annona* and this system is that each soldier had specific earmarked land which provided his supplies and payments.

3.6 The Planned Germanic War and the Assassination of Alexander Severus in 235

As noted above, the vast majority of the Roman land forces were marched from the East via the Balkans so that it was secured before the main Roman army was assembled along the Rhine frontier for a major invasion in 235. Before this however, Roman central command made thorough preparations for the war. New recruits were raised and trained and the invading forces were assembled close to the border. In addition, Alexander Severus celebrated his 'Parthian Victory' in Rome to gather support for his regime in 233–4. The extant sources claim that the Romans were finally ready to launch the massive campaign in early 235, but then something happened. According to Herodian, Julia Mamaea and her advisors thought it preferable to buy the peace with gold rather than invade and therefore cancelled the campaign. Aelius Lampridius adds that there were those who claimed that Julia Mamaea's plan was to lead the soldiers back to the East against the Persians, but he maintains that this was only propaganda spread by Maximinus's supporters. I agree with Brian Campbell that if Alexander was planning to invade Germania, it is probable that the promises of gold to the Germans reflect Roman attempts to ensure that the Germanic tribes would not be able to unite their forces against the Romans.[38]

However, there exists strong circumstantial evidence that supports the claim of Herodian that the German campaign was abandoned after the bridge over the Rhine had already been built. The first of these consists of the already mentioned *Kestoi* of Julius Africanus, if it was written in about 233–4, which is likely. The text can be used as evidence of Alexander and his advisors seeking to learn the lessons of the campaign in 231–33 and were planning to attack the Persians again. The second concerns the events that took place in Gaul in 234 and then in Italy in 238. The key texts are those by Herodian (8.6) and Julius Capitolinus (*HA MB* 12.2ff.). According to Herodian, German *symmachoi* (allies) came to assist Pupienus Maximus in Ravenna against Maximinus Thrax in 238 because they had warm feelings towards him from his term as their governor. Their presence is confirmed by Julius Capitolinus. It would therefore be clear that these Germans flocked to help Pupienus against Maximinus Thrax because of their fond memories of him. The only time such fond memories could have been formed was when Pupienus had defeated the Germanic invaders in 233–4. This means that he had given the defeated enemy very lenient terms of peace, and it is probable that Alexander had actually marched to Mogontiacum/Mainz only to confirm these terms so that he could then lead the army back to the east against the Persians. The subsequent invasion of Germanic territory by Maximinus Thrax would naturally have caused intense hatred among the Germanic tribesmen, who therefore eagerly sent assistance to Pupienus in 238. In sum, it is very likely that Herodian was correct in his claims.

The situation would have been opportune for a war against Persia. There was an opportunity for success in the east because Ardashir had suffered a defeat both when fighting against the Armenians and against the Romans and was fighting against his other enemies in 235. It is therefore quite probable that it was not merely propaganda of Maximinus that Alexander wanted to abandon the campaign in the West and march against Persia. The problem with this is that it does still sound like Maximinus's propaganda because the negotiations referred to had also taken place under Caracalla to divide the enemy, not to mention the similar negotiations preceding the Persian campaign. There is therefore no particular reason to think that the situation would now have been any different, except that Maximinus was able to exploit this for his own purposes among the inexperienced recruits. Regardless, in light of the extant evidence the case for the abandonment of the German campaign is stronger than the case against it.

Whatever the truth, the soldiers were apparently upset because they considered the abandonment of the Germanic war cowardly. The soldiers had been assembled near the border in readiness to exact vengeance on those who had attacked their homes. They could also expect to be bribed with donatives during the campaign, not to mention the prospect of obtaining booty and military glory, and they had not received any. On top of this, if we are to believe Aelius Lampridius, Alexander, Julia Mamaea and their advisors had once again committed the same blunder they had at Antioch, namely they had disbanded some local legions for their behaviour (which must once again mean drinking and whoring). This is indeed a distinct possibility. It is further supported by Eutropius who notes that Alexander enforced severe military discipline and disbanded whole legions.[39]

'Alexander having brought with him a large body of Moors, and a huge number of bowmen from the east, some from Oshroene, and some deserters or mercenaries from the Parthians… Against the Germans these kinds of warriors were particularly useful [*Alexander and his staff were clearly competent*]… But … in close combat… the Germans were often a match for the Romans. While he was thus employed, he… thought proper to send an embassy to the enemy to discuss peace terms with the offer to accept reasonable demands that he could meet because he had plenty of money… The Germans were avaricious… which caused Alexander to attempt to buy peace rather than run the risk of war. But the Roman soldiers opposed this waste of time. They thought that Alexander had no intention of waging war, but rather amused himself in chariot racing and other idle diversions at a time when the insolence of the Germans required punishment. [*All of the above is likely to be propaganda spread by Maximinus and his henchmen among the soldiers. Firstly, the use of diplomacy to divide the enemy was standard practice and had been used for example by Caracalla. Secondly, the offering of the terms appears to follow the same pattern as was shown on the previous occasion. Thirdly, in the context of Caracalla, chariot racing was not considered bad by the soldiers but rather entertainment offered by the Emperor to the soldiers*]… There was in the army one Maximinus… Alexander put Maximinus in charge of exercising the recruits… which office Maximinus executed with great diligence; and won the love of the soldiers… to this he added other

popular motives to gain their affections, such as liberal gifts and posts of honour…
[*It is clear that Maximinus had started to plan the revolt from the beginning of his command*] the young soldiers, of whom most were Pannonians [*Herodian 8.5.6 adds the 'barbarian' Thracians to this list who were either barbarian settlers on Roman soil or just Thracians. In my opinion it is practically certain that we are here speaking about barbarians settled in Thrace, so Maximinus was put in charge of their training because he was their compatriot.*[40] *On the basis of the use of the Pannonian phalanxes as a vanguard (Herodian 7.8.11, 8.2.2) it is practically certain that these consisted of horsemen. In this case the use of the word phalanx/phalanxes cannot be used as conclusive evidence that the vanguard consisted of infantry because it is clear that vanguards always included cavalry and in this case the vanguard marched so fast as to be several days in front of the main army which included infantry. It is clear that this phalanx must have consisted solely of mounted men. In other words, Alexander and his advisors now created the cavalry army that I have referred to in my biography of Gallienus and in my article of the reign of Decius*], admired Maximinus's courage… and despised Alexander as one ruled by his mother… clothing him [*Maximinus*] in a purple robe, saluted him emperor… At first he refused the offer, and threw off the purple [*this was mere show*]… but… he accepted the honour… he [*Maximinus*] enjoined them to… advance upon Alexander before he had the least information, to surprise the soldiers and bodyguards… When he had excited their alacrity, and confirmed their affection by doubling their pay, promising great gifts and donatives, and remitting all their punishments, he put them in motion, and led them to the camp of Alexander and his attendants not far off…When the news of Maximinus's approach was brought to Alexander he was panic-stricken… he sprang out of his royal pavilion, weeping and trembling… He exclaimed at Maximinus unfaithfulness and ingratitude… charged the young recruits… of treason… The soldiers and guards about him all that day shouted in his favour and attended him, promising to hazard their lives in his protection; but when the night had passed and they were told that Maximinus was at hand… Alexander came forth again… and, having called the soldiers together… the soldiers at first indeed promised to stand by him; but soon after fell off by few and few; refusing to take arms; And some of them demanded to have the military prefect, and Alexander's household executed because they had ordered the retreat [*The retreat may mean the postponement of the campaign in the aftermath of the disbanding of legions mentioned by Aelius Lampridius. The retreat would presumably mean the taking apart of the already assembled pontoon bridge over the Rhine. The anger against the military prefect suggests that Aelius Lampridius is correct in stating that the principal reason for the mutiny was excessive disciplining of the soldiers*]… Others said that his mother was… a woman of insatiable avarice, she hoarded treasure and had rendered Alexander odious to the army by clandestine peculation and unreadiness to distribute donatives. [*It is possible that these complaints were spontaneous reactions of the soldiers, but it is also possible that there were operatives of Maximinus among the soldiers enflaming their passions. What appears certain is that the soldiers accompanying Alexander had real grievances in the form of excessive discipline instituted by the military prefect, which was made worse by a stingy attitude to the granting of donatives*]… But when Maximinus's army came into sight, and exhorted their brothers-in-arms

to quit their service to a stingy mean-spirited woman and a pusallinimous boy, a slave to his mother… deserting Alexander, went all over to Maximinus; and unanimously saluted him emperor. The poor trembling… Alexander… returned to his tent; and… waited for the executioner, upbraiding his mother as the cause of his misfortunes… Maximinus… dispatched a tribune with some centurions to murder Alexander and his mother [*Aelius Lampridius HA Alexander 61, 62.5 claims that the killers consisted of the barbarian guard. Maximinus had obviously served in this unit so this is not surprising.*] and all of his entourage who resisted.' Herodian 6.8.1ff., tr. by Hart 261ff. with changes, corrections, additions and comments.

In sum,[41] when one takes into account the likely demotion from the position of *dux ripae* to the post of trainer of recruits of Pannonian and Thracian origin, it is probable that Maximinus Thrax started to harbour revenge against Alexander Severus from the start. It is also likely that the claim that it was Alexander's timidity that had caused the defeat of the southern division during the Persian war was not mere propaganda for Maximinus Thrax but that he really believed that his defeat had been caused by the timidity of Alexander so his disgraceful demotion in the ranks was a personal insult – the real culprit was Alexander.

The new recruits, most of whom were Pannonians, naturally idolized the impressive looking goliath Maximinus Thrax and easily believed whatever he told them. Maximinus spared no opportunity to endear himself to the troops with his personal example – he shared their hardships and was well-known for his courage. This was in great contrast to the reputation of Alexander. The disasters during the Persian war that could be claimed to have resulted from Alexander's cowardice together with the advertised attempt to buy the peace could now be used to enflame the anger especially of the recruits. As if this was not enough, the military prefect had disciplined the bodyguards while Julia Mamaea and Alexander had not bribed the soldiers sufficiently. This is what bothered the veterans most. The long peace had diminished the number of donatives and the shameful buying of the peace from the Germans promised the continuation of the same. When the soldiers then claimed Maximinus as Emperor, he acted as if he was reluctant to accept, but it is clear that this was just stage-managed theatre. It was therefore in about March 235 that Maximinus launched his well-planned coup. Maximinus bribed the soldiers by doubling their pay, by promising an enormous bonus in cash and kind, and by cancelling all punishments. Maximinus's forces were stationed not far from the camp of the Emperor somewhere near the city of Mainz/Mogontiacum. On the basis of Aelius Lampridius (*HA Alex.* 59.6), Julius Capitolinus (*HA Max.* 74–5) and Victor (24.4) it has been suggested that the camp was located in Vicus Britannicus (Bretzenheim near Mainz)[42] or in a place called Sicilia near Mainz because Aelius and Victor claim that the place was Sicilia in Britain or Gaul. Unlike Alexander, Maximinus did not hesitate in the least, but led his loyal followers against the legitimate Emperor. Maximinus's aim was to overpower the soldiers and bodyguards of Alexander either with bribes or surprise so that Alexander, Julia Mamaea and their supporters could be killed with one surgical blow. When Alexander learnt of what had happened he burst out of his tent and tried to convince his men to stay loyal, and they promised to do so.

After this Alexander and his men spent a nervous night, and then when the news of the approach of Maximinus's army came at dawn, Alexander assembled his men on the parade ground to try to convince them to fight. However, Maximinus's henchmen had been preparing for the coup. The soldiers began to desert the colours one by one. Some of them demanded the execution of the military prefect (possibly the Praetorian Prefect)[43] and Alexander's household; they accused them of retreat while others accused Julia Mamaea of avarice. When the recruits of Maximinus then became visible and started to shout insults and called for the soldiers to leave the strings of a woman and join the army of a man, the soldiers of Alexander deserted en masse. Alexander fled to the imperial tent where he clung to his mother and wept and blamed her for his fate. When the army had then hailed Maximinus as *Augustus*, he sent a tribune (chiliarch) and centurions to kill Alexander and Julia and anyone who attempted to resist. The assassins, who appear (*HA Sev.* 61.3) to have consisted of the members of the Germanic bodyguards (either the *Aulici* or *Germanici/Equites Singulares Augusti* or new personal guards of Maximinus Thrax formed out of the Germanic settlers of Thrace), killed Alexander, Julia and all those who they thought to be their friends or favourites, including both praetorian prefects. Some of the latter managed to avoid detection for a while, but the henchmen of Maximinus soon found them and killed the whole lot. In fact Maximinus launched a savage purge of all of those who he considered potential threats to his rule. The reign of Gaius Julius Verus Maximinus began with bloodshed and it was to end in bloodshed.

3.7 The Inheritance of Alexander Severus and Julia Mamaea

It was largely thanks to the ill-conceived prudish military disciplining of the soldiers, most importantly the Praetorians and other bodyguard units, in conjunction with the avaricious behaviour of Julia Mamaea, that the Emperor and his friends and family lost their lives. Julia Mamaea should have followed the policy of her mother Julia Maesa and bribed the soldiers.

However, it is still clear that Alexander and his mother should be considered to have been good rulers. They were just too 'good' in bad times. The successes of the northern army corps together with the Armenians and the Roman main army against Ardashir I in 232–3 also prove that with the murder of Alexander the Romans lost a golden opportunity to destroy the Sassanian Empire in its bud. The details provided by the *Kestoi* of Julius Africanus prove that the Romans had learnt their lessons, and the enlargement of the cavalry army following the Persian war would have made the Romans even readier for such a campaign than they had been in 233. Indeed the most important legacy of the deceased emperor Alexander, Julia Mamaea, and their advisors, was the creation of the first truly large cavalry field army of the Roman Empire.

The best evidence for the creation of the cavalry army is that the Pannonian and Thracian recruits that Maximinus Thrax trained appear to have consisted of mounted men and that the main striking forces serving under Maximinus consisted of cavalry. Therefore the first truly sizable cavalry field army of the Roman Empire consisted of the following: Pannonian and Thracian cavalry trained by Maximinus; Moorish cavalry; regular Roman cavalry in regular gear or in *clibanarii* gear; Oshroenian, Armenian and Parthian mounted archers; and units of bodyguard cavalry (Praetorians, *Equites Singulares Augusti*, and *Aulici/Scholarii*). This cavalry army was to serve Maximinus with distinction during his foreign wars and it was this cavalry force that was destroyed with Decius in the disastrous battles of Beroea and Abrittus in 251 and then recreated by Gallienus. It is possible that some of the Pannonian units created by Alexander survived the disasters of Decius so that they formed the core of the Dalmatian cavalry under Gallienus.

As regards the soldiers, the only way to satisfy this greedy bunch was to provide them with sizable bribes in the form of salary and donatives and war booty gathered from defeated enemies. This Maximinus set out to achieve.

Left: Moorish cavalry without bridles in the Column of Trajan.
(source: Cichorius Plates)

The Moors were famous for unbridled cavalry javeliners. However, contrary to the popular image in antiquity and today in reality not all of them were unbridled.

Below are examples of Moorish cavalry with bridles drawn after images and photos in Hamdoune's book (*Les auxilia externa africains des armées romaines*, Montpellier 1999)

Stele of Nonius Julianus,
Ala Milliaria, 3rd century, garrisoned at Benian.
Note the use of the bridle

Horseman of Chemtou
Note the use of bridles and horned saddle.
(drawn after a photo in Hamdoune, slightly simplified;
likely to date from the principate)

A coin of Hadrian depicting Mauretania
Note that this coin depicts bridled cavalry.

A stele depicting a Moor.
Note that this coin depicts bridled cavalry.

Chapter Four

Maximinus Thrax (AD 235–38)

A bust of Maximinus Thrax in Louvre. Source: Duruy.

A statue of Maximus Caesar, son of Maximinus. Source: Duruy.

4.1 Maximinus Thrax secures the Throne[1]

The first task of Gaius Julius Verus Maximinus was to secure his position. He needed to purge the supporters of Alexander from all positions of power. The persecution of Christians, which Maximinus started immediately, formed a part of this project. Notably, the governor of Moesia Inferior, C. Messius Quintus Decius Valerianus, the instigator of the future great persecution of Christians, was a loyal supporter of Maximinus to the bitter end.[2] Maximinus knew all too well why Alexander Severus had fallen from power. He had used all of Alexander's failings to gain the throne. Maximinus needed to prove himself a warrior by leading the men to victories. He needed to bribe the soldiers so he needed to obtain money. Maximinus also knew that as a barbarian of low birth he would never be acceptable to the Roman elites, so he intended to rule them by fear, which suited his bloodthirsty temperament.

Eusebius (6.26) claims that the reason for the persecution of Christians was that most of Alexander Severus's household consisted of Christians. Maximinus however did not launch a widespread persecution like Decius later. His persecution consisted only of the enforcement of already existing laws and regulations. Furthermore, Maximinus did not target ordinary Christians but only the leaders of the Church and in most cases even these appear to have been only exiled rather than killed. Therefore it is clear that Maximinus saw his own actions mainly as a necessary security measure against the supporters of Alexander. However, later Christian tradition claims that Caecilia Paulina, the wife of the Emperor, tried to restrict Maximinus's violent hatred towards the Christians so Maximinus killed her. This has usually been classified as Christian propaganda, but it may have happened. It would have been entirely in character for Maximinus to kill his wife if she opposed his policies. Maximinus did not want to appear as a man who took advice from women as Alexander Severus had. Whatever the truth, Caecilia Paulina soon died and was consecrated *Diva*.[3]

Left: A coin depicting Caecilia Paulina as consecrated *Diva*. Source: Cohen.

The first to suffer the wrath of Maximinus were the friends (*amici*) of Alexander and the sixteen members of his council that had been elected by the Senate. Some were killed, others were exiled or merely removed from office. This was necessary for the success of the coup. Herodian adds that because of his low birth Maximinus did not want to be near nobles. He wanted to be surrounded by his army. In my opinion, this was a security measure. Maximinus dismissed the entire staff that had served Alexander. Most were executed for treason because Maximinus suspected them of disloyalty.

Then a plot against the life of Maximinus was discovered. According to Herodian, it was not known if the plot was real or invented by Maximinus to get rid of potential enemies while obtaining their property. The claimed plotters consisted of centurions and senators. They planned to enthrone Magnus, a patrician of consular rank. The centurions in question must have consisted of the *aulici/scholarii* and/or of the *evocati Augusti* and/or of the *praetoriani* and/or some other unit stationed at Rome during peacetime. The senators obviously included many who had previously held high positions under Alexander. If the plot was real then the *primus motor* behind the conspiracy was Magnus. The plan was that when the building of the pontoon bridge over the Rhine was completed and Maximinus crossed it, the soldiers who were guarding the bridge would cut it behind Maximinus with the idea that the barbarians would kill him. Maximinus had all those suspected of being party to this conspiracy arrested and executed. This obviously gave him a windfall of cash with which to bribe the soldiers.

After this followed the mutiny of the Oshroenian mounted archers, who were upset by the murder of Alexander.[4] The persecution of Christians, if it preceded the revolt, would have had a role in this, because many of the Oshroenians were Christians. According to Herodian (7.1.9ff.), the Oshroenians forced Quartinus to usurp power. He had been a friend of Alexander with consular rank and had been dismissed from the army by Maximinus. Quartinus was unwilling to accept this less-than-welcome honour, but the plotters, led by Macedo the former commander of the Oshroenians, forced him. According to Trebellius Pollio (*HA Tr.* 23), the rebel's name was Titus, and on the basis of this it has been thought that the name of the man was Titus Quartinus. The sources unfortunately fail to give us any details of when where and why the revolt took place and how it progressed. The only detail that we have is Trebellius Pollio's (*HA Tr.* 23.1) statement that it lasted for six months. Trebellius Pollio (*HA Tr.* 23.1–3) also states that Titus was made Emperor by the Armenian bowmen and by the former tribune of the Moors. It is easy to think that Pollio has made a mistake, but if we assume that he is correct, then it would be easy to understand why the revolt lasted for six months (confirmed by the lateness of Maximinus's campaign against the Germans). The Moors, Armenians and Oshroenians consisted of highly mobile elite cavalry so it is easy to see why it would have been very difficult for Maximinus to force them into a decisive fight. Notably, Herodian states that Quartinus had been dismissed from the army – had he been the commander of all of these forces, the Moors, Armenians and Oshroenians?

The best educated guess for the progress of the revolt is that the Oshroenians had been particularly friendly towards Alexander and his mother and that one of the first measures that Maximinus took as Emperor was the dismissal of the entire top brass of this unit including its commander Macedo, and that this caused the forming of the plot. Whatever the reason and circumstances had been, Macedo soon regretted having rebelled because he entered the tent of Quartinus one night and killed him. According to Herodian, Macedo then brought the head of Quartinus to Maximinus in the hope that he would reward him. Maximinus, however, executed Macedo because he considered Macedo as the ringleader of the mutiny who had then murdered the unwilling victim of his own plot.

According to Herodian, the above revolts against Maximinus embittered him further and he became even more savage than before.

4.2 The Foreign Wars of Maximinus in 235–38[5]

Once the revolts against his rule had been solved, Maximinus began the long planned campaign. It was now about mid-summer 235. See the attached Map of the Campaigns in 235–41.

> 'His [*Maximinus's*] countenance was stern and formidable; and the size of his body was colossal that he could hardly be matched by any of the most athletic Greeks, or the stoutest and most pugnacious barbarians. [*According to Julius Capitolinus HA Max. 6.8 Maximinus was 8 feet 6 inches tall. Pearson quite rightly suggests that he suffered from acromegaly.*] Having settled the abovementioned disturbances [*the*

conspiracies against him], he put himself at the head of his troops and marched fearlessly over the bridge to attack the Germans. He had an enormous army, consisting of almost all the Roman power, a great number of Moorish javeliners, and Oshroenian and Armenian archers, some of whom were his subjects [*these would have been Oshroenians and Armenians living inside the Empire while the following filoi and symmachoi were presumably Armenian allies*], others his friends/ auxiliaries [*filoi*] and allies [*symmachoi*]; And all the Parthians in Roman service, whether mercenaries, deserters or captives. This vast multitude had been first collected by Alexander, but then augmented and disciplined by Maximinus. The best troops against the Germans seemed to be the javeliners [*akontistai*] and archers because they attacked with incredible speed before the Germans were aware and then retreated again with equal ease. Maximinus advanced deep into the enemy's country; and meeting no opposition (for the barbarians retired at his approach) he laid waste all the fields, especially those of corn, which was then ripe [*this dates the campaign to mid-summer 235*]; set fire to the villages; and permitted his soldiers to ransack and plunder without hindrance. For the cities and houses of the Germans are easily destroyed by fire as they have very few stones or bricks, but build chiefly with timber… Maximinus advanced a long way in this hostile manner, driving off the cattle, and giving all the herds they met to his army [*This undoubtedly pleased the men*]. For the Germans retired from the plains and any unwooded areas, and hid themselves in the woods and stayed in the marshes so that they could attack the enemy and fight in these areas where the thick foliage provided good covering against the javelins and missiles, and the deep marshes were very dangerous for the Romans who were strangers to the area; but, on the contrary, the Germans could easily run through them, as they were well acquainted with the country; knew what parts were unpassable, what hard; and usually ran through the water up to their knees. Besides, the Germans are very expert swimmers…

This part of the country… was the principal scene of action; and here the emperor himself bravely began a battle. For having attacked the Germans near a vast and deep marsh, into which the enemy was retreating in flight, the Roman troops were afraid to pursue, Maximinus himself first rode into the lake, that took his horse up to the belly [*The horse which carried Maximinus must have been huge in size, not any smaller than the largest horses that later carried the Medieval knights. This shows that the Romans possessed large horses suitable for shock combat*]; and made a great slaughter among the barbarians who resisted him; till the rest of the soldiers, animated by his example, and fearing the reproach of deserting their sovereign fighting in their cause, plunged into his assistance. And now a general battle ensued… Great numbers fell on the Roman side, but the barbarians lost almost their whole multitude, the Roman prince eminently distinguishing himself in action till the ponds and bogs were filled with dead carcases, and the lake red with blood; so that the battle looked like a naval battle to the infantry fighting there. The battle ended, Maximinus not only dispatched letters to the senate and people… an account of his personal prowess; had the whole battle painted in huge pictures, and hung up before the Senate House… There were several battles after this [*one was the now famous battle of Harzhorn*] in which he won great honour, exposing his own person and attacking the enemy with sword in hand; But as the season of the year was far advanced, he thought proper to lead the army into winter quarters; and carrying off the prisoners and plunder returned to Pannonia. He resided all the winter at Sirmium, a large city in those parts [*Herodian has left out the campaigning against the Sarmatians and others in this region*]; where he made the necessary preparations for the ensuing campaign; threatening… to cut off and reduce all the German nations as far as the Ocean… Arms are taken up against you [*this is taken from the speech that Herodian puts into the mouth of Maximinus on the occasion of the revolt of Gordian I*]… not by the Germans, whom we have so often conquered [*this refers to the war of 235*], nor by the Sarmatians [*this means the campaigns conducted in 236–7*], who are every day our supplicants for peace; Even the Persians, who but lately were overrunning Mesopotamia [*in 230*], are now very quiet… being taught the danger of raising disturbances by the renown of your arms and the greatness of my actions, which they always found sufficient to winstand their utmost efforts while I commanded the camps on the banks of those rivers [*this refers to the period during which Maximinus had been dux ripae*].' Herodian 7.12.1ff.,7.8.4, tr. by Hart 270ff., 289 with changes, corrections, additions and comments.

'He [*Maximinus*] passed into Germany with all his army: The Moors, Oshroenians, Parthians, and all those that Alexander Severus had mustered out of the countries of the east… for the eastern auxiliary archers were of greater use against the Germans than any other force. The preparations of Alexander Severus for this war had been great, but yet Maximinus added greatly to it. He passed the Rhine, and entered Germany. He burned villages of the enemy for three or four hundred miles about [*The seventeenth century translation of Bernard has preserved the correct reading. As noted by Pearson on p.108 modern editors and translators like Magie have preferred the later versions of the text over the earlier Palatine Codex. This is unjustified as Pearson quite rightly notes.*]. He drove their cattle, killed large numbers of barbarians, took innumerable prisoners and made the army rich with plunder. He would certainly have reduced all the country of Germany under Roman rule had not the Germans sought shelter from the forests and swamps. He did a great deal with his own hand; He had indeed been cut off in a lake, in which his horse stuck fast, and the enemy surrounded him, but that his men came timely up to his rescue [*This is the same battle as mentioned by Herodian*]. It was a piece of his barbarian rashness to think that an emperor ought always to fight with his own hand [*In truth, his behaviour was modelled after that of Caracalla, the darling of the soldiers. Note, however, that Maximinus is criticized for the behaviour that the soldiers had expected from Alexander Severus*]. Therefore, a sort of naval battle was fought in the swamp and large numbers were killed. So Germany being conquered, he wrote an account of it to the Senate and People of Rome to this purpose: "It is impossible, Fathers of the Senate, to express all that we have done: For 400 miles we have burnt the villages of the Germans, driven away their cattle, taken prisoners, and slain all who opposed us, and fought a battle in a swamp. We would have penetrated their forests had not the depth of their swamps prevented the passage." [*This suggests that the advance was blocked by the difficulty caused by constant fighting in difficult terrain*] Together with this, he ordered pictures of this war… to be drawn and laid before the Senate… In all his other engagements, which were many, he came off always conqueror, and took a great amount of booty, and many prisoners. He says in another letter which he sent to the Senate thus: "In a short time, Fathers of the Senate, I have fought more battles than any of the ancients ever did. I have brought away as much booty from the enemy's country into our own as exceeds all manner of expectation; And so many captives that dominions of the Empire are scarcely sufficient to hold them." From Germany he came to the city of Sirmium intending to make war upon the Sarmatians; and his ambition was to reduce the northern parts as far as the Ocean [*Baltic Sea*] into obedience of the Roman Empire. Which if he had lived, he would have done, says Herodian [*The above account has clearly been taken from Herodian, but there is still material which is not in his text*], out of prejudice against Alexander Severus.' Julius Capitolinus *HA Maximini* 11.7ff. tr. by Bernard, 13ff. with changes, corrections, additions and comments.

With the exception of what the coins have preserved for us and archaeology in Harzfeld has unearthed, the above is all that we know of these great campaigns against Germans and others. The above accounts prove that Alexander Severus and his staff had analyzed the situation correctly and had assembled a force that was ideally suited to defeating the Germans in their native hiding places. They had basically created the first permanent cavalry army, consisting of the Oshroenian, Armenian and Parthian mounted archers, Moorish mounted javeliners, regular Roman cavalry forces and 10,000 Romans equipped as *clibanarii*. On the basis of the cavalry armies later used by Gallienus and the East Romans the minimum size for this force would have been about 30,000 horsemen, but it is likely that there were even more than this. Alexander and his staff had assembled a massive infantry force on the border as well, so the Romans possessed a truly impressive combined arms force capable of facing anything the Germans could pit against them. It is probable that the so-called strengthening of this force by Maximinus consisted solely of the recruits that he had been put in charge of training by Alexander. The results prove that the campaign had been meticulously planned.

The Germanic tribesmen knew that they could not face this force on equal terms in the open so they resorted to guerrilla warfare in which they exploited the terrain by retreating into the forests and swamps while the Romans destroyed and pillaged everything they found on their marching route. There was constant fighting and skirmishes, but no real battles. Maximinus showed his personal fighting skills in most of these encounters to prove his worth as a warrior-prince. This situation persisted until the Romans had penetrated 400 miles into enemy territory. It was presumably approximately there that the Romans finally managed to force the retreating enemy into a pitched battle, but even this took place in a swamp, a location that favoured the Germans. When the Romans proved unwilling to pursue the retreating foe into the swamp, Maximinus personally charged after the enemy. But his horse became stuck in the mire and the Germans were able to surround him. When those behind saw this, they became ashamed and charged after their Emperor and saved him so that the Germans were defeated. Soon after this Maximinus began his journey back. The depth of the invasion means that Maximinus's armies had faced a series of Germanic tribes including the Chatti, Alamanni, Hermunduri, Thuringi and possibly also the Lombards and Suebi. Note however that it is probable that at least the Hermunduri and Suebi should be considered to have belonged to the Alamanni (All-Men) Confederacy.

En route back the same situation persisted, namely that the Romans had to fight their way out. The Germans fought a series of skirmishes and lesser battles in all of which the Emperor fought as if he had been a common soldier to prove himself to the men. We know one of these locations thanks to finds made by German archaeologists. This place is Harzhorn.[6] It is located 350 km from the Roman base at Mainz/Mogontiacum. The finds (arrowheads and ballista-bolts) made there suggest that the Romans were at this time retreating back to their own territory. The location was ideally suited to blocking the route of retreat. It was located on a major ancient route (now the A6 autobahn) located between two hills (the Harzhorn, the Harz mountains) so that it was possible to post the blocking force on the hills. Archaeological finds have been located only on the eastern hill and not on the western hill so it is possible that the Germans occupied only it, but this is uncertain because the eastern hill has suffered a series of landslides. The finds on the site show that the Romans concentrated their archery and ballistae shots at particular points on the hills. The arrows are more widely distributed than the ballistae bolts. Notably, some of the arrowheads are of the three-sided type typically used by the Oshroenians. Archaelogists have speculated that the likeliest reason for the targeting of these locations is that some Germanic chieftains stood on those places. The easternmost tip of the western hill has the largest concentration of finds. The likeliest reason for this concentration is that the Romans sought to pin down the Germans on the hill while they made a breaktrough along the ancient route between the hills. Once they got past the opening they started to shoot arrows and ballistae bolts from behind. This shows nicely how the Romans were able to operate their *carroballistae* as mobile artillery platforms.[7] The defence of the hill appears to have collapsed once the Romans made their breakthrough so the Romans were able to advance up the hill. See the map on p.xx. However, the concentration of hobnails from Roman leather sandals and military boots shows that there was also some hand-to-hand fighting before the Romans were able to force their way uphill. The archaeological finds on the smaller hill just behind the main Harzhorn hills show that during the retreat phase some of the Germans became isolated there because it has missile hits from different directions. The archaeologists suggest that the encounter on the hills was a short one lasting no more than about half an hour, so this would have been one of the skirmishes mentioned above.

Above left: A coin of Maximinus Thrax celebrating his German Victory. Source: Duruy.
Above right: A coin of Maximinus and his son Maximus Caesar celebrating the German Victory. Source: Cohen.

Once back in Roman territory, Maximinus marched his forces to Sirmium to spend the winter there in preparation for a campaign against the Sarmatians who needed to be punished for the invasion they had undertaken in 233. On 19 March 236 Maximinus designated his son Maximus as his successor with the title *Caesar* to secure his own standing among the army. They now had a dynasty to look forward to. The appointment of the Emperor meant that the soldiers were bribed with a donative. Maximinus appears to have developed an offensive grand strategy the goal of which was to subject all lands up to the Baltic Sea under Roman rule. Once inside Roman territory, he sought to secure his position by two means. Firstly, he kept the army close to him because his position was entirely reliant on its support. Secondly, he appointed Marcus Pupienus Africanus Maximimus, the youngest son of Marcus Clodius Pupienus Maximus, the *Praefectus Urbi*, as *consul ordinarius*. He held the consulship at the same time as Maximinus himself so this was a great honour. The likeliest reason for this appointment is that Maximinus wanted to keep the elder Pupienus, the City Prefect, happy. Pupienus was a man of great importance at this time so it was very important to flatter him. This flattery, however, appears to have taken place against the background of removing the elder Pupienus from office because we find another man in this office in 238. Maximinus's aim was to secure his own position in Rome while he was not there in person. As noted by Xavier Loriot, Maximinus hoped he could pacify the hostile elements within the Senate with the help of some influential members of the Senate who were kept in office or promoted. This did not work in a situation in which his policy was otherwise hostile towards the Senate. In Rome his principal henchman was the Praetorian Prefect Vitalianus, who should probably be identified with Publius Aelius Vitalianus, the recent governor of Mauretania Caesarensis. The removal of the elder Pupienus from office secured Vitalianus's standing in Rome.[8]

Unfortunately we lack details of the Danubian wars that took place in 236–8. All we have are the extant inscriptions and statements that the Sarmatians repeatedly used to sue for peace. Maximinus planned to continue his campaigns until all the territory up to the Baltic Sea was in Roman hands. We know that several military detachments earned the honorific title *maximiana* at this time. Similarly we know that Maximinus Thrax earned the titles *Dacicus Maximus* and *Sarmaticus Maximus* together with the salutation *imperator III* and probably also *imperator IV* in 236. This means that he fought at least in Pannonia and Moesia Superior, but the inclusion of Dacians suggests that he may also have fought in Moesia Inferior and Dacia. Maximinus appears to have fought against the same enemies in 237 so that he earned the *imperator V,* and *imp. VI* salutations. This means that he achieved outstanding military successes against the Dacians and Sarmatians, but that is all that we know.[9] Maximinus Thrax could therefore look forward to contuing his highly successful military campaign in 238, but this was not to happen thanks to his own serious and unforgivable mistakes.

The continuous fighting in the north meant that Maximinus Thrax needed money from whatever source possible to finance his wars and bribery of the soldiers. The mistakes he made on this field proved very costly as we shall see. Maximinus believed that his military successes and the propaganda celebrating them would bring him the support and acceptance of not only the soldiers but also of the elites and common people. This was a mistake as well. His imperial propaganda announced *Victoria Augusti* and *Pax Augusti* and the beginning of a new dynasty with the appointment of his son as

Caesar, but none of this was sufficient when he angered his audiences with his oppressive policies. One of these was also the conscription of new recruits in north Italy to replace those lost during the wars. There exists evidence for at least two conscriptions (*dilectus*) of the *iuventus Italica* for the region of Aquileia and one can surmise that there were similar conscription efforts elsewhere.[10] As we shall see, the conscription of Italian youth for military campaigns may actually have helped the enemies of Maximinus in Italy in a way that he did not expect. It is possible that if the *legio IV* (*Parthica?*) – that had been raised and trained by Maximinus Thrax so that it had become his 'personal legion' – was destroyed with the southern column during Alexander's Persian campaign, that Maximinus Thrax now recreated it with the conscripts raised in Italy. This, however, is mere speculation on my part.

3rd century heavy infantry equipped with heavy javelins, *spatha*-swords, armour, shields, and helmets. The socketed *pila* heavy javelins that they carry were primarily meant for use against infantry. The typical *pilum* tactic was to throw those at the enemy after which the men used their swords. However, these could also be used as thrusting weapons. This was typically done when the enemy attacked with cavalry. In that case the rear ranks usually threw their *pila* at the approaching cavalry while the front ranks used theirs as thrusting weapons.

© Dr. Ilkka Syvänne 2020
(adapted from earlier drawings of Dr. Ilkka Syvänne for this book)

Archaeological finds from Harzhorn prove that the Roman heavy infantry used the socketed *pila* (sing. *pilum*) at the battle of Harzhorn in 235.

Below left: 3rd century Hedderheim-type cavalry helmet (drawn partially after Mattesini)

Below right: Roman helmet. Friedberg in Hessen in the Museum of Darmstadt (drawn after Lindenschmit)

Chapter Five

The Year of the Six Emperors (238): Maximinus Thrax, Gordian I, Gordian II, Balbinus and Pubienus, Gordian III[1]

Coin of Gordian II
Note the hoplite.
Source: Beger 1696

| Gordian I according to Duruy | Gordian II according to Duruy |

5.1 Gordian I and Gordian II usurp power in about February – early March 238[2]

The reason why Maximinus Thrax failed rests both in the legacy of Alexander's reign and in his own actions. The end of Alexander and Julia Mamaea had proved that the Emperor needed to satisfy the needs of the army which consisted of two elements. Firstly, the Emperor needed to prove himself an able commander and warrior. Secondly, he needed to keep the soldiers well rewarded. Maximinus succeeded in the fields of war and war booty and he was also able to bribe the soldiers with money and donatives. However, it was in the way Maximinus obtained the necessary money that caused his downfall.

'[*Maximinus*] would have obtained immortal fame had not his cruelty and barbarity to his subjects eclipsed his martial glory. For what availed it to have cut off the barbarians when more murders were committed at Rome and in the provinces of the empire? What was the advantage of taking plunder and captives from the enemy and then despoiling his subjects of their lawful properties? ...Nor was anyone put on trial by an informer, but he was immediately stripped of fortune... under pretence of supplying money to distribute to the soldiers. His ears were always open to every malicious calumny... upon slightest and most frivolous slanders [*he*] would order commanders of armies and provinces, men of consular diginity, men of triumphal honours to be seized and hurried in carriages without attendants and brought to him, night and day, from the East and West, or, if it so chanced, from the most southern parts to Pannonia where he commonly resided. Then, after degrading and insulting them, he condemned them either to death or exile.

As long as he practised these cruelties on single persons, and the tragedy affected only the sufferer's family, the people of the cities and provinces cared very little. For the distress of the great and wealthy does not cause concern for the common people, but often even caused rejoicing among the worthless men of evil minds, because they envy the prosperity of those who seem happier than themselves. But after having reduced many illustrious families to beggary, not content with private rapines, which he thought inconsiderable and trifling, he broke in upon the public funds, seizing into his own possession all the city funds reserved for food supply and cash distribution for poor citizens, and funds set apart for the support of the theatres and other public festivals. All the consecrated gifts of the temples, effigies of gods, statues and armoury of heroes, decorations and ornaments of the city; in a word, everything composed of valuable metals was melted down and turned into money. The people resented this and mourned to see their city ransacked... Some of them were brave enough to resist and attempt the defence of the temples; choosing rather to die before the altars than to stand and see their country ravaged. Hence arose great confusion throughout all the cities and provinces; the hearts of the common people swelled with resentment. Nor, indeed, did the soldiers themselves much like what was being done; being perpetually reviled and upbraided by their relations and families alleging that it was their fault that Maximinus did all this mischief. [*Caracalla had been wise enough to limit his extraordinary taxes to the rich. He apparently understood that the soldiers were recruited from the ranks of the common people.*] Herodian 7.3.1ff. tr. by Hart 274ff. with changes, corrections and comments.

In early 238 these matters reached boiling point in Africa. Maximinus had sent his agent of the privy purse (*rationalis*) together with tax-gatherers to gather extraordinary taxes from the province to finance his wars and fulfil his promises to the soldiers. There was no other alternative, quite possibly because his predecessor Alexander Severus had lowered the taxes. The reason why Maximinus paid so much attention to North Africa was that it was one of the most important sources of provisions in kind for the army.[3]

At the time, the proconsul of this senatorial province was Marcus Antonius Gordianus Sempronianus Romanus, better known as Gordian I or Gordian the Elder, a man known for his wealth and noble birth. According to Julius Capitolinus, Gordian's father was Maecius Murullus and his mother Ulpia Gordianus, so on his father's side he descended from the famous Gracchi and on his mother's side from the Emperor Trajan. On the

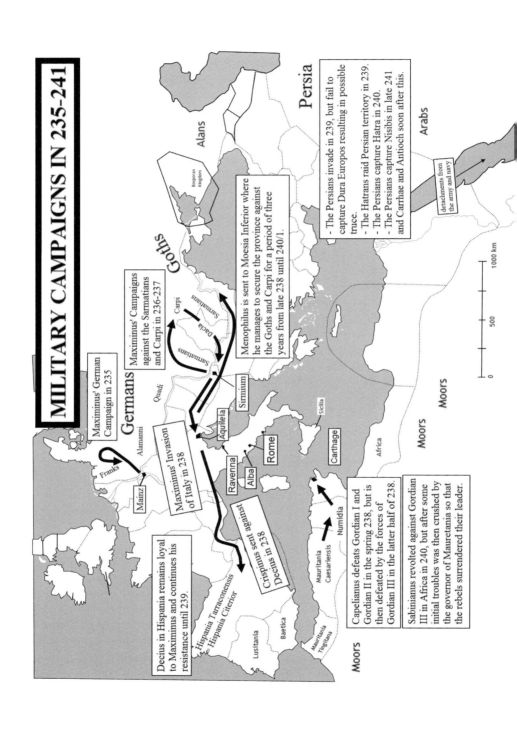

MILITARY CAMPAIGNS IN 235-241

Germans

Maximinus' German Campaign in 235

Maximinus' Campaigns against the Sarmatians and Carpi in 236-237

Goths

Carpi

Dacia

Sarmatians

Sarmatians

Quadi

Alamanni

Franks

Mainz

Maximinus' Invasion of Italy in 238

Aquileia

Sirmium

Ravenna

Alba

Rome

Crispinus sent against Decius in 238

Menophilus is sent to Moesia Inferior where he manages to secure the province against the Goths and Carpi for a period of three years from late 238 until 240/1.

Decius in Hispania remains loyal to Maximinus and continues his resistance until 239.

Hispania Tarraconensis

Hispania Citerior

Lusitania

Baetica

Sicilia

Carthage

Africa

Moors

Numidia

Mauretania Caesariensis

Mauretania Tingitana

Moors

Capelianus defeats Gordian I and Gordian II in the spring 238, but is then defeated by the forces of Gordian III in the latter half of 238.

Sabinianus revolted against Gordian III in Africa in 240, but after some initial troubles was then crushed by the governor of Mauretania so that the rebels surrendered their leader.

Alans

Bosporan kingdom

Persia

- The Persians invade in 239, but fail to capture Dura Europos resulting in possible truce.
- The Hatrans raid Persian territory in 239.
- The Persians capture Hatra in 240.
- The Persians capture Nisibis in late 241 and Carrhae and Antioch soon after this.

Arabs

detachments from the army and navy

Moors

0   500   1000 km

basis of his cognomen, Gordianus, it is clear that he also had some family connection with Asia Minor. In Rome he owned the famed House of Pompey and in the provinces more land than any other subject. Gordian had received his governorship under Alexander Severus, but he had been allowed to keep his office, presumably because Maximinus did not consider him a threat as he was very old. In 238 he was 80 and one of the most influential senators, one of the best-connected men in the Empire, and with plenty of money to bribe. He was a cultured man who had written poetry and a text called the *Antoniniad* – the lives of Antoninus Pius and Marcus Aurelius, both of whom he admired greatly – and other prose eulogies of all the Antonines which would then presumably include Commodus and the fictitious Antonines, the Severans who consisted of Septimius Severus, Caracalla (Antoninus Magnus), Elagabalus (Antoninus) and Alexander Severus. These writings would have flattered the emperors from Caracalla onwards, under whom he had served.[4]

Gordian had two children. The eldest was the 66-year-old Marcus Antonius Gordianus Sempronianus Romanus, better known as Gordian II or Gordian the Younger. He acted as Gordian the Elder's legate in Africa. The second child was Maecia Faustina. She had been married to Iunius Balbus and from 238 was a widow. They had an 11 or 13 or 16-year-old son called Marcus Antonius Gordianus, better known as Gordian III.[5] She and the grandson had stayed behind in Rome. The Younger Gordian had a distinguished career behind him. He acted as his father's legate because the other senators thought that the 80-year-old needed the help of his son to perform his duties as governor of a province. Julius Capitolinus gives us details of the life of the old man which strike true. According to him, Gordian was sparing in his consumption of wine and even more sparing of food. He dressed elegantly. In the summer he bathed four or five times a day and in the winter twice. As a rich man, he would have the time to do so. Gordian the Elder was also known for his 'love of sleep'; he would doze off at the table in presence of his friends.[6]

The idea that the Emperor was levying extraordinary taxes in Africa did not sit well with the Senate or with Gordian the Elder. The exactions were also targeted against Gordian's own vast properties there. Consequently, according to Julius Capitolinus (*HA Gord.* 7.2), Gordian the Elder and the Younger both voiced their disapproval of Maximinus's actions to the agent, and the agent threatened to kill them. However, the sources, Julius Capitolinus included, portray the following events as if the Gordiani did not have any role in them. Their claim is that the agent of Maximinus was then killed as a result of a popular reaction to his ruthless methods of tax gathering. In my opinion this version is possible, but I would suggest that it is far likelier that the Gordiani were behind the murder, especially so because Julius Capitolinus specifically notes that the *rationalis* (the agent of the privy purse) threatened them with death. Julius Capitolinus (*HA Gord.* 7.2) also claims that the young killers of the *rationalis* were helped by a number of soldiers. In my opinion it is probable that these soldiers consisted of the detachment of soldiers serving under the Gordiani. In other words, it is more than likely that with the help of his son, Gordian the Elder schemed his own and his son's elevation to power.[7] Herodian however, like the others, claims that the initiative for the murder came from the rich young men of the noble Carthagian families:

'The *rationalis* then of Libya among other acts of violence, having fraudulently condemned some young men of good birth and fortunes, endeavoured to extort money from them; and to strip them of all their patrimonies… which the young gentlemen bearing very badly promised to bring him the sums demanded, if he would indulge them with three days time in which space they formed a conspiracy of all who either had suffered, or were afraid of suffering,… and ordered all their supporters, tenants and farmers in the country to come to them in the night with clubs and axes. The tenants readily obeyed their landlords, and came together into the city before the break of the day. A very large multitude was soon collected… Gentlemen… ordered their servants to follow them… Themselves, with their daggers concealed in the folds of their garments, proceeded to the *rationalis*… and, rushing upon him unawares, stabbed him. Upon which the guards drew their swords and endeavoured to revenge the death, but the whole multitude of rustics pulled out their clubs and axes and bravely fighting for their masters in a little time put the soldiers to flight. [*This account does not include any role for the soldiers mentioned by Julius Capitolinus, but as noted there is every reason to suspect that the retinue accompanying the Gordiani was also involved.*]

Matters having thus far well succeeded, the young gentlemen, knowing themselves engaged in a desperate cause… concluded their only means of safety consisted of making an even bolder attempt… They therefore resolved to make the governor of the province a partner in their problem [*Julius Capitolinus HA Gord. 7.4ff. states that a decurio called Mauritius held an assembly on his farm near Thysdrus and convinced the other conspirators to choose Gordian as Emperor. If this information is true, then it is probable that he was in collusion with the Gordiani*]… Accordingly, they came to the proconsul's house about midday attended by all the multitude. His name was Gordian, an old man, …he was 80 years of age… Gordian was residing in leisure at his own house [*in Thysdrus near Carthage, modern El Djem in Tunisia*]… The young men and the mob with their swords in their hands forced their way in and found Gordian on a couch, and immediately gathering around him threw the purple robe over his shoulders and saluted him Augustus. The astonished Gordian… prayed them to spare an old man… one of the young men, who was superior to the rest in birth and force of eloquence, ordered his companions to be silent… spoke to the old man: "If you embrace the present opportunity… you will add new lustre… But if you deny what we ask… fate has fixed this day for your last." [*Gordian*] willingly enough accepted the offer choosing the future danger before the present and thinking that as he was very old… it would be no great loss if he would happen to be cut off in the enjoyment of imperial honours.' Herodian 7.4.3ff. tr. by Hart 278ff. with changes, corrections, additions and comments.

The above, like all of the sources, Julius Capitolinus (e.g. *HA Gord.* 9.2) included, claim that the murder was a spontaneous reaction of the young landowners of Carthage and that they forced Gordian the Elder to become their Emperor. The young landowners are called *Iuvenes* by Julius Capitolinus, which implies that they consisted primarily of the paramilitary citizen militia. However, on the basis of the information provided by Julius Capitolinus himself, I am inclined to suspect that the prime movers behind the killing were still the two Gordiani. This also receives support from another piece of circumstantial evidence which is that Gordian the Younger was not present in Thysdrus at the time his father was declared Emperor. He was serving as his father's legate at Carthage (*HA Gord.* 9.6). I would suggest that it was Gordian the Younger at Carthage who orchestrated the events in the background while his elderly father rested (or rather slept through the events) nearby at Thysdrus so that he could maintain deniability. It is hard to believe that Gordian the Younger would have remained inactive when a band of rustics under the leadership of local young Carthagian nobles had murdered the Emperor's *rationalis* in the city where he was serving as a legate. It is clear that when the killers then supposedly held a council in which it was decided that they should ask Gordian the Elder to don the purple, the younger Gordian was pulling the strings in the background. It is also very likely that it had been the detachment of soldiers serving under Gordian the Younger that had assisted in the murder. The fact that the elder Gordian was in Thysdrus enabled the plotters to act as if they had forced the reluctant Gordian to take the throne.

Whatever the truth, it is clear that the plotters acted as if they were working from a playbook prepared for a usurpation. Julius Capitolinus gives us two versions of when Gordian II was appointed co-ruler with Gordian I. The first is that Gordian I appointed his son co-ruler at Thysdrus and then travelled to Carthage. The second is that Gordian I travelled to Carthage and it was only there that he nominated his son Gordian II as his co-ruler. These two versions can be reconciled if one assumes that Gordian I appointed his son as co-ruler immediately at Thysdrus, but then made his son ceremoniously co-ruler by enrobing him in purple only when he reached Carthage. It was then after Gordian I had reached Carthage that he sent an embassy bearing letters to Rome. According to Julius Capitolinus, the Africans gave both the title *Africanus*.[8]

The embassy sent to Rome had two purposes: to canvass support among the senators, soldiers and populace to his cause; and to assassinate the supporters of Maximinus by stealth before they could react. Now the Gordiani were able to cultivate the contacts they had made in the course of their very long careers. It is probable that the revolt of the Gordiani took place some time in March 238, but 21–24 February has also been suggested, or alternatively even as late as 7 April.[9]

According to Julius Capitolinus (*HA Gord.* 9.7), the chief of the Senate, Valerian, the later hapless Emperor, received the embassy of the Gordiani, but Zosimus (1.14) claims that Valerian was actually one of the envoys sent to Rome. It is unlikely that Valerian, who at the time was about 43–48 years of age, would have been the Chief of the Senate. Therefore we should consider Julius's statement as a Freudian slip. Valerian was later the Chief of the Senate under Decius. On the basis of this it is probable that Valerian was one of the envoys of Gordian[10] or at least his supporter. Letters were also sent to their noble friends. The Senate was convened into a secret session by consul Junius Silanus. At the session, there were no clerks, public servants or officers of the census. The clerks, and probably also the other public servants, appear to have had internal security/police duties besides their other duties. The senators themselves performed the duties of these officials. Prefect of the City (*Praefectus Urbi*) Sabinus somehow got wind of the proceedings, but chose to keep away, probably because he wanted to wait and see. It is likely that he had some sort of internal security role in the city, like earlier Urban Prefects, and had therefore immediately learned of the secret session taking place. The consul informed the

Senate of the events that had taken place in Africa and read the letters of the Gordiani. As a result the Senate gave a secret decree (*senatus consultum tacitum*) in favour of the Gordiani. They elected twenty men between whom they apportioned the districts of Italy to be guarded against Maximinus – the *vigintiviri*. Loriot and McMahon note that their existence is confirmed by inscriptions as *XX Viri Ex S.C. Rei Publicae Curandae*. Everyone who killed the enemies of the Gordiani was promised a reward. Everyone took an oath of silence until the business was completed. However, Maximinus immediately learned everything. He got a copy of the Senate's secret decree, which indicates that he also had his supporters inside the Senate. These supporters would have undoubtedly consisted mainly of the Illyrian senators and of those who favoured a soldier on the throne and/or a persecutor of Christians. The supporters of the Gordiani in the Senate must have consisted of a great variety of people, whose only common denominator was their hatred of the upstart barbarian Emperor Maximinus. All the rich senators feared for their lives and for their properties. The traditionalists abhorred the thought that the barbarian would continue to rule them. The sympathisers of the Christians and closet Christians definitely wanted an end to the rule of their persecutor.[11]

We know the names of four or six members of the *vigintiviri*. The best known are the future emperors Clodius Pupienus Maximus and D. Caelius Calvinus Balbinus; and L. Caesonius C. f. Quir(ina) Lucillus Macer Rufinianus and L. [V]alerius Claud(ia) [Maximus] Acilius Priscilianus. The background of the two emperors will be discussed later in the appropriate place. Here it suffices to say that both were highly ranking patricians at this stage of their career. The latter two were Italians and patricians, and both had illustrious ancestors and careers that had prospered under the Severans. It has also been speculated that C(?) Tullius Menophilus and Rutilius Pudens Crispinus, the men who were tasked with the defence of Aquileia, were also members of the *vigintiviri*. This suggestion has not been accepted by all, but I am inclined to accept this on the basis of what Julius Capitolinus stated on the role of the members of the *vigintiviri*. It is clear that the membership was based on perceived ability and nobility. All were clearly eminently qualified for the tasks they were now given by the Senate.[12]

It is clear that the Second Sophists, and philosophers and their sympathisers, were also in favour of the cultivated Gordiani. Both father and son favoured philosophers and Gordian the Elder was known for his admiration of Antoninus Pius and Marcus Aurelius. He had even written a history of their lives. He is said to have studied Plato, Aristotle and may even have been the Antonius Gordianus to whom Philostratus dedicated his *Lives of the Sophists*.[13]

The principal threat to the aspirations of the Gordiani and their backers in the Senate was the Praetorian Prefect Vitalianus, but the conspirators had formed a plan to get rid of him. According to Herodian it was Gordian himself who recognized the danger posed by Vitalianus and who then formed the plan to kill him. Herodian states that Gordian gave the task of assassinating Vitalianus to his provincial *quaestor*, a young man who was brave and strong. He was given some centurions and soldiers to assist him. Was this man Valerian? This is a possibility because Zosimus claims that he was one of the envoys sent, but he would not have been young by any means. Apparently just before or simultaneously with the secret session of the Senate or immediately after it, the assassins/soldiers went to meet the Praetorian Prefect with a forged letter purporting to come from Maximinus. They went to meet him early in the morning while it was still dark so that there were not many people around. The envoys said that they also had further information, not in the letter, to be told only in secret. Vitalianus led the soldiers/assassins to a distant portico (Julius Capitolinus) or room (Herodian), where the killers cut him down. They then ran from the scene and claimed to the few Praetorians present that they had killed Vitalianus by command of Maximinus. The guards believed this because Maximinus was in the habit of ordering secret assassinations. According to Herodian the soldiers then ran to the Sacred Way where they displayed the letters written by Gordian to the consuls and to the people. They also spread the rumour that Maximinus had been killed. Julius Capitolinus, however, claims that the assassins immediately went to the Camp of the Praetorians where they displayed the letters and images of the Gordiani.[14]

The news of the revolt in Africa and the Senate's support for it appears to have reached Maximinus some time in late March or April, but later dates have also been suggested.[15] It came as a horrible surprise to Maximinus. According to Herodian, when Maximinus learnt of the situation in Rome he remained inactive for the first two days, during which he held discussions with his advisors, and it was only on the third day that Maximinus acted and summoned his army for a speech and instructions. Julius Capitolinus gives us more details of what happened. When Maximinus Thrax learnt the news, he went mad with fury and screamed incoherently, dashed himself against walls, sometimes threw himself on the ground, drew his sword as if to kill the Senate with it, tore his purple robes, and then beat up a member of the *aulici* in his fury. He then blamed his son Maximus for the situation because he had not gone to Rome when he had ordered him. It is clear that this accusation was unfair. I agree with Pearson (pp.142–3) that it is likelier that the son would have ended up as the first victim of the revolt. Then Maximinus's friends led him away to his room so he would not do anything foolish. Maximinus then began to binge drink wine with the result that he lost his memory so badly that his friends had to tell him the very same things again in the morning. When he had recovered from his hangover, Maximinus consulted his advisors and then adopted a course of action consisting of two elements. Firstly, he and his advisors expected that Italian resistance would collapse immediately if they made a blitzkrieg invasion of Italy: they considered Italian civilians to be an unwarlike rabble easily scared. This was to prove a fatal mistake. Secondly, they combined this blitzkrieg operation with simultaneous messages promising all sorts of nice things to those who abandoned the revolt. This did not work either. Maximinus announced that he would start the campaign the next day, which was the fourth day after he had received the news. He also bribed the soldiers to increase their enthusiasm.[16]

As noted above, at the same time as he started to organize the campaign, Maximinus sent several envoys in succession to the City Prefect Sabinus, followed with an embassy armed with promises of all kinds. But the Gordiani's embassy promised more and, more importantly, they were trusted. They promised a huge bounty to the soldiers and also promised they would be generous to the people. On the basis of Julius Capitolinus, the first messages of Maximinus were sent to City Prefect Sabinus, and they included a copy of the Senate's secret decree. Maximinus naturally demanded that the Prefect take the appropriate action, but in vain. The Prefect sat on the fence as long as he could. When the threatening letters from Maximinus arrived, he decided to act. His decision was to side with the Senate. So he made an address to the people and soldiers saying that Maximinus was indeed dead. The general session of the Senate believed him and declared the Gordiani emperors. They then ordered all informers, false accusers, and personal agents and friends of Maximinus to be put to death. The people did this eagerly, and threw the victims into the sewers. Some unscrupulous people took the opportunity to exact vengeance on their personal enemies or their creditors. Sabinus, the Prefect of the City with consular rank, attempted to put a stop to the rampage, but only with the result that he was clubbed to death and his corpse left lying in the street.

When the truth of the situation became known and the senators learnt that Maximinus was alive it was too late to repent. The Senate dispatched letters and delegations of senatorial representatives and well-known members of the equestrian order to the provinces to secure their support for the Senate and the Gordiani. Most of the provinces rebelled against Maximinus because he had made himself hated. The henchmen of Maximinus, his friends, the administrators, generals (*duces*), tribunes, and soldiers were everywhere put to death on the orders of the Senate. Strategically the most important of these provinces were those bordering the Rhine because their change of allegiance enabled Maximus Pupienus, one of the special XX senators that took charge of the defence of Italy against Maximinus Thrax, to obtain German allies[17] from across the Rhine. It is a pity that we do not know if he dispatched his message to the Germans now or only after he had become Emperor. However, there were also provinces which stayed loyal and either killed the envoys or sent them to Maximinus.[18] These included Numidia under Capelianus and Hispania Citerior under Q. L(?). Decius Valerinus (probably the future emperor Decius).[19] It is probable that Decius sided with Maximinus because he hailed from the Balkans and hated Christians.

On the fourth day after having learnt of the revolt, Maximinus started his campaign to crush it. The best and most detailed description of this operation comes from the pen of Herodian:

'After distributing large sums of money… [*Maximinus*] set out at the head of a numerous army consisting of all of the Roman forces, and a great multitude of other soldiers; among whom was no inconsiderable number of Germans whom he had subdued by arms or brought over as allies and auxiliaries. He likewise took with him all the war engines and artillery pieces and other things that he had intended for use against the barbarians; and made slow marches because of all the baggage carts and necessities choking all the roads. He had no time to make the usual preparations, because this expedition to Italy was sudden and unforeseen. Therefore, he had to furnish the army with what was needful en route by improvising. It was because of this that Maximinus decided to send ahead the Pannonian phalanxes in whom he placed his chief trust because they had first recognized him as emperor, and because they always seemed willing to hazard everything in his service. They were instructed to advance in front of the main body and occupy the advantageous positions in Italy [*Even if one cannot be absolutely certain, it is very likely that these Pannonian phalanxes consisted of fast moving cavalry whose mission was to secure the important passes over the Iulian Alps, but the subsequent account of Herodian fails to state that as we shall see*]. Herodian 7.8.9ff., tr. by Hart 291ff. with changes, corrections, additions and comments.

In the meantime important developments had taken place both in Africa and in Rome.

5.2 The Death of the Gordiani in March 238[20]

The usurpation of the Gordiani had progressed well in Rome, Italy and in most of the provinces, but not quite so well in Africa itself. Maximinus had appointed a senator called Capellianus/Capelianus as governor of Numidia. This province had a strong garrison force the most important elements of which were the *legio III Augusta* and the Moorish light cavalry. His army was therefore stronger than that of the Gordiani. Gordian the Elder was an old enemy of Capelianus thanks to some legal dispute and when Gordian became the Emperor he dismissed Capelianus from office. Capellianus reacted to this by declaring his loyalty to the Emperor Maximinus Thrax. The two sides were unevenly matched. Capelianus had a professional army while Gordian I was unable to take the field in person, so he had to give command of the citizen militia, which was strengthened with some soldiers, to his militarily inexperienced son.[21]

Julius Capitolinus paints Gordian II as a good looking person who had taken his studies seriously. He was also considered to be very kind: if he saw any of the boys flogged at school, he cried out of sympathy. As an adult he enjoyed the riches he possessed to the full. He was very fond of wine that was spiced with roses, mastic, wormwood[22] or other herbs, and of cold drinks, and he ate enormous amounts of fruits and greens. He ate sparingly otherwise. He never married, but his sex life was lively: he is claimed to have had twenty-two concubines and three or four children with each. It was thanks to this that he had two apt nicknames: Priam (father of fifty sons in Iliad) and Priapus, the god of fertility. He lived his life in constant revelry and was extremely fat,[23] but his father did not have anything to say against this. The son's rise up the ladder of the senatorial offices was swifter than that of his father, which is not surprising in light of the influence wielded by his father. However, it would be wrong to say that Gordian the Younger had any particular ambitions before becoming an Emperor – after all, he served as his father's legate in Africa at the age of 66. This makes it clear that the usurpation of the Gordiani was merely a reaction to the threat posed by the *rationalis* of Maximinus. It is also clear that Gordian lacked the necessary military background and experience to confront Capellianus at the head of his professional soldiers. Gordian II the Younger was no Maximus Pupienus.

The accounts of Herodian and Julius Capitolinus are largely in agreement with what happened next, but since Herodian gives us the longer account I quote him below. This account is important because it demonstrates the relative strengths of the professional army vis-à-vis the citizen militia consisting of the *Iuvenes*. It also gives two different versions of the death of Gordian I.

'[*Capellianus*] having summoned the army together and persuaded them to keep their oath of allegiance to [*Maximinus*], marched against Carthage with a great number of stout soldiers in the prime of their age, well armed and furnished with everything necessary to war; and through their martial experience gained in many considerable fights with the barbarians fit to undertake the most important battles. The news of Capellianus's approach struck great terror into Gordian and very much alarmed the Carthagians, who depending more upon numbers than good discipline for victory issued out of the city in universal multitude to draw up and engage with Capellianus.

But when Gordian saw him advance to the city, the old man (as some report) giving up everything for lost, because he knew Maximinus's power, and seeing nothing in Libya sufficient to match it, fell into despair and hanged himself. However, his death was concealed and his son chosen to head the multitude who drew up and engaged. The Carthagians were much superior in number, but all raw and ignorant of war,... destitute of arms and engines of war. Every one brought from home a little sword, an axe and hunting spears. The available skins and sawed wooden stakes of any shape were used to make shields... In contrast the Numidians were dextrous javelin-throwers, and such excellent horsemen that they rode without bridles and managed the speed of their horses only with a rod. The Carthagians were therefore soon defeated; for not being able to sustain the violence of the first attack, they threw away their arms and fled with precipitation, thrusting and trampling over one another in the confusion so that more were killed by their own than by the enemy. Gordian's son... fell in the general slaughter... nor could young Gordian's body ever be found. For out of this routed multitude only a few were able to get again into Carthage and escape by dispersing and hiding themselves throughout the large and populous city. The rest were crowded at the gates and striving to get in first they were all either hit by javelins or cut to pieces by the hoplites [*these would be the legionaries of the legio III Augusta*]. The city rang with horrible shrieks and lamentations of women and children... Others relate that old Gordian, who remained at home by reason of his great age and weakness, being informed that Capellianus had entered the city, and seeing everything in a state of desperation, went into his room... and there took off his girdle from his waist, fastened it in a noose around his neck and so finished his life...

Capellianus, having entered Carthage, put to death the principal persons who had escaped the battle. He pillaged the temples, and spared neither private nor public treasures. After which he went to the other cities that had destroyed the dedications of Maximinus, and having put to death their magistrates and leading citizens, he drove the lower class out of the territory. The fields and villages were handed over to the soldiers to burn and plunder under the pretence of treason against Maximinus, but his real secret intent was to canvass the support of the soldiers for himself, if Maximinus's fortunes would take the wrong turn.' Herodian 7.3ff., tr. by Hart 292ff. with changes, corrections, additions and comments.

In sum, Capellianus crushed the revolt with great efficiency and brutality and treated Roman territory as if it was enemy territory. Herodian implies that Capellianus's real intention was not to support Maximinus but rather to place himself in such a position as to be able to usurp power himself if the opportunity presented itself. The only real achievement of the two Gordiani was that they forced the Senate, the Roman people and all those who had supported their usurpation to continue on the road they had chosen.

5.3 The Emperors of the Senate Pupienus and Balbinus; and the Emperor of the Gordian Faction Gordian III (March or early April 238)[24]

| A bust of Balbinus according to Duruy (presumably before he gained weight) | A bust of Pupienus according to Duruy (the best commander of his day) |

News of the deaths of the Gordiani was received with great dismay by the populace and Senate of Rome. They knew that Maximinus Thrax would not show them any mercy for their treachery. Therefore they decided to continue along the path they had chosen. The Senate decided that they must immediately choose new emperors. Therefore the senators assembled at the Temple of Jupiter Capitolinus (Herodian 7.10.2) or Temple of Concord (*HA MB* 1.1)[25] and held a closed session in the inner sanctuary. After this the senators made a preliminary selection of the candidates (means probably the *vigintiviri* as suggested by Whittaker[26]) after which they held a vote in which many candidates were eliminated before the vote ended, selecting Clodius Pupienus Maximus and D. Caelius Calvinus Balbinus as the next emperors. It is clear that the death of the Gordiani in Africa had taken place so soon after the election of the *vigintiviri* that they were still in Rome when the news arrived. According to Zonaras (12.17), Pupienus was 74 and Balbinus 60 at the time of their accession. Both had illustrious careers behind them. Pupienus had had a long and very distinguished military career and his service as *praefectus urbi* was seen in favourable light by the conservatively minded senators because he had shown himself to be an impartial and intelligent man with 'sober habits' as befitted a man who held high positions under Alexander Severus. As we shall see this view was not universally accepted. There were those who thought that he had been far too harsh. Pupienus therefore represented the military faction within the Senate, but it is not surpring that he was elected because he was the most distinguished military commander alive and the

Senate needed such a man to take charge of the operations. The second of the candidates, Balbinus, hailed from a patrician family. He had held the consulship twice and had been provincial governor without complaints. He was the candidate of the civilian faction within the Senate. Their special skills complemented each other so that one could be expected to fight wars while the other administrated the Empire from Rome.[27]

According to Herodian, while the above proceedings were taking place people started to gather around the Capitol. He suggests that this was done on behalf of the friends and relatives of the Gordiani. The events prove that Whittaker (Herodian, 228) is correct in saying that the Gordian faction had a strong control of the *plebs urbana*. The likeliest reason for this control would be wealth. It is quite possible that the Gordiani owned the houses in which the people lived, that they employed large numbers of them in the businesses they owned, and they had enough wealth to pay the *plebs* to fight on their behalf. At the instigation of the Gordian faction the mob armed themselves with sticks and stones, occupied the road that led to the Capitol and voiced their disapproval of the Senate's actions – in particular the choice of Pupienus because they considered him to have been too severe during his tenure as *praefectus urbi*. The mob threatened to kill the new emperors and demanded that a member of the Gordian family be chosen as Emperor. The emperors assembled around them the young men of the equestrian order (*iuvenes*, *iuventutes*) and anyone with any military experience and tried to force their way out of the Capitol, only to be forced back by a shower of stones. Then someone came up with the idea of raising the grandson of Gordian as Emperor. According to Herodian this was a trick meant to fool the people. It probably means that the 11- or 13-year-old Gordian was considered too young to be a threat and therefore a safe choice. The emperors accepted the idea and sent some of their supporters to fetch the son. They placed the son on their shoulders and carried him through the mob which started to proclaim him as Emperor. Once in the Capitol, the Senate voted him *Caesar* because he was too young to be made *Augustus*. This satisfied the people for the moment and the emperors were able to make their way to the Imperial Palace.

According to Julius Capitolinus, the sequence was slightly different. He claims that the two emperors were chosen in the Temple of Concord and that they then went to the Capitol to sacrifice after which they summoned the people. The people and soldiers (on the basis of later events likely to be Praetorians) who were with them responded by demanding Gordian as their Emperor. This request was met and Gordian was brought to the House of the Senate and declared *Caesar*.

It is impossible to be certain which of these versions is correct, but at least the end result is known. The Senate had chosen the two *Augusti* while the Gordian faction had forced them to nominate Gordian III as *Caesar*. Julius Capitolinus notes that the sources were in disagreement concerning the age of Gordian at this time. Some claimed he was 11, others stated that he was 13, while Junius Cordus claimed that he was 16. Most modern historians, like Herodian, consider 13 to be the correct age. The reason for the modern concensus view is that Gordian started to demonstrate his independence as an 'adult' three years later, which would have meant that he had attained the age of 16 with the *toga virilis*. This is indeed the likeliest of the alternatives, but not conclusively so. Whatever the truth, it is clear that Gordian III was young and still under the guidance of his mother, relatives and their friends at the time of his accession to power.

Xavier Loriot has identified some of the likely members of the Gordian faction. He suggests that the Carthagian consul L. Domitius Gallicanus Papinianus, C. Flavius Iulius Latronianus, C. Octavius Appius Suetrius Sabinus and M. Aedinius Iulianus belonged to it. He suggests that Gallicanus belonged to this group on the grounds that he clearly had a pivotal role in the creation of hostility between the soldiers (meaning primarily the Praetorians) and populace, which will be discussed later. Latronianus became *praefectus urbi* in 239/40 which makes it probable that he belonged to this group. Sabinus, the personal friend of Caracalla and *consul ordinarius* in 214, became consul again in 240 with the same implication. The former praetorian prefect of Alexander Severus, Iulianus, is also claimed to have had an active role in the events of 238 with the implication that he too was a member of this group. In short, this power block included men who had risen to prominence under the Severans.[28]

Pupienus and Balbinus needed money fast to pay for the war against Maximinus and also to pay for the promises they had made, which included the payment of 250 *denarii* for each person in Rome to celebrate their rise to power. They also needed to pay the customary *donativum* to the soldiers when new emperors were appointed. Pupienus and Balbinus adopted an ingenious solution. They readopted the expedient invented by Caracalla by reintroducing the two-*denarius antoninianus* coin. However, they diluted the silver content of the coin even further than Caracalla. Caracalla's *antoninianus* had weighed on average 5.02 grams with a silver content of 510⁰/00, but the coins minted by these two emperors weighed only 4.75 grams with a silver content of 490⁰/00. Herodian states that the two emperors ruled the city efficiently and sensibly. The decision to reintroduce the *antoninianus* was certainly one instance of that. The two emperors did not have to resort to extraordinary confiscations of property to obtain money, but could use the existing silver supply by diluting it.[29]

Xavier Loriot also notes that the Senate and new emperors stressed their connection to the Senate in their propaganda. Pupienus and Balbinus were emperors chosen by the Senate. Their coins celebrated this and their strict equality of powers, with the legends Concordia, Fides, Pietas Mutua and Patres Senatus. The senatorial connection was very real, but as we shall see their propaganda of mutual solidarity and equality was pure propaganda.[30]

Julius Capitolinus claims that Clodius Pupienus Maximus had risen to power from the ranks of the plebs and that some claimed that his father's name was Maximus and that by profession he was a blacksmith. This Maximus then had a wife called Prima with whom he sired Pupienus and four boys and four girls, but the latter all died before the age of puberty. Pupienus was then raised and edcuated in the house of his kinsman Pinarius. Once Emperor, he rewarded Pinarius with the office of Praetorian Prefect. The aim was clearly to secure the support of the Praetorians behind Pupienus, but it is probable that Balbinus appointed the other prefect with the same idea. If this appointment happened immediately on Pupienus's accession, then the appointment may have had political implications, which I will discuss below. As a student Pupienus paid very little attention to grammar and rhetoric and showed interest only in soldiery subjects, so he rose through the ranks to become military tribune and commander of many military units (*numeri*). It was then that Pescennia Marcellina adopted Pupienus as a son and paid the expenses related to praetorship. This relationship may suggest that the young and handsome Pupienus seduced an elderly rich woman to improve his lot in society. After this, Pupienus served as proconsul of Bithynia, Greece and Gallia Narbonensis followed by service in the east in 231–3, special commands in the Balkans and Gaul in 233–4, and Urban Prefecture after that. He was also consul twice. His personal habits reflected his stern military countenance. He loved food but was sparing in his drinking of wine and in affairs of love as befitted a man who had risen through the ranks during the conservative reign of Alexander Severus. He was a tall fit man with a stern, gloomy look on his face. However, he is claimed not to have been cruel or unmerciful. Julius Capitolinus claims that he never joined any conspiracies and trusted no-one else's opinions except his own.[31]

The second of the emperors, D. Caelius Calvinus Balbinus, had very noble birth. He had served with equal distinction in civilian life as Pupienus in the military. Balbinus had managed the civil administration of Asia, Africa, Bithynia, Galatia, Pontus, Thrace and the Gauls, and even served as a *dux* of an army. He is claimed to have been good, righteous and modest in his life and it was this that had endeared him to the other senators. Balbinus claimed to have descended from the famous Cornelius Balbus Theophanes[32] and there is no reason to doubt this. He was tall, he was very rich, and loved pleasures excessively. Balbinus was very fond of food and love, which is in evidence in his extant coins, busts and statues. He was known for his eloquence and poetic skills. He was loved by all for his manners. It is therefore not surprising that he was elected as Emperor by the Senate.

Once this succession had been solved there was the question of how to deal with the approaching Maximinus Thrax. The Senate and Balbinus both agreed that Pupienus, with his extensive military experience was the man for the job, so Pupienus was entrusted with the task of fighting the war while Balbinus remained behind in Rome. Julius Capitolinus notes that the Senate sent at the same time men of the rank of consul, praetor, quaestor, aedile, and tribune to all districts to make certain that every town and city was well stocked with supplies, arms and that the defences and walls were ready to receive the enemy. The Senate also ordered that all provisions outside the cities and towns were to be gathered inside the walls so that the enemy would not be able to obtain supplies. True to his character, Pupienus set out to accomplish his mission with speed and diligence. It is obvious that he was the man behind this strategy, which was to defeat Maximinus with guerrilla warfare fought from within the Italian cities while Maximinus's army starved. Pupienus also arranged for a blockade of the supply routes and harbours. Most of the provinces sided with the Senate and the new emperors. Maximinus was entering a trap.

The fact that the provinces bordering the Rhine sided with the Senate meant that Pupienus was able to obtain reinforcements from his Germanic friends. Pupienus himself settled in Ravenna where he began to gather an army to face Maximinus Thrax. Maximinus had made the mistake of advancing into Italy in the hopes that he would be able to gather provisions en route, but he now faced a terrain in which everything edible had either been destroyed or taken inside the cities. This meant that he had to capture Aquiliea if he wanted to obtain supplies, or that he would have to continue his march past in the hopes that he would be able to obtain supplies from some other source, which in fact was not possible. On top of this, once Pupienus had enough men, which were en route to Italy at the time Maximinus approached, he would start harassing Maximinus's army.

Herodian (7.12.1ff.) has misplaced one important part of this process. Alongside the commanders that were sent to organize the defence of the Italian towns and cities, the Senate naturally ordered new recruits to be enrolled all over Italy. All of the youth groups (*iuvenes* and *iuventus/iuventutes*) and the paramilitary citizen militia were called to arms and then armed with whatever makeshift weapons could be found on the spur of the moment. In my opinion it is probable that Maximinus Thrax had already called some of these to arms because, as noted, there is evidence for at least two such groups for the area of Aquileia. This means that it is probable that the new emperors were able to use already assembled conscripts against Maximinus. According to Herodian, Pupienus took most of these with him while the rest were left behind to guard and protect Rome – this last mentioned must be a mistake for the leaving of the rest of the new recruits to guard their respective cities. However, since Herodian places the above to take place only after the fighting between the Praetorians and populace in Rome (see below), it is clear that some of these citizen militias were transferred to Rome to fight against the Praetorians and other soldiers.

In the meantime, after Pupienus left, Balbinus had troubles in Rome.[33] Maximinus had left behind a garrison in Rome consisting of the soldiers (i.e. Praetorians) who were about to be discharged from service. Some of these men saw that people were gathered in front of the Senate House (Curia Iulia) and went there unarmed but still wearing their military uniforms and cloaks. They and the populace then gazed inside through the open doors, but then two or three of the Praetorians, the most curious ones, entered and passed beyond the Altar of Victory which was forbidden. Then one of the senators, one Gallicanus from Carthage, of consular rank, and Maecenas, a former *dux* of praetorian rank, stabbed and killed two of the Praetorians with the daggers they were carrying – all senators carried daggers at this time as a security measure. When the other soldiers saw this they ran away because they feared the size of the crowd around them. Then Gallicanus came out of the House and shouted to the crowd to pursue and kill the soldiers who were the enemies of the Senate and Roman people and allies of Maximinus. The people were happy to comply and ran after the soldiers and pelted them with stones. The soldiers, however, were too quick and despite suffering some casualties managed to enter the Praetorian Camp and shut the gates behind them. Once inside, the soldiers armed themselves and defended the walls against the populace.

Then Gallicanus urged the mob to arm themselves from the public armouries and as they did so he opened the gladiatorial barracks and led the gladiators against the Praetorian Guard. In addition, all spears, swords, axes and anything that could be used as a weapon was collected from private houses and workshops and used to arm the people. After this Gallicanus and Maecenas led the armed mob against the Praetorian camp with the intention of storming it. The soldiers, however, had long experience of fighting and were protected by walls and shields so it was easy for them to drive the mob away with arrows and long spears. The notable points here are that the soldiers were clearly trained to fight with bows and that they also possessed long spears (the '*dorasi makrois*' of Herodian). The latter lends some support to one of my previous suggestions, namely that the *argyroaspides* and *chrysoaspides* of Alexander Severus probably consisted of the Praetorians. The defenders of the Praetorian camp, however, cannot have consisted solely of the members of the *praetoriani* (Praetorian Guard) because the *urbaniciani* (Urban

Cohorts) and possibly other bodyguard units such as the *evocati Augusti* were housed in the same barracks. Julius Capitolinus (*HA MB* 10.5) makes it clear that the barracks also housed veterans. This means that all of the units housed there joined the fight and that it is also possible that they were included in the ranks of Alexander's Golden and Silver shields to make the overall number of these phalangites the ideal 16,384 men, but it is still likelier that they were the *praetoriani*. When the soldiers saw that the people and gladiators were in retreat with their backs turned towards the Camp, the soldiers opened the gates and sallied out. The gladiators put up a fight and all were killed along with huge numbers of armed civilians. The soldiers pursued the defeated foes for a short distance and then returned to the camp.

This incident infuriated the Senate and people. Balbinus had proved ineffectual as a military leader. He issued an edict which begged the people to lay down their arms and accept a truce, while he promised the soldiers an amnesty for their deeds. Julius Capitolinus notes that when Balbinus tried to calm the populace and stretched out his hands, he was almost hit by a thrown stone, and according to some he was actually hit with a club. In short, neither side listened to his pleas.

The Senate acted on its own initiative and ordered some of the youth groups to march to Rome to assist the Senate against the soldiers while the people were furious over the fact that so few soldiers had defeated them and the soldiers were angry at the people for their hostile attacks. The Senate also appointed generals (*strategoi/duces*) to take charge of the forces collected against the soldiers housed in the Praetorian camp. The generals the Senate chose were clearly up to their job. They ordered all of the channels of water supply into the camp cut off to force the soldiers to surrender through thirst. They achieved this by creating a diversion. The mob and militias were ordered to attack while the chosen men either cut off the pipes or blocked them. The soldiers realised their predicament, threw open the gates and made a desperate attack. This resulted in a short but fierce battle which ended in the flight of the people. This time the soldiers pursued the fugitives deep inside the city. The mob was no match for the professional soldiers in hand-to-hand fighting, but by taking up positions in the upper storeys and roofs of the houses they managed to inflict casualties by showering the soldiers with tiles, stones and broken pots. Many of the houses had wooden balconies. The soldiers then set the houses on fire, and since the houses stood in rows side-by-side the resulting conflagration burned down most of the city. According to Herodian, many rich people became paupers as a result of this. The situation was then exploited by criminals and poor people who joined with the soldiers to loot the houses of the rich. At that moment Maximinus Thrax and his army reached the neighbourhood of the city of Emona, which was considered a part of Italy.

Herodian unfortunately fails to state how this fight ended. Julius Capitolinus (*HA MB* 9–10) provides us only with a confused account according to which the veterans and Praetorians rioted twice, the first of which was ended by parading Gordian III in front of the soldiers and populace; in the latter case, which involved the cutting of the water pipes, he fails to state how it ended. If we assume there was just one revolt, which Julius has confused, then we may make the assumption that the parading of Gordian III before both parties resulted in some sort of truce. As noted above, the Gordian faction had some unknown influence over the mob and some of the soldiers. The other two possibilities are that the soldiers were pacified as a result of thirst or that they agreed to give up the fight only later when they realized the hopelessness of their position at the latest after the death of Maximinus. My own educated guess is that we should unite the two instances of Julius, because Herodian describes this only as a single riot, which was ended by the Gordian Faction.

The above account admits the making of speculations, which result from the appointment of Pinarius as Praetorian Prefect by Pupienus. If Pupienus left Pinarius behind in Rome and did not take him with him to the north, then it is possible to think that the fighting between the soldiers and populace could have been Pupienus's attempt to overthrow Balbinus so that the two or three veterans who entered the House of the Senate had actually been sent inside as assassins and that they were killed by the two armed senators. The resulting fight between the soldiers and populace would then have been fought on behalf of Pupienus – and we should not forget that the other major corps inside the Praetorian Camp consisted of the Urban Cohorts which had been under Pupienus as recently as 236. However, there are two important things that speak against this interpretation. Firstly, it is probable that Pupienus took his own Praetorian Prefect with him while Balbinus would surely have appointed a Praetorian Prefect of his own. Secondly, as we shall see, the Praetorians appear to have been particularly hostile towards Pupienus, probably because of his reputation as a disciplinarian. Therefore there is every reason to believe that the fighting between the soldiers and populace was not the result of Pupienus attempting to murder Balbinus.

Xavier Loriot (1975a, 718–20) has suggested an explanation for this strange incident. In his opinion it is quite possible that the instigator of this fighting, L. Domitius Gallicanus Papinianus, was actually acting on behalf of the Gordian faction so that he directed the hatred of the mob towards the Praetorian Guard to separate the senatorial emperors from the Praetorians posted in the city. This suggestion is attractive in its simplicity and logic. The Gordian faction had already demonstrated its ability to control the mob when Gordian III was appointed *Caesar* and now it used the very same mob as supporters of the Senate and its emperors against the Praetorian Guard. When this is connected with the claim of Julius Capitolinus that the parading of Gordian III pacified the two sides, it becomes even more likely that the whole incident was the handiwork of the Gordian faction. The mob was easily pacified with the appearance of Gordian III and the Praetorians could likewise be pacified by his appearance because he was not the Emperor of the Senate – the killing of the veterans had shown that the Senate was the enemy of the Praetorian Guard, and the supporters of the Gordiani within the ranks of the *praetoriani* were then used to manipulate the rest. In short, even though one cannot entirely preclude the possibility that the trouble resulted merely from a misunderstanding and accident, I would still suggest that Xavier Loriot is correct in his suggestion. The Gordian faction had now managed to create a rift between the Praetorians and the Senate that worked to their benefit. The Praetorians had now been turned into supporters of Gordian III.

5.4 Maximinus Thrax reaches Italy in April 238[34]

In the meantime Maximinus had continued his march towards Italy, but by the time he was approaching Emona the generals Crispinus and Menophilus, who had been put in charge of Aquileia, had reached it and had started making preparations while the other Emperor, Maximus Pupienus, had taken residence in Ravenna where he was collecting forces against Maximinus. These events are described in some detail by Julius Capitolinus (*Max.* 20.7ff.; *MB* 2.1ff, 9.1ff.; *Gord.* 22.1ff.) and with fewer details by other later sources, but the most detailed and best of the accounts is that of Herodian, who was a period author, and because of this I quote him below and on the following pages:

'As soon as Maximinus drew near to the borders of Italy [*this is still on the other side of the Iulian Alps*], he dispatched scouts to search whether there were any ambuscades concealed in the mountains, thickets or wooded places, while he himself brought down the army into the plain and formed the following disposition. The infantry were ranged into a large shallow rectangular formation [*This agmen quadratum or hollow square is also mentioned by Julius Capitolinus twice in Historia Augusta, Maximini Duo 21.1, and in Maximus et Balbinus 2.4*)], not exactly a square, but front longer than the sides so as to occupy a greater extent of the plain. The baggage, beasts of burden and carts were taken into the centre, and he brought up the rear with all bodyguards (*these doryforoi spear-bearers would be the cavalry boyguards consisting of the aulici, praetoriani and equites singulares Augusti*). On the wings rode the *alae* of *cataphractarii* [*'tôn katafaktôn hippeôn ilai' meaning the 10,000 clibanarii created by Alexander*], the Moorish javeliners, and the Eastern archers. There was besides a great number of German cavalry that he brought with him as auxiliaries. These he aways placed in the most advanced posts to receive the first attacks of the enemy, not only because they were troops of great spirit and courage in the beginning of a battle, but as they were barbarians and not so valuable as his other forces [*This solution took into account two things: the Romans considered the barbarians expendable; the sixth century Strategikon advised that the Germans were bold and brave in the beginning of the battle but then lost fighting spirit if the battle lasted for long.*].

In this disposition the army marched with great regularity and caution over the plains. [*The use of the hollow oblong/square formation was the standard combat formation and marching formation at this time. For details, see Syvänne, Caracalla, esp. Appendix 2.*] The first town of note they reached was Emona situated at the extremity of the plain before the foot of the Alps. At his approach, the scouts and dispatched parties came in with the intelligence that the inhabitants had deserted the town after setting fire to the doors of the temples and housing and taking with them or burning all the provisions and necessities or magazines in the town leaving nothing [*This proves that the Pannonian phalanxes had taken a different route or even more likely that they had just bypassed it in an effort to reach the Iulian Alps before the enemy had chance to block them*]... Maximinus was highly pleased at this news hoping that the other cities would do the the same... But the soldiers were very differently affected, having dreadful apprehensions of famine even at their first entrance [*The soldiers were correct. Maximinus did not understand the implications of this move by the enemy*]. The army rested that night... at sunrise they advanced to the Alps... they gained the passes without any opposition which made them descend into the plain with great alacrity... Maximinus now hoped to carry all before him because the Italians had lacked confidence to hold this difficult terrain... [*In truth the Pannonian phalanxes had cleared the route before the enemy could occupy the passes*]… When they had reached the plain, scouts arrived again with intelligence. This time they told that Aquileia… had shut its gates and that the Pannonian phalanxes [*The suggested dates for the arrival of the Pannonian vanguard before the city of Aquileia vary from March to May. See Pearson, 228–9*] which Maximinus had ordered to advance before the rest of the army, had invested the place, and made several attempts to take it by storm, but without success; and that despairing of carrying the city, they had raised the siege and were sorely harassed in their retreat by the enemy with showers of arrows, stones and other missiles. Maximinus was very angry with the Pannonian generals [*strategoi* = *duces*] for their poor combat performance and hastened to the scene with his whole army in the expectation that he could take the city without any difficulty.' Herodian 8.1.1ff., tr. by Hart 303ff. with changes, corrections, additions and comments.

The Marching Formation of Maximinus Thrax in 238

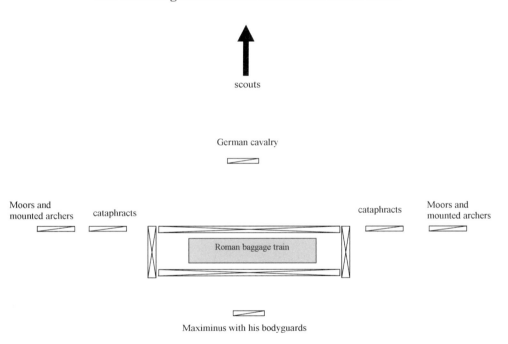

5.5 The siege of Aquileia in about April/early May(?) 238

The exact date Maximinus began the siege of Aquileia in person is not known with certainty and it depends on how one dates the beginning of the revolt of Gordian I and Gordian II. The suggested dates vary from April to May and the end of the siege varies from May to July. In my opinion the likeliest alternative is that the siege of Aquileia by Maximinus lasted from April to May. The only detailed description of the siege comes from the pen of Herodian:

'Aquileia has always been a very important and populous city…the size of which was now swollen by refugees… the old walls were in ruins… yet, as the present necessity required they had repaired the walls, and strengthened them with additional defences by erecting towers, battlements and bulwarks. Having fortified the city with these walls, and shut the gates, they assembled on the walls and kept continual guard night and day; whereby they made a gallant defence and repulsed the enemy, every assault they made. The defence of the place was committed to two generals of consular rank chosen out of the Senate, one named Crispinus and the other Menophilus. These had with great foresight imported large quantities of all sorts of provisions… nor was there any lack of water because the city abounded with wells and fountains, and a river ran all round the walls, serving… as a good fosse. [*See the accompanying map on page 99*]

Maximinus… thought it proper to send some officers as envoys… He had in his army a tribune, a native of Aquileia whose children and wife and all his family were blocked up in the city… thinking that the citizens would be easily convinced [*to open their gates*]… [*However*] Crispinus exhorting the citizens…prevailed with the people to persist in their defence… Crispinus was encouraged… by several good omens… soothsayers… divinations… oracles… foretelling victory [*This was a standard ploy to encourage the fighters. It is clear that Crispinus was not personally encouraged by these things but used them to raise the morale of the defenders*]. The Aquileians worship Beles, … and some say the image of this deity appeared several times to Maximinus's soldiers in the air fighting in defence of the city. Whether such an apparition was really seen by any or whether they raised the story to palliate the shame of so great an army yielding to a multitude of undiscipline citizens, far inferior to them in number… I cannot determine [*In my opinion it is possible that the sights of this deity were also produced by Crispinus. For other examples, see my biography of Aurelian and Probus*].

The ambassadors returned from their fruitless errand. Maximinus was inflamed with anger and resentment and accelerated his march with all possible speed. But then his advance was blocked by a large and broad river with a strong current at a distance of sixteen miles from the city, because the season of the year had melted the accumulated winter snows of the neighbouring mountains… [*so*] that it was now rendered impassable for the army. The Aquileians had demolished the bridge… Thus destitute both of bridge and boats, the army halted in much dismay. Some of the Germans, strangers to the strength and rapidity of the Italian rivers and imagining that they flowed gently into the plain as rivers usually did in their country,… were rash enough to plunge in with their horses accustomed to swim, but were soon carried away by the force of the stream and all perished in the waters. [*This implies that the Pannonian phalanxes had crossed the river before the melting snows had made it impossible for the cavalry to cross or before the bridge was broken.*]

For two or three days, therefore, Maximinus was forced to encamp, and having cast up entrenchments all round the camp to guard against any surprise, he continued on his side of the river contriving how to throw a bridge over it. As timber was very scarce in those parts, and there were no boats to fasten together to form a bridge, he was at loss what to do. However, some of the engineers came and informed him that there were a great number of round and empty wine barrels in the deserted fields… These … might serve as good pontoons. They would not be swept away because they were fastened together with brushwood laid on top of them over which soil would be placed and levelled. This design was put in execution with Maximinus supervising the work and crossing of the river after which the army advanced towards the city.

Finding all the suburban houses and villages deserted, they began to destroy the vineyards and cut down and burnt all the trees… The army being fatigued, Maximinus thought it proper not make an immediate assault; so they stayed outside the range of arrows. Maximinus divided his army into *lochoi* and phalanxes [*Both terms are problematic, but it is clear that in this case lochos meant a smaller unit while the phalanx a larger unit like a legion*] and invested the whole city with each unit being allocated a section of the front [*It is probable that a significant portion of the cavalry was on the opposite side of the river because they were less useful in sieges, but still valuable for the blocking of the city*]. After giving one day's rest, he began the siege. All kinds of siege engines were applied and the walls were assaulted by main force; in a word, no form of siege warfare was left unattempted; and hardly a day passed without several assaults (for the whole army invested the place and closed it in, as it were in a net) but they always met stout and obstinate resistance. For the Aquileians had… brought their wives and children into bulwarks and towers where they opposed and repelled the assailants… But the houses in the suburbs… were demolished by the enemy and the materials were used to construct siege engines. Maximinus struggled night and day to make a breach in some part of the walls… With this resolution both he and his son, whom he had created Caesar, rode continually round the army, exhorting, encouraging, promising and even beseeching his soldiers to carry on the work with spirit and activity. But the Aquileians still maintained their posts, throwing down rocks and fire bombs made by mixing pitch, oil, sulphur and bitumen which were poured into empty jars. These they had in great numbers upon the walls, and as soon as the enemy approached, they set fire to the combustibles and let fly volleys at once which dispersed among the soldiers like showers of fire. The scalding pitch with the other ingredients penetrated through the naked parts of their bodies and spread further till the men tore off their burning breastplates while the leather and wooden parts [*means shields*] caught fire and were burnt. So you might see the soldiers disarming themselves… Hence a great number of soldiers had their faces, hands and other exposed parts scorched or they lost their eyesight. The besieged also flung down lighted torches dipped likewise in pitch and resin and which were tipped with arrowheads meant to stick into the siege engines… [*Julius Capitolinus HA MB 11.3, 16. 5 adds after Dexippus that the women of Aquileia cut their hair to make bow strings to shoot arrows. This is obviously a topos which stresses the commitment of the defenders, but I would still suggest that it really happened because one of the emergency measures during sieges was to use women's hair to make torsion catapults/ballistae or hand-crossbows if there were not enough animal tendons.*]

For the first few days the fight seemed tolerably equal, … but at length Maximinus's army grew tired and their spirits sunk… On the other hand, the

Aquileians continually gathered new strength... The long fight gave them experience and courage and they now began to despise the army. They scoffed at the soldiers and insulted Maximinus as he rode around the walls abusing him and his son in the most insulting manner... Maximinus became ever angrier and not being able to take vengeance against the Aquileians, he vented his anger against his own commanders for cowardly or ineffective attacks... But this... served only to make him odious to the exasperated soldiers and more contemptible to the enemy... Besides the Aquileians were plentifully supplied with all kinds of provisions... The army, on the contrary, were in the utmost scarcity having cut down all the fruit trees about the place and having laid waste the fields and countryside... Wherefore some of the soldiers, indeed, lay in temporary tents, but the greatest part of the army was exposed to the open air and endured the rains and the heat of the sun, and at the same time they were distressed by famine [*Maximinus had clearly arrived in Italy poorly prepared for what he faced. This was incompetent. They had carried not more than about twenty days supplies, which ran out fast, and not even enough tents. The destruction of houses in such a situation was less than wise*] having no magazines of corn or forage, destitute of supplies because the Romans had taken care to block all the roads of Italy... and the Senate had sent officers of consular rank at the head of chosen troops... to lay an embargo on all kinds of vessels and keep a strong guard at the ports and havens. Maximinus was therefore unaware of what was taking place in Rome, for all the roads, paths and byways were diligently guarded... So that the army that seemed to besiege was in reality besieged itself. For they could neither take Aquileia nor if they raised the siege could they march to Rome for want of ships and carriages... Rumours were likewise spread... that all Illyrians and barbarian nations in the east and south were raising armies... against Maximinus... The army being in this extremity of distress and dejection while Maximinus was resting in his tent, ... the soldiers belonging to the camp on Mount Alba [*legio II Parthica*], whose children and wives were left there [*This suggests that Pupienus was using their families as hostages to convince them to change sides. This was a masterful ploy by a masterful commander*], came to the resolution to kill Maximinus... with this bold design they came in a body to his tent about midday, the life-guards also conspiring with them [*They too had families that could be used as bargaining chips*], and having pulled down his images from the military standards, as Maximinus and his son were coming out of the tent, ... they refused to hear anything he said but immediately killed both [*Epitome 25 claims that Maximinus's daughter was also killed*] and after them his Military Prefect and all his close friends. After treating their bodies with all kinds of indignities and trampling them underfoot, they exposed them as prey to the dogs and birds. The heads of Maximinus and his son were sent to Rome.

The death of the emperor put the whole army into utmost confusion. Nor was the deed approved by all of them. The Pannonians and Thracian barbarians who had raised Maximinus to power were particularly angry. But as it was impossible to undo what was done... they went to the walls in a pacific manner and told the Aquileians that Maximinus was killed... [*Julius Capitolinus HA Max. 23.6: '... put their heads on poles, showed them to the Aquileians.'*] But the two generals would by no means suffer the gates to be opened [*They undoubtedly suspected a ruse*], but exposing to their sight the images of Maximus [*Pupienus*], Balbinus and Gordian Caesar to be cheered... They likewise opened a market on the walls where the soldiers might buy all sorts of necessaries... the horsemen carrying the head of Maximinus... found the emperor Maximus [*Pupienus*] waiting in Ravenna, where he was mustering his picked troops from Rome and Italy, and no small numbers of German allies sent to him by their states... [*Pupienus*] performed sacrifices of thanksgiving... [*and*] sent away the horsemen with the heads to Rome.' Herodian 8.2.3ff., tr. by Hart 306ff. with changes, corrections, additions and comments.[35]

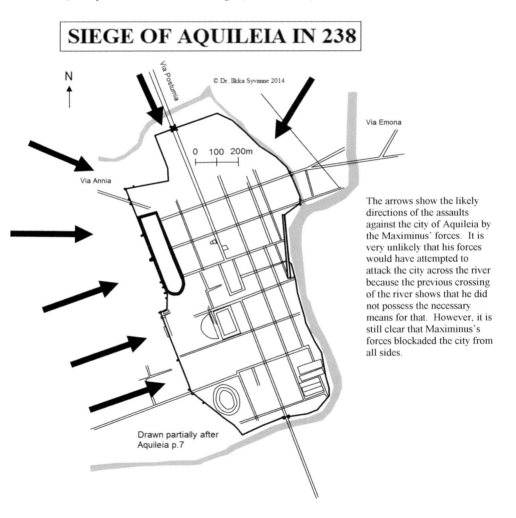

The arrows show the likely directions of the assaults against the city of Aquileia by the Maximinus' forces. It is very unlikely that his forces would have attempted to attack the city across the river because the previous crossing of the river shows that he did not possess the necessary means for that. However, it is still clear that Maximinus's forces blockaded the city from all sides.

The defensive strategy adopted by the Senate quite probably at the instigation of Pupienus had proved itself highly successful. The massive army of Maximinus Thrax consisting of professional elite forces had been defeated by civilian paramilitary forces. The Senate and Italian population showed once again why the Romans had conquered themselves an Empire. Pupienus had outgeneralled Maximinus and his staff. It is more than likely that Pupienus had been in contact with the legionaries of the *legio II Parthica* and the bodyguards of Maximinus Thrax via some couriers/agents (members of the *frumentarii*?) and that these couriers had then instigated the assassination by noting that their families were under Pupienus's control. In short, I would suggest that this was a special operation by men who acted as Pupienus's agents who are likely to have consisted of men of the same units that committed the murder but who had previously been left behind at Alba and Rome.

5.6 The Legacy of Maximinus Thrax

One legacy of the first low-born soldier emperor Maximinus Thrax was the further strengthening of the already existing divisions within the Roman society. The rise of this barbarian soldier had caused the rise of Roman patriotism among the senators and populace especially in Rome and Italy but also elsewhere with the result that the Senate had raised its own emperors. The soldiers naturally resented this because they considered the raising and overthrowing of emperors their exclusive right. The rest of the century was dominated by the power struggle between the noble-born emperors usually favoured by the senators and the low-born soldier emperors usually favoured by the army. It ended in the victory of the army. The only real anomaly to this pattern is the reign of the nobly born Gallienus who was intensely disliked by the Senate because of his favouritism of the army and soldiers. A second of the defining matters of the third century was the attitude towards Christianity, but this question divided both the noble born and the lowly born according to their personal attitude towards this religion. It ended in the victory of Christianity under Constantine the Great in the fourth century.

The army that Maximinus Thrax left behind was essentially the same as had been created under Alexander Severus with its strong emphasis on the use of large cavalry armies and of spear-armed hoplites against the Persians. The continued existence of hoplite-type forces in 238 is proved by Herodian's reference to the long *dory*-spears used by the soldiers in Rome in 238. However, it is still clear that the vast majority of the infantry continued to be armed with cylindrical rectangular or oval shields with a single handle, helmets reaching down to their shoulders, heavy *pila*-javelins, a short version of the *hasta*-spear (ca. 2.5 m) and *spatha* (long double-edged sword) and *semispatha* (short double-edged sword). This was the army that then fought under Gordian III and Philip the Arab against their enemies.

Maximinus Thrax had also reinforced the already existing expectation among the soldiers that their emperors would lead them from the front. It is therefore not surprising that we find many of the subsequent emperors fighting in the front ranks – including for example Gordian III, Philip the Arab, Decius and Gallienus. The emperors were no longer only generals but also soldiers and warriors. This was the legacy of both Caracalla and Maximinus Thrax.

ulia Maesa. (*Source: Bernoulli*)   Julia Mamaea. (*Source: Bernoulli*)   Orbiana. (*Source: Bernoulli*)

Alexander Severus depicted in three coins at different points in his life. (*Source: Bernoulli*)

Maximinus Thrax depicted in two coins. (*Source: Bernoulli*)   Maximinus Thrax and his son Maximus. (*Source: Bernoulli*)

Left: Gordian I
Right: Gordian II
(*Source: Bernoulli*)

Balbinus. (*Source: Bernoulli*)

Pupienus. (*Source: Bernoulli*)

Furia Sabina Tranquillina, wife of Gordian III and daughter of Timesitheus. (*Source: Bernoulli*)

Gordian III. (*Source: Bernoulli*)

Philip the Arab. (*Source: Bernoulli*)

Otacilia Severa, wife of Philip the Arab. (*Source: Bernoulli*)

A coin of Alexander Severus depicting Mars Ultor on the reverse struck in 232. Note the hoplite equipment and the use of units called Silver and Gold shields (*HA Alex*. 49.5). Note also that the muscle armour is made out of scales. (*With the kind permission of the Ancient Coin Traders, ancientcointraders.com*)

A coin of Alexander Severus depicting Mars Ultor on the reverse struck in 232. Note the hoplite equipment. (*With the kind permission of the Ancient Coin Traders, ancientcointraders.com*)

Philip the Arab
(*Source: Bernoulli*)

Jotapianus, usurper under Philip. (*Source: Delaroche*)

acatianus, usurper under Philip. (*Source: Delaroche*)

Philip Jr. (*Source: Delaroche*)

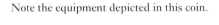

Note the equipment depicted in this coin.

Philip the Arab. (*Source: Delaroche*)

Note the equipment depicted in this coin.

Philip the Arab, Philip Jr. and Otacilia.
(*Source: Delaroche*)

This coin celebrates Philip's victory over the Germans and Carpi (Germanicus Maximus, Carpicus Maximus).

Two sculptures depicting the emperor Alexander Severus. (*Source: Bernoulli*)

'He [Alexander Severus] had the strength and height of a soldier and the vigour of the military man who knows the power of his body and always maintains it.' Aelius Lambrides [HA Alexander 4.4, tr. by Magie p.185.]

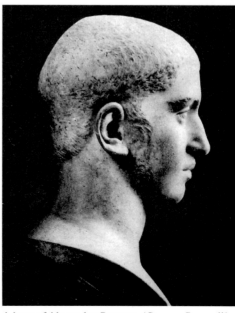

A coin depicting Alexander Severus and Julia Mamaea. (*Source: Bernoulli*)

A bust of Alexander Severus. (*Source: Bernoulli*)

A bust of Julia Mamaea, mother of Alexander, Vatican. (*Source: Bernoulli*)

A possible bust of Orbiana, wife of Alexander, Louvre. (*Source: Bernoulli*)

A bust of Maximinus Thrax. (*Source: Bernoulli*)

A bust of Pupienus, Bracchio Nuovo. (*Source: Bernoulli*)

statue of Pupienus, Louvre. (*Source: Bernoulli*)

A bust of Balbinus, Vatican.
(*Source: Bernoulli*)

bust of Gordian III, Villa Albani.
ource: Bernoulli)

Philip Sr., Otacilia, and Philip Jr.
(*Source: Bernoulli*)

A bust of Gordian III from two angles, Louvre. (*Source: Bernoulli*)

A bust of Philip the Arab, Berlin. (*Source: Bernoulli*)
Note that the nose and parts of the ear and clothing are modern restorations.

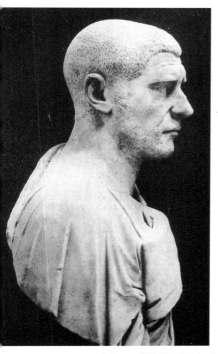

A bust of Philip the Arab, Bracchio Nuovo. (*Source: Bernoulli*)

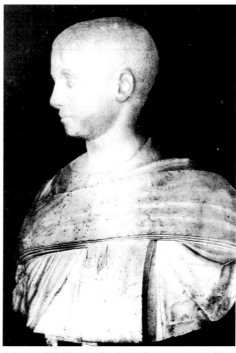

bust of Marcia Otacilia Severa, wife of
hilip the Arab, Munich. (*Source: Bernoulli*)

A bust of Philip Jr., Capitol. (*Source: Bernoulli*)

A bust of Marcia Otacilia Severa, wife of Philip the Arab, British Museum. (*Source: Bernoulli*)

A bust of Philip the Arab, Louvre.
(*Source: Bernoulli*)

A bust of Decius. (*Source: Bernoulli*)

Bronze head of Alexander Severus. (*Public Domain / Wikimedia Commons / Ophelia 2*)

A statue of Balbinus. (*Picture © Giovanni Dall'Orto / Wikimedia Commons*)

Maximinus Thrax. (*Author's painting*)

Gordian III. (*Source: Bernoulli*)

Left: Pupienus. (*Public Domain / Wikimedia Commons / user Jastrow*)

Below left: Gordian I. (*Public Domain / Wikimedia Commons / user Jastrow*)

'In height he was characteristically Roman. He was becoming grey, with an impressive face, more ruddy than fair. His face was fairly broad, his eyes, his countenance, and his brow such as to command respect. His body was somewhat stocky. In character he was temperate and restrained; there is nothing you can say that he ever did passionately, immoderately, or excessively.' *HA Gord.* 6.1-2, tr. by Magie, 391.

Below right: Gordian III. (*Photograph © Marie-Lan Nguyen / Wikimedia Commons (user Jastrow)*)

Bust of Gordian. (*Public domain/
Wikimedia Commons/user Slick*)

Philip the Arab. (*Author's painting*)

Philip the Arab (Hermitage). (*Author's
painting*)

Alexander Severus. Sources: A statue, with *Historia Augusta* (Alex. 29.2, 40.11). Alexander always wore bands on his legs and used white trousers and not scarlet ones as emperors usually did. Note the Star of David and Cross on the wall. Alexander and his mother showed great interest in both Judaism and Christianity. Alexander, however, did not convert to either, so Philip the Arab became the first Christian emperor. (*Author's drawing*)

Philip the Arab. Sources: A bust combined with typical gear used by the emperors with Christian symbols added. (*Author's drawing*)

© Dr. Ilkka Syvänne 2020

Above left: A member of Alexander Severus's *argyroaspides* (Silver Shields).
Above right: A member of Alexander Severus's *chrysoaspides* (Gold Shields).

The reconstruction is based on their names (*HA Alex*. 49.5). Julius Africanus's *Kestoi*, Alexander Severus's coins, use of scale armour, and depictions of soldiers in the so-called Ludovisi Sarcophagus dated ca. 251– Examples of these and a full analysis can be found in the text. I have made the educated guess that the Silver and Gold Shields consisted of the Praetorian Guard (identifiable from the scorpions); I have guessed that the Silver Shields depicted Alexander the Great on their shields because he had created a unit with this name; and I have guessed that the Gold Shields had Alexander Severus depicted on their shields because he was their creator. (*Author's drawing*)

Shapur I vs. Gordian III

This illustration represents a hypothetical reconstruction of the combat between the *shahanshah* Sapor and *Caesar Augustus* Gordianus III (emperor Gordian III) at the battle of Mesikhe (Pērōz Šāpur, Victoric Shapur, mod. Anbar) in 244. According to Sapor's inscription ŠKZ, Sapor destroyed *Caesar* Gordian the great battle at Mesikhe in which the Roman army (including Goths and Germans) was annihilated. has long been recognized that the Persian version exaggerates the scale of the Roman defeat because Roman sources prove that the army was able to retreat from Persian territory and that Gordian died route home. For a fuller discussion, see the text. I have taken some artistic liberties in this illustration joining the claim of Sapor that he killed Gordian at the battle of Mesikhe with the claims that Gordian from a horse and broke his hip and died. In other words, I have taken Sapor's claim literally that it he who caused Gordian to fall from his horse, which is by no means impossible though we do not ha any specific information from the other side to confirm it. The uniforms, helmets and equipment in t illustration have been adapted quite freely from period coins, statues, busts, reliefs, silver plates, came and sarcophagi. The 'balloons' depicted on Sapor, which are sometimes shown on the horses and riders, usually interpreted as decorative pieces, but I have here made the educated guess that they could actua be protective pieces used against archery at the same time, namely silk balloons like those later used by Japanese Samurai against the Mongol invaders. Please note that this interpretation is very controvers (*Author's drawing*)

A coin of Balbinus celebrating his generosity to the people and soldiers. Source: Cohen

A coin of Pupienus celebrating the peace brought by him. Source: Cohen

A statue of Pupienus in Louvre. He was still a physically fit man despite his 74 years of age. Source. Duruy.

A coin of Pupienus celebrating his position as emperor chosen by the Senate. Source: Cohen

5.7 Pupienus, Balbinus and Gordian III from April/May to 7 June 238[36]

According to Julius Capitolinus (*HA Max.* 24.5–6), when the horsemen carrying the heads of Maximinus and his son arrived at Ravenna, Pupienus at once dismissed the German allies and sent a laurelled letter to Rome.[37] Julius Capitolinus has nothing more to say about the Germans, but one may make the educated guess that Pupienus gave the Germans some money as a form of thanks before dismissing them to ensure that they would not pillage Roman territory on their way back home. The Germans must also have been in a joyous mood because their hated foe Maximinus Thrax was now dead. Pupienus had remained inactive at Ravenna largely because he had been waiting for the arrival of these Germans, which were then after all not even needed. However, on the basis of Herodian, we know that Pupienus did not dismiss all of his German allies, but took a significant number with him to Rome. Regardless, I see no reason to doubt the general veracity of Julius Capitolinus's statement that Pupienus dismissed his German allies which must have been so numerous that he could not take all of them to Rome. The arrival of the heads of Maximinus and son was joyously received in Rome, and if there was any resistance left, it ended now. Balbinus sacrificed a hecatomb (large sacrifice) and ordered that gods should be worshipped in every town to thank them for their help.

In the meantime, Pupienus left Ravenna and went through the lagoons of the River Po to Aquileia which opened its gates to him. The Italian cities showed their joy by sending delegations of prominent citizens to Aquileia to do homage to Pupienus and shower him with flowers. The army that had been besieging Aquileia came to show their obedience to Pupienus too with demonstrations of peace. Herodian adds that in truth most did not do that out of genuine feeling, and he is undoubtedly correct in this. Most of the soldiers gathered before Aquileia were resentful and angry that their choice as Emperor had been killed while the emperors chosen by the Senate were in power. Pupienus did nothing else for the first two days after his arrival but perform public sacrifices in honour of the gods, but on the third day he assembled the entire army on the plain and addressed the troops from a dais constructed for this purpose. It is possible that Pupienus did this only on the third day to test the mood of the soldiers before taking the risk of appearing before them in person. Herodian states that Pupienus reminded the soldiers of their sacred military vow to obey the Romans, the Senate and their emperors. The Empire was not the private property of the Emperor but the common property of the Roman People. The fact that there were now two emperors worked for the benefit of the Empire if there were any crises. He also promised a complete amnesty for all and a very generous sum of money. These last two were undoubtedly the most important parts of his speech.[38]

After this, Pupienus spent a few days organizing necessary matters, which included sending most of the soldiers back to their provinces and their permanent stations, the idea being to scatter the army as fast as possible so that it would cease to be a threat. Julius Capitolinus (*HA MB* 12.3) notes that Pupienus stayed in the area for a while to make certain that everything was safe up to the Alps and that none of the barbarians who had favoured Maximinus would cause any trouble. Julius was presumably referring to the Thracians (probably mostly barbarian settlers of Gothic and Alan descent), German auxiliaries (obtained during Maximinus's campaigns), and possibly also the Pannonians.[39]

I would suggest that the above activities should be connected with the need to subjugate the provinces that had sided with Maximinus, and possibly also with the Gothic invasion of Thrace.

After the death of Maximinus, coins and inscriptions started to celebrate the *Victoria Augustorum*. According to Loriot, there is evidence that the following provinces celebrated their victory: Baetica, Germania Superior, Achaia, Thessalia, Epirus, Thrace, Pannonia Inferior, Asia, Pontus-Bithynia, Lycia-Pamphylia, Cilicia, Cappadocia, Coele-Syria, Egypt, and Mauretania Caesarensis.[40]

This list is obviously incomplete. As noted by Loriot, most of the provinces and persons would have immediately rallied to the winning side. However, there are two provinces in which this appears not have been so. Capelianus continued to oppose the new regime in North Africa and the fighting there appears to have continued until the first months of the sole reign of Gordian III when the *legio III Augusta* was disbanded as a punishment. Unfortunately there are no details of how he was finally defeated. The second of the provinces which appears to have continued to resist against the new regime is Hispania Citerior, the legate of which was Q. L. Decius Valerinus. There is evidence in milestones that recognize the 6th and 7th acclamations of *imperator* for Maximinus, which Bersanetti connects with the victory of Capelianus over the Gordiani, but the 6th has also been connected with Maximinus's victories in the Balkans, leaving the 7th acclamation for the victory over the Gordiani. There also exist stones with the datings *TR P IV* and *TR P V* indicating tribunician powers for Maximinus Thrax for 238 and 239. This has led to the conclusion that Decius could have maintained fictive obedience towards the Emperor of the soldiers even after Maximinus's death until 239. As P.W. Townsend has suggested, this conclusion receives support from the cursus of Rutilius Pudens Crispinus who was '*[dux] bello Aquil[iensi]*' after which he was immediately appointed '*leg(atus) Aug(usti) pr(o) pr(aetore) provinc(iae) [Hispaniae Cite]rioris et Gallaecia[e]*'. As noted by Loriot, if the imperial government decided to send one of its best generals to Spain it is clear that it required an energetic man in charge, but he also notes quite correctly that this does not necessarily mean that Crispinus was forced to use armed force to defeat the last supporters of Maximinus. In light of the fact that Decius survived, it is likelier that he surrendered to Crispinus without a fight as Birley notes. However, just like Loriot in 1998, I would not entirely preclude the possibility that Decius continued to resist the new rulers for several months even after the death of Maximinus. However, it is still clear that even if Decius continued to resist and fight until 239 that he surrendered to Crispinus in return for amnesty. Otherwise it would be very difficult to understand why he survived. Unsurprisingly, he appears not to have held any offices under Gordian III.[41] Note however that there are differences in the inscriptions for the man modern research has identified as the Emperor Decius: Q. L. Decius Valerinus (in Hispania) and C. Messius Quintus Decius Valerianus (in Moesia in 234). This makes it possible that we are actually dealing with two different men, probably related to each other, so that the former, Q. L. Decius Valerinus, actually continued his resistance in Hispania until 239 and was then killed. In my opinion the likeliest date for the dispatch of Crispinus to Spain is when Pupienus and Crispinus were both at Aquileia. Pupienus would then have chosen soldiers from the army that Maximinus had brought to Italy sufficient to defeat Decius.

Julius Capitolinus mentions on the basis of Dexippus that the Carpi waged a war aginst the Moesians during the reign of Pupienus and Balbinus, and that the Scythian (i.e. Gothic) war began with the Scythians destroying the city of Istria/Histria (Istros, mod. Dobrudja). The fragment of Peter the Patrician proves that command of the campaign was given to Tullius Menophilus. It also suggests that Menophilus somehow managed to remove the invaders, both the Carpi and Goths, from Roman territory. The fragment, translated by Banchich, states that the Carpi envied the annual subsidies the Romans paid to the Goths.[42]

'The Carpi, the nation, envying the subsidies paid annually to the Goths, sent a delegation to Tullius Menophilus arrogantly demanding subsidies. The man was *dux* of Moesia and used to drill the army daily. And since he had learned of their arrogance beforehand, he did not receive them for many days, giving them permission to observe in safety the soldiers being drilled. And during the delay, in order to reduce their presumption, after he had taken a seat on a lofty tribunal and surrounded himself with the most imposing men of the camp, he received them, making no account at all of them, but in the middle of their speaking about the delegation he kept talking continuously about other things, just as if he had other more important business. [*This was a standard stratagem. For another example, see the campaign of Carus in my biography of Aurelian and Probus. The idea was to demonstrate to the envoys that the Romans had nothing to hide and that they considered them absolutely inconsequential. The sight of the Roman soldiers drilling and training demonstrated to the envoys the very high quality of their opposition.*] Those who had been ignored said nothing else except: 'Why do the Goths receive such payments from you and we do not receive any?' And he said: 'The emperor is master of much wealth, and he shows favour to those who are in need of it.' And they proposed, 'Let him hold us, too, among those in need and give such things to us. For we are better than them.' And Menophilus laughed and said, 'I need to inform the emperor... After four months come here to this spot... and receive an answer.' Then he departed and again began drilling the soldiers. And the Carpi came after four months, and when he had made a similar show to them, he devised another delay of three months. And again, in another camp, he received them in the same way and gave them an answer, 'So far as a compact goes, the sovereign gives to you absolutely nothing. But if it is a welding you require, after you have departed, throw yourselves face down and implore him and it is probable that you will be hammered.'[43] And with irritation they departed, and, with respect to the province of Menophilus, which he had obtained for three years, they kept quiet.' [*In other words, after the initial troubles were over, Menophilus pacified the entire area for the period of his rule. The incident recorded shows him as an excellent commander who knew how to handle the situation and how to use stratagems. The constant drilling of the soldiers also suggests that their combat readiness remained high, so high as to convince the enemies to maintain the peace.*] Peter the Patrician, F 170, tr. by Banchich, 2015, 111 with my comments added inside parentheses.

The above information has been interpreted by Loriot and others so that the transferral of the army from Sirmium to Aquileia had created a power vacuum which was then exploited by the Carpi and Goths with the result that Pupienus and Balbinus dispatched Tullius Menophilus, one of the defenders of Aquileia, to Moesia Inferior to defend it against the invaders. Drinkwater suggests that Menophilus defeated the Carpi by bribing the Goths to abandon their alliance with the Carpi. He also suggests that Menophilus was probably recalled in disgrace by 241.[44]

I would suggest that Menophilus was actually dispatched by Pupienus when both men were at Aquileia together, and I would suggest that it was then that Pupienus gave him a part of the army that Maximinus had brought there. It is clear that Menophilus did indeed bribe the Goths with money to abandon their alliance with the Carpi, but I would not preclude the possibility that he had first fought against them inconclusively (but probably still with some success) and only then paid them. I agree that it was the breaking of the alliance that enabled Menophilus to defeat the Carpi decisively. The defeat that the Carpi suffered was clearly so serious that there was no need to pay them any money.

I also consider it unlikely that Menophilus would have been recalled in disgrace in about late 240 or early 241. Rather it is far likelier that he was simply removed from office because he belonged to the senatorial faction that lost its power when Timesitheus became the Praetorian Prefect of Gordian III in about 240/1. It is likelier that it was the removal of Menophilus from office that caused the invasions of 241. It was his fame as a superb commander that had kept the Carpi and Goths in check.

Once everything was secure, Pupienus took with him the bodyguards (*doryforoi*) of Maximinus (meaning primarily the *praetoriani*, *equites singulares Augusti*, and the *aulici*) and others who had served under Maximinus (meaning mainly the *legio II Parthica*) and then returned to Rome. According to Herodian, Pupienus also took with him his German allies because he trusted that they would stay loyal to him. However, my educated guess is that Pupienus took with him only a select body of Germans to serve as his personal trusted bodyguards and dismissed the rest back to their homes. It is unlikely that Pupienus led a large body of Germans into Rome when he acted as Emperor of the Roman People and the Senate. It is far likelier that he took a select body of about 2,000–3,000 horsemen to serve in the same capacity as the *equites singulares Augusti*. These Germans were valuable as a counterbalance against the existing bodyguard units and *legio II Parthica* if these showed any signs of disloyalty.

Herodian states (8.7.8) that when Pupienus approached Rome, Balbinus, Gordian *Caesar*, the Senate and people came out to meet him and welcomed him back with cheers and shouts of joy. Pupienus was publicly thanked in a special session of the Senate after which the emperors Pupienus, Balbinus and Gordian III went to their Palace. Julius Capitolinus (*HA MB* 12.4ff.) claims that Pupienus was greeted by the twenty representatives of the Senate and that because Pupienus had taken up Maximinus's army he came to Rome with a huge train and multitude. This statement has been doubted, for example by Magie (*HA MB*, pp.470–71), because Herodian specifically states that Pupienus sent the army back to their quarters in the provinces, which is not to be doubted because the scattering of the massive field army would have been a sensible safety measure against possible problems. However, the statement of Julius Capitolinus should still be accepted because at least the Parthian deserters are unlikely to have had specific garrisons designated to them because Alexander Severus had brought those units from the East, and it is possible that there were also other similar units. What is practically certain is that after the reign of Alexander Severus there existed some sort of cavalry army at the disposal of the Emperor because we find one operating under the Emperor Decius in 249–51.[45] It would have been these in conjunction with the *legio II Parthica*, *praetoriani*, *equites singulares Augusti*, *aulici* and Pupienus's Germans that would have made up the multitude. There would have been about 20,000–23,000 men in the regular units alone, in addition to which would have come the Germans of Pupienus and some of the cavalry units raised by Alexander Severus.

The new emperors faced five sources of troubles. Firstly, Pupienus and Balbinus were at odds with each other. Secondly, the Gordian faction was working to get rid of both Pupienus and Balbinus. Thirdly, the soldiers, mainly the Praetorians, were resentful that the Senate had appointed emperors. Fourthly, the emperors needed money to pay the donatives. Fifthly, the Sassanians were known to be preparing an invasion[46] presumably with the intention of exploiting the Roman civil war which was shorter than they probably expected.[47]

The most immediate problem was probably the donatives promised to the soldiers and populace. As noted above, this was solved by reintroducing the two-*denarius antoninianus* coin. It was the ancient equivalent of printing money. Decisions such as these made the senators, equestrians and people in general happy, but this did not include the soldiers who still seethed with anger because the Senate had given them two emperors of noble birth. The presence of Pupienus's German bodyguards in Rome infuriated them still further, because they knew that they could be used against them if they attempted anything. Herodian also notes that the soldiers suspected that Pupienus could try to disarm them, as Septimius Severus had done to the murderers of Pertinax, and then replace them with Germans. Herodian was primarily referring to the Praetorians. The soldiers could no longer maintain their silence after they had reached Rome and started to voice their grievances and fears openly. This resulted from the public insults that the senators levelled at the soldiers, ridiculing the soldiers' choice of Emperor while thanking themselves for their wise choice of rulers. The soldiers felt ridiculed. This was soon exploited by the Gordian faction who managed to convince the soldiers to back the claim of Gordian III and murder the emperors chosen by the Senate.

The sources make it clear that Balbinus was envious of the fame won by Pupienus and that the two men disagreed with each other. Balbinus thought that Pupienus had actually had less trouble than he, because he Balbinus had faced a civil war in Rome while Pupienus had just sat at Ravenna. It had been the citizens of Aquileia and their commanders Crispinus and Menophilus who had won the war for Pupienus. This was obviously unfair, but it is easy to see why Balbinus would have thought so. In addition, Balbinus felt that he should be given precedence over his colleague because of his noble birth and earlier second consulship. Pupienus on the other hand thought that he should be given precedence over his colleague because of his term as *praefectus urbi* and great reputation. Both were wise enough to avoid public demonstrations of their disagreements, but it was still common knowledge. Both were also wise enough to pay public respect to the Senate, to institute some good new laws, and to hear lawsuits as was expected of them. All the while, the Praetorians were seeking an opportunity to kill Pupienus and Balbinus, but were prevented from doing so by the presence of the German bodyguards.

As new emperors, both wanted to prove themselves as well qualified for their job by fighting wars on behalf of the Roman commonwealth, as was expected by the Senate, people and soldiers. They decided to divide their duties so that Pupienus would march against the Persians, and Balbinus would attack the Germans while Gordian III would stay in Rome. This may imply that Pupienus intended to betray his German allies now that he no longer needed them, but it is more likely that the intention was to attack some other Germanic tribes and use Pupienus's German friends as allies. Since the sources do not mention any trouble for the German frontier, and the Persian attack against the Romans came only in the winter/spring of 239, it is clear that both operations were meant as pre-emptive strikes that would bring military glory to both emperors. This was a wise policy. The military campaigns would give the emperors the opportunity to bribe the soldiers with donatives while the campaigns would bring military glory not only to the emperors but also to the soldiers, not to mention the spoils of war. The pre-emptive strikes had the advantage that they gave the Romans the initiative of when and where to fight. This was especially wise in the conditions prevailing in antiquity where the transferral of troops took a long time. Even more so because the redeployment of Roman troops often created a power vacuum. The simultaneous attack against the Germans and Persians meant that the Romans were well prepared on both of their major frontiers and were presumably prepared to conscript more men if necessary. But it was not to be, because the Gordian faction incited the Praetorians to attack the two emperors.

5.8 The Murder of Pupienus and Balbinus in about June/July 238.

There are two slightly different versions of what happened next. According to Herodian (8.8.4ff.), the personal ambitions of the two emperors were the chief cause of their downfalls, because when the Praetorians advanced to the Palace with the intention of killing Pupienus, and Pupienus wanted to summon the German allies who were in Rome, Balbinus opposed him because he thought that Pupienus's intention was to use the Germans against him. The two men then started arguing with each other and were still doing so when the Praetorians burst in. The *aulici* had abandoned their posts. The Praetorians stripped the two men naked and dragged them away from the Palace. The Praetorians beat them, jeered at them, pulled their beards and eyebrows, mutilated their bodies and dragged them to their camp. Their intention was to torture the two men to death. When the German allies heard this, they grasped their weapons and gave chase, and when the Praetorians heard this, they murdered both men and exposed their mutilated bodies for all to see on the road. They then lifted up *Caesar* Gordian III, proclaimed him *Augustus*, and took him to the Praetorian camp and shut the gates. When the Germans then learnt of this, they returned to their quarters.

Julius Capitolinus (*HA MB* 14.1ff.) stated that his account was based mainly on Herodian, but since it includes some important details missing from Herodian it is worth recounting his version too. According to him, the Praetorians had been on the lookout for an opportunity to kill the emperors and the suitable occasion came when there were some scenic plays which required the attention of the *milites* and *aulici* so that the emperors were at the Palace alone with the Germans. The *milites* here mean the *praetoriani* who were clearly not party to the plot and the *aulici/scholarii* who were likewise loyal. The members of both of these units were therefore distracted somewhere else when the attack was launched. It is probable that the distraction was caused by the scenic plays and that the troubles requiring the attention of the soldiers was caused by the mob controlled by the Gordian faction. The demands of public order then caused someone to dispatch the guards away from the Palace so that the two emperors became vulnerable. Julius Capitolinus's account therefore explains why there were not guards present at the Palace, which Herodian's does not. This gave the conspiring soldiers (*milites*, i.e. the *praetoriani*) the opportunity they had been looking for. They rushed from their camp to the Palace and when the news was brought to Pupienus he immediately summoned the Germans who were with Balbinus in another part of the Palace. This is clearly a mistake. The two emperors appear not to have had German allies in the Palace, or at least not enough to prevent an attack by the Praetorians. It is therefore clear that the summoning of the Germans meant their summoning from their billets either inside the city as was claimed by Herodian or from outside the city as was claimed by Julius Capitolinus, not from inside the Palace. Julius Capitolinus then continues that Balbinus suspected that Pupienus intended to use the Germans against him and refused to cooperate at first but then began to ponder over it. This quite clearly proves that the Germans were not inside the Palace. While the two emperors argued with each other, the *milites* (i.e. the Praetorians) arrived, captured Balbinus and Pupienus and declared the young Caesar Gordian III as *Imperator* and *Augustus*. The two emperors were then killed and left in the street when the conspirators learned of the approaching Germans. The plot of the Gordian faction had worked like a dream.

In sum, the likely course of events is that the Gordian faction managed to convince most of the Praetorians to back them and then coordinated the efforts to murder the two senatorial emperors. The opportunity came when the scenic plays enabled the Gordian faction to use their mob for the creation of public disturbances which required the attention of the Palace Guards (both the *praetoriani* and *aulici*). This left the two emperors vulnerable to attack. The Gordian faction knew that the two men would not be able to agree to the calling of the Germans when they were vulnerable to an attack. Then they were able to launch their attack with the Praetorians.

5.9 Pupienus and Balbinus as emperors

Herodian and Julius Capitolinus are both correct to state that the deaths of the two senatorial emperors were undeserved. The two men had served the Roman Republic well.

Horus spearing crocodile, which probably serves as a model for the Dragon-spearing St. George. Note the equipment and lack of shield. The cavalry had units equipped with shields or without them just like they had cavalry with or without armour. Source of the image: Duruy.

As emperors Pupienus had defeated Maximinus Thrax and had dispersed Maximinus's defeated army safely back to the provinces while Balbinus had survived the civil war in Rome. After this, both had managed to calm down the soldiers with a sizable bribe, the donative, which they could pay without resorting to extraordinary measures, simply by reintroducing the *antoninianus* coin. Their plan to conduct pre-emptive strikes against their enemies was also laudable. But it is an entirely different issue how matters would have progressed from there because both men were quarrelling with each other and seeking supreme power. It is entirely possible that had they survived the plot they could have ended up fighting a civil war against each other.

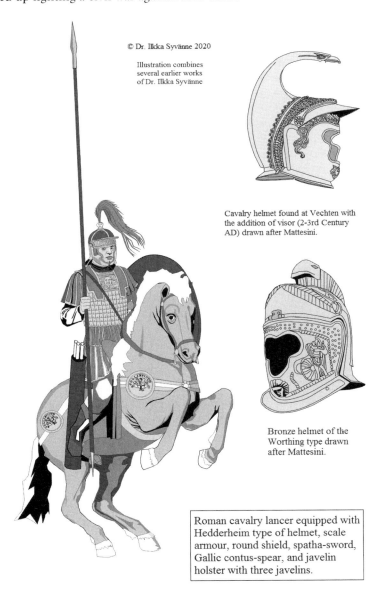

© Dr. Ilkka Syvänne 2020

Illustration combines several earlier works of Dr. Ilkka Syvänne

Cavalry helmet found at Vechten with the addition of visor (2-3rd Century AD) drawn after Mattesini.

Bronze helmet of the Worthing type drawn after Mattesini.

Roman cavalry lancer equipped with Hedderheim type of helmet, scale armour, round shield, spatha-sword, Gallic contus-spear, and javelin holster with three javelins.

Chapter Six

Gordian III (AD 238–44)

A bust of Gordian III according to Duruy

A coin of Gordian III depicting him mounted. Source of image: Cohen

6.1 Early Reign of Gordian III from 238 until 241: The Modern View[1]

The Sources

Imperator Caesar M. Antonius Gordianus *Pius Felix Invictus Augustus*, better known in the English world as Gordian III, began his sole rule on 7 June 238, but in truth he was emperor only in name for the first three years. The sources for these first three years are very sparse. Basically all that we have are the very short references to the circumstances of Gordian's rule by Julius Capitolinus in the *Historia Augusta Gordiani Tres* (*HA Gord.* 22.1ff.) and even shorter texts of Zosimus (basically the same as in the *HA*), Zonaras, Peter the Patrician, extant laws of Gordian in the *Codex Iustinianus*[2] and some inscriptions. The prejudiced view towards the *Augustan Histories* has caused it not to be used by the vast majority of modern historians except when its contents can be confirmed from other sources. This has led to a twisted view of the reign, which I will set out to correct. However, I will first represent the consensus view of modern historians before turning to the evidence provided by Julius Capitolinus in the *Historia Augusta*.

The Creation of a New Bodyguard Unit in 238

Modern historiography has largely neglected the evidence provided by the later 'Byzantine/East Roman' sources for the reign of Gordian. This evidence shows that it is probable that either Gordian or the caretaker government acting on his behalf reformed the already existing units of *scholarii/aulici*. In the confused text of the *Chronicon Paschale* (Niebuhr ed. p.501) *Gordianus Augustus* created an *arithmos* (*numerus*) of *candidati* (elite bodyguards dressed in white) by selecting full-grown impressive men from the ranks of the *scholarii*. He called the *schola* of his *arithmos* (*numerus*) 'seniores'. These were the sixth *schola*. This would imply that the creator was Gordian I, but it is clear that this results from some confusion in the original source or sources. It would also be very odd if Gordian I had access to bodyguards posted in Rome. Cedrenus (Niebuhr ed. p.451) states that it was after Balbinus and Pupienus that Junior (i.e. Gordian III) was the first to create *candidati* and *protectores* and the *tagma* of *scholarii* that were called *iuniores*. The extant Greek text is ambiguous and allows many interpretations so that it is possible to think that the *candidati* and *protectores* were created by selecting men from the sixth *schola*, but it is also possible to think that the *candidati* and *protectores* were selected from the *scholarii* to act as officers for the new sixth *schola*. In light of the subsequent reform of the same corps under Philip the Arab (see the reign of Philip after Niebuhr ed. *Chronicon Paschale* p. 502) the latter is actually the likelier interpretation with the implication that Gordian strengthened the *scholae/aulici* with the addition of a new unit. However, this is by no means conclusive. It is similarly possible to think that we are here dealing with 'schools' of *candidati* drawn from the ranks of *scholarii* so that there would have been a school of *candidati* for each school of *scholarii*, and that the *seniores* and *iuniores* in this case mean senior and junior 'schools' (*scholae*) of *candidati* within each 'school' of *scholarii*.

Since it is known that the *scholae* appear in the sources for the first time during the reign of Septimius Severus, it is possible to speculate that he had formed the first *schola* out of the 600 chosen bodyguards of his in 193 (Dio 74.15.3), and that Caracalla and Geta would have formed the second and third *scholae*, Elagabalus the fourth and Alexander Severus the fifth so that Gordian would indeed have formed the sixth *schola* as stated. Whatever the exact details, my own suggestion is that it is very likely that the sixth *schola* was added in 238 when Gordian and the faction behind it would have needed a special corps to protect Gordian and his mother against possible assassins among the bodyguards hired by the former supporters of Pupienus and Balbinus.

The Ruling Circles and Politics in 238–41

Modern historians have established that between 238 and 241 the Roman Empire was in the hands of the Senatorial Party that had risen against Maximinus Thrax, but such that the leading element within it was now the Gordian faction. The new ruling elite consisted of both senators and equestrians who sought to re-establish the situation that had existed under Alexander Severus. It also included a small number of people who had been appointed to their posts by Maximinus Thrax but who had changed their allegiance soon enough to avoid being removed. In short, these historians do not accept the version which is given in the *Historia Augusta*. Xavier Loriot states that we can identify the following senators and equestrians from epigraphic evidence.[3]

1) M. Acilius Aviola, an aristocrat who was a consul together with Gordian III in 239.
2) C. Octavius Appius Suetrius Sabinus, a partisan of Septimius Severus and Caracalla, a *consul ordinarius* in 214, a proconsul of Africa ca. 225–30, and a consul together with Gordian in 240. For his outstanding career under Caracalla, see Syvänne, *Caracalla*, 172, 188, 215–6, 219.
3) Clodius Pompeianus, an aristocrat who was a consul together with Gordian in 241.
4) Caesonius Lucillus, an ex-vigintivir who became proconsul of Africa after 240/1.
5) Tullius Menophilus, an ex-vigintivir and governor of Moesia Inferior in 238–240/1.
6) Rutilius Pudens Crispinus, an ex-vigintivir and governor of Hispania Citerior in 238–41.
7) L. Domitius Gallicanus Papinianus, the man who created the animosity between the Senate and mob on the one side and the Praetorians on the other; governed Germania Inferior in about 240 and succeeded Crispinus as governor of Hispania Citerior in 241.
8) C. Flavius Iulius Latronianus, one of the *clarissimi pueri* who had sung the *Carmen saeculare* in 204 and was *consul suffectus* and *pontifex* priest under Alexander Severus. He was nominated *praefectus urbi* in about 239/40.
9) M. Aedinius Iulianus, Praetorian Prefect in 233 was still held in esteem in 238.
10) L. Flavius Honoratus Lucilianus became *magister* of the *fratres arvales* in 240.

The young Gordian III was therefore guided to demonstrate his respect to the Senate and its ancient rights and privileges. It was because of this that Gordian's administration introduced legislation that protected the liberty of individuals and communities while freelance informers, which the senators considered their greatest personal threat, were suppressed with new laws. Gordian III received the best education money could buy, so there was substance to the propaganda that represented him as a cultured philhellene in contrast to the barbarian brute Maximinus. The fact that the senatorial block sought to bring back the good old days of Alexander Severus meant that it sought to govern without resorting to any extraordinary measures to obtain funds. Therefore they continued to mint the debased *antoninianus*-coins while reducing the tax burden. However, they did this by lowering its standard even more than ever before.[4]

According to Xavier Loriot, Gordian's regime advertised its generocity by distributing money four times with the text *liberalitates Augusti*, and the sum of money distributed, 350 *denarii* per person, was greater than the 250 *denarii* per person distributed by Pupienus and Balbinus. The idea was to secure the loyalty of the army and people behind the new emperor and ruling circles, and by and large this appears to have been successful. The regime also favoured festivities connected with religion and it is probable that the personal likings of young Gordian had a role in this. In 242 he instituted *Agon Minerviae* in Rome and encouraged cities in particular in Italy and Greece to organize similar festivities. The existence of *Gordianeia* is attested in the cities of Athens, Aphrodisias and Side, and other festivities are attested also for Beroea and Thessalonica.[5]

All of this required money. The administration obtained this by debasing the coins. According to Loriot, the gold *aureus*, which in about 235 had weighed about 6.45 grams, weighed about 5.04 grams in 240. The silver *antoninianus* that had weighed 4.75 grams with a silver content of $490^0/00$[6] under Pupienus and Balbinus, weighed about 4.48 grams with a silver content of $435\text{–}450^0/00$ in about 239/40. As a result, the copper *denarius* tended to disappear entirely from circulation. The tetradrachma of Syria and drachma of Alexandria had a similar fate. On the basis of this it has been speculated that there was rampant inflation in prices and salaries, but the researchers of this question still caution that we do not have any documentation to give specific numbers.[7] I would add to this the comment that increasing the amount of money in circulation tends to improve the economy and not the other way around. Indeed my personal view is that this question belongs largely to the field of speculation based solely on the lowering of the silver content and weight. The evidence that the soldiers and people would not have accepted the money at its face value is based solely on the simultaneous disappearance of the copper coins, the minting of which became less profitable when the silver coins were practically the same as the copper coins. It is also dangerous to draw too drastic conclusions on the basis of the above because it is entirely possible that the new debased *antoninianus* bought exactly the same amount of things as before if the populace continued to accept it at its face value. The evidence from the period 215–35 actually suggests this. There were no murmurings from the soldiers when Caracalla introduced his *antoninianus*; there were no troubles after 219 when the government stopped using it; and there were no revolts resulting from the reintroduction after 238 when the coin was brought back into circulation. This suggests a situation in which the soldiers and populace at large accepted the coins at their face values.

The Senatorial Party brought the army back into imperial control with several measures. The *legio III Augusta* that had supported Capelianus against the Gordiani was cashiered in infamy and its soldiers spread out to other units throughout the empire (see below). The supporters of the new regime naturally received most of the important military commands to make certain that the army stayed loyal. Their sole qualifications for the posts consisted of their perceived loyalty to the Senate and Severan Dynasty and the new Gordian Dynasty. Xavier Loriot lists the following: Tullius Menophilus in Moesia Inferior; L. Domitius Gallicanus in Germania Inferior; D. Simonius Iulianus in Dacia between 241–4; Attius Rufinus in Coele-Syria; Egnatius Lucilianus in Britannia Inferior in 238–41;[8] M. Domitius Valerianus in Arabia in 238–41 (not to be confused with the Emperor Valerianus); Q. Petronius Melios (*legio XXX Ulpia Victrix*); L. Luxilius Sabinus (*legio X Gemina*) and so forth. Most of these lacked the necessary military qualifications for their posts. Their sole recommendation was their perceived loyalty, or as we shall see on the basis of the *Historia Augusta*, their readiness to bribe the eunuchs. The soldiers were compensated by improving their legal status with new edicts. The events prove that these measures were relatively successful. There was only one military mutiny before 244.[9] Perhaps the fresh memory of the humiliating defeat suffered by the professional soldiers at the hands of the Italian *iuventutes* and senators had a role in this – the events of 238 had proved to the soldiers and their professional officers that they could not defeat the united front consisting of the People and senators. Furthermore, the soldiers and their families were Romans with shared views of what was right and wrong – and Maximinus's policies had clearly been wrong.

Military Troubles in 238–41
The new administration was forced to deal with military problems immediately. As noted already, the crushing of Capelianus in North Africa took until the fall of 238 to achieve, after which the *legio III Augusta* was disbanded. This did not pacify this area because Sabinianus revolted in Carthage in 240. The usurpation threatened the grain supply of Rome. However, the procurator of Mauretania Caesariensis Faltonius Restitutianus, despite his initial troubles with the conspirators, eventually crushed the rebels so decisively on behalf of Gordian III that all of the rebels came to Carthage where they surrendered Sabinianus to the governor and asked for forgiveness.[10] It is probable that they were granted this because we hear of no further troubles. The fact that the governor received the rebels at Carthage means that he had gathered together the forces under him after which he had marched to Numidia and then to Africa and that he had inflicted a crushing defeat on the enemy so that he was able to capture Carthage. This success is not surprising in light of the fact that the governor of Mauretania possessed the largest forces in the area after the disbanding of the *legio III Augusta*. Similarly, Decius appears to have been able to hold out against Crispinus until early 239 before he was forced to surrender in return for a pardon.

North Africa faced other very serious troubles too. It faced the endemic threat posed by the Moors who conducted razzias against cultivated areas and cities in coastal areas. This was large scale banditry. The principal threats consisted of the Autololes and Baquates in Mauretania Tingitana, the Bavares of Mauretania Caesarensis, the Musulmanes of Numidia, Gaetuli and Aethiopians of Sahara, Garamantes of Fezzan/Tripolitania and Marmaridae of Tripolitania and Cyrenaica. See the Berbers Map in the Maps Section. The Moors consisted of lightly equipped cavalry armed with two or three javelins/spears and of similarly lightly equipped infantry. Typically their only form of protective equipment was a shield. The Moors also possessed archers and there were differences between the tribes, but their standard combat methods were surprise attacks and ambushes; if the Romans managed to collect adequate numbers of soldiers, the Moors fled to the desert. If the Moors were forced to fight they usually built marching camps protected by rings of animals tied together using them for refuge. If possible they hid some forces nearby to act as ambushers. The Moorish infantry could fight in tight phalanx formations, but due to their lack of drill and lighter equipment they were no match for the Romans. The Moorish javeliner cavalry specialized in skirmishing tactics and was also no match against a determined Roman cavalry attack. However, the Moors still posed a strategic threat because they could make surprise raids and then disappear into the deserts and mountains. The Severans had solved the strategic problem by pushing the frontiers further into the desert where they had built a number of fortresses (*castella*). The garrisons posted in these fortresses were usually assisted by detachments sent from the *legio III Augusta*, which had its main base at Lambaesis. See the Map of the Roman Fortifications in Africa in the Maps Section. The Romans used walls built across the routes of movement both to make it easier to tax the people and to control the movements of the raiders.[11]

The disbandment of the *legio III Augusta* led to trouble because after this there were no longer legionary detachments supporting the other garrison forces. The *vexillatio militum Maurorum Caesariensium Gordianorum*, which was posted as its replacement in Lambaesis, was not large enough to act as its real replacement. The *burgus* located at Gheria-el-Gharbia in Tripolitania was apparently the first to suffer because it was attacked and partially destroyed by the Garamantes either in late 238 or early 239. There is also evidence for the permanent abandonment of the *castellum* located at Dimmidi in the autumn of 238. Loriot is undoubtedly correct in stating that there were no longer enough men to man this outpost, so the men were concentrated where they were most needed. The new withdrawn line of defence consisted of two fortresses located at Doucen and Sadouri and the road connecting them. Both were repaired or enlarged by the legate of Numidia T. Iulius Antiochus in 242, and the *numerus Palmyrenorum* was tasked to guard this section. It is possible that the *fossatum Africae* was lengthened at the same time, but this is contested by several historians who suggest that this took place during the second century. An inscription from the reign of Philip the Arab from Kasr Duib of Tripolitania describes the situation after the disbandment of *legio III Augusta*. This document states that each of the sectors of the frontier was now placed under *praepositus limitis* (an acting commander of the frontier sector) and all of these were placed under the imperial legate of Numidia.[12] This has been used to suggest a change from mobile defence to territorial defence, but is by no means conclusive in this respect. In my opinion, it is far likelier that this meant only a change of titles that reflected the situation better – the only real difference was that the legate of Numidia no longer had the legion at his disposal. The rural population was mobilized for the defence of their own respective areas and their villages fortified. This arrangement concerned also the *coloni* of the imperial domains.[13]

The extant inscriptions from Mauretania Tingitana show that the Romans faced serious troubles in this area. The Baquates and Bavares were particularly active there during this period. The inscriptions from Volubilis show that there were at least two or three bouts of problems between 239 and 241. In 239 M. Ulpius Victor conducted peace negotiations with some anonymous princeps of the Baquates. Victor is attested in this province between about 230 and 245 and he held the extraordinary title of *procurator Augusti pro legato*. The extent of the trouble is evident from his title, because it signifies that he had in his service legionary detachments probably drawn from Hispania Citerior.[14]

Zonaras (12.17) claims that someone called Pompeianus usurped power for a period of less than two months after Pupienus (Maximus) and Albinus (Balbinus) had been killed. Zonaras notes that Pompeianus was killed, but he did not know by whom or how. If this is true, then there was another usurpation against Gordian III of which we know nothing, but the problem with this is that the account of Zonaras is hopelessly confused: that Balbinus succeeded Pompeianus and that Balbinus was then killed after three months when Gordianus arrived in Rome from Africa. The 79-year-old Gordianus then died of old age and was succeeded by his similarly named son. As is obvious this account is so hopelessly confused as to make the reference to the usurpation of Pompeianus practically meaningless. However, I would still consider this very likely, because there were many other provinces besides Hispania Citerior and Numidia/Africa that had supported Maximinus Thrax against the Senate and it is easy to see that a governor of such a province could have decided to try their luck just like Capelianus and Decius. It is possible to think that the troubles with the Scythians in the Balkans were connected with this usurpation and that Menophilus dealt with it too, but this is obviously pure speculation.

Modern historians usually think that the campaign of Maximinus Thrax had largely secured the Rhine frontier, but this is only partially true. The land frontier appears to have been relatively secure, but the money treasures dated to the period 238–44 that have been found in the northern and north-western regions suggest that the Germans had not stopped their raids. Most of these finds are located along the coast and the Pas-de-Calais, which suggests that they resulted from piratical raids either by the Franks or Saxons – in my opinion the latter alternative can be discounted because the Saxons began their raids much later. However, there is evidence for the existence of Frankish piratical activity and I would suggest that this is the likeliest group of raiders in this case. Some historians have suggested that this resulted from some local troubles caused by local brigands, by the rapacious behaviour of soldiers, or by some unknown slave revolt. In the absence of written sources this is also possible, but I would still consider the likeliest culprit to have been the Frankish pirates.[15]

Tullius Menophilus, who had been dispatched to Moesia Inferior by Pupienus, faced trouble in both Dacia and Lower Danube, but he was able to defeat the invaders by concluding a separate peace with the Goths, which in its turn allowed him to inflict a decisive defeat on the Dacian Carpi. The peace was then maintained thanks to the above-mentioned stratagems and yearly payments to the Goths. This enabled Menophilus to strenghten the defences in the area with fortifcations and diligent drilling of the soldiers. He managed to maintain the peace until he was dismissed from service in about 240/1 when the new Praetorian Prefect Timesitheus overthrew his supporters in Rome. The removal of Menophilus from office, the man whom the enemies feared, appears to have led to an almost immediate invasion of Roman territories.

Modern historians[16] have sometimes accepted the statements of Zonaras (2.18) and Syncellus (AM 5731) that Ardashir/Artaxerxes I captured Carrhae and Nisibis during the reign of Maximinus Thrax, but this is a mistake, as I will make clear later. Herodian (7.8.4–5) states in no uncertain terms that the Persians had not invaded at the time Maximinus Thrax began his campaign against the Gordiani in 238 and Julius Capitolinus (*HA Gord.* 23.4–6) confirms this by stating that the Persians invaded only in 241. However, the latter is true only for the start of the main Persian invasion which led to the capture of Nisibis, Carrhae and Antioch; it is not true that the war started only then, because the Persians had already attacked Dura Europos in 239 and had captured the allied city of Hatra between 14 April 240 and 31 March 241. My own suggestion is that the siege of Hatra began and ended during the winter of 240/1, and that the entire siege may have taken place during the year 241 because it was only then that the Persian war started according to Julius Capitolinus, but this date is obviously based on the time when the news reached Rome. These were not considered important enough to merit the personal attention of the Emperor.[17]

On the basis of *Codex Iustinianus*, which places Gordian III in Antioch on 1 April 239, Xavier Loriot has suggested that he indeed was there on that date. As an additional proof of this visit, he notes that a series of coins that depicted the equestrian type of ADVENTUS AUGUSTI was minted in Rome in about 240. This suggests that Gordian visited the East in 239 and then returned to Rome probably the next spring. The problems with this are that the dates and locations in the *Codex Iustinianus* are known to be inaccurate and the ADVENTUS coin could result from a return from some other place. However, when this evidence is taken together the case for a visit to the East in 239 is still stronger than the case against it. Therefore I accept Loriot's suggestion. This would mean that Gordian III and the court were in the East at the same time as the Persians engaged the *cohors XX Palmyrenorum Gordiana* in combat at Dura Europos 30 April 239. The Persian attack failed so it is easy to see why Gordian did not have to stay in the area.[18] It is possible that it was during his visit of the East that Gordian III made the military appointments criticized in the *Historia Augusta*, for which see the next chapter.

In my opinion it is quite probable that the Roman court and the Persians concluded some sort of truce while Gordian was in the East because al–Tabari (i.827ff.) claims that after this Sapor I was waging a war in Khorasan in about 239–40. This was then exploited by the ruler of Hatra who raided Persian territory in 239. This raiding then served as the reason for the siege of Hatra by Sapor in 240–41. This implies that the two sides had probably concluded some sort of truce in 239 that enabled Gordian III to return to Rome and Sapor I to march to Khorasan and that this truce was then broken by the greedy Arabic ruler of Hatra.

6.2. Early Reign of Gordian III from 238 until 241:

The Historia Augusta *Taken into Account*[19]

Even though the above account has its merits, there is one problem with it. The view presented above has failed to take into account the information provided by the *Historia Augusta* to the extent that it deserves. There is nothing inherently improbable in the description of the circumstances of Gordian's early reign to merit this. It is because of this that the above account needs the addition of subtle nuances and qualifications.

According to Julius Capitolinus, Gordian III (i.e. the Gordian faction) was able to secure his position very soon after the murder of Pupienus and Balbinus. However, thanks to the fact that Gordian III was young the actual power was in the hands of his mother and her favourites. This shines through most clearly in the two letters included by Julius Capitolinus, one from Gordian to Timesitheus and one from Timesitheus to Gordian, dated to 241 or after. It is possible that the letters are forgeries of Julius Capitolinus, but not conclusively so, and most importantly it is obvious that their contents are still accurate on the basis of common sense. Gordian was young and not in control of his own decisions during his first years as Emperor. It is very likely that he was controlled by his mother as Alexander Severus had been.

'[*Gordian was*] assisted with the counsels of so excellent father-in-law [*This refers to the period after 241 when Gordian had married the daughter of Timesitheus. Julius calls him Misitheus, but the former is the correct version of his name*] [so] nothing in his rule seemed childish or despicable; ... nor did he allow his favours to be sold by the eunuchs and servants of the court with the connivance or ignorance of his mother. We have a letter of his father-in-law written to him and another from him written to his father-in-law... the letters are these: "To my Lord and Augustus, from Timesitheus his Prefect and Father-in-Law. It is a pleasure for me to obeserve that the blot has been removed from your reign, I mean the eunuchs and those who pretended to be your friends (but who were really your greatest enemies) who bought and sold everything for money... the commands in the army were given through the favour of the eunuchs and men were denied their due rewards for their labours, or when the men who should have been slain or set free were judged by money handed to the eunuchs, when the treasury was exhausted, and when plots and cabals were fomented to deceive you... while evil men... prevented the access of men of virtue and honesty... and on the contrary insinuating others into your favour, ... and sold your secrets for money. ... The gods be thanked that you have reformed the state [*this refers to the situation after 241*]."' HA Gord. 23.7ff. tr. by Bernard 60ff. with changes, corrections, additions and comments.

'The Emperor Gordianus to Timesitheus my Father my Prefect. Were it not for the almighty gods to protect the Roman Empire, the eunuchs would have ruined that and me by selling and buying as though we would be under a hammer. I now see very well that Felicio was not fit to command the Praetorian Guard, which I gave him; nor Serapammon to be trusted with the Fourth Legion [*Both of these persons are otherwise unknown, but this doesn't mean that they didn't exist. We do not know the names of all of the important persons of the third century. The inclusion of the IV legion in the list lends credence to the text because, as noted above, it is probable that it had been created by Alexander Severus for his eastern campaign and it is probable that it was stationed there after 238. The great successes of the Persians in the East in 241 could easily have been caused by the appointment of incompetent men such as Serapammon in charge of the forces there. The Romans lost Nisibis, Carrhae and Antioch in 241 and it is probable that they lost many other places as well. It is easy to imagine that the legio IV under Serapammon could have been posted in one of these cities as its garrison force and if this Serapammon performed very poorly it is probable that the fall of the city resulted from that. The most likely locations for this legion would therefore have been Nisibis or Carrhae or Antioch. Nisibis, however, is the least likely because of reasons stated later*]. I am sensible enough not to give any further examples [*In other words there were several similarly incompetent generals in the East and elsewhere*] that I have done many things that I should not have done; And I thank the gods that thanks to your just and true suggestions, I have understood my error and that I know the things which have been not known to me. What could I have done when even our mother was betraying us and took counsel with Gaudianus, Reverendus, and Montanus and [*These too are otherwise unknown, but this does not mean that they didn't exist. We do not know the names of all of the eunuchs of the Palace so we cannot dismiss the information as has usually been done.*] then on the basis of these witnesses either recommended or did not recommend persons to me. My Father, I would desire you to search for the truth of things. An emperor is in a miserable condition if the truth is hidden from him because he cannot walk out among the people to examine matters himself, so out of necessity he has to rely on what is said to him and then believe what he has heard or what the majority opinion has confirmed.' Julius Capitolinus, *HA Gord.* 25.1ff. tr. by Bernard 62ff. with changes, clarifications, corrections, additions and comments.

The above demonstrates that in 238, after the deaths of Maximus Pupienus and Balbinus, effective control of the Empire was in the hands of Gordian's mother Maecia Faustina and her favourite eunuchs Gaudianus, Reverendus and Montanus. The eunuchs seem to have sold offices and imperial secrets in the open market to fill their pockets. Contrary to the consensus view of modern historians, the reasons for accepting this version are stronger than the case against it. It is obvious that when the ruler was not old enough to rule that the real power was in the hands of his mother just as it had been under Alexander Severus, and there is nothing improbable that an Empress would have relied on her inner circle when making decisions or appointments. Consequently, thanks to the corruption, incompetent men were appointed as generals. This, however, concerns only those appointments that were made outside the inner circle belonging to the Gordian faction. The men who belonged to this faction or whose support was important to maintain were kept in their positions until 241. These men included the highly competent generals Crispinus and Menophilus, so it is clear that the problem of military incompetence was not universal – rather it appears to have concerned only the appointments to the commands in the East and to the position of the Praetorian Prefect.

The appointment of Felicio as Praetorian Prefect appears to have been the worst of the nominations resulting from the corruption.[20] This Felicio is not known outside the *Historia Augusta* and therefore usually considered fictitious. However, this silence is not conclusive because we do not know the names of all of the praetorian prefects even for the reign of Gordian III. It is unlikely that the Gordian faction led by Maecia Faustina would have entrusted so important a position as that of praetorian prefecture to only one person at a time. This means that we do not know the names of the other praetorian prefects before 242. Modern historiography has established the known praetorian prefects of the reign of Gordian III as follows according to the list of Katrin Herrmann and Ensslin:[21]

238 Aedinius Aelianus	(source: Ensslin, *CAH*, 82)
20 September 239 Herodotus	(source: Cod. Ius. 5.11.2)
21 May 240 Domitius	(source: Cod. Iust 8.30.2, Johne)
27 August 240 Ammonius	(source: Cod. Iust 6.45.2)
241–3 C. Furius Sabinus Aquila Timesitheus	(source: Johne)
242/4 C. Iulius Priscus (brother of Philip the Arab)	(source: Johne)
243–4 M. Iulius Philippus	(source: Johne)

On the basis of the above list, the man who is called Felicio by Julius Capitolinus could be Herodotus, or Domitius, or Ammonius, or their co-prefect. The important point is that Julius Capitolinus states that this Felicio had a dominant position among the praetorian prefects before 241 just as Timesitheus was to have after him. Therefore it is probable that this Felicio was the military prefect of the pair of praetorian prefects while the ones named above are likely to have been the legal experts whose names were thereby preserved. The ousting of Felicio from his position is to be connected with the failure of the Roman army in the East during 240–41.

Julius Capitolinus notes that the Fourth Legion was entrusted to Serapammon, and that other military commands were also entrusted to persons solely on the basis of their readiness to bribe the eunuchs. As noted above, the Fourth Legion had been raised by Alexander Severus before his eastern campaign, which means that it was meant as a garrison force for one of the cities in the region. On the basis of this it is clear that the Praetorian Prefect Felicio and the incompetence of Serapammon and the other appointees of the corrupt court were blamed for the loss of Nisibis, Carrhae, Antioch and some other cities to the Persians in 240–2. It is also very probable that many of the eunuchs, freedmen, equestrians and senators promoted by Gordian's mother were either closet Christians or openly so.

6.3 The Persian War in 241–44

The Persians invaded in strength in 241–2 and achieved almost unprecedented successes. This required the personal attention of the Emperor and his Praetorian Prefect, and because of this the administration paid less attention to other matters, such as legislation. According to Xavier Loriot's calculation, out of a total of 222 or 275 laws of Gordian preserved in the *Codex Iustinianus* only 61 date from the period after January 241.[22]

The Persian Invasion in 240–42
The Persians invaded the Roman Empire in strength under the leadership of the crown prince Sapor/Shapur I in 240–41. Their first object was the allied city of Hatra, which had a Roman detachment to support its ruler. The reason for the invasion is provided

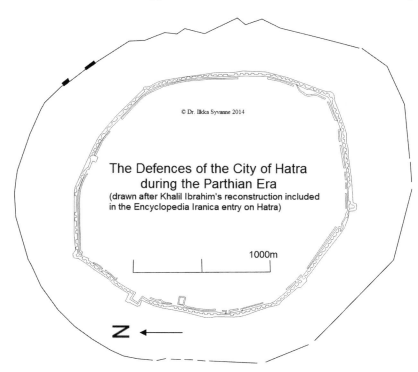

© Dr. Ilkka Syvänne 2014

The Defences of the City of Hatra
during the Parthian Era
(drawn after Khalil Ibrahim's reconstruction included
in the Encyclopedia Iranica entry on Hatra)

1000m

N ←

by al-Tabari. According to him, king/sheik Daizan of Hatra, together with his Qoda tribe, had exploited the absence of Sapor, who was at that time in Chorasan, by raiding Persian territory. As a result, Sapor's first step was to punish the insolent Arab. Hatra had formidable defences, but then luck smiled on Sapor. The daughter of Daizan, Nadira, fell in love with the *shah* and betrayed the city. Sapor butchered the Qoda tribe and some other Arab tribes that had supported Daizan. He also wedded the fair maiden, had rough sex with her, and then had her killed by having her tied by her hair to the tail of a horse.[23]

A number of sources claim that the founder of the Sassanian Empire Ardashir I rewarded his son by nominating him as his co-ruler after the capture of Hatra in about 240–1. Some historians have accepted this at its face value while others have not. The problems associated with this question are discussed in some detail in my co-authored book with Katarzyna Maksymiuk, but personally I am of the opinion that there are not necessarily any real problems with the evidence and that it is possible to reconcile them. It is clear that on the basis of the Iranian tradition there could be only one 'royal fire' at a time so that Ardashir I and Sapor I could not have been equals. However, as I note in the book it is possible to see in this the same kind of arrangement as prevailed in the Roman Empire when father and son were both *augusti* – the former obviously was the de facto ruler even if both had theoretically equal powers. Therefore, in practice the co-regency meant only that the ruler designated a successor for himself which the mighty men of the Persian Empire still needed to accept after the death of Ardashir.[24]

Artaxerxes/Ardashir giving power to his son Sapor/Shapur I. Source: Texier

Despite the fact that al-Tabari (i.826) claims that Sapor marched against Nisibis in the eleventh year of his reign and then marched to Khurasan/Chorasan because there were troubles and then returned after he had solved the troubles, it is clear that the events that al-Tabari describe took place in 241–2. The reasons for this are that Sapor conquered

Nisibis because its wall split on its own and because the troubles in Chorasan can also be connected with the events preceding the capture of Hatra. Al-Tabari does not state why the wall split on its own, which leaves open the following options: 1) The walls collapsed due to neglect; 2) The walls collapsed because of an earthquake; 3) or the walls collapsed because the Persians had undermined them. However, when this piece of information is connected with the information provided by Julius Capitolinus (*HA Gord.* 26.1–3, see also below) of the events that took place in the Roman Empire in 241–2, namely the massive earthquakes that hit the Roman Empire, it becomes obvious that we are here dealing with a major earthquake occurring against the East Anatolian Plate which is located close to Nisibis. According to al-Tabari the siege had lasted a long time because Nisibis had a garrison of Roman troops, which means that the Persians were really lucky in that the walls were split asunder in the earthquake. It was thanks to this that the Persians were able to gain entry to the city where they then killed the Roman soldiers, made slaves of the women and children, and captured the Emperor's war chest.

This raises the question of who was in charge of the Roman garrison posted in Nisibis. If the garrison consisted of the Fourth Legion under the above-mentioned Serapammon, it would definitely be an exaggeration to call him incompetent in the manner that the letter preserved in Julius Capitolinus claims. The earthquake would have made it difficult to defend the place. The account preserved in al-Tabari raises the possibility that Serapammon and others who had been nominated at the instigation of Gordian's mother and eunuchs were just made scapegoats for the loss of the cities in the East, most of which apparently fell at least partly thanks to the destruction of the walls in the massive earthquake that hit the area in about 241/2.

The accounts of Zonaras (2.18) and Syncellus (AM 5731) make it clear that Sapor exploited his success further by capturing Carrhae. Julius Capitolinus (*HA Gord.* 26.3ff.) adds that after this Sapor I invaded Syria and even captured Antioch. Most modern historians do not accept the capture of Antioch because the sole source for this is the *Historia Augusta*, but I see no reason to doubt it.[25] Furthermore, it is probable that Sapor also captured a number of other garrisoned or not garrisoned cities in this area, even if the sources fail to mention this. Obvious locations are the cities between Antioch-Hatra and Carrhae-Nisibis and other cities close by. This implies that at least the legionary garrisons at Resaina (*III Parthica*) and Singara (*I Parthica*) ended up in Persian hands.[26] It is also possible that the legionary garrison at Sura (*XIV Flavia*) was lost. The other important cities that fell into Persian hands were surely Edessa, Beroea, Zeugma, Hierapolis, Barbalissos, and Seleucia on the coast. If the earthquake had caused damage to the walls of these cities too, it is easy to see why all of them fell with relative ease if the commanders in charge were not up to their tasks. The gravity of the losses suggests that the court appointees were probably not only scapecoats for the defeats but really were incompetent as generals. The fact that Sapor was forced to march to the East before Nisibis fell means that the capture of Nisibis must have taken place late in 241 with the implication that the capture of the other places took place probably in early 242. However, the speed with which the Roman defences collapsed cannot be entirely explained by the earthquake because after the fall of Nisibis the men in charge of the other cities certainly had enough time to make repairs before the arrival of the Persian army if their defences had suffered as a result of the earthquake. Therefore it is clear that there was some truth in the accusations of incompetence among the court nominees, but probably not quite to the extent that the letter preserved by Julius Capitolinus claims. It is probable that the defeats suffered in the East gave Gordian III and his mentor Timesitheus the chance to blame those in positions of power so that they were able to get rid of their opponents in the military and the imperial court.

After the capture of Antioch luck smiled on the Romans because the Persian invasion, which was advancing ever deeper into the Roman Empire, was halted by the death of the founding father Ardashir in 242. Sapor I had to halt his campaign until such time that he would be able to obtain the confirmation of his position from the magnates and magi. This Sapor I appears to have obtained without trouble because Ardashir I had already made him a co-ruler in 241 and the victories achieved against the Romans made his position strong. However, he still made promises to the mighty men of the state and distributed riches to the people (the landed and militaty classes) and any prominent persons, soldiers, noble and humble, aristocracy and people.[27] In other words, Sapor acted in the same manner as Roman emperors and bribed all those whose support he needed.

The problems in Africa and in the east and north were not the only troubles that Gordian faced in 240–42. As already noted, Julius Capitolinus (*HA Gord.* 26.1) notes that there was a severe earthquake in which entire cities with all their inhabitants disappeared in the openings of the ground. This can be dated roughly to late 241. As will be made clear below the likeliest locations for this massive earthquake are the areas close to the East Anatolian Plate. The frightened people of Rome offered vast sacrifices to the gods, and the Sibylline Books were consulted and everything stated in them was done. As a consequence, according to Julius Capitolinus (*HA Gord.* 26) and his source, the otherwise unknown historian Cordus, the spread of the worldwide evil was halted. It is probable that Cordus included in this the spread of Christianity which was now stopped for a while. There were pogroms of Christians throughout the Empire; but obviously this is uncertain.

The most important consequence of the calamities of the year 241–2 was actually not the physical earthquake, but the earthquake that shook up the governing structures of the Roman Empire. The inexperienced court appointees to the military commands were accused of gross incompetentence in the face of the renewed Persian attack. The crisis reached such proportions that the 16-year-old Gordian III took the reins of power into his hands with the help Timesitheus. It is uncertain whether this momentuous change took place before or after consulting the Sibylline Books; in my opinion it is practically certain that the idea for consulting the Sibylline Books came from Timesitheus and that he and Gordian III both exploited its 'message' to get rid of their political opponents.

The Rise of Timesitheus in 241

It is unfortunate that we do not know the exact circumstances in which Timesitheus became the trusted advisor of Gordian III and how he was then appointed as Praetorian Prefect and in which circumstances the marriage between Furia Sabinia Tranquillina, the daughter of Timesitheus, and Gordian III took place. What is known with certainty is that Gordian III did indeed marry Timesitheus's daughter in the spring of 241[28] and that this marriage sealed the relationship between the two men, and that the new Praetorian Prefect Timesitheus was then the man who controlled the Roman Empire in the name of his son-in-law Gordian from the year 241 onwards.

Xavier Loriot notes the important positions that Timesitheus had held before becoming Praetorian Prefect, some of which have already been noted above. These positions prove that Timesitheus had been a trusted and loyal servant of the Severan Dynasty and that he continued to hold important positions under Maximinus Thrax. He was a man of great ability. His name implies that he had Hellenic origins, and it has been suggested that he was either a Syrian or Arab because he had been favoured by the Severans and because he promoted the careers of Iulius Priscus and Philippus Arabus (see below), or that he had connections with Anatolia like the Gordiani. This together with his connection with the Severan Dynasty would have put him in close contact with governmental circles and the entourage surrounding Gordian III, and this in its turn enabled him to gain the trust of the young Emperor.[29]

It is possible to think that the rise of Timesitheus resulted from the love of Gordian for Timesitheus's daughter and that Timesitheus then used this to his own advantage, or that when Felicio and the court appointees in the East had proved incompetent that Gordian lent his ear to the advice of Timesitheus who accused Gordian's mother and the eunuchs of the disasters, or that Gordian just realized that he needed Timesitheus's help to be able to get away from the influence of his mother and her friends. It is possible that all of the above played a role. However, in my opinion, in light of the fact that the marriage between Gordian and Tranquillina took place in the spring of 241, the likeliest reason for the rise of Timesitheus is that the relationship was based on the love felt by Gordian towards Furia Sabinia Tranquillina and that the father-in-law Timesitheus was able to use this to his own advantage by pointing out how Gordian's mother had manipulated him. In other words, Timesitheus succeeded in the same situation that had faced Seius Herennius Sallustius Barbius earlier. Alexander Severus had abandoned his wife Sallustia Barbia Orbiana and stayed loyal to his mother Julia Mamaea, but Gordian III remained true to his wife Furia Sabinia Tranquillina and abandoned his mother Maecia Faustina. The principal difference between these two cases was the fact that Timesitheus was able to point out the failings of the people Gordian had appointed on the basis of the advice given by his mother. In light of what happened in the East it was easy for Timesitheus to blame the mother Maecia Faustina and her favourite eunuchs Gaudianus, Reverendus and Montanus and their appointees Felicio, Serapammon and others for the disasters. The fate of the dutiful mama's boy Alexander Severus could be used as a warning example and undoubtedly was. It is also practically certain that it was the idea of Timesitheus to consult the Sibylline Books which could then be used against their enemies within the court and administration and army. The end result of this was that Gordian and Timesitheus were able to remove from office all those whom they considered to be their political opponents. It was then that the military commanders closely associated with the previous power block lost their positions.

Timesitheus sought to strengthen his own position by reinforcing the position of Gordian III. The strengthening of Gordian's powers meant the strengthening of Timesitheus's own powers because Gordian listened to his advice. The heroes of the siege of Aquileia, Crispinus and Menophilus were removed from office despite or rather because of their acknowledged military skills. Their replacements consisted either of careerists who could be expected to be loyal to Timesitheus and Gordian despite the removal of the previous faction from power, or of career military men who were needed

Left: A statue of Tranquillina as Ceres. Source: Duruy

Above right: A coin of Tranquillana. Source: Cohen

where there were military troubles. This means that most of those who had been in prominent positions in the past continued to occupy important positions after 241. They included L. Caesonius Lucillus who after his proconsulate of Africa ended in about 241/2 became *electus ad cognoscendas vice Caesaris cognitiones* in about 244/4; L. Domitius Gallicanus who replaced Crispinus in Germania Inferior; L. Catius Celer, the legate of Thrace and consul in 239/40, who became governor of Moesia Superior in 242; … us L. f. Annianus who had an active role in the war against Maximinus Thrax and became *leg(atus) leg(ionis) XXII Primig(eniae) P(iae) F(idelis) Gordinae* (stationed at Mogontiacum/Mainz) in 242. C. Attius Alcimus Felicianus, an equestrian officer whose career consisted of various fiscal positions under Elagabalus and Alexander Severus saw his career prosper once again under Gordian III; he became head of the *ratio privata* in 239, then Prefect of the *vigiles* and head of the grain supply in Rome in place of the praetorian prefects in 241. Out of the six ordinary consuls for the year 242–4 four belonged to the Severan aristocracy. The consul for the year 224, Ti. Pollenius Armenius

Peregrinus, was married to the daughter of Flavius Latronianus who is attested to have been *praefectus urbi* slightly after 238.[30] The Roman upper classes were a tight knit group, as befitted the Gordiani, the family named after the Gordian knot.

Not unnaturally the inner circle of the Hellenic Timesitheus appears to have consisted mostly of men who were originally from Greek speaking parts of the Empire. Two were Arabs of equestrian origins, C. Iulius Priscus and M. Iulius Philippus (the future Emperor Philip the Arab born ca. 204) from Trachonitis, the sons of a sheik named Marinus. Of these two, Priscus became Praetorian Prefect before his brother Philip, so he was Timesitheus's colleague at least from 242 onwards. If the *Eis Basilea* is dedicated to Philip the Arab, then it proves that Philip was a philhellene who had received a first class education. It is clear that these two brothers had a great influence in the imperial court from about 241/2 onwards, and that Priscus must have been a very influential advisor of Timesitheus and Gordian III. Some historians think that Philip the Arab may have been appointed to the position of *praefectus Mesopotamiae* with the command of *legiones I* and *III Parthica* and their auxiliaries in 242, but this is uncertain. It is equally possible that Philip was just one of the *duces* temporarily put in command of some of the units. Whatever his position was in 241/2, it was important enough for him to rise to the position of Timesitheus after the latter's death. The protégé of these two Arabian brothers, Claudius Aurelius Tiberius, was appointed tribune of one of the cohorts of *vigiles* in the capital in 241. The brothers were clearly placing their own men in positions of importance. The other men who belonged to the inner circle of Timesitheus included Cn. Domitius Philippus (not to be confused with the abovementioned emperor Philip), possibly of Macedonian roots, who was appointed Prefect of the *vigiles* in 241, and then *dux/stratelates* of Egypt in 242 with extensive powers to organize the sending of supplies from Egypt for the army campaigning against the Persians in 242. Timesitheus also promoted Valerius Valens, the Prefect of the Fleet of Misenum, as acting commander of the *vigiles* in 242–243/4, while Aurelius Basileus was appointed Prefect of Egypt in about 242–5. C. Iulius Alexander obtained temporary command of the detachments of the Praetorian Fleets of Misenum and Ravenna during the *expeditio orientalis* against the Persians, after which he was promoted to *stolarchus/praefectus classis praetoriae Misenatium* at the beginning of the reign of Philip the Arab in which position he is attested to have been in 246. All of these were equestrians of Greek or oriental background and therefore hailed from the same regions as Timesitheus and the Gordiani.[31]

As noted by Xavier Loriot, this did not mean that men from other regions would not have been able to gain Timesitheus's favour – it means only that the men with similar background were more likely to be favoured. Faltonius Restitutianus, the man who defeated Sabinianus in 240, was one of those whose origins were not in the Greek-speaking world, but this did not prevent him from becoming Prefect of the *vigiles* in 243 or 244.[32]

The Preparations of the Persian War and the Fighting in Raetia and the Balkans in 242
The Persian attack against Hatra in the winter of 240–41 provided a casus belli for the Romans, and the subsequent success of the Persian invasion stressed the urgency of the situation. Timesitheus and Gordian III appear to have started their preparations for the campaign in 241 so that everything was ready in the spring of 242. Having been in charge

of the logistics of Alexander Severus's Persian war Timesitheus was well prepared for the task. The preparations were on a massive scale. Provisions were deposited in magazines along the route of march and grain fleets were prepared in Egypt under the newly appointed special officer Cn. Domitius Philippus whose title was *dux*. The grain of Egypt was particularly important for the success of the operation being the primary source of grain for the armies operating in the East. The plan was to march the army through the Balkans to Asia Minor and from there to Seleucia and Antioch. The detachments drawn from the Praetorian Fleets of Misenum and Ravenna and corveed civilian ships provided logistical assistance. The crossing of the straits from Europe to Asia was undoubtedly supported by the detachments provided by the Praetorian Fleets and by the ships of the local *Classis Pontica* and by the surviving ships of the *Classis Syriaca*. The grain fleet from Egypt met the army either when it was crossing into Asia or when it reached the Seleucia/Antioch area.[33] In my opinion it is also very likely that Timesitheus not only filled the ranks of existing units with new recruits but also raised new units including legions because this had always been standard practice when conquering new territories and as we shall see this was the grand strategy adopted at this time.

The campaign plans also had a psychological element. Whereas the Persians had evoked their Achaemenid past, the Romans turned their eyes to the archaic past. Gordian opened the doors of the Temple of Janus to signify that a war had been declared. He also borrowed from the Hellenistic traditions in 242 by celebrating an *agon Minerviae* in honour of *Athena Promachos*, the protector of the combatants at the battle of Marathon against the Persians. In my opinion this celebration of the battle of Marathon suggests that Gordian probably still had in his service the *argyroaspides* and *chrysoaspides* of Alexander Severus, in other words the men equipped as the Greeks/Macedonians of Julius Africanus. Gordian minted coins with oriental themes like the *Sol* with the globe that was presented as guarantor of AETERNITAS, and coins with the text Oriens AUGUSTI. Other coins had *Jupiter Stator*, the god that captured the enemy, on the reverse, or *Apollon* the god who presided over wars fought against barbarians of the Orient. Some coins presented Gordian in military attire while others showed the Emperor under the protection of Hercules.[34]

After all the preparations had been performed, the Emperor then presided over the religious ceremonies which invariably preceded a campaign, after which he and his prefect left Rome to begin the campaign. Detachments were collected from the forces posted on the Rhine and Danube frontiers and then concentrated somewhere in the Balkans. Loriot suggests that the forces were concentrated either in Sirmium or Viminacium, but if the Sarmatians invaded Pannonia (see below) the place of concentration must have been further to the north-west e.g. in Aquileia, Emona, Poetovio, Celeia, Neviodunum or Siscia.[35]

There were troubles along the Danube that Gordian and Timesitheus had to solve before proceeding against the Persians. The removal of the previous military commanders by Timesitheus and Gordian III appear to have caused troubles both in Raetia and the Balkans in 241–2, or at least that is my educated guess based on the sequence of events and evidence that we have. The finds of coin hoards in Raetia dated to between 241 and 244, and the destruction of the *castellum* of Künzing in Raetia not far from Noricum, has caused some to speculate that the Germans (i.e. the Alamanni) invaded Raetia in 242.[36] In my opinion this suggestion receives support from the list of defeated enemies in the epitaph of Gordian III quoted later. It includes the Germans among the enemies that Gordian defeated and the invasion of Raetia appears to be one of the candidates for this claim, but it is also possible that the Germans in question were the Quadi or some other Germanic tribe that had joined the invaders in the Balkans that Gordian and Timesitheus then defeated in 242.

Xavier Loriot suggests that Pannonia did not face enemy invasions at this time so the troubles in the Balkans concentrated solely on the two Moesias, Dacia and Thrace.[37] The inclusion of the Sarmatians among the foes defeated by Gordian in the list of Julius Capitolinus, however, suggests that Pannonia also faced an invasion. It is probable that it was the removal of the feared Menophilus from this area that was the root cause of the invasion of these very same areas by the Carpi, Goths, and Alans. The reason for the invasion of Pannonia by the Sarmatians – and probably also by the Marcomanni or Quadi or Vandals if the Germans defeated by Gordian were these – is not known, but it may have resulted from the removal of its commander just as was the case further East.[38]

The only source that provides us with any real information regarding the combat in the Balkans is Julius Capitolinus and it is therefore worth analyzing his text without the prejudices that one usually encounters among modern historians:

> 'After the earthquake and in the time of the consulship of Praetextatus and Atticus [242], the doors of the Temple of Janus were opened (which was a sign that war had been declared) and Gordianus marched upon an expedition against Persia. He took so great an army with him and such a quantity of gold that he could easily conquer the Persians either with his auxiliaries or with his regular soldiers. He passed through the province of Moesia and so into Thrace where he conquered as he went and whosoever barbarians disputed his passage, he fought them, routed them and drove them before him.' Julius Capitolinus, *HA Gord.* 26.3–4., tr. by Bernard p.63–4. with changes, corrections, additions and comments.

At the very end of his book on the Gordiani, Julius Capitolinus adds very important information regarding the campaign conducted by Timesitheus and Gordian III against the invaders in the Balkans – an inscription that the soldiers put in the tomb of Gordian. This piece of information has usually not been accepted, because it includes a pun on Philip. This results solely from the misplaced distrust in everything that the *Historia Augusta* claims. As I have noted many times, the *Historia Augusta* is an unreliable source, but unless there are very strong reasons to doubt its information there is no reason to disregard its information. Roman soldiers are known to have ridiculed their commanders so there is no reason to doubt the contents on the basis of this. Rather it is the other way around – the pun lends support for its reliability. Secondly, there is nothing inherently incredible in the claim that the enemies could have invaded as far south as Philippi as is claimed by Magie (p.447). A few years later the same groups of invaders advanced much further south during the reign of Gallienus.

> 'This was therefore the life and end of the three princes of the name of Gordianus. The two first were killed in Africa; the third upon the borders of Persia where

at the castle of Circesium, which is upon the Euphrates, a tomb was built by the soldiers for him with this inscription, written in Greek, Latin, Persian, Hebrew and Egyptian languages that all the world might read and understand it: "To the honour of the Emperor Gordianus, Conqueror of the Persians, Conqueror of the Goths, Conqueror of the Sarmatians, Queller of Mutinies at Rome [*This presumably means the problems in 238*], Conqueror of the Germans [*This may refer to the abovementioned invasion of Raetia presumably by the Alamanni which was then apparently defeated by the local commander, or to Gordian's personal campaign against them*], but not the Conqueror of Philippi." For the Alans had defeated him in a disorderly battle ['*tumultuario proelio*'] in the Plains of Philippi [*in Macedonia*] and had forced him to retreat and the two Philippi had killed him. [*It is clear that this defeat and retreat in the plains of Philippi was not decisive, because the enemies were still forced to withdraw from Roman territory. It is therefore probable that the disorderly battle refers to a cavalry combat that ended badly for the Romans who were then forced to seek safety from inside the infantry hollow square. The presence of the steady infantry formation would have then changed the situation so that the Alans were eventually forced to retreat from the Roman lands before the march continued to the East. The reference to the defeat suffered by Gordian in person suggests that he had taken personal charge of the cavalry fight. The saving of the situation would have been the handiwork of Timesitheus. This is confirmed by Julius Capitolinus at Gord. 27.2, which refers to Timesitheus's accomplishments from the war in the Balkans up to the reconquest of Nisibis.*] It is said that Licinius defaced this tomb at the same time as he seized imperial power, because he pretended to descend from the two Philippi. Most excellent Constantine, all this I have therefore investigated in order that you should not be unacquainted with anything that might seem anywise to be worthy of the knowledge of your Majesty.' *HA Gord.* 34.1–6., tr. by Bernard 72–3 with changes, corrections, additions and comments.

The texts of Julius Capitolinus and Peter the Patrician (F 170) therefore make it clear that Timesitheus defeated the Sarmatians, Carpi, Goths, Alans and probably also the 'Germans' (Marcomanni and/or Quadi and/or Vandals) in the Balkans. It is probable that Timesitheus defeated the Sarmatians somewhere in Pannonia and, if they were accompanied by some Germanic group like the Macromanni and/or Quadi, then these were also defeated there. It is possible that Timesitheus crossed the Danube and marched through Sarmatian lands to Dacia where he then defeated the Carpi, after which he marched to Thrace where he engaged the Goths and then their client tribe the Alans in the plain of Philippi in Macedonia. The other possibility is that Timesitheus marched from Pannonia to Macedonia where he engaged the Alans and from there to Thrace where he engaged the Goths and from there north either to Moesia or Dacia or east of Dacia where he then engaged the Carpi. The sources do not specify what type of combat formations were used, but it is probable that the Romans used their standard combat formation, the hollow infantry square with large cavalry forces posted outside.

If one combines the standard Roman combat formation with what we know of Alan tactics it is possible to make some educated guesses regarding the battle in the plains of Philippi. The diagram on page 131 with its caption describes the Alan drill used by

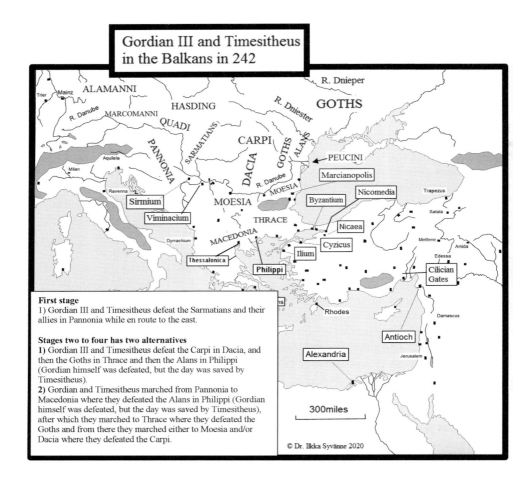

Gordian III and Timesitheus
in the Balkans in 242

First stage
1) Gordian III and Timesitheus defeat the Sarmatians and their allies in Pannonia while en route to the east.

Stages two to four has two alternatives
1) Gordian III and Timesitheus defeat the Carpi in Dacia, and then the Goths in Thrace and then the Alans in Philippi (Gordian himself was defeated, but the day was saved by Timesitheus).
2) Gordian and Timesitheus marched from Pannonia to Macedonia where they defeated the Alans in Philippi (Gordian himself was defeated, but the day was saved by Timesitheus), after which they marched to Thrace where they defeated the Goths and from there they marched either to Moesia and/or Dacia where they defeated the Carpi.

300miles

© Dr. Ilkka Syvänne 2020

the Romans. This combat tactic can also be seen in the Column of Trajan so there is no reason to doubt that the Sarmatians and Alans employed it. When this is put into the context of period Roman tactics it is probable that the Alans lured Gordian to send his cavalry forward with their skirmishing *koursores*, and when the Romans then pursued the retreating Alan *koursores* they peppered them with arrows from a relatively long range. The battle then became disorderly and the Alan *defensores* charged forward against the disordered Romans and forced them to flee inside their hollow infantry square. The steadiness of the Roman infantry then forced the Alans to abandon any further attempts against the Romans. Readers, however, are advised that this is based only on my learned educated speculation and not on specific details provided by the sources, which are quoted.

The list of defeated foes and the list of foreigners in Roman service in the *SKZ* of Sapor I has caused some modern historians to speculate that Timesitheus and Gordian raised auxiliary forces from the ranks of their defeated foes so that they now added a number of Goths and Germans (Marcomanni and/or Quadi and/or Vandals and/or Alamanni?) to the army.[39] This is very probable in light of the previous and later instances in which the

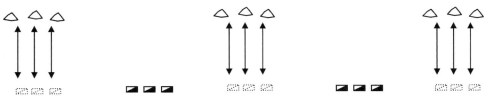

Roman Alan Drill.
(Not to scale! Shows only the principal and not all of the units)
The cavalry arrayed in one line consisting of *moirai* of *koursores* and *defensores*. The *moirai* (at most 2,000–3,000 men) were arrayed c.60–120 metres apart. The moirai would have consisted of the *tagmata/banda* (c. 200–400 men). The *koursores* (initially deployed as rank-and-file oblongs) were used as pursuers or skirmishers (now in irregular order) in front of the array. If the enemy attacked, the *koursores* turned and feigned flight by performing a sudden about turn, or by counter-galloping through the files or by having the unit wheel right. The use of irregular order/loose wedge would have enabled all these variants. After the feigned flight, the *koursores* together with the *defensores* attacked the pursuers either frontally or the *koursores* attacked their flanks.

Romans enlist the Gothic cavalry lancers for use against the Persians – Gothic lancers in particular were very useful in this capacity.

It is probable that the defeat of the Goths enabled Timesitheus to renew the previous treaty that had existed between the Romans and Goths when Menophilus had been the governor because Jordanes notes that at the beginning of Philip the Arab's reign the Romans paid 'tribute' to the Goths. This means that Timesitheus sealed the peace treaty with the Goths by agreeing to continue to pay the 'tribute' in return for the Goths handing over to him a large body of cavalry lancers. This treaty meant that the Goths directed their agression towards their other neighbours in the course of the years 243–45, which are described in the sources as follows:

'Thus by blood and not by right did the Emperor Philip raise himself [*in 244*]. In the meantime, Argaithus, King of the Scythians [*i.e. Goths*], ravaged the kingdoms adjoining him, unto which he was encouraged especially by the death of Timesitheus by whose counsels the Empire had been so well governed [*This means that the Goths had attacked the Roman client kingdoms, but not yet actual Roman territories, which took place only under Philip's reign, as we shall see*]. Julius Capitolinus, *HA Gord.* 31.1–2, tr. by Bernard, 69.

'Now the Gothic race gained great fame… in the Scythian land on the shore of Pontus, holding undisputed sway over great stretches of country, many arms of the sea and many river courses. By their strong right arm the Vandals were often laid low; the Marcomanni held their footing by paying tribute and the princes of the Quadi were reduced to slavery. Now when the aforesaid Philip – who with his son Philip, was the only Christian emperor before Constantine – ruled over the Romans… He withheld from the Goths the tribute due to them.' Jordanes, *Getica 89*, tr. by Mierow, 74.

It was therefore the peace treaty and the payment of tribute that kept the Goths from invading Roman territories. However, they committed one unforgivable thing in Roman eyes which was that they became too powerful, and this required a Roman response.[40] It was a standard Roman operating principle to destroy any power close to their borders which had become too large and powerful, and in this case there were also other pressing reasons for a Roman response, namely that the Goths had subjected the neighbouring tribes, the Marcomanni and Quadi, to paying tribute, while the Romans saw these as their client tribes. Furthermore, when the time came for the Roman response, it took place under Philip the Arab, who as a new emperor had previously concluded a humiliating peace with the Persians (which he did not keep, as we shall see) and needed victories in foreign wars to justify his right to rule.

The Roman counterattack against the Persians in 242–44

Gordian III and Timesitheus continued their journey to the East after the barbarian raiders had been defeated and auxiliary forces had been obtained from them. The route they took can be reconstructed on the basis of ADVENTVS coins. According to Loriot this establishes a route Nicaea (Nikaia), Nacolea (Nakoleia), Antioch-in-Pisidia (Antiocheia), Iconium (Ikonion), Gates of Cilicia (Pylai Kilikiai), Tarsus (Tarsos), and Antioch (Antiocheia). Kettenhofen includes the same information but suggests an alternative route, which is included in the accompanying map: The Persian War under Gordian III 242–44. The coins struck in the East enable us to pinpoint the time of arrival of Gordian and Timesitheus in Syria. It took place during the last months of 242 because the *antoninianus* coins minted at Antioch have the text TR P V which gives us that year. The coins and a papyrus enable us to date the arrival of the Roman army at the Euphrates to the spring of 243. Loriot suggests that the Romans crossed the river at Zeugma and then reoccupied Carrhae (Karrhai), and then recaptured Edessa (if it had been lost to the Persians). Gordian appears to have restored the Oshroenian kingdom by installing Abgar X Soros as its ruler because there is a number of *sesterces* and *dupondii* in existence with the profile of Gordian III on the front with the reverse text of *Basileius Abgaros*. The modern view is that the Romans continued their march from there towards Resaina (Rhesaina) where they engaged the Persians in a battle which the Persians decisively lost with the result that they evacuated Nisibis, Singara and all of Mesopotamia. But then at the end of the spring or beginning of the summer of 243 a disaster struck: Timesitheus, the architect of these victories, died of illness and was succeeded as Praetorian Prefect by Philip the Arab.[41]

Xavier Loriot has suggested on the basis of the text of Agathangelos that the Armenians reinforced the Roman legions posted in Cappadocia and inflicted a series of minor defeats on the Persians while the above took place so that the two armies then met up at Nisibis.[42] This is quite possible, but there are serious problems with the Armenian sources including that of Agathangelos. Agathangelos (18–36) mentions the counter-offensives conducted by the Armenian King Khosrov the Great against the Persians, but fails to put them in their right context. The only specific points that can be identified with any degree of certainty are the counter-operations conducted by Khosrov against Ardashir/Artaxerxes immediately after 224 and the defeats of Sapor just before he dispatched Anak (means the Evil) to assassinate Khosrov in about 253–6.[43] Moses

Khorenatsi (Thomson ed. pp.211–23) bases his account partially on that of Agathangelos but adds some details missing from him. The problem with his account is that he places the events taking place in Armenia to the reigns of the wrong Roman emperors. This means that Moses (pp.218–9) claims that the first time that Khosrov received help from the Romans took place under Philip the Arab whereas it in truth this happened under Alexander Severus and again under Gordian III as suggested by Loriot. On top of this Moses credits the advance as far as Assyria and Ctesiphon to the forces led by Khosrov the Great and not to the Romans as he should. See also Chapter 3. The problem with this account is compounded by the fact that both Agathangelos and Moses connect this Roman help with the situation that existed in the immediate aftermath of the death of the last Parthian king of kings Artaban V and the rise of Ardashir/Artaxerxes I and follows it with the account of the murder of Khosrov the Great in about 253–6. In light of this, it is impossible say what role the Armenians played in this war beyond the general statement that it is very likely that Khosrov the Great served as an ally against his arch-enemies the Sassanians. He may have done this in the manner suggested by Loriot, namely by joining forces with the Romans, or by conducting a separate campaign against the Persians in Media thereby distracting a part of their force there. The problems posed by the Armenian texts are further discussed in the context of the events that took place under Philip the Arab because there are strong reasons to suspect that at least a part of Moses' account really belongs to his reign and that he mixes it up with material that belongs to the very beginning of the conflict between Khosrov the Great and Artaxerxes.

The great victories achieved by Timesitheus and Gordian III were commemorated in Roman propaganda by minting a series of coins in Rome celebrating Felicitas Temporum and Secvritas Perpetua while the mint at Antioch struck coins with Saecvli Felicitas with the image of Gordian as a soldier with a lance and globe of power. The inscriptions in the cities of Asia celebrated Gordian as the new Sun which would bring peace. It was not only propaganda, because the Romans expected that the successes would continue.[44]

Julius Capitolinus adds some important pieces of information to the above, as follows:

'From there [*Thrace*] he [*Gordian III*] continued to Syria and advanced to Antioch, which was then in Persian hands. Here he engaged the enemy in several battles and drove out Sapor the Persian king. [*This is confirmed by Festus (22.2) and Eutropius (9.2) who also refer to several battles won by Gordian III against the Persians. This suggests that there were several battles before the decisive battle at Resaina. This is something one would expect. The Persian cavalry would have harassed the Romans from the moment they reached the vicinity of Antioch and they would have continued this up to Resaina where they had assembled their main army in readiness to engage the by then weakened Romans. The decisive battle, however, did not end as the Persians expected*] After this he regained the possession the cities of Artaxerxes, [*This is confusion of the death of the founder of the Sassanian dynasty Artaxerxes/Ardashir with the name of a city. However, it is also possible that the Persians had renamed one of the conquered cities in honour of the founding father so that there really was a city called Artaxerxes at the time. It is impossible to know what city Julius meant, but on the basis of the order of the names it was clearly en route from the Cilician Gates to Antioch.*] Antioch, Carrhae, and Nisibis that had been parts of the Persian Empire. Indeed the King of Persia became so frightened of the power of the Emperor Gordianus that though he was provided with great forces both from his own lands and ours, he voluntarily withdrew his garrisons from our cities and left them to their inhabitants intact; nor did he plunder them [*This means that the Persians fled very fast after their defeat at Resaina. Although, it is possible that they did not plunder the cities for another reason which is that they intended to return*]. All this was accomplished by Timesitheus, the Father-in-Law and Prefect of Gordianus. In fine, the Persians who had made themselves feared even in Italy retired back to their own kingdom as a result of Gordianus's campaign, and all the East submitted to the obedience of the Roman Empire. ... The account sent by Gordianus himself to the Senate of this expedition thanks his Prefect and Father-in-Law Timesitheus thus... "Fathers of the Senate, To add to the victories which we obtained in our passage into the east, which each merits a triumph, we have delivered the necks of the Antiochians from the Persian yoke and have removed from them the kings and laws of Persia [*The Romans saw the Persian way of life, which was based on the strict observance of Zoroastrian laws, as oppressive*[45]]. We have reconquered Carrhae and other cities to the Roman Empire, and we have come up to Nisibis; and if the gods favour us, we shall proceed further to Ctesiphon. I pray for the good health of Timesitheus, my Father-in-Law and my Prefect of the Guard, by whose conduct and leadership we have achieved these and we hope to finish the rest also. It is for you to decree thanksgivings and to recommend us to the gods and to give thanks to Timesitheus." When this was read in the Senate, they decreed to Gordianus chariots drawn by four elephants ... and to Timesitheus a chariot with six horses.' Julius Capitolinus, *HA Gord.* 26.5–27.10., tr. by Bernard p.64–5 with changes, corrections, additions and comments.

The principal addition of Julius Capitolinus to the version presented by modern research is his statement that the Romans and Persians fought several battles and not only the one battle at Resaina in 243. As noted above in the comments, this is to be expected. The Persians harassed the advancing Romans with their cavalry until they reached the neighbourhood of Resaina. This delay was necessary also because Sapor was not on the scene when the Romans reached Asia thanks to the fact that after the death of his father he had needed to obtain the support of the magnates and people for his rule. The battles before the main battle near Resaina therefore consisted of cavalry skirmishes, the idea of which was to weaken and demoralize the Romans before the decisive battle.

None of the sources – Ammianus Marcellinus (23.5.7), who is the only one to mention the battle of Resaina by name, or Julius Capitolinus – give us any details of this decisive encounter beyond the fact that the Persians were commanded by Sapor I and that the Romans routed the Persians. There are basically two ways the period Romans could have fought against the Persians: 1) The Marathon manner in which the frontline consisted of the cavalry outer wings, hoplite flanks and legionary centre with reserves posted behind; 2) The hollow infantry oblong/square with cavalry posted outside. Both are plausible.

There are two reasons why the Marathon tactic could have been successful against the Persians: Firstly, the Persian army was exceptionally static because it included infantry that had been used both during the sieges and as garrison forces. Secondly, the Persian king of kings had decided to fight a decisive battle. The fact that the Persians would have had infantry behind their cavalry means that it was possible for the Roman cavalry wings to tie the Persian flanks in place until the Roman hoplites on the flanks reached the Persian lines, followed soon after this by the legionary centre. The infantry charge forward would have consisted of jogging and running, depending on the enemy archery: If the volley of arrows was approaching, then the men ran forward to be inside the arc and if the volley had not been shot or was still far away the men jogged or walked depending on the distance to be covered. This tactic enabled the Romans to reach the Persian cavalry relatively intact because the Persian cavalry could not retreat and avoid contact; if it did, they only retreated behind their own infantry that then enabled the Romans to attack the Persian infantry forces and camp where the cavalry would be regrouping. I suspect that this is what happened and was the reason for the Persian defeat. The Persian cavalry could not exploit their speed and mobility and ability to flee when their infantry forces were present on the battlefield. However, it should be noted that the Romans could have exploited the same tactical advantage even if they had deployed their infantry as a hollow oblong/square because one of the standard offensive tactics with the square array was to send the front portion forward to assist the cavalry against the enemy. This would have resulted in similar situation as the above when the Persian cavalry could not continue its retreat in nomadic manner.[46] Readers, however, are advised that the above is pure speculation based only on known combat tactics.

The next stage in Roman plans was to continue the campaign along the Euphrates up to Ctesiphon, but it was not fated that Timesitheus would lead it. The most detailed account of this comes once again from the pen of Julius Capitolinus, but it misses important references to a battle fought at Mesikhe for which there is evidence in the *SKZ* of Sapor I and indirectly in the texts of John of Antioch, Malalas, Syncellus, Festus, Aurelius Victor, Jerome, Georgius Monachus, Cedrenus and Zonaras. This question is given greater attention right after the quote.[47]

'But this felicity did not continue long. Most say that Timesitheus died through the plotting of Philip, who was made Praetorian Prefect after him, but some say that he died as a result of sickness… So advantageous had been the ministry of this great man that there was no frontier city of major size that had not been furnished with stores of provisions consisting of cheap wine, grain, bacon, barley and straw for a year. Lesser towns had stores some thirty, some for forty days and some for two months, and even the least had been provided with supplies for fifteen days. When he was the Praetorian Prefect, he continually examined the arms of the soldiers. He never allowed an old man to remain in service. He inspected the camps and their trenches himself and he frequently visited the sentries during the night. All loved him because he was so equal a friend to both the Emperor and the Empire. The tribunes and *duces* had such regard for him that they never failed in their duties before him nor disputed his orders. [*The successes achieved prove this to be correct. Timesitheus was clearly respected for his great skills and possessed the authority to have his orders obeyed.*] Philip, who succeeded him in his place as Praetorian Prefect, for some reasons feared him and it was this anxiety that caused him to plot with doctors against his life. He achieved this in the following manner: Timesitheus was suffering from diarrhoea and the doctors ordered him to take a potion to stop it. And, they say that the doctors changed the dose and gave him something that increased the flux to such a degree that he died. [*This account has usually been suspected as hostile innuendo against Philip after the fact, because diarrhoea is one of the typical illnesses in that area, indeed it is the most typical illness for all soldiers in all places. But if Philip was indeed the culprit, then the reason for his fear might have been that Timesitheus had suspected him of corruption and/or of Christian sympathies.*]

After the death, which happened under the consulship of Arrianus and Pappus [in 243], Philip the Arab was made Praetorian Prefect in his place. A low-born man, but proud and arrogant and not able to contain himself in so sudden a rise to office and excessively good fortune, he soon began to form designs to turn the soldiers against Gordian… He did this in the following manner… Timesitheus had stored up vast quantities of supplies everywhere… but Philip brought the army into places where there were no provisions [*He marched the Roman army northwards on the eastern side of the Euphrates where there were no magazines of supplies, because this area was officially considered a part of Persia. On the opposite western shore from the city of Dura Europos northwards, the Roman army would have been on Roman soil with its magazines full of supplies*], … and he diverted away the grain-ships. [*In other words, Philip prevented the ships from bringing supplies to the army which was on the eastern side of the river. The defeat at Mesikhe (see later) was by no means a decisive major defeat as it has sometimes been claimed to have been on the basis of Sapor I's propaganda statement, and the retreat away from the Persian territory was not difficult – the Persian cavalry was completely impotent to oppose the retreat of the Roman infantry in a situation in which the Romans had enough supplies left. The Roman army was suffering from lack of victuals only because of Philip's personal ambitions.*] This he did to make the soldiers hostile towards Gordianus… Philip added yet to their resentment and caused a rumour to be spread that Gordianus being so very young was not a person of sufficient ability to govern the Empire… He corrupted the *principes* [*leaders of the army*], … till at last they openly demanded that Philip be made Emperor, which the friends of Gordianus immediately opposed vigorously, but when the army was in a condition of starving for want of provisions, the Empire was entrusted to Philip, and it was agreed that he should reign together with Gordianus, and should be as if he were the guardian of the young prince. Philip… began to act very arrogantly towards Gordianus… so he [*Gordianus III*] assembled in the presence of Maecius Gordianus, his kinsman and Praetorian Prefect, [*otherwise unknown but not necessarily fictitious because Gordian III would surely have wanted a new Prefect in this situation*] the officers and soldiers of the army together and complained to them… he achieved nothing. Next he asked the soldiers to choose between them, but Philip prevailed by intriguing so that Gordian came second in the vote. Then he offered to be content with the office of *Caesar*. This was also denied. Then he asked to be Prefect of Philip. But this was also denied. His last prayer was his life as a *dux* in Philip's service. Philip had almost consented to this… but when he considered the affection which the Senate and People of Rome, the whole of Africa and Syria, and indeed the whole Empire felt for Gordianus, … he thought that it could one day happen that the army… might fancy to reintroduce him again… and therefore he ordered him to be carried out of sight (Gordianus crying as he went) and to be disrobed of purple and killed… Thus by blood and not by right did the Emperor Philip raise himself. In the meantime, Argaithus, King of the Scythians [*i.e. Goths*], ravaged the kingdoms adjoining him, unto which he was encouraged especially by the death of Timesitheus by whose counsels the Empire had been so well governed [*This means that the Goths had attacked Roman client kingdoms, but not actual Roman territories yet, which took place only now under Philip's reign, as we shall see*]. Philip, willing to conceal the circumstances of his rise to power by bloody means, sent a letter to Rome with a quite different account in which he said that Gordianus had died of a sickness and that as for himself the army had elected him Emperor. The Senate was easily deceived… They accepted and proclaimed Philip Emperor [*Probably the sickness of Gordian to which Philip was referring means the falling from the horse and crushing of the thigh that Zonaras, Cedrenus, Georgius Monachus and Malalas claim killed Gordian. It is clear that this was only an excuse meant to fool the Senate, as is stated here. The real culprit for the killing of Gordian was undoubtedly Philip, as claimed by Julius Capitolinus, Aurelius Victor, Ammianus Marcellinus, Eutropius, Festus, Epitome de Caesaribus, Syncellus, John of Antioch, Jordanes and by one version of Zonaras.*[48] *As we shall see, the version put forth by Philip was probably not accepted quite as easily as stated by Julius Capitolinus or by Eis Basilea 5–6.*]. Julius Capitolinus, *HA Gord.* 28.1ff., tr. by Bernard p.65ff. with changes, corrections, additions and comments.

According Zosimus (1.17.2), Timesitheus was renowned for his learning. John Marvin York (p.12) has also suggested that the reason Julius Capitolinus mistakenly calls Timesitheus with the name Misitheus has resulted from the existence of a hostile version of Timesitheus's career (likely to date from the reign of Philip the Arab) because it is clearly a corruption of the Greek *misotheos*, which means 'God-hater', godless, hating the gods. When these pieces of information are combined with the fact that the famous neo-Platonist Plotinus was accompanying the expedition (Porphyry 3), it is quite possible to think that Timesitheus was also a neo-Platonist and that the above-mentioned consultation of the Sibylline Books and the halting of worldwide evil should be interpreted as measures taken against Christians by the 'God-hater' Timesitheus. In fact, the persecution of Christians under Gordian III is confirmed by both Cedrenus and Scutariotes who state that Leonides was martyred under him.[49] It is very likely that this persecution started when the learned Timesitheus took the reins of power. The persecution, however, was not severe because Julius Africanus and many other Christians still prospered under Gordian III, but this does not mean that Christians like Philip (probably a closet Christian at that time) would not have reason to fear. The key piece of information in Porphyry regarding the conspiracy of Philip is that when Gordian was killed in Mesopotamia, Plotinus was able to save himself only with great difficulty by fleeing to Antioch. This suggests that Plotinus had been attached to the imperial retinue of Gordian III probably by the learned Timesitheus so that the flight of Plotinus had been caused by very real fears when a Christian took the throne.

Porphyry's biography of Plotinus is also valuable for another reason. According to him, Plotinus had been eager to learn the Persian and Indian philosophies and so joined the army at the age of 38 years. This suggests that the strategy that Timesitheus and

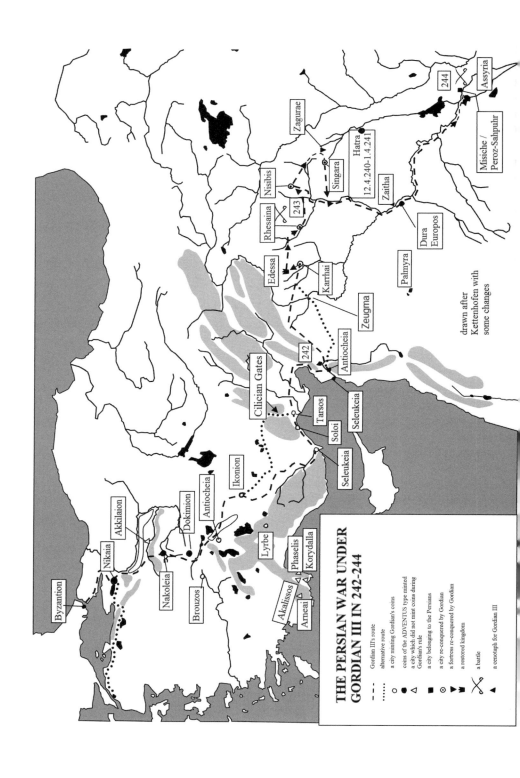

THE PERSIAN WAR UNDER
GORDIAN III IN 242-244

- - -   Gordian III's route
· · · · · alternative route
○   a city minting Gordian's coins
● ◁   coins of the ADVENTUS type minted
△   a city which did not mint coins during
        Gordian's rule
■   a city belonging to the Persians
⊙   a city re-conquered by Gordian
▶   a fortress re-conquered by Gordian
▲   a restored kingdom
✗   a battle
▲   a cenotaph for Gordian III

Byzantion

Nikaia

Akkilaion

Nakoleia

Dokimion

Antiocheia

Brouzos

Ikomion

Lyrbe

Akalissos

Arneai   Phaselis

Korydalla

Cilician Gates

Tarsos

Soloi

Seleukeia

Seleukeia

242

Antiocheia

Zeugma

Edessa

Karrhai

243

Rhesaina

Nisibis

Zagurae

Singara

Hatra
12.4.240-1.4.241

Zaitha

Dura
Europos

Palmyra

244

Misiche /
Peroz-Sahpuhr

Assyria

drawn after
Kettenhofen with
some changes

Gordian III adopted towards Persia was nothing less than the conquest of the entire Persian Empire in the manner of Alexander the Great. In other words, they followed in the footsteps of practically all Roman emperors who sought to make war against Persia – worship of Alexander the Great was alive and well. As noted above, this suggests the raising of new units and legions and not only the addition of barbarian *foederati* like Goths and Germans.

In sum, Julius Capitolinus claims Philip the Arab was in great fear of Timesitheus and therefore plotted to kill him. This has been doubted for good reasons because diarrhoea was and is certainly a very typical problem for persons not accustomed to the local water and food and secondly because in light of the subsequent plotting against Gordian it is easy to accuse Philip of similar activities before this.[50] There is no way of knowing for certain whether the story is true, but if we assume that it is, then it would imply that Philip the Arab, and probably also his brother Priscus, who was the junior Praetorian Prefect, were constantly in fear of their lives either because they were guilty of corruption and/or because they were closet Christians.[51] Zosimus (1.18.3) confirms that Philip had achieved his position by dishonourable means.

In sum, I find Julius Capitolinus's claims plausible enough to accept because the Christian Philip had very real reasons to be afraid. Philip and Priscus, however, were lucky. When the Romans reached Nisibis, Timesitheus started to suffer from diarrhoea and it was this that gave Philip the chance he had been waiting for. Timesitheus was told by his doctors to take a potion as medicine. Doctors of the time quite often came from the Greek-speaking East, and it is possible that they were also closet Christians, which might have made them easy to bribe. The doctors then, it is said, changed the potion, Timesitheus duly died, and Philip was chosen as his replacement, probably as a result of his brother's recommendation.

However, it is possible to suspect this account. How would Julius Capitolinus have known these facts? It is impossible to answer this conclusively. But the circumstances certainly support the claim that Philip was behind the death of Timesitheus. As a closet Christian Philip would have had reason to fear Timesitheus, and the end result does have the earmarks of two brothers plotting to increase their power. Philip's brother Priscus, as sole Praetorian Prefect, was in a position to prevent a thorough investigation of the cause of Timesitheus's death, which after all looked natural, and he was influential enough to have his brother nominated as co-prefect.

If we identify the Emperor in the anonymous *Eis Basilea* (*To the Emperor*) with Philip the Arab, it is possible that Philip and his brother purged the administration immediately. This text was previously mistakenly included in the corpus of Aelius Aristides, but it is now recognized that the author is anonymous. Historians have not found a consensus of who the dedicatee of this text is; it has been suggested that he is Antoninus Pius, Marcus Aurelius, Commodus, Macrinus, Philip the Arab or Gallienus. Most, however, consider the dedicatee to have been Philip the Arab and I agree with this view.[52] This text (13) states that when the ruler (i.e. Philip) became associated with imperial duties as an official of the Emperor, he recognized that 'many functions of the imperial service were not being decently or conscientiously administered but that a great deal of stubbornness, arrogance and lack of discipline had arisen… he did not permit the situation to continue or grow worse. Instead, like a physician healing the sores and ills of a huge, sick body, or like a rider attempting to control the wildness and recalcitrance of a strong and difficult horse… he again and again restrains and checks, he worked on the realm effectively with an eye to its interests. Such, then was the sort of man he was before he ruled.'[53] This suggests two things. Firstly, Philip and his brother apparently accused the members of the previous administration of incompetence and replaced them with their own men and thereby removed Timesitheus's men from all positions of importance. On the other hand, the restraining of the difficult and impulsive horse can be seen to imply the restraining of the eagerness of the young Gordian, who as we shall see appears to have been far too eager to lead cavalry charges against the enemy. It is also quite probable that Philip purposely delayed the beginning of the campaign to the onset of winter in 243 because the mostly European soldiers of the Roman army fought better during that season.

The Battle of Mesikhe in February and the murder of Gordian III in about early March 244
The details of what happened when Gordian and Philip the Arab then led the Roman army south along the Euphrates against the Persian capital Ctesiphon are shrouded in mystery. What we know is that the Roman army advanced downstream along the river without any significant opposition until they reached the city of Mesikhe. It is probable that the Persians scorched the earth. Then, according to Sapor's inscription *SKZ*, he defeated and killed Gordian, and annihilated the Roman army in a great battle. The claims of Sapor can easily be shown to be false.[54] The Emperor did not die there, and Sapor definitely did not annihilate the Roman army. But Mesikhe was the furthest limit of the Roman advance, which means that Sapor did effectively stop the Roman onslaught, and achieved enough of a victory to name the city Peroz-Sapor (victorious Sapor) with some justification, but the victory was not quite of the magnitude claimed by him. Some of the sources[55] claim that Gordian drove his horse forward in battle to exhort his men, and that his horse stumbled and fell on him, crushing his thigh, and he died as a result. It is possible that the Emperor may indeed have been injured in the course of the battle, but he did not die as a result of this. He died later as a result of a plot by Philip the Arab.[56]

   None of the sources give any specific information of how the two sides fought at the decisive battle of Mesikhe beyond the statements that the Romans lost, Gordian probably fell from his horse and was injured, and that Philip the Arab apparently saved the army through his actions, if the anonymous *Eis Basilea* (*To the Emperor, The Encomium of Philip the Arab*), which has been falsely attributed to Aelius Aristides, can be used as evidence of this. Its sections 13–15 are used to shed light on this battle, namely the following quotes. Translations of all the other sources except the Anonymous are by Dodgeon and Lieu (REF1, pp. 43–4); the translation of the Anonymous 14–5 is by Swift (p.275–6). I have added comments inside parentheses.

   Malalas apud Synopsis Sathas: 'He [*Gordian III*] in the battle against the Persians was brought down from his horse and crushed his thigh. On his return to Rome, he died from it (i.e. the wound) in his fiftieth year.' [*This is a mistake. The age is wrong in addition to which modern historians have recognized for a long time that it is probable that the death resulting from the fall of the horse is likely to have come from the report that Philip sent to the Senate. For this, see REF1, p.357 n.23*]

Syncellus: 'Gordian… afterwards routed Shapur, the king of the Persians and the son of Ardashir, in battle and brought Nisibis and Carrhae under subjection… But as he was approaching Ctesiphon, he was murdered by his own troops at the instigation of the Prefect Philip.'

Cedrenus: 'He [Gordian III] died after falling from his horse and crushing his thigh.'

First version of Zonaras: 'They wrote that he [*Gordian III*] campaigned against the Persians and fell in with them. He drove his horse forward in battle, exhorting his men and stirring them to feats of courage. The horse stumbled and fell on him, crushing his thigh. [*This suggests that Gordian III led a cavalry charge in person, which failed possibly because his horse stumbled*] He therefore returned to Rome and died from the fracture after a reign of six years.'

Second version of Zonaras: 'He [*Gordian III*] marched against the Persians and joined with them in battle…. He vanquished his foes and recaptured Nisibis and Carrhae… Then while on his way to Ctesiphon, he was murdered through the treachery of Philip, the Praetorian Prefect… Scheming to provoke the soldiers to revolt, he reduced the food-provisions of the soldiers, giving the impression that this was at the command of the emperor. Some say that he (Philip) withheld the corn which was being conducted to the camp so that the soldiers would be oppressed by shortages and they would then be roused to mutiny.'

The anononymous Eis Basilea 14–15: 'When all mankind had been set in motion and, … was on the move to another land [*This refers to the invasion of Persian territory*]; when the empire was tossing as in a great storm or earthquake and then foundering like a ship being carried off to the ends of the earth where governors and kings had previously gone astray and had finally given up after they encountered, as in a labyrinth, many grievous difficulties and were cut off from the road back, unable to return, he it was who, seeing all this, did not like an unskilled pilot, permit the Empire… to run her dangerous course. [*This refers to the stage in the campaign in which the Romans had reached the area near Mesikhe and Ctesiphon where the canals formed a labyrinth. It also implies that the Persians had probably opened their sluices so that the Romans had become isolated and that the Persians had also posted their army behind the Romans thereby blocking their route of retreat*] Rather, as the most experienced of emperors and one of superior intelligence, he first checked and stopped the headlong rush in that direction, then brought her back and secured her at anchor. [*This suggests that Gordian probably led an impetious cavalry charge against the Persian army and that Philip then saved the day after Gordian's cavalry charge had failed, and that he also convinced Gordian to abandon his plan to continue the march towards Ctesiphon*] And, now, like a ship surviving a violent storm, the state lies at anchor in the greatest safety while he conducts and manages the affairs of the Empire in a way… not only reverent towards the gods and just towards men, but who possesses temperance, self-control, prudence and all other virtues.'

Battle of Mesikhe in 244
(probable battle formations)

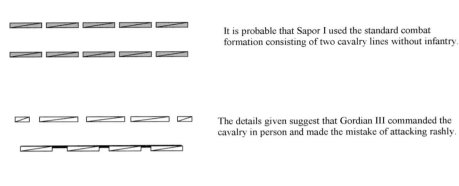

It is probable that Sapor I used the standard combat formation consisting of two cavalry lines without infantry.

The details given suggest that Gordian III commanded the cavalry in person and made the mistake of attacking rashly.

Roman baggage train

The fact that Philip the Arab saved the day suggests that he commanded infantry which was probably deployed as a hollow oblong to protect the baggage train and footmen.

When the above information is combined with the other sources, and with terrain and military probability, we can arrive at a likely course of events, but which, it should be warned, is still only my best educated guess based on period combat tactics. When the Romans reached the neighbourhood of Mesikhe in early 244, they faced a labyrinth of canals, and their route of retreat was probably blocked by two things. Firstly, that the Persians opened their sluices and isolated the Roman army in the maze of canals and flooded terrain. Secondly, that the Persians placed their cavalry army behind the Romans and blocked their route of retreat. Gordian III then led an impetious cavalry attack against the Persians in the course of which his horse fell and he fractured his thigh. It is possible that the defeat of the Roman cavalry attack resulted from this fall, but it is possible that it would have been defeated anyway, because the Persians had chosen the battlefield. The situation was then saved by the steady hand of Philip the Arab, but he was not able to defeat the enemy like Timesitheus had done at Philippi in 242. It is probable that he was in charge of the infantry, which would probably have been deployed as a hollow oblong/square for marching. The fleeing Roman cavalry was received inside the hollow oblong/square and the steadiness of the Roman infantry made it impossible for the Persians to achieve anything. This may have been similar to what happened in the fields of Philippi in 242. It is unlikely that the 'Roman hoplites' would have had any special role in this battle. Now Philip managed to convince the impetuous young Emperor to abandon his rash plan to continue the march to Ctesiphon, which the Romans could undoubtedly have achieved, but only with the result of making their situation quite hopeless, in the same manner as Julian did in 363. It would have been impossible for the Romans to besiege Ctesiphon in the presence of the Royal Persian Army. Had the Romans tried this, they would have been annihilated. The accounts of *Eis Basilea* and Julius Capitolinus suggest that Philip the Arab became a co-emperor of Gordian III soon after the disaster at Mesikhe, which would have shown the soldiers that Gordian was young and rash and would need the steady guidance of Philip to lead them.

It was during the retreat that Gordian III was killed as a result of the plot of Philip the Arab. Julius Capitolinus and Zonaras claim that Philip directed the grain ships with their provisions away from the marching army and that Philip lowered their food rations. Zosimus (see below) states that when the Emperor with the army was near Carrhae and Nisibis, Philip directed the ships further inland so that the army would be oppressed by hunger and be therefore easily provoked to mutiny. The implication is that this was done when the army had already retreated to Roman territory or was close to it. The fact that the tomb of Gordian is located at Zaitha means that the Romans were back in their own territory because the city of Dura Europos was located south of it.[57] The opposite shore where Zaitha was located was obviously considered Persian territory, but in practice it was not really controlled by the Persians. The reason for this was that with their navy the Romans controlled the River Euphrates up to Dura Europos so it is clear that Philip could have easily brought supplies for the Roman army had he so wished. It is unlikely to be a coincidence that the abovementioned temporary *praepositus* of the Praetorian Fleets C. Iulius Alexander was rewarded with the permanent command of the Fleet of Misenum as its Prefect by Philip after this (attested in this position in 246) and I would suggest that Alexander's successor as its Prefect Aelius Aemilianus (in 247) could also have taken part in the plot.[58] It is likely that this Alexander was in charge of all naval operations during the eastern campaign and was the man who directed the ships away from the army as instructed. One wonders if this C. Iulius Alexander was related to the brothers M. Iulius Philippus and C. Iulius Priscus? Philip had kept the Roman army on the eastern side of the River Euphrates, which did not have Roman magazines full of supplies – but there would have been magazines full of supplies on the opposite side of the river because it belonged to the Roman Empire. In light of the evidence, it is very likely that Philip directed the Roman ships somewhere else so that the Roman army would start to suffer from famine. This would have worked especially well if the Roman army was already suffering from food shortages as a result of the opening of the canal sluices by the Persians and as a result of their scorched-earth tactics. It was this that Philip exploited. He prevented the arrival of further supplies, and blamed Gordian. Philip also spread rumours that Gordian was too young and inexperienced to lead the Empire, which was confirmed by his recent defeat and now by the lack of provisions. What was needed was a seasoned and experienced man who could rule with skill. With these measures and well-placed bribes he won both the officers and the men over to his side. They then demanded that Philip be made co-emperor with Gordian, which Gordian was forced to accept, but this was only the first stage in Philip's plan.

There were probably two reasons why Philip was chosen as Emperor instead of his probably older brother Priscus: The usual assumption is that Philip had a son while Priscus probably did not. However, Zahran has noted that this conclusion may be wrong because an inscription in Philippopolis suggests that Priscus may have had a son. She suggests that the reason for the choice of Philip was that he was known for his moderation while Priscus was known to be strict. The second reason would have been that it had been Philip who had fraternized with the soldiers and officers so it was he that they favoured. John Marvin York has suggested that Philip may have had a better claim to the throne thanks to his marriage to a woman called Marcia Otacilia Severa whose name may imply a connection with the Severan family, but other historians disagree. Bowersock claims that the *cognomen* Severa implies that she must have come from a family of Arabs that had been favoured by Septimius Severus while Körner quite correctly suggests that the name of her father or brother was Severianus, and indeed this Severianus was later appointed vice-regent of the Balkans by Philip. Philip would have married Otacilia probably in the 230s and their son Marcus Iulius Severus Philippus (Philip Jr.) was probably born in about 236–38.[59]

When Philip started to treat Gordian arrogantly, Gordian attempted to convince the soldiers to choose him, but the disastrous conduct of the war and the dearth of supplies had made the soldiers resentful towards him, so that this attempt ended only in his death. On the basis of *Eis Basilea*, it is clear that the two brothers had already placed their own men in all of the important positions in 243 so it is not surprising that they were in full control of events. Philip and Priscus were clearly superb plotters and schemers. The murder of Gordian took place after 13 January 244, but before 14 March 244 because the *Codex Iustinianus* names Philip as the Emperor for the latter date but not for the former. This means that it took place probably in late February or early March 244, the latter being the usual assumption.[60]

Potter (236) is completely wrong to think that it would be odd if the campaign had taken place in the rainy season. Firstly, the mostly European soldiers suffered less from this than from the heat of the summer. Secondly, the Romans possessed a fleet so they were able to cross the Euphrates and other rivers at will. Thirdly, and possibly most importantly, the rain weakened the glue of the composite bows and made the Persian archery less effective against the Romans. In sum, the timing of the campaign to the winter was well chosen and shows that the staff in charge of advicing the young Gordian III was up to its task. It is very probable that Gordian III's principal advisor was none other than Philip the Arab, but it is possible or even probable that the plan had already been made when Timesitheus was in charge.

The same events are described by Zosimus as follows. He adds the obvious piece of information missing from the above, which was that Philip bribed the soldiers handsomely to secure his position:

'Philip was a native of Arabia, a nation in bad repute, [*The sources are very biased against Philip and the Arabs in general, but the actions of Philip certainly contributed to such views. Note, however, that, his ambitions and actions were not really that different from the actions of all usurpers*] and had advanced his fortune by no very honourable means [*This implies corruption*]. As soon as he was fixed in his office, he aspired at the imperial dignity, and endeavoured to seduce all the soldiers that were well disposed to innovation. Observing that abundance of military provisions was supplied, while the emperor was staying about Carrhae and Nisibis, he ordered the ships that brought those provisions to go further up in the country, in order that the army, being oppressed with famine, might be provoked to mutiny. His design succeeded… He therefore made peace with Sapores [*Sapor I*], and marched towards Rome; and as he had bound the soldiers to him by large presents [*This means the standard bribes in the form of a donativum*], he sent messengers to Rome to report that Gordianus had died of a disease [*i.e. of the fall from the horse that broke his thigh*].' Zosimus 1.18.3–19.1, tr. anon 1814, p.13 with changes, corrections and comments.

According to Julius Capitolinus (*HA Gord.* 33.4–5), Philip and his brother Priscus had nine important accomplices in the murder of Gordian, all of whom participated actively in the killing by using their swords – the fact that all nine used their swords against Gordian III made them equally guilty and therefore loyal to each other. This lends credence to the story because it is something that one would expect to happen in such circumstances. Capitolinus claims that after the two Philippi had died, all of them killed themselves using the very same swords that they had used in the killing of Gordian. This could of course be thought of as a borrowing from the fate of the murderers of Julius Caesar, but as such it is not at all improbable. It is entirely plausible to think that the men who had participated the murder of Gordian chose to kill themselves rather than be subjected to the treatment that awaited them after the Philippi had died.

The murder of Gordian was initially hidden from the Senate by Philip. He claimed that Gordian had died as a result of illness, namely from the fall from the horse that had broken his thigh, and that the army had chosen him, Philip, as Emperor. According to Julius Capitolinus, he did this to obtain the acceptance of the Senate and the Senate was deceived by these words and confirmed his accession to power. Philip knew what had happened in 238 and wanted to make his accession secure. It was also important for him to maintain his claim to be a legitimate successor of Gordian, so he demanded that the Senate deify Gordian. However, the later 'Byzantine' sources have preserved an alternative account of the very beginning of Philip's rule, which we shall treat later in its proper place. There were those who opposed the rise of Philip.

After the death of Gordian, Philip and the soldiers then raised a tomb in honour of Gordian III. This tomb was located at Zaitha and it had the abovementioned commemoration if we are to believe Julius Capitolinus, and in light of the typical jesting of the Roman soldiers it is entirely possible that the tomb did indeed carry that text. The ashes of Gordian were taken to Rome.

6.4 Gordian III as Emperor

From the point of view of the Senate and Roman populace the reign of Gordian III had marked a return to normalcy that had prevailed under Alexander Severus, but its achievements were still modest. Because he was young Gordian III was quite ineffectual as emperor. He was under the guidance of his mother and eunuchs for the first three years, 238 until 241, after that he was under the guidance of his father-in-law Praetorian Prefect Timesitheus until Timesitheus's death in 243, and after that he was under the guidance of Philip the Arab.

Xavier Loriot's assement of the six years of Gordian's rule is to the point. Excluding the foreign wars of the latter half, he is correct to state that it marked a period of relative calm within the Roman Empire. The administration managed to bring calm after the tumultaneous years of 235–38. The army and Senate were both satisfied with their position and Timesitheus restored imperial authority back to where it belonged, namely to the ruler. The imperial administration also showed concern for the wellbeing of its subjects. The short reign saw a massive increase in the number of laws which restored the traditionalist institutions and abolished the abuses that had marked the reign of Maximinus Thrax. However, Loriot's view of the state of the army under Gordian III is bleak. The mediocrity of its commanders, to which he refers, was primarily caused by decisions made on the basis of political expediency. There was one significant exception, as Loriot notes: Timesitheus, who showed great talent both in the fields of logistics and combat. Loriot is quite correct to compare him with Corbulo and Avidius Cassius.[61] There was always talent present, but as in all armed forces, it was far more typical for those in power to promote mediocre but loyal men rather than take the risk of promoting talented persons who could then usurp power. This problem had been present ever since the first century AD, so it was not a new phenomenon and there is no reason to accuse solely the administration of Gordian for its failings.

1. A coin of Gordian III celebrating his generosity to the people.
2. Gordian III addressing the troops. Note the rectangular and six-sided shields, which can also be found from the Ludovisi Sarcophagus and Dura Europos paintings.
3. Gordian III crossing from Europe to Asia.
4. Gordian III's coin celebrating his 'virtus'. Note the round 'hoplite' shield.
Source of the images: Cohen

The politically expedient but poorly made appointments to the important military commands during Gordian's first three years in conjunction with the massive earthquake of 241 led to serious troubles in the East, and the removal of Menophilus from office in the Balkans caused additional troubles there. All of these the able Timesitheus corrected before his death, but the campaign that Gordian III and Philip led against Persia ran into insurmountable problems, and to Gordian's death thanks to the plotting of Philip. It was left for Philip to save the Roman army and the situation. This was something that he wished for and was also capable of delivering, unlike the young and rash Gordian. The only personal contribution of Gordian to the wars fought appears to have been to lead two unsuccessful cavalry charges, that required the intervention of Timesitheus in the fields of Philippi and the intervention of Philip the Arab at Mesikhe. Gordian III was no Alexander the Great who demonstrated his great military talents at the age of eighteen in the battle of Chaeronea in 338 BC. The Roman Empire was certainly in steadier hands under Philip than it had been under Gordian III. Regardless, it is one of history's what ifs: what if Timesitheus or Gordian III had been allowed to live longer? It is quite possible that the Romans would have fared far better than they did. Philip, however, was still far more competent as a ruler than the young Gordian was. Gordian III was a dutiful brave youth who could have become a great Emperor, but this is something that we shall never know, thanks to the personal ambitions of Philip the Arab and his brother Priscus.

Left: Young Gordian III.   **Right:** Philip the Arab
Drawings by Piranesi

Chapter Seven

Philip the Arab, the First Christian Emperor
(March 244–August/September 249)

| Philip the Arab Sr. according to Duruy | Philip the Arab Jr. according to Duruy |

The reign of Philip the Arab is among the least known of the important reigns of the third century. This results, funnily enough, from the fact that we no longer possess the information provided by the *Historia Augusta* because there is a lacuna at this point that covers the reigns of Philip, Decius and most of the reign of Valerian. All that we have are some scattered and all-too-often contradictory and irreconcilable short references in period or later sources and in coins, papyri and inscriptions. Readers are therefore advised to keep in mind that the following discussion is based on very meagre sources, but I will note these difficulties in the text by including quotations from the sources with their problems.

7.1 Securing the Throne and the Troubled Frontiers in 244

The most immediate problem facing Philip the Arab after his accession was how to secure his acceptance as Emperor both in the East and West. He needed to quickly conclude a truce/peace with Persia while still retaining his credibility so that he could march to Rome to secure his and his son's accession to power.

Peace with Persia in 244
Philip's negotiating position vis-à-vis Sapor I was actually not bad because by the time of Gordian's death the Roman army was already in the area controlled by the Roman navy and hence safe from any Persian attempts to harass it. This is confirmed by Eutropius (9.3) who states that Philip brought the army safely to Roman territory. It is clear that Philip was eager to end the war as fast as possible. He may have begun negotiations before he crossed into Roman territory proper which took place when the army reached the official border at Circesium before 14 March 244.[1] The sources give us two different versions of the terms and what Philip then did. Some of the Roman sources claim that Philip the Arab concluded a shameful peace and handed Mesopotamia and Armenia over to the Persians; other sources claim that he handed over to the Persians only those parts of Armenia that belonged to the independent Armenia ruled by Khosrov the Great. The sources such as Zonaras which claim that Philip handed over Mesopotamia are surely wrong because it is clear that Rome kept Timesitheus's reconquests, Oshroene and Mesopotamia, unless of course Philip promised these areas but never delivered his promise. The cities of Edessa, Resaina and Nisibis struck coins in the name of Philip and his successor Decius so this is certain not to mention the fact that Philip's brother Priscus held the office of governor of Mesopotamia afterwards.[2] Sapor's *SKZ* states that Philip sued for peace and paid a ransom of 500,000 *denarii* to Persia and became a tributary nation with the implication that Philip may have promised to pay a yearly tribute.

A ransom was paid for the release of the Roman captives.[3] Mireille Corbier (p.357) has calculated that 500,000 *denarii*, equal to 10,000 lbs of gold, was to be paid for the release of the captives. This would seem a large sum of money; however, it needs to be put in context. According to a fragment of Olympiodorus (frg. 41.2, Blockley ed.), many of the fifth-century senatorial families had yearly incomes of 4,000 lbs of gold, plus produce with a market value of 1,320 lbs of gold, so it is clear that the Emperor was able to pay this amount of money without undue difficulties. The sum was huge for the Persians, but not for the Romans. Furthermore, the return of their comrades pleased the soldiers.

In other words, if the terms of the truce/peace did not include Mesopotamia, but only that part of Armenia which did not belong to Rome, Philip could justifiably claim that he did not cede any Roman territory to the Persians and actually returned as a victor from the campaign because the Romans had previously reconquered all the lands lost in 240–42. However, as will be made clear below, if Philip did promise to hand over Mesopotamia, he did not keep his word – his intention was just to fool Sapor to gain time, and in this he succeeded. It is clear that Philip had been less than honest in all of his dealings with Sapor. Whatever the terms were, Sapor I was happy with the result. After all, he had been worsted quite badly before he had been able to save the situation at Mesikhe. It was in his interest to have the Romans away from his lands. The terms promised were more than enough to satisfy the Persians, but Armenia was an independent kingdom and it was not for the Romans to promise it to the Persians.

On the basis of the accounts of *Oracula Sibyllina*, Zonaras and *SKZ* we know that Philip the Arab did not keep his word to Sapor I, which is not surprising in light of

Philip's character, and there is no reason to criticize him for this. It was wise for him to conclude the peace with Sapor I, start securing his throne, and then break the treaty immediately after it had served its purpose.

Oracula Sibyllina:
'But when first the wolf will confirm solemn oaths with the flock against the white-toothed dogs, then he will violate the truce; injuring the woolly sheep, he will cast aside the treaty; and unlawful battle of overbearing kings will take place in wars. Syrians will perish horribly; Indians, Armenians, Arabs, Persians, and Babylonians will kill one another because of mighty battles. But when first the Roman Ares will destroy the German Ares, conquering the oceanic destroyer of souls, then indeed, the Persians, arrogant men, shall have war for many years, but victory will not be theirs [*This may mean that Philip fought against the Germans in the Balkans in 246 before he ordered Priscus to assist the Armenians, but it is possible that the war started before this because Philip had not handed over Mesopotamia. The former, however, is likelier. This account also makes it clear that the Persians lost this war and this is confirmed by the Armenian accounts*]. English tr. by York, 56–7 slightly changed to follow the better translation in REF 1, 46.

Zonaras describes the events as follows:
'Then, after he had returned, Philippus came into control of the empire of the Romans. During his return, he appointed his son Philippus colleague in his sovereignty. After he had established a truce with Sapor, the ruler of the Persians, he concluded the war against the Persians, having ceded to them Mesopotamia and Armenia [*The ceding of Mesopotamia did not take place in practice*]. When he recognized that the Romans were upset because of the transfer of the territories, after a bit he set the treaties aside and seized the territories [*I would suggest that it is likelier that Philip never intended to keep his promises to the Persians*].' Zonaras 12.19, tr. by Banchich/Lane, 46–7.

Moses Khorenatsi has preserved for us the following problematic account of the events that took place during the reign of Philip the Arab, but he has mixed it with material that belongs to the years 224–29.

'After Artashir, the son of Sasan, had killed Artavan and gained the throne, two branches of the Pahlav family called Aspahapet and Suren Pahlav were jealous at the rule of the branch of their own kin, that is, of Artashes, and willingly accepted the rule of Artashir… But the house of Karen Pahlav,… opposed in war Artashir… As soon as Khosrov, king of Armenia, heard of the troubles he set out to aid Artavan… the sad news of Artavan's death and the alliance of all the Persian troops and nobles – both of his own family the Parthians and of the Pahlavik, except the branch of Karen. To the latter he sent messengers and then returned to our country… [*all of the above belongs to the year 224*] and immediately made haste to inform Philip, the Roman emperor, seeking help from him. Because there were troubles in Philip's empire, he was unable to spare any Roman forces to give military assistance to Khosrov [*This *suggests the year 246*]. But he helped him by means of a letter ordering that he be given assistance from every region. When they received this command they came to his support from Egypt and the desert, from as far as the shores of the Pontic Sea [*On the basis of the sources quoted in this book (see above and below) it is probable that Philip did indeed send assistance to Khosrov so that I am inclined to accept this part of the text to have been based on real events but in such a manner that Moses has mixed events with each other*]. Having acquired such a multitude of troops he marched against Artashir, and giving battle put him to flight; he took from him Assyria and other lands where he had a royal residence. Again he sent through messengers to his own kin the Parthian and Pahlav families, and to all the forces of the land of the Kushans… Aspahapet and Surean did not agree, so Khosrov returned to our land… Then came… word that "your kinsman Vehsachan with his… the Karen Pahlav had not given obeisance to Artashir…" yet his joy was short-lived; for the sad news quickly arrived that Artashir himself with his united forces had caught up with them and slaughtered all the branch of the Karean Pahlav… save one youth [*The fight between Ardashir and Karen Pahlav in all probability belongs to the early reign of Ardashir*].' Moses Khorenatsi, Thomson ed. and tr., pp.218–9 with my comments added.

In sum, it is clear that Philip I the Arab lied to Sapor I only to secure the eastern border for the period he needed to secure the throne by going in person to Rome, which may also have required the subdual of two usurpations against Philip, as I will discuss below. Philip left his brother Priscus in charge of the whole East as *rector orientis* and travelled to Rome. Notably, before leaving he created new fully armoured cataphract cavalry units to protect the eastern frontier.[4] He had clearly witnessed with his own eyes the effectiveness of the Sassanian heavy cavalry.

Sapor I has also preserved for us evidence of the duplicity of Philip the Arab in his *SKZ* inscription, which Dodgeon and Lieu (REF1, p.30) translate as follows with underlining added: 'And the Caesar (Philip I?) <u>lied again</u> and did injustice to Armenia.' In short, Philip the Arab acted as a wise ruler should. He fooled the gullible foe with a one-time payment of money and promises to hand over either Mesopotamia and Armenia, or only Armenia. The payment of money was a small price to pay for Philip for the chance of securing his throne; the fooling of the Persian ruler must have been the frosting on the cake, thrown in Sapor's face. The lying <u>again</u> in the case of Armenia suggests that Philip had lied about something before this, which I interpret to mean the ceding of Mesopotamia. The injustice in the case of Armenia meant that Philip ordered his brother Priscus to give all the assistance that Khosrov the Great needed against the Persians, and it is clear that Khosrov achieved great successes with these forces. However, if he did advance as far as Assyria this time too, it is clear that this was done under the leadership of Priscus, which added credence to Philip's claims of Persian victories. This Romano-Armenian offensive against the Persians should probably be dated to about late 244/245–249, or alternatively 246–49 if the Germanic victories of the *Oracula Sibyllina* are dated to have taken place before these – and in light of Sibyl's text and the circumstances leading to the revolt against Priscus (see later) the latter dating should be preferred. The great Roman victories against the Persians during the reign of Philip are confirmed by the *Eis Basilea* (36) which dates from about April 248.

Why did Philip promise so many concessions to the Persians when the Roman army had already safely reached Roman territory? Would the need to secure confirmation by the Roman Senate have been enough to justify them? There are reasons to believe this was not so, but there were usurpations against Philip in the West immediately after the news of the death of Gordian III, and it was the urgency of the situation that made it necessary for Philip to make those concessions. This question will be discussed in greater detail below.

The Creation of a New Unit of Bodyguards
It is possible that Philip the Arab sought to secure his position at the very beginning of his reign by creating a new personal unit of bodyguards. According to *Chronicon Paschale* (Niebuhr ed. p. 502), Philip the Arab and his son created an *arithmos* (*numerus*) of *candidati* by enrolling into it select youths from the ranks of the *scholarii*. They called them the *schola* of the *tagma* with the title *iuniores* after Philip the father. They were called the seventh *schola*. The text is unfortunately ambiguous and it is possible to think that the

Two coins of Sapor I at the corners and a propaganda relief of Sapor I depicting the emperor Gordian III as corpse, Philip begging for peace and Valerian as captive. This is pure propaganda. Gordian III was not killed by Sapor I as he claimed and Philip actually emerged as victor despite having first sued for peace. Philip the Arab had betrayed his promises at the first opportunity he got and Sapor I lost the war that followed up. Source of the drawings: Rawlinson.

arithmos of the *candidati* would have been selected from the *scholarii* of the seventh *schola*, or that the select *candidati* formed the core for the newly created seventh *schola*. One possibility is that this *schola* was the *ala Celerum Philippiana* of Philip the Arab, but it is more likely that we are dealing with two separate units. Whatever the exact details, on the basis of this and on the basis of need to secure one's own person, it is probable that Philip the Arab created a personal unit of bodyguards, the seventh *schola*, to secure his and his son's life against such members of the former imperial bodyguards who did not approve of the manner in which Philip had attained his position. The text also implies that this seventh *schola* included two schools of *candidati* (*seniores* for the father and *iuniores* for the son).

Usurpations against Philip in early 244?
The later 'Byzantine' sources – Zonaras, George the Monk, Scutariotes/*Synopsis Sathas*, Cedrenus and Joel Chronographus – preserve a version according to which Marcus the Philosopher and Severus Hostilianus usurped power against Philip the Arab in 244. In addition to this, we possess coins of usurpers bearing the names Mar. Silbannacus and Sponsianus that are sometimes dated to the reign of Philip the Arab.

> **Zonaras (12.18) has the following account:**
> 'Philip immediately leaped into the rulership. When the slaughter of Gordian was announced to the senate, it assembled to choose another prince. And it immediately proclaimed as Caesar a certain philosopher, Marcus. He died suddenly before setting foot to the principate, while he was dwelling in the palace. After his death, Severus Hostilianus [*Seuêros Stilianos*] gained power for the rulership of the Romans. But he was not yet near consolidating this, when he fulfilled a necessity [i.e. he died]; when he had a vein open because he was ill he died.'
> English tr. by York, 52–3 with my comment added inside parenthesis.

> **George the Monk:**
> 'And after Ounior [Gordianus III], Marcus reigned 2 years. And after Marcus, Ioustillianus reigned 2 years and, when he had opened a vein, poured forth his blood while asleep, and… died. And after Ioustillianus, Philippus reigned for 6 years.'
> English tr. by Banchich/Lane, p.84.

> **Cedrenus:**
> After him [Gordianus III], Marcus 3 years. After Marcus, Hustilianus two years. And, when he had opened a vein… died. After him, Philippus reigned 7 years.'
> English tr. by Banchich/Lane, p.83–4.

John Marvin York has accepted the above to refer to real usurpations occurring at the very beginning of Philip's reign and that Philip gained the Senate's acceptance only thanks to the fact that he had been able to bring back the army intact and that he used this to intimidate the Senate. However, there are serious problems with this, which are that Körner has demonstrated conclusively that the names of both usurpers are the result of confusion and corruption of the names in the extant sources. Marcus the Philosopher

(Markos Filosofos) is clearly a corruption of the name of Philip the Arabs (Marcus Iulius Philippus = Markos Filippos) while the inclusion of the name of Severus Hostilianus among the usurpers results from the name of Decius's son C. Valens Hostilianus Messius Quintus.[5] In short, it is clear that the names of the usurpers preserved in the 'Byzantine' sources are the result of confusion and mix-up of persons. However, does this mean that there were no usurpations against Philip at the very beginning of his reign that would have required the conclusion of the peace with Persia with whatever terms possible? This brings up the problem of the extant coins minted in the name of Mar. Silbannacus and Sponsianus.

As I have already noted in my biographies of Gallienus and Aurelian and Probus, there are two coins extant which attest to the existence of an otherwise unknown Emperor called Silbannacus.[6] The interpretation of who he was is entirely based on a numismatic analysis of the coins, and since this is an uncertain art there are as many interpretations as there are researchers. It has been suggested that Silbannacus ruled for some time between 240 and 260, with the reigns of Philip the Arab, Decius and Gallienus being considered the likeliest, so that it is possible that the coins were minted in Rome, or by some unknown mint possibly in Lorraine. As I have already noted, it is ultimately impossible to pinpoint exactly when and where Silbannacus usurped power, so it is even possible that he could have been the unknown usurper in Britain under Probus. However, if we assume that this usurpation took place roughly at the time Philip was emperor there are two possibilities. Firstly, that his name is Gallic; the reverse of the coins has the text Victoria Aug. with Mercurius suggesting that he was an unknown commander on the Rhine frontier. The second of the alternatives is that he was the Marcus (note M Aur Silbannacus and Mar Silbannacus) who was nominated by the Senate and that his name Marcus Aurelius Silbannacus then became confused with the name of Philip the Arab in the later 'Byzantine' sources. In my opinion this is the likeliest alternative, but not conclusively so. The second of the alternatives was originally suggested by Hartmann and it connects the usurpation of Silbannacus with the civil war in Gaul mentioned by

This head is my sketch of the obverse of the British Museum coin of Silbannacus

Only two coins attest to the existence of this otherwise unknown emperor Silbannacus. These bear the following texts:
1) British Museum Version Found in Lorraine ca.1937
Obverse: IMP M AVR SILBANNACUS AVG
Reverse: VICTORIA AVG with Mercurius
2) Found near Paris in ca. 1996
Obverse: IMP MAR SILBANNACVS AVG
Reverse : MARTI PR/OPVGT with Mars

Eutropius for the very beginning of the reign of Decius, which Decius then suppressed. Unless new evidence surfaces, this question is unfortunately unsolvable, but if there was a usurpation by a victorious commander of the Rhine frontier at the very beginning of Philip the Arab's reign at least that would explain why Philip was prepared to buy the peace from the Persians when there was no urgent need for it. Furthermore, as will be made clear below, there is evidence for fighting on the Rhine frontier in 244 which would have enabled Silbannacus to claim the victory depicted in his coins.

The second of the usurpers dated to the reign of Philip the Arab on the basis of coin finds is Sponsianus – similarly otherwise unknown. In 1713 two gold *aurei* bearing the name Sponsianus were found in Transylvania together with the coins of Gordian III and Philip the Arab, which has led some historians to the suggestion that he was a usurper under Philip. These coins are actually so problematic in their details that in the nineteenth century Cohen declared them to be modern forgeries. The reason for this is that the reverse of the coin depicts an image borrowed from coins minted by C. Minucius Augurinus from the *gens Minucia* (family of the Minucii) that are datable to 187 BC. The inclusion of the Republican era reverse has led Hartmann to suggest that Sponsianus was the leader of senatorial resistance against Philip the Arab. In opposition to this Meckler and Körner have quite correctly noted that it is unlikely that senatorial opposition of the period would have used a Republican-era reverse from a coin celebrating the family of Minucii because there existed emperors – Pupienus and Balbinus – quite recently

Left: A coin of Sponsianus. Source: Cohen
Right: A coin of Sponsianus. Source: Delaroche.

chosen by the Senate and it would have been more logical for the usurper supported by the Senate to use images from their coins. Meckler and Körner also note that the use of such a reverse would have been of interest only to the *gens Minucia* and that it is probable that this family had died out long ago. These counter-arguments as such are solid, but in my opinion not conclusively so because it is not impossible that Sponsianus could have claimed to have descended from this ancient senatorial family and that he wanted to celebrate his connection with it – much stranger things have happened in history than this. Furthermore, there exists period evidence for troubles in the precise area where the coins were found, namely the Danube frontier.

The evidence which may connect the above-mentioned rulers with real life usurpers of the reign of Philip the Arab consists of archaeological finds along the Rhine and Danube frontiers. On the basis of these, Xavier Loriot has noted that the Alamanni had burned the fort of Saletio in 244 and that for the same period (Loriot has 245?) there is also evidence for troubles with the Quadi and that several hoards of coins have been found in Romania datable to 244 and after.[7] Perhaps the hoard which has the coins of Sponsianus among the coins of Gordian III and Philip should be included in this same category? In short, there is evidence of fighting in the precise areas in which it has been suggested Silbannacus and Sponsianus usurped power and it was one of the typical features of the third century that victorious commanders usurped power. This means that there is strong circumstantial evidence for their existence for the reign of Philip.

On the basis of this I would suggest that the likeliest date for the usurpation of Marcus Silbannacus is the early reign of Philip the Arab and that he had achieved some significant enough successes against the Alamanni in early 244 to enable him to declare victory in his coins and to usurp power with the support of the Senate. It is probable that he was the enigmatic Marcus of the 'Byzantine' sources, but not a philosopher because this addition results from the confusion of the names.

I would also suggest that Sponsianus was a usurper from the early reign of Philip the Arab who had also achieved some significant enough successes against enemies along the Danubian frontier for him to be able to proclaim himself Emperor. I would connect him with the mysterious Severus Hostilianus of the 'Byzantine' sources and that the *Seuêros Stilianos* (Severos Stilianos) of Zonaras would have resulted from a confusion of Severus Sponsianus with Decius's son C. Valens Hostilianus Messius Quintus. The use of the name Severus by Sponsianus would have enabled him to claim connection with the Severans, as Philip's wife Otacilia Severa did.

In short, it would have been the usurpation of Marcus Silbannacus and support for him by the Senate that forced Philip the Arab to make the concessions to the Persians noted above. The years in the sources may be taken to mean months so that it is possible that Marcus Silbannacus ruled for two months and was then killed in the Palace and that Severus Sponsianus then usurped power in the Balkans but was then either killed by his doctors with excessive bloodletting or as a result of having cut his own veins in an act of suicide after having ruled for another two months. The other alternative is that both men usurped power simultaneously so that the usurpations against Philip the Arab lasted for two months. This is actually likelier. The extant accounts suggest that Philip the Arab managed to kill both men by special operations much akin to the way he had achieved his own power. If this set of conjectures, which is based on the existence of mutually supporting circumstantial evidence, is correct then it is clear that Philip the Arab was a master of unorthodox warfare and deserves our full admiration for the great skill he showed in this. The fact that both usurpers, Marcus Silbannacus and Severus Sponsianus, were killed so fast in special operations enabled Philip the Arab to betray Sapor I immediately and not hand over Mesopotamia as promised. In short, I would suggest that the case for early usurpations against Philip the Arab is far stronger than the case against it. The *Eis Basilea* (9) claims that Philip showed clemency towards those who had plotted against him. This must mean that Philip forgave those who had supported the usurpers in order to calm the situation.

The reorganization of the East and Balkans and the journey to Rome in 244
The peace negotiations with Sapor I, the special operations to get rid of the usurpers, and the reorganization of the defences in the East so that Philip could march to the West would have preoccupied the very beginning of Philip's reign.

Having fooled Sapor, while still in the east Philip assumed the titles *Parthicus Maximus* and *Persicus Maximus*, and the mint of Antioch struck coins with the legend *pax fundata cum Persis* to indicate that Philip had brought peace to the region.[8] This was actually fully justified. Philip had pacified the region with false promises and a relatively small sum of money. He then made the Persians pay for their foolishness by granting Khosrov the Great the assistance he needed possibly in late 244/245–249, or more likely in about 246–49, the latter dating being likelier.

We possess two texts, one by Aurelius Victor and another by Zosimus, that describe Philip's actions immediately after he had concluded the peace with Persia and had started to celebrate his Persian victory. Unfortunately neither of these gives us the full picture.

According to Aurelius Victor:
'And so Marcus Julius Philippus… settled affairs in the east [*he appointed his brother Priscus as rector orientis*], founded the town of Philippopolis in Arabia, and came to Rome (with his son).' Victor 28, tr. by Bird, 29 with a comment added.

Zosimus describes what happened next:
'On his arrival at Rome, having made the senate his friends, he thought it most politic to confer the highest posts to his closest relatives. From this motive he made his brother Priscus, general of the Syrian armies, and entrusted the forces in Moesia and Macedonia to his brother-in-law Severianus. [*It is clear that this account is inaccurate. Philip would certainly have already left his brother in charge of the eastern armies when he left and then appointed his brother-in-law as commander of the forces in the Balkans when he marched through it. However, it is possible that the claim is accurate from the 'official' point of view such that the appointements were only confirmed officially after the Senate had recognized Philip as Emperor in Rome*]' Zosimus 1.19.3, tr. by anon. 1814, p.13 with a correction and comment.

When the above two texts are taken together, it is clear that before Philip set out to Rome to obtain the confirmation of his position in person from the Senate, he reorganized the defences in the East by appointing his brother Priscus into the special command of

CITY OF PHILIPPOPOLIS IN ARABIA

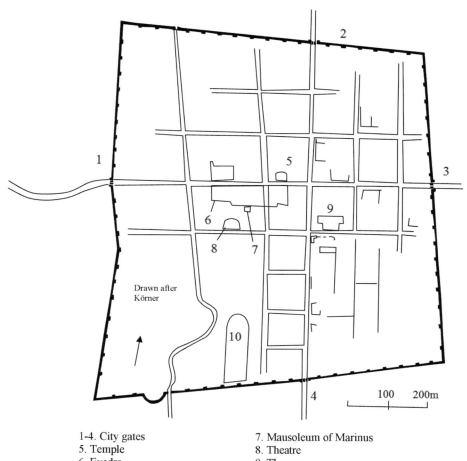

1-4. City gates
5. Temple
6. Exedra

7. Mausoleum of Marinus
8. Theatre
9. Thermae
10. Stadium

rector orientis. This was an extraordinary office: in practice he was in charge of governing everything in the East as if he was Emperor himself. Philip also bribed the cities of Nisibis and Singara with the addition of Julia to their names, and renamed Neapolis in Palestine as Colonia Iulia Neapolis, and Bostra (the capital of his native province of Arabia) as Colonia Metropolis. He also stopped at Damascus, which was promoted to colonial rank. These cities together with Philip's birthplace (see below) formed a line of defence against the Persians, so rewarding them was not a coincidence. It is also probable that Philip promoted Odaenathus of Palmyra to the Roman Senate. Philip's next stop was his birthplace Shahba in Arabia. He renamed and refounded it as Philippopolis. He ordered it rebuilt as a true city with defensive walls, aqueduct, thermae and theatre, and established an imperial sanctuary to celebrate the memory of his father *divus Marinus.*

However, the favouritism of Philip's birthplace caused resentment elsewhere.[9] In my opinion it was thanks to the fact that both usurpers were killed in special operations that Philip the Arab was able to spend slightly more time in the East than would have otherwise been the case. The killing of the usurpers also enabled Philip to declare victory against the Persians because he was no longer under any compulsion to honour his promises to the Persians.

According to Eusebius (6.34), Syncellus (AM 5737) and Zonaras (12.19), Philip visited a church on some unidentified Easter. Most historians who accept Philip the Arab as a Christian think that it was in 244, which means that Philip would have celebrated the Christian Easter probably at Antioch already on 13 or 14 April 244. The reason for this suggestion is that an unknown Arian historian whose work is included in the fragments of Philostorgius states that Leontius, Bishop of Antioch, was later executed by Decius because he had denied entry to the church by Philip and his wife who were both Christians because Philip had murdered Gordian III. The important point here is that they might have been baptized just before this took place, but this is uncertain because the first source to mention this, Eusebius, does not give any date or place for the event. It is possible that Philip was actually baptized only later in about 247/8 and that his visit to the church at Easter took place on 2 April 248. The reason for this suggestion is that in 248–49 Philip was clearly unwilling to lead military campaigns in person, which could have been the result of his recent baptism. Possibly Philip felt pangs of conscience after his Balkan campaign, but it is equally possible to think that he felt pangs of conscience immediately after the murder of Gordian and would have sought forgiveness by confessing his sins. The latter is most likely. In short, when Philip and his wife attempted to enter the church the man in charge of the congregation did not let him in because Philip was a known sinner. Philip was told to confess his sins and to sit in the area reserved for penitents. With this he implied that Philip had committed very great sins and crimes that had to be confessed. The crime in question was probably the murder of Gordian III. The Emperor is said to have been humble and confessed and then joined the others in prayers.[10] Christianity was very convenient as a religion for a sinner. All he needed to do was to confess and do penance and all was forgiven. The implications of his Christianity soon became evident to all. Eusebius describes this very important event as follows.

Eusebius 6.34
'He [Philip], there is reason to believe, was a Christian, and on the day of the last Easter vigil he wished to share in the prayers of the Church along with the people; but the prelate of the time would not let him come in until he made open confession and attached himself to those who were held to be in a state of sin and were occupying the place for penitents. Otherwise, if he had not done so, he would never have been received by him in view of many accusations brought against him. It is said that he obeyed gladly, showing by his actions the genuine piety of his attitude towards the fear of God.' tr. by Williamson/Louth, 206–7.

Once Philip had visited his birthplace, he started his journey to Rome. Philip went through Antioch to Lycia-Pamphylia and from there to Bithynia after which he crossed

1. Philip the Elder's coin celebrating the Peace with Persia.
2. Philip the Younger's coin with father and son on the reverse (stressing piety, sense of duty)
3. Philip the Younger's coin propagating him as a soldier and general. Note the equipment worn by the soldiers, which is suggestive of the continued existence of Alexander's hoplites, but not conclusively so. See also the Plates.
4. Otacilia's coin celebrating her chastity.
Source: Cohen.

the straits to Thrace. Everywhere along the route he was received with celebrations. At Beroea (Augusta Traiana) there exist inscriptions which include his titles *Parthicus Maximus* and *Persicus Maximus* and name his wife Otacilia Severa with the title *Augusta*. While in the Balkans Philip entrusted the forces there to his brother-in-law Severianus in the same manner as he had done in the East.[11] There was a need to appoint a loyal relative in charge of the Danube frontier with the powers of vice-regent in the aftermath of the usurpation of Severus Sponsianus.

Philip reached Rome after 23 July 244[12] and immediately began a policy of rapprochement with the Senate. The Senate duly confirmed his position and officially granted him the titles *Parthicus* and *Persicus Maximus* while he himself issued coins (*pax fundata cum Persis*) proclaiming peace with Persia. To gain legitimacy for his rule, he also had the Senate declare his father divine, his son Philip *Caesar* and his wife *Augusta*. Declaring his father Marinus as divine and therefore Emperor was unprecedented but not really that different from the fictive adoption of the Severans into the Antonine imperial family by Septimius Severus. The naming of Philip Jr. as *Caesar* associated him with his father in imperial legislation and he is for the first time named in a law on 15 August 244. Philip Sr. wanted to stress that he had given the populace a dynasty and minted coins with the title *de pia mater pivs filivs* (patriotic/dutiful son of a patriotic/dutiful mother). He also struck coins to stress his son's future role as *Imperator Augustus*.[13]

7.2 Internal Policies 244–48

As we have seen, Philip secured his position with two key appointments. His brother Priscus was appointed de facto regent of the East and his relative Severianus was given command of the Balkan armies with the same functions. In other words, the vast majority of the armed forces were placed under the direct control of Philip's relatives. We do not know the names of the praetorian prefects under Philip and it is possible that they also held these positions. As regards the other personnel choices, these appear to have been meant to please the important senatorial factions while also securing the rise of Christians or pro-Christian elements back into power. Philip also promoted the careers of those who had been sidelined either by the Gordiani or Timesitheus. The names of the ordinary consuls suggest that Philip's helpers or the people whose opinions he courted included at least Fulvius Aemilianus and Ti. Pollenius Armenius Peregrinus (both ordinary consuls in 244); C. Maesius Titianus (ordinary consul in 245); C. Allius Albinus and C. Bruttius Praesens (both ordinary consuls in 246); and L. Fulvius Gavius Numisius Aemilianus (brother of Fulvius Aemilianus *consul ordinarius* in 244.) and L. Naevius Aquilinus (both ordinary consuls in 249). With the possible exception of Naevius Aquilinus, all of these families were already prominent during the reign of Septimius Severus or Caracalla so there was continuity in this respect. Furthermore, all of these families were Italian or Sicilian (Titianus) in origin just like the bulk of the other office holders. This implies that Philip courted in particular the Italian families unlike the previous administration that had favoured the families with roots in the Hellenic East, although obviously there were some from these and other areas who held high positions under Philip. C. Bruttius Praesens and L. Fulvius Aemilianus and his brother probably came from the family of the Bruttii from Lucania, which implies a very prominent role for this family under Philip. The appointment of C. Messius Quintus Decius Valerianus (the future Emperor) as *praefectus urbi* in about 248–49 also proves that Philip promoted the careers of known enemies of the Gordiani to higher positions.[14]

Though Philip showered money on his birthplace, he did not forget the other provinces, Italy or the capital either. Roads were built in the provinces to facilitate the movement of soldiers, farmers and merchants. For Rome, he built a water reservoir on the other side of the Tiber at Trastevere to ease water shortages. This work benefited mostly the Jewish district of Rome and therefore the location where most Christians were located too. He generously distributed money to the people. Despite being a Christian, he also performed the religious duties of a pagan Emperor. It is clear that he acted like Constantine the Great and his succesors in the following century. They were Christians but at the same time they were pagan high priests who performed their religious duties as pagan emperors of the Roman Empire. It is a simplistic view of humanity to think that a Christian emperor would not be able to maintain the façade of pagan worship to keep their pagan subjects happy. It is no different from the behaviour of the Roman commanders who manipulated their simple-minded soldiers with gods and omens.[15] The rise of Philip the Arab had meant the rise of the pro-Christian faction of the Severan era back into the positions of power, but Philip was not a bigot – he knew that it was wiser to unite Christians and pagans under his rule. There is evidence for a reform of the state financial structures so that the state assessed the property and produce of the taxpayers more accurately, and how many persons there were to perform liturgies so that the state knew better how to organize them. However, at the same time, he increased the control of the central government over the local authorities and removed exemptions from taxation. This was detested by all those affected. The sons of the *decuriones* were forced to undertake the tax gathering duties of their fathers in their own communities. This secured a steady income for the state because the *decuriones* were personally responsible that the state got its taxes. This reform was apparently the handiwork of two equestrian chiefs of the *rationales* called Claudius Marcellus and Marcius Salutaris. The reform removed the abuses that had been exploited by tax gatherers and others under Maximinus Thrax, but at the same time it tightened the grip of the central government over the corrupt local elites, which they detested. They could no longer abuse their powers so easily. Local resistance to the ever tightening grip of the central bureaucracy created a centrifugal tendency, which the bureaucrats failed to grasp because they were operating on the principle now known as Parkinson's law. They thought that they were correcting abuses with additional controls, but in truth they were only creating additional costs and problems which in turn created a need for additional controls in an ever increasing cycle.[16]

The reign of Philip the Arab saw further deterioration in the quality of coins, which probably reflects his need to bribe the soldiers while keeping the senators happy by not resorting to extraordinary taxation. By 246/7 he had introduced a new, lighter version of the gold coin, and the silver coins were also debased. According to Potter, under Philip the maximum silver content of *antoninianus* ranged between 44 and 31 per cent while it had varied between 47 and 37 per cent under Gordian III while the average weight of the coin remained the same. This means that Philip could mint more gold and silver coins than had been the case before. This, however, appears to have been insufficient to meet the demands because Philip introduced stricter fiscal administration on the local aristocracies. Potter is correct when he notes that this did not necessarily mean better government. The centralizing tendencies present in all bureacracies, the Roman one included, driven by the need to pay the armed forces and fighting of wars, upset the delicate balance of power between central and local government. Local aristocracies reacted with ever increasing hostility towards these tendencies, for example by nominating emperors of their own.[17]

In the field of legislation, Philip paid particular attention to civil rights. At the very beginning of his reign he granted a general amnesty for the exiled like so many other emperors had done before him in the hopes of gaining their support. He decreed that appeals could only be made to the Emperor if the praetorian prefects or their deputies had made a decision in the case. As noted, he reformed the state treasury and its practices. Philip and his administration were not as busy in the field of legislation as had been Gordian III's administration: there exist only 78 Edicts of Philip in the *Codex Iustinianus* while there are 275 or 271 or 222 laws of Gordian in the same *Codex*, depending on the person who counts them. However, he was still the second busiest legislator of the era from 235 until 284, which means he took his duties seriously. Furthermore, while the legislative work of Gordian III's reign was largely the work of his subordinates, it is likely that as former Praetorian Prefect Philip was personally responsible for many of the decisions taken.[18] Körner lists the laws preserved in the *Codex Iustinianus* as follows:

Maximinus Thrax (235–238)	4 Edicts
Gordian III (238–244)	271 Edicts
Philippus Arabs (244–249)	78 Edicts
Decius (249–251)	8 Edicts
Trebonianus Gallus (252–253)	2 Edicts
Valerian and Gallienus (254–268)	89 Edicts
Claudius II (268–270)	1 Edict
Aurelian (270–275)	6 Edicts
Probus (276–282)	4 Edicts
Carus, Carinus and Numerianus (282–284)	25 Edicts

7.3 The Wars in 245–47

Philip had another important problem: the frontiers faced a series of threats. As noted above, he did not honour his treaty with Persia. He had solved this problem by giving his brother Priscus the power to do what was necessary. Priscus did this in conjunction with the Armenians and secured this front, their combined forces inflicting a series of defeats on the Persians from 245/6 onwards.

As noted above, there is evidence that the Alamanni had torched the Roman fort at Saletio (mod. Seltz in Alsace) in 244, which I connect with the events that led to the usurpation of Marcus Silbannacus. We do not know what caused this or what Philip did after Marcus Silbannacus had been killed. It is possible that this problem had already been solved by Silbannacus or that it was now solved with a new agreement, or that the Germans that Philip defeated by 246 (celebrated in coins with *Germanicus Maximus*) were the Alamanni, and that these victories were achieved by Philip or his general in the area.

At about the same time as this happened there was also fighting between the Quadi and Roman troops in about 245. These problems would have been handled either by Philip in person or by his brother-in-law Severianus. There exists an edict dated 12 November 245 which places Philip at Aquae, which has been identified as a city in Dacia Inferior, which means that Philip could have fought against the Quadi while en route there. The victory over the Quadi could be the reason for the subsequent adoption of the title *Germanicus Maximus*. The location suggests trouble with the Carpi, and there is evidence for this in other sources. The needs of the Army of Dacia were met by minting coins there during the summer 246. It is therefore in the Balkans that we find Philip from 245 onwards.[19]

The War in the Balkans in 245–247

We know very little about the war that erupted in the Balkans in 245–47. None of the sources provides a detailed and logical account of the events. The abovementioned information suggests that Philip the Arab faced a series of enemy invasions in the Balkans in 245 and that he had marched from Rome to Aquae in Dacia Inferior by 12 November 245. The route taken and the subsequent adoption of the title *Germanicus Maximus* in 246[20] suggests that Philip had marched to Dacia through such lands that had either Germanic invaders like the Alamanni, Quadi and Marcomanni, or alternatively that he engaged the Goths in 245–6 and gained the title *Germanicus Maximus* as a result. In

Dacia Philip would then have fought against the Carpi. It is possible that Philip the Arab had purposely provoked a war in this area or at least had provoked a war with the Goths because Jordanes claims that Philip stopped paying the customary subsidies.[21]

Let us begin with the account of Jordanes:

'He [*Philip*] withheld from the Goths the tribute due to them; whereupon they were naturally enraged and instead of friends became his foes. For though they dwelt apart under their own kings, yet they had been allied to the Roman state and received annual gifts. [*The description of this situation best fits the situation prevailing in 245 after the Goths had enlarged their territories at the cost of Roman allies so that the Marcomanni and Quadi had become tributaries of the Goths. Standard operating procedure for the Romans in such cases was to destroy the enemy before it became too powerful. Refusal to pay tribute to the Goths was sure to cause an outbreak of hostilities so Philip would have the war he wanted and for which he could collect adequate forces in advance. I doubt the reason for the refusal to pay was financial because the sums the Romans paid in such cases were very small in comparison with the yearly income of a single senatorial family. The problem with this is that subsequent details provided by Jordanes actually fit the situation prevailing in 248–249, which suggests the possibility that Jordanes has confused two different wars with each other, one taking place in 246/7 and another in 248/9 resulting from the usurpation of Pacatianus, or that he has confused all events between 244 and 250*]. …Ostrogotha [*The overall king of the Goths*] and his men soon crossed the Danube and ravaged Moesia and Thrace. [*It is possible that this refers to the events of 245–7 when Philip achieved victories against the Carpi and Quadi-Germans. In fact it is possible that the Goths invaded in 245 and then again in 246 or 247 (described below) depending on how one dates the events of the Carpic war. Even if Jordanes is referring to the reign of Philip, it is also possible that this means the invasion of the Balkans in 242, which was defeated by Timesitheus. However, it is still likelier that Philip did indeed fight against the Goths also in 245*] Philip sent the senator Decius against him. And since he could do nothing against the Getae [*Goths*], he released his soldiers from military service and sent them back to private life, as though it had been by their neglect that the Goths had crossed the Danube. When, as he supposed, he had thus taken vengeance on his soldiers, he returned to Philip. [*It is possible that Jordanes has confused the events of 249 and 245 with each other because this account best fits the period immediately after the death of Pacatianus in 249 when Philip had sent Decius to the Balkans to punish the rebels, and suggests that Decius was unable to defend the area against the Goths if the Goths had invaded in 248/9, with the result that he returned to Rome while Philip went in person to the Balkans, as can be found in the account of John of Antioch which will be quoted later in the context of the events of 248–49. The other alternative interpretation is that Jordanes has confused events so that Decius actually only purged the army after the revolt of Pacatianus, as the other sources state, and then returned to Rome, as John of Antioch's account claims, and that the Gothic invasion then took place in 249 forcing Philip to take care of the problem in person, as also suggested by John of Antioch's account. In either case this would mean that Decius usurped power in Rome while Philip was in the Balkans, but the problem with this is that there exists an alternative version for these events. It is also possible to think that Jordanes has confused the revolts of Sponsianus and Pacatianus so that the sacking of the Roman soldiers actually took place in 244 and they then convinced the Goths to invade in about 245/6. Similarly it is possible that Decius was sent to the Balkans in 245 for reasons that I will elaborate below. This is the likeliest alternative. Regardless of which of the versions is true, it is clear that Jordanes has left out the setbacks suffered by Goths because it is clear that they were forced to retreat from Roman territory by November 245. Unfortunately these accounts are so confused that it is impossible to achieve any certainty]* But when the soldiers then found themselves expelled from the army after so many hardships, in their anger they had recourse to the protection of Ostrogotha... He received them, was aroused by their words and presently led out three hundred thousand armed men, having as allies for this war, some of the Taifali [*a client tribe of the Goths*] and Astringi [*Hasding Vandals*] and also three thousand of the Carpi, a race of men very ready to make war and frequently hostile to the Romans... Besides these tribes, Ostrogotha had Goths and Peucini from the island of Peuce, which lies in the mouth of the Danube... [*The figure of 300,000 men is quite credible for the combined forces of the Goths, Taifali and Vandals plus others*] He placed in command Argaithus and Gunthericus, the noblest leaders of his race. They speedily crossed the Danube, devastated Moesia a second time [*This could refer to the years 246/7 or 249; the second time obviously means that there was first time, which is likely to mean the invasion resulting from the refusal to pay subsidies by Philip in 245 rather than the one crushed by Timesitheus.*] and approached Marcianople, the famed metropolis of that land. Yet after a long siege they departed upon receiving money from the inhabitants... From this city, then,... the Getae returned after a long siege to their own land, enriched by the ransom they had received [*In truth this was a meagre achievement for an army of 300,000 men. There exists an alternative account of this siege in the extant fragments of Dexippus. There are several possible ways to interpret this. Firstly, if Jordanes had confused the different wars, as appears quite possible, then this could mean that this buying of the peace from the Goths took place in 246/7. It is known that Philip took the titles of Germanicus Maximus and Carpicus Maximus after the 245–7 war, which may imply that he did not take the title Gothicus Maximus because he had not defeated them but had bought a peace. If this is what happened then it is easy to see why the soldiers in the Balkans nominated Pacatianus as their Emperor in 248. Philip had first provoked the Goths to a war by refusing to pay the subsidies and then still bought them off. In such a case it is possible that Philip was employing the stratagem described by Julius Africanus, but which was not known to the soldiers. A fuller discussion follows below. The problem with this is that it is possible that the title of Germanicus Maximus hides inside also a victory over the Goths. Furthermore, the evidence also fits the circumstances of the year 249. If Philip was fighting against the Goths and others in the Balkans in 249 and Decius usurped power in Rome, it is easy to see why the citizens of Marcianopolis would have been forced to buy their freedom. On the other hand it is possible to think that Philip himself advised them to do so because he needed to return to Italy and the Goths were willing to accept the payment because of the presence of the Emperor and his army. The problem with this is that John of Antioch's account suggests that Philip had achieved a complete victory over the Goths in 249. On the basis of this it is likelier that the siege of*

Marcianopolis took place in about 246–7. Whatever the date, it is still clear that Philip's performace against the Goths was better than the performance of Decius when he became Emperor – had Philip ruled, it is probable that the Romans would never have faced the disaster that took place under Decius in 251]. Now the race of the Gepidae was moved with envy... and made war on their kinsmen... These Gepidae... dwelt in the province of Spesis on an island surrounded by the shallow waters of the Vistula... Fastida, king of the Gepidae, stirred up his quiet people to enlarge their boundaries by war. He overwhelmed the Burgundians, almost annihilating them, and conquered a number of other races... He unjustly provoked the Goths... [*Had Philip bought their services against the Goths so that he could use his forces against Decius? In my opinion this is likely if this event took place in 249, but it is also possible that it took place in 246–7. The latter option is likelier.*] The Gepidae hastened to take arms and Ostrogotha likewise moved his forces against them... They met at the town of Galtis, near which the river Aula flows, and there both sides fought with great valour; indeed the similarity of their arms and of their manner of fighting turned them against their own men [*this suggests that the Gepidae employed primarily cavalry forces armed with spears and to a lesser extent with bows*]. But the better cause and their natural alertness aided the Goths. Finally the night put an end to the battle as a part of the Gepidae were giving way... Fastida, king of the Gepidae, left the field of slaughter and hastened to his own land... The Goths returned victorious [*i.e. the Goths won by not losing*]... and dwelt in peace and happiness... so long as Ostrogotha was their leader. After his death, Cniva divided his army [*This took place in 250,[22] which means that the Goths were preoccupied with the war against the Gepidae from 247 until 250, or alternatively for the rest of 249 until 250 depending on how one interprets the above. The state of peace prevailing under Ostrogotha after the battle between the Gepid   ae and Goths suggests that it is likelier that the Gothic war with two invasions of Roman territory took place in 245–246/7 – it would be strange to state that there was peace as long as Ostrogotha was their leader if this peace lasted only a few months! It is because of this that I will below reconstruct the Gothic war to have taken place in 245–246/7 while I still also give the alternative reconstruction in its rightful place. Furthermore, if Philip employed the stratagem of Julius Africanus described below it is easy to see why the Goths would have been paralyzed from ca. 247 until 250]*' Jordanes, *Getica* 89–96, tr. by Mierow, 76–9 with changes and comments.

'After he had undertaken a war against the Scythians, the emperor Philippus returned to Rome. [*The reference to Scythians here and in the text of John of Antioch frg.226 quoted later from the translation of Banchich both imply that this war was fought against the Goths. However, thanks to the problematic nature of the information provided by these sources, especially by Jordanes, it is possible that Philip fought against the Goths only later in 249 rather than now in 245–246/7]*' Zonaras 12.19, tr. by Banchich/Lane, 47.

When one combines this with the above quoted prophecy of the Oracula Sibyllina that Philip would defeat the German Ares, conquering the oceanic destroyer of souls, and after that begin the war against the Persians, it is possible to think that Philip defeated the Quadi and others in Pannonia and after this he defeated the Goths and their allies (Scythians of Zonaras) in a war that he provoked by refusing to pay subsidies, all in 245–246/7, so that he was able to take the title of *Germanicus Maximus* in 246/7. The other two alternatives are that Philip fought against the Goths twice, once in about 245–246/7 and then again in 249; or that he fought against the Carpi in 245–6 and only then against the Goths in 247. If he fought against the Goths in about 245–7, it is possible that the above-mentioned ransoming of the city of Marcianopolis resulted from the simultaneous invasion of the Dacian Carpi which would have required Philip's attention elsewhere. However, this is also uncertain, because Jordanes was in the habit of hiding unwelcome reverses suffered by the Goths. It is entirely possible that the Goths had been forced to flee Roman territory and that the Gepids then attempted to exploit the weakness of the Goths.

There is an even likelier explanation for all of the above. It is probable that Philip had indeed stopped the payments to the Goths to provoke a war in 245. The Goths would naturally have ordered their allies to assist them so that the Quadi, Marcomanni, Vandals and Carpi invaded at the same time under the king Ostrogotha. It is probable that Jordanes has misunderstood why Decius arrived in the Balkans because we know that Philip was at Aquae in Dacia in November 245. It is probable that if it was Decius (but it could be anyone) who sacked Roman soldiers in 245, that Philip's plan was to infect those Roman soldiers (Goths, Alans etc) with plague that he knew would flee north to join the Goths when cashiered, but, as said, Jordanes's account is not secure. What appears certain, however, is that Philip had defeated a number of enemies en route to Aquae and that he had forced Ostrogotha to flee from Thrace and Moesia. It is probable that it was then in 245/6 that Philip crushed the Carpi in the manner described below because the Goths had only 3,000 of them in 246–7. When the Ostrogoths renewed their invasion in 246, it is quite probable that Philip's plan was to destroy them by waging germ warfare and that it was because of this Philip allowed the ransoming of Marcianopolis after which the Goths were allowed to return to their lands unmolested. It is quite probable that Philip did not engage those besieging Marcianopolis because he had already infected them with the plague thanks to the fact that the soldiers sacked by Decius had carried it to the north and probably also because Philip continued the same strategy during the second invasion. The reason for this conclusion is that when the Goths subsequently invaded Roman territory in 250/1 they suffered from the plague which they then spread to the Romans.[23] An outbreak of sickness would explain why there was probably peace between the Romans and the Goths of Ostrogotha between 247 and 250. Philip the Arab was definitely an expert in underhand methods in warfare, but possibly this is an instance in which Roman ingeniuity backfired. As a high ranking Christian, Philip the Arab undoubtedly had read the *Kestoi* of his fellow Christian and author Julius Africanus and its recommendation to use a rudimentary form of germ warfare both in defence and attack.[24] I would suggest that it is very likely that its recommendations were now put to use. This action closely resembles the recommendations of Julius Africanus to feed enemy prisoners poisoned food and then release them to contaminate their fellow soldiers and then their civilian population, or to leave contaminated food and/or drink for the enemy to consume. It seems very likely that this happened now as a result Philip's secret command.

If Philip did indeed use this stratagem, it shows him as an expert of unorthodox warfare and in light of his earlier actions I would suggest that this is the likeliest alternative for his actions. He would have first provoked the Goths into action with his refusal to pay the subsidies, after which he would have sought to contaminate the food and drink available to the invaders. However, I would suggest that it is probable that these measures did not work as planned and that it was because of this that the Roman soldiers of barbarian origin were infected and sacked so that they could carry the disease north. Consequently, when the Goths then renewed their invasion in 246, the Romans knew that they were already infected so the Romans chose to pay them to leave. However, this does not preclude the possibility that the Romans once again sought to infect the Gothic besiegers of Marcianopolis in like manner if the previous attempts had not yet worked to their satisfaction. In such a case the ransoming of Marcianopolis would have happened once Philip was sure that the germs had been released among the invaders but before they had the chance of spreading them among the Romans. The fact that the massive Gothic army was able to advance only as far as Marcianopolis suggests that Philip was fully prepared to receive the invasion and close by. It is very likely that Philip followed this stratagem with another, even if it is not explicitly mentioned by any of the sources, which was that he induced the Gepidae against the Goths, possibly by using the same stratagem as Justinian used later, namely by claiming that the Goths had been given the subsidies promised to the Gepidae as a ransom for Marcianopolis – at least this would explain why the Gepidae were envious of the ransoming of the city. Furthermore, the inciting of the Gepidae against the Goths would have subjected them to the germ warfare too so that the plague would have spread ever further into the barbaricum.

If the *Eis Basilea* was dedicated to Philip the Arab on the Millenary Celebrations in April 248, as appears very likely on the basis of the dedication and contents of the text, then it confirms my speculation:

'most valuable is his [*Philip's*] good judgment and sagacity in war. Though he was aware that men who make a display of being formidable and warlike think it essential to conquer in battle and not by laying careful plans, he did not imitate or emulate them. He thought it right to employ arms against one's own kind – for it is a noble thing to conquer these by valour [*this may imply that Philip had needed military force against the usurpers at the beginning of his reign, but it is even likelier that it means the crushing of the revolt in Alexandria in late 247, for which see the discussion below*] – but against the barbarians to use adroit planning. He recognizes… that even the one who led countless hordes against the Hellenes and for whom neither land nor sea provided room enough was no match for the wits of a single man [*Swift is correct that this refers to Xerxes and Themistocles, but I would suggest that it also refers to the Gothic invasion and Philip*]. Wherever it is possible to prevail by strategy, what need is there running risks? … the Emperor thinks it proper not to imitate those who are senseless and reckless, but to remain steadfast in the face of the barbarians through careful planning… [*In my opinion this implies the use of germ warfare to destroy the Goths and other barbarian invaders through intellect rather than brawn*] He demonstrated his power to prevail over them not only by reason of his intelligence and general education, but also by his valour. [*This means that Philip also fought battles*] Wherever the Celts, the strongest and most bloodthirsty men under the sun, had effrontery for all kinds of acts, they now make obeisance to their lord [*Swift suggests that this refers to the Germans defeated in 246, but they could equally well be the Bastarnae*]. Only the name of this race survives [*Swift suggests that the race which survives must be the Dacian Carpi. For these, see the discussion below. However, if the Celts and this race mean the same group then it is possible to think that they are the Bastarnae who had joined the Goths in the invasion. If this is the case, we lack the details of this combat].' Eis Basilea 32–5,* tr. by Swift, 280–1 with my comments added.

In sum, the case for the use of germ warfare is relatively strong. But if Philip used this stratagem, it backfired with a vengeance, because in truth the Romans did not really understand even the rudimentary basics of bacteriological warfare. They only understood that one could spread contamination via food and drink and by air to people who would then infect others, but they did not understand that the germs that were supposedly harmless to the Romans could mutate into a more contagious form, and they apparently did not understand the consequences of the plague to the societies into which it spread. The panic resulting from the epidemic at first paralyzed the societies infected, but after that it caused a mass movement of peoples against the Roman frontiers along the Danube and then the Rhine which the Romans were unable to fully contain when the Roman armies were under an incompetent leader such as Decius proved to be – obviously Philip could not foresee that he would be overthrown by such a man. In 250 the Goths brought back with them a more virulent and deadly version of the plague than the Romans had spread to them.

By 247/249 Philip had attained the titles *Germanicus Maximus* and *Carpicus Maximus.* The only details of the fighting that we have consist of Zosimus's description of the combat between Philip and the Carpi, and we know that Philip was back in Rome in the summer of 247 because the Roman mint struck coins with the title Adventus Augg(ustorum).[25]

There exists an alternative account for the siege of Marcianopolis in the extant fragments of Dexippus (*Skythika frg. 22*). It is usually thought that this siege took place in about 248 and this has also been the conclusion of the latest editor and translator of Dexippus, von Günther Martin (p.17). According to Dexippus, when the Goths invaded Roman territory they thought that they could easily capture Marcianopolis, but its inhabitants had prepared themselves well under the guidance of Maximus, who was a man devoted to philosophy, but who at this time took the duties of a general and soldier. He instructed the citizens in the preparations for the siege and told them to protect themselves with shields and parapets when the enemies launched their bombardment of the city. When the Goths arrived, they collected enough stones and launched their attack. They bombarded the city with stones, spears and arrows but with no result because the citizens were well protected by their defences. The citizens did not respond to this attack but remained behind their defences. When the ammunition had been spent, the Goths grew despondent, withdrew and pitched camp nearby. The Goths remained there for a few days and when their spirits had recovered they repeated their attack, surrounding the city in close formation. This time Maximus ordered the citizens to respond with missiles. The citizens, whose spirits had been uplifted by their previous success, now raised a war cry and let loose their missiles, the stones and arrows, inflicting a great number of casualties among the Goths. It was impossible to miss the Goths because they were so tightly arrayed. The Goths had achieved nothing and withdrew. On the surface this account would seem to contradict what Jordanes states, but it is probably only a

Siege of Marcianopolis in about 246-247

Marcianopolis (shown with churches and cemeteries) according to Alexander Minchev. It is clear on the basis of the size of this "metropolis" that it did not require the presence of all of the Goths and their allies, which means that some of those were raiding other areas while this siege continued.

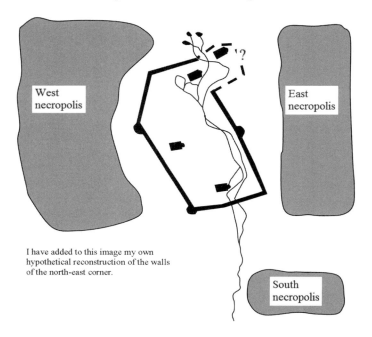

I have added to this image my own hypothetical reconstruction of the walls of the north-east corner.

fragment of the original account of the siege. It is likely that the siege became prolonged, as Jordanes states that after the intial attack had failed the Goths were paid to leave. In this way the abovementioned stratagem of germ warfare could go into action, or that there were two sieges, one in 245 and another in about 246–7.

We possess slightly better evidence for the war against the Carpi in about 245–7 in Zosimus but even this describes only a single battle. It is therefore worthwhile to quote the text of Zosimus at length:

'Thinking that he had by these means established himself in the possession of the Empire, he [*Philip*] made an expedition against the Carpi, who had plundered all the country about the Ister. When an engagement took place, the barbarians not being able to withstand the impetious charge of the Romans ['*machés de genomenés ouk enegkontes hoi barbaroi tên prosbolên,*' *with the implication that the Roman frontline attacked in close order*] fled into a fortified place [*a marching camp in the form of a wagon laager/carrago or fort?*] in which they were besieged. But finding that their troops, who were dispersed in various directions [*This implies a cavalry battle in which the fleeing and pursuing cavalries had dispersed*] had again rallied in a body, they resumed their courage, and sallying attacked the Roman army. [*This would mean that the first Roman cavalry line had lost its cohesion during the pursuit so the regrouped Carpi could exploit this with a counterattack*] Being unable to bear the brisk onset of the Moors, the Carpi sued for peace, to which Philip assented, and marched away. [*The onset of the Moors means the use of the cavalry reserves posted in the second line. It is unlikely to be a coincidence that Gallienus also commanded the Moors in person in a cavalry battle. See Syvänne, Gallienus, 70–5. It is also probable that the Pannonians/ Illyricians, Foederati and legionary vexillationes were in the same places in the first cavalry line as we find them in the sixth century Strategikon*]' Zosimus 1.20 tr. by anon. 1814, p.13 with changes, corrections, additions and comments.

The above account is very important because it implies in no uncertain terms that Philip the Arab was using standard Roman cavalry tactics with two lines against the Carpi. This is the same array that we subsequently find in use by the Emperor Decius. The place of the Moors is also the same as in the battle array of Gallienus in the battle of Mursa in 258. The Emperor Gallienus commanded these in person and their location corresponds with the location of the *optimates* in the sixth century military treatise *Strategikon*. It is therefore very likely that Philip commanded these elite troops in person as Gallienus did a bit later.[26]

The quote is also important because it is the only text that describes the fighting methods of the Carpi in any detail. It shows them fighting like their neighbours the Quadi, Vandals, Sarmatians, Alans and Goths. It is clear that the Dacian Carpi had copied the cavalry tactics used by their neighbours. However, this does not conclusively prove that they did not have infantry because the Vandals and Goths certainly had. Furthermore, we know from later sources that even such famed light infantry soldiers as the *Sklavenoi* (Slavs) possessed excellent cavalry forces that could raid Roman territory without the involvement of their infantry.

This means that Philip the Arab attacked the Carpi with a large cavalry army consisting of two cavalry lines in which he was in personal command of the Moorish cavalry in the second line while the seventh *schola* served as his personal bodyguard in the centre of the second line. The initial attack with the cavalry formed in close order forced the Carpi to flee back to their marching camp/fort, but the pursuit and the presence of the fortified camp/fort in front of the pursuing Roman cavalry disordered them to such an extent that the Carpi were able to regroup and counterattack. The disordered Romans were unable to withstand this attack so Philip had to order his reserve of Moorish cavalry forward. Even if Zosimus fails to state this, it is probable that the other units of the second line were also ordered forward. If the only unit that counterattacked consisted of the Moors, then there are two possibilities. Firstly, that the cavalry forces in this case consisted of ca. 5,000–15,000 men so that there was only one or two divisions in the reserve, but this is very unlikely on the basis of the known sizes of cavalry armies used at this time, for which see my biography of Gallienus. Secondly, if the Moors formed the reserves of the centre, then it is possible that only those Romans who had been in the centre of the front line had been forced back by the presence of the fortified camp/fort, so it sufficed to counter the enemy attack with only Moors. This alternative and the alternative in which all units of a

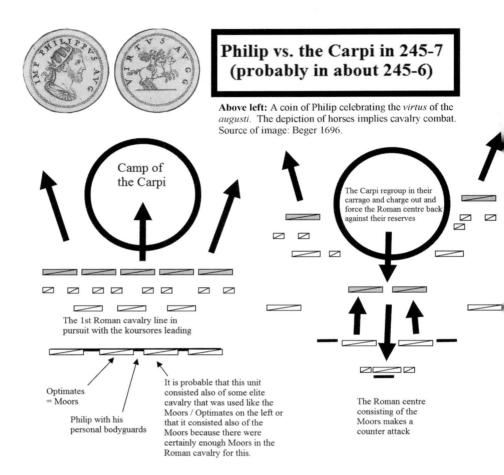

Philip vs. the Carpi in 245-7 (probably in about 245-6)

Above left: A coin of Philip celebrating the *virtus* of the *augusti*. The depiction of horses implies cavalry combat. Source of image: Beger 1696.

Camp of the Carpi

The Carpi regroup in their carrago and charge out and force the Roman centre back against their reserves

The 1st Roman cavalry line in pursuit with the koursores leading

Optimates = Moors

Philip with his personal bodyguards

It is probable that this unit consisted also of some elite cavalry that was used like the Moors / Optimates on the left or that it consisted also of the Moors because there were certainly enough Moors in the Roman cavalry for this.

The Roman centre consisting of the Moors makes a counter attack

large cavalry army had been ordered to make a counterattack are likelier, but the likeliest is the one in which the round shape of the wagon laager/carrago would have enabled the Carpi to break up the Roman centre so that the Roman counterattack was conducted only by the reserves of the centre. This version is the one reconstructed. The counterattack was a success and the Carpi sued for peace. I would suggest that this battle took place in 245–6 and that it was because of this crushing defeat that only 3,000 Carpi joined the Goths in 246. It was then after these successes in 245–7 that the Philippi could return to Rome victorious.

From the point of view of Roman military history the important point here is that Zosimus's text shows Philip employing the very same cavalry tactics as are in evidence under Decius and Gallienus, for which see my biography of Gallienus. As noted above, it is probable that the increased importance of the cavalry in warfare started under Alexander Severus, that he increased its numbers very significantly, and we find his successor Maximinus Thrax employing cavalry as his main striking force against the Germans. However, it is still clear that Maximinus Thrax and then Gordian III both employed significant numbers of infantry to support their cavalry while we find Decius

A coin depicting Philip Sr., Otacilia and Philip Jr. with the text *Germanicus Maximus* and *Carpicus Maximus* on the reverse dated to the year 248. The coin celebrated the great victory of Philip the Arab against the Germans and Carpi. Source: Cohen.

employing only cavalry without any infantry support against the Goths. Does this mean that the change in which the Romans employed only large forces of cavalry for major battles without any infantry support dates from the reign of Philip the Arab? This would make Philip the Arab the major reformer of Roman combat methods. However, in my opinion this is taking the evidence a bit too far. We do not know if the cavalry described by Zosimus had infantry posted in its support somewhere further to the rear or inside a marching camp. Furthermore, the Romans already used independently operating cavalry forces during the Republican era and also during the early Principate. For the latter, see for example my article dealing with the Germanic wars of Germanicus in AD 13–16 available online at *academia.edu*. In sum, I would suggest that the Romans were always prepared to use cavalry for combat alone if the situation allowed it, so Philip the Arab's actions were not without precedent, but I would still suggest that Philip now set a precedent for his successors Decius and Gallienus that it was wiser to employ a very large cavalry force against invaders that used only cavalry forces. Under a capable leader like Gallienus this worked well, and in fact it initially worked quite well under Decius when he used the tactic of feigned flight against the Goths. But when his successes had gone to his head, he was fooled by the very same trick.[27]

As already noted, the Adventus Augg(ustorum) coins prove that Philip had returned to Rome by the end of the summer 247. The father and son returned as victors and the coins announced Felicitas Impp with the Civic Crown. The latter symbol was usually used as a recognition by the Senate for merits that benefited the entire city of Rome. It was apparently then that Philip Sr. raised his son Philip Jr. to the rank of *Augustus* to celebrate their victory over the Germans and Carpi because Philip Jr. still had the title of *Caesar* in an inscription dated to 11 July 247, but had the rank of *Augustus* in the fourth Egyptian year of his father, so Philip Jr. must have been nominated *Augustus* before 30 August 247.

Philip also distributed his second '*liberalitas*' to the populace on this occasion. Philip the Arab must have been elated and prepared to celebrate the thousandth Anniversary of Rome in 248.[28]

The Other Fronts in 245–48

As noted already, Philip the Arab appears to have given his brother Priscus the order to provide assistance for the Armenians in about 245–6 with the result that the combined armies of Armenia and Rome fought with great success against the Persians in 245/6–9. This required money and Priscus appears to have used heavy-handed means to obtain it because he soon faced a revolt, as we shall see.

On the basis of the creation of the office of *praepositus limitis* for one sector of the Tripolitanian *limes* during the reign of Philip in about 244–47 and the position of *procurator* of the *limes Tripolitanus* for M. Aurelius Comius Cassianus and Lucretius Marcellus in 248, this sector faced a serious nomadic threat at that time. This must have been caused by the dissolution of *legio III Augusta* by Gordian III, which had seriously weakened the defences and had resulted in the abandonment of the outer defence posts and in the partial redeployment of the remaining troops.[29]

There were also troubles in Italy where Philip sent marines from Ravenna to Petra Pertusa on the Umbrian coast to clear the brigands and presumably also the pirates from this area. The date of this policing operation is uncertain.[30] This means that the local resources had not been enough to police the coastal areas and the sea so that the intervention of the professional navy and its marines was needed.

7.4 The Apogee of Philip's Reign: The Millenary Celebrations in April 248

When Philip returned from his Balkan campaign, the Senate gave him the abovementioned titles and confirmed his son's appointment as *Augustus*. His wife Otacilia was named *mater Augusti et castrorum et senatus et patriae*. After this he presided over the secular games and millennium celebrations of Rome with a great pomp and style.[31]

The 1,000th anniversary of Rome was an important opportunity for public propaganda. It is probable that the celebrations took place in April 248 because the millenary year began on 21 April 247 (when Philip was still fighting in the Balkans) and was completed on 21 April 248. The coins date the celebrations to the year 248. This was an opportunity for him to make a public display of his generosity and benevolence to the populace. He duly delivered a no-expenses-spared secular games, and distributed his third '*liberalitas*' to the populace. The festivities lasted for three days and three nights and included theatrical performances on the Campus Martius, 1,000 pairs of gladiators fought, and there was a display of numerous exotic animals some of which were killed.[32] This was undoubtedly the apex of Philip the Arab's career.

> *Jerome (Eusebius-Hieronymus) describes the festivities as follows:*
> 'When the Philips were ruling, the thousandth year of the Roman city was completed. Because of this solemnity, innumerable wild animals were slain in the Circus Maximus [*Julius Capitolinus lists these, but only because Philip committed*

A coin of Philip the Arab celebrating the 1000th Anniversary of the city of Rome and Saecular Games. The COS III dates this to the year 248. Source: Cohen.

a sacrilege when doing so, as is noted by York on p.61. The animals in question had originally been collected for the triumph of Gordian III's Persian war]; theatrical games were performed in the Campus Martius for three days and three nights, while the populace watched.' Dated incorrectly to the year 249, tr. by York, p.60 with two changes and one comment.

The celebrations were also the occasion during which Philip the Arab demonstrated his devotion to conservative values which were in vogue among significant sections of the pagan senatorial class at this time. It was easy enough for the Christian Philip the Arab to share these values.

Aurelius Victor describes the event as follows:
'They [*father and son Philip*] celebrated the thousandth anniversary of the city with games of all kinds… but it was celebrated with none of the customary festivities, so drastically has the concern for Rome diminished day by day. In fact they say that this was announced at that time by prodigies and portents… For when some victims were being sacrificed according to pontifical law, female genitals appeared on a hog's abdomen. This the soothsayers interpreted to predict the decadence of later generations and the aggravation of vices. The emperor Philip, because he thought that this would prove false and then again because he had caught sight of a young boy prostitute resembling his son as he happened to walk past him, took very honourable measures to abolish the practice of male prostitution. Nevertheless it still survives, for if circumstances are altered it is practised even more outrageously as long as men seek more avidly whatever is dangerous and forbidden.' Aurelius Victor 28, tr. by H.W. Bird, 29–30 with comments added.

Below and right: Coins of Philip celebrating the Secular Games.
Source of images: Cohen

The prohibition of male prostitution that accompanied the festivities is confirmed by the *Historia Augusta* (*Elagabalus* 33.6; *Alexander* 24.4), and it was a sign of the times which were dominated by conservative prudish views of what was appropriate and what was not. Philip apparently did not only prohibit male prostitution, but also prostitution in general, closing the brothels. The change in attitudes took place after the reign of Elagabalus and was very much in evidence under Alexander Severus, but in truth its origins were even earlier, the best proof of this being Cassius Dio's reaction to Caracalla's behaviour at Alexandria. Dio disapproved in the strongest possible terms to Caracalla's reaction to homosexual practices in Alexandria; Caracalla had only voiced his disapproval of homosexual behaviour while Dio would have wanted to see homosexuals killed – it must have been a horrible shock for a man like Dio and his ilk to see the bisexual behaviour of Elagabalus.[33] This was an era of societal conservativism which reached its apogee under Decius and Valerian who sought to restore the 'good old times' by persecuting Christians and other deviants while old customs and religious practices were brought back – after all, this had been the policy under Gordian III. Philip not only prohibited male prostitution but also homosexuality and castration.[34]

The *Eis Basilea* appears to have been presented to Philip on the occasion of his millenary celebrations in April 248. This text shows that Philip had been very successful as Emperor until then. He had defeated the barbarian invaders and the Persians. He had been dutiful, just, affable, calm and easy to approach. He had showered the soldiers with donatives so they were happy to serve under the strict discipline imposed on them by Philip the Arab. The soldiers were no longer allowed to spend their free time in the lap of luxury. Philip hardened the soldiers through relentless training and forbade them from plundering the property of Romans when marching through their lands or when billeted in their houses. This also meant that it was easier for the state to get its revenues because they had not been stolen by undisciplined soldiers. These laudatory comments, however, were said too soon because the soldiers revolted in 248. One wonders whether the prudish attitude to sex demonstrated by the legislation had a role in this so that the bribery of the soldiers with money was not enough to satisfy them when their sexual needs were not fulfilled.

The *Eis Basilea* also shows that Philip made every effort to please the senatorial class so that it would support him and his family. He appears to have allowed freedom of speech: his spies, who circulated in all of the cities, were not to persecute people for their opinions. The text also praises Philip for his self-discipline: he was not a slave of food or sexual desires. This indeed seems to have been the case, and it shows in his legislative work. He seems on the whole to have behaved like a Christian was expected to in his personal life if one overlooks his treacherous side.[35]

7.5 The Egyptian Revolts in 247–49 and the Usurpations of Jotapianus and Pacatianus in 248–49

The celebrations of the millenary year and happiness of the occasion did not last for long. The Emperor received horrible news soon enough, probably in the latter half of 248. The sources give us conflicting and irreconcilable versions of what happened, which will be quoted below. What is certain, however, is that there were revolts in Alexandria in 247–49 and that usurpers emerged against Philip the Arab in 248–49. I begin the account with a description of the people of Alexandria and circumstances which led to these revolts.

The circumstances that led to the revolt in Alexandria are discussed in some detail by John Marvin York and it is worth including his translation of the relevant section of *Oracula Sibyllina* on which he bases his analysis. The text has been partially translated and analyzed in REF1 (46–7, 359) and I include some changes, comments and additions on the basis of this.

Oracula Sibyllina 13.56–78 (43–78 in York)
'So also the Persians will be far from achieving victory on that day, so long as the beloved nurse of the Italians, situated in the plain of the Nile, send a portion of produce to the seven-crested Rome… so many years will she willingly give thee measure… Another distress for the greatly suffering Alexandrians will I sing, destroyed by the battle of shameless men, those formerly mighty, becoming craven and feeble, will submit to peace, because of the cowardice of their leaders and wrath against the Assyrians [*York p.66 suggests that this should be interpreted as a revolt of the Alexandrians against the heavy taxation needed for the war against the Persians and for feeding the populace at Rome. He also suggests that the Alexandrian revolt was defeated by force*]… and a torrent of River will destroy them utterly, and He, coming to a citadel of Caesar, will injure the Canaanites [*York pp.66–7 suggests that this means the Jews of Dura Europos. This seems like a good guess but other cities are also possible; the Oracle looked to the future, namely the capture of Dura Europos or some other city by the Persians in the 250s. In my opinion, this account may also imply that 'cowardly' Priscus was forced to sign a peace treaty with the Persians or that he just stopped his campaign because Alexandria revolted and there were no supplies available for the continuance of*

the war and that Priscus then squashed the revolt. The likeliest interpretation is that Priscus was forced to abandon his campaign without the signing of any peace treaty with the Persians because Sapor would not have believed anything that the Romans promised at this stage. This would then have enabled Sapor I to capture some fortress of 'Caesar'. However, it is also possible that this refers to the situation after Priscus and Philip had been killed because the account appears to refer to the invasion of Roman territories that took place under Decius]. The Pyramus shall water the city of Mopsus, where there will fall the Aegaeans, because of the strife of mighty men [*On the basis of Polemius Silvius (Chron. Min. 1.521) John Marvin York (pp.67–8) suggests that this refers to the usurpation of Jotapianus: he would have started his revolt in Cappadocia and advanced from there to Syria where he would then have been killed in uncertain circumstances while Philip was still alive*]. Wretched Antioch, the exacting Ares [*Priscus*] will not leave thee while the Assyrian war will last; for in the houses will dwell a military leader of men who will make war on all the arrow-shooting Persians [*This probably implies that the soldiers were billeted in the city as long as the war against Persia lasted which was the entire period from ca. 246 onwards, with the implication that Priscus continued the Assyrian/Persian war as long as he was in charge*]; and he himself [*i.e. Priscus*] comes from the royal house of the Romans. Now adorn yourselves, cities of Arabia… Bostra and Philippopolis… ye who have listened too much to them, wretched, when, afterwards, that your final day is to approach [*York (pp.70–1) is quite correct to note that the adorning of these two cities caused envy and anger and was one of the reasons for the populace to join the revolt against Priscus and Philip*]. Now for the strife-loving Alexandria I will sing the direst battles; many of the common people then will perish, townsmen put to death by uncitizen-like fellows [*this would be Priscus once again*], citizens battling for the sake of malicious strife; for them swift and fearful Ares will cease from war [*This suggests that Priscus indeed halted his campaign against the Persians to punish Alexandrians with bloodshed*].' tr. by York, 65–73.

The revolt of Alexandria is confirmed by the letter of St. Dionysius Bishop of Alexandria to Fabius of Antioch which has been preserved by Eusebius. The principal reason of the revolt would have been the heavy taxation introduced by Priscus and by the central government to pay for the war fought against the Persians and to feed the populace at Rome, but there was another equally important reason too. York is correct to note that the letter refers to a pogrom against the Christians that took place under Philip the Arab without his approval at the instigation of some nameless prophet and worker of mischief. The terror against the Christians remained intense for a long time during which they were tortured, burned and their property stolen, but the pogrom ended when the Christian rulers exacted vengeance against the persecutors. This means that one of the reasons for the revolt in Alexandria was the favouritism of Christians and Christianity by Priscus and Philip, and that this had caused a counter-reaction in Alexandria where the populace had been incited to a pogrom of Christians by some unnamed prophet. The pogrom against the Christians was a revolt and Priscus punished the culprits by the sword. In my opinion, it is probable that this unnamed prophet is Macrianus, the teacher and guild-leader of the Egyptian magicians who later incited the Emperor Valerian to begin a persecution of Christians and who then usurped power against Valerian's son Gallienus.[36]

The date of the revolt in Alexandria is uncertain. It is usually assumed on the basis of the letter preserved by Eusebius to have taken place roughly in 248/9, but on the basis of the above quote of *Oracula Sibyllina* it is possible that it actually took place in late 247 or early 248. Perhaps both alternatives are true so that the revolt started in late 247, was crushed with much bloodshed, and the area remained troublesome even after that. In fact, modern research has confirmed that there were pogroms in 247, 248 and again in 249, so apparently Priscus had been unable to pacify the situation so that it required constant imperial intervention.[37]

In my opinion, on the basis of circumstantial evidence (friendships and events), it is quite possible or even probable that there was a large scale cabal of pagan 'magicians' at work at this time, which included the above-mentioned prophet Macrianus, Valerian (the future Emperor) and most importantly Decius (the future Emperor) and that the plan was to overthrow Philip and his brother Priscus. This cabal operated just as effectively and covertly as the cabal of Christians had worked under Philip and Priscus when they got rid of Timesitheus, Gordian III, Marcus Silbannacus and Severus Sponsianus. It is uncertain whether the usurpers of 248–9, Jotapianus and Pacatianus, belonged to this cabal or not, but it is entirely plausible.

The above reference to the cowardly leaders and halting of the war suggests that Priscus only halted his campaign against the Persians to crush the Alexandrian revolt, because the same text also mentions the continued successes of the Romans against the Persians and the hardships this caused for the populations in the East in the form of taxation. The statement that Priscus (and apparently his soldiers) continued to be billeted in Antioch suggests strongly that he did not conclude any peace with Persia. When the above text is taken together with the evidence given by Zosimus (quoted below) it is clear that the over-taxation of Egyptians and Easterners in general to pay the costs of the war effort of the Romans and Armenians against Persia caused such dissatisfaction in the East that it led to the usurpation of Jotapianus against Philip and Priscus; and this against the background that the brothers still had plenty of money to adorn their native lands and cities with buildings. This was not a wise policy. *Eis Basilea* (16) claims the exact opposite, namely that Philip had lowered taxes and reduced wasteful spending. Admittedly this text is a panegyric, but there are still good reasons to accept this statement because Philip did indeed reduce wasteful spending, but he did this by placing the local elites under stricter supervision of the central government and also removed some of the tax exemptions both of which naturally caused resentment. In short, Khosrov the Great of Armenia and *rector Orientis* Priscus were highly successful in their war against the Persians and advanced all the way to the Persian capital, but the cost of this war was so great that Priscus and the central administration over-taxed or rather over-controlled the Easterners, which manifested itself for this first time in the revolt of Alexandria (and presumably of Egypt as a whole) against the Christian rulers in 247 or 248, which was crushed with brute force. After this the Easterners in Asia Minor raised a usurper called Jotapianus possibly in Cappadocia against Priscus and Philip. The debasing of coinage that took place under Philip the Arab was clearly insufficient to meet the demands for money on the eastern front. It should have been debased more drastically.

The usurper Jotapianus is mentioned in three sources: Aurelius Victor (29.2), Zosimus (quoted below) and Polemius Silvius (*Chron. Min. 1*, p.521). The coins give us his full name: M. F. Ru. Iotapianus. The usurper claimed descent from Alexander, which either means that he claimed descent from Severus Alexander or Alexander the Great. Körner has proposed after Syme that he may have belonged to the royal house of Commagene which had queens with the name Iotape I and Iotape II so he would have claimed to be descendant of Alexander the Great. The royal house of Commagene had lost its autonomy and throne under Vespasian. Most scholars, however, contest this and suggest that Jotapianus claimed descent from the Severan dynasty of Emesa and Alexander Severus. I find the arguments of Körner likelier. What is certain is that this usurpation was not made by the army but by the local population with the support of some local military detachments in the East and that it was a popular reaction against the policies and taxation of Priscus and Philip. It is unlikely to be a coincidence that the usurpation started in Asia Minor, the power base of both Timesitheus and the Gordiani. Polemius Silvius states that the usurpation began in Cappadocia and it is indeed likely that he marched from there towards Syria as has been suggested by York and that entire units of soldiers joined the revolt. It is also possible that the usurpation took place at the same time as one of the revolts of Alexandria and Egypt and that it was because of this that the squashing of the revolt took place only towards the end of Philip's reign despite the fact that Priscus must have possessed far greater numbers of men than Jotapianus. The city of Antioch, however, appears to have remained in Priscus' hands. We do not know what happened to Priscus, but in my opinion it is possible that it was he who defeated or stalemated Jotapianus, that Jotapianus was ultimately killed by his own soldiers, and that Priscus managed to survive until his own brother was killed.[38]

York has suggested that the usurpation of Jotapianus and revolt of Alexandria may have been instigated and supported by Persian special operatives. There is no need for this speculation because the overtaxation and favouritism of Christians and Arabia would certainly have been enough to cause troubles and revolts. But if we speculate that he is correct, then this leads to some interesting propositions. It is clear that he has a point because the Persians had special operatives in the Roman East, the best evidence of which are the actions of Myriades-Mereades-Cyriades in Antioch in about 252/3, which has also been noted by York.[39]

If we assume that Persian operatives were active in Alexandria (because this was the logistical hub of the Roman Army of the East and its supplies were needed to support the war effort of both Rome and Armenia) they would have been in contact with Macrianus,

A coin of Macrianus
the Elder.
Source of the image:
Cohen.

the prophet, teacher and guild-leader of Egyptian magicians, who then instigated the pogrom of Christians. This same man was then in charge of provisioning Valerian's army during the Persian wars. If he served as a Persian operative, it is possible that he instigated Valerian to begin the persecution of Christians to weaken Valerian's support in the East where most of the Christians were. It is also possible that he introduced germs into the food supplies, because the Roman army started to suffer from the plague at the decisive moment during Sapor's campaign against them. It is also possible that he advised Valerian to advance against Sapor with far fewer men than the enemy when this was not necessary so that he was then defeated, and after that to meet Sapor I in person to negotiate so that Sapor I was able to capture Valerian. Notably, he remained behind and did not join Valerian. It is also notable that immediately after the capture of Valerian, Macrianus retreated from Samosata to Emesa and thereby opened the invasion route for Sapor. And it is also notable that Macrianus did nothing when the forces of Herodes, the son of Odaenathus, defeated the Persians by the Orontes River, which ran past Emesa. Furthermore, he did nothing to hinder the retreat of Sapor I from Roman territory in a situation in which Ballista, Odaenatus and the garrison of Edessa all took action against the retreating Sapor. And still further, when Odaenathus was then pursuing the Persians to Ctesiphon, Macrianus usurped power and thereby forced Odaenathus to abandon his campaign against the Persian capital and march back against the usurper.[40]

In sum, there is plenty of circumstantial evidence to suggest that Macrianus may have been a Persian special operative working for Sapor I. This would make Sapor one of the most skilled users of special operations of this era, as I and Katarzyna Maksymiuk have already suggested because of other actions of his[41]. The evidence for this new addition to Sapor's CV, however, is uncertain at best even if it is clear that it has its merits. It is indeed very odd that everything that Macrianus did was beneficial to the Persians! If he was a Persian agent, then he deserves to be placed among the most successful ones in history.

An interesting point here is that we do not know what happened to Priscus after the usurpation of Jotapianus, because there is no mention in any source. Aurelius Victor (29.2) notes that the head of Jotapianus was brought to Decius at the beginning of his reign and that he had been killed by the soldiers. Victor follows this immediately with the statement that Lucius Priscus, who was governor of Macedonia, usurped power when the Goths invaded. This took place in 250. Dexippus (*Skythika* frg. 23) also refers to this. The Emperor Decius sent a letter to Priscus who had withdrawn to Philippopolis, to convince him to remain loyal to him and not usurp power. The usual assumption is that this Lucius Priscus of Victor and Priscus of Dexippus is T. Iulius Priscus, and this was also my assumption in my biography of Gallienus (pp.31–3). However, is this really so, or should we identify him with the brother of Philip? It would have been all too easy to confuse Lucius Priscus and Iulius Priscus with each other. If this is the case, then Julius Priscus would have negotiated with Decius from a position of strength because he was in charge of a victorious army that had just defeated the Persians, Alexandrians and Jotapianus. It is easy to see that Decius would have wanted to find a way to reconcile himself with Priscus. The governorship of Thrace and Macedonia in return for surrender and the head of Jotapianus would have been a small price to pay. Furthermore, the transferral of the hated Priscus from the East and from his loyal forces to Thrace would have been a wise policy decision. It is also easy to see why Decius would have become worried about the prospect of usurpation when Priscus and his soldiers had taken a place of refuge in a city named Philippopolis in 250. Even though this city was so named after a king of Macedonia, it was also synonymous with the name of Philip, and indeed this Priscus did usurp power in this city, but was then killed by the Goths when they betrayed him. Unfortunately we do not know if the above speculation is correct or not. Therefore it is probably safest to think that Philip's brother was killed by his own soldiers very soon after Decius gained power.

1. Usurper Jotapianus claiming victory, which he probably achieved initially.
2. Usurper Pacatianus.
3. Usurper Pacatianus.
4. A coin minted at Philippopolis depicting Marinos/Marinus, the name which was used by Zosimus for the usurper in Moesia and Pannonia. If the Philippopolis is the Thracian one, then it is probable that he is Ti. Claudius Marinus Pacatianus. However, if he is not Pacatianus, then he is some unknown usurper from the same area who died without leaving any mark in history. However, according to Cohen (Vol.5, p.228) it is far likelier that the Philippopolis is actually the city named after Philip the Arab in Arabia so that this Marinus / Marinos would then be his father. I agree with this view.
Source of the images: Cohen.

In the Balkans, trouble was brewing roughly at the same time. For some unknown reason an officer named Pacatianus assumed the purple (see the images of the coins). If one of the Gothic invasions mentioned by Jordanes took place at about this time, as is usually assumed,[42] it is possible that the soldiers wanted their own emperor against the impending invasion of the Goths, or simply because they and the pagan traditionalists among them did not want to see an Arab Christian as emperor of Rome. However, in my opinion the likeliest reason for the usurpation is the one that I have already suggested above, namely that Philip had first provoked the Goths to a war in about 245–7 and that he had then bought them off by allowing them to receive a ransom for Marcianopolis and then allowing them to leave unmolested. This would have been a greater offence to the manliness of the local soldiers than had been the postponement of the German war by Alexander Severus which had been exploited by Maximinus Thrax. It is easy to see how such a situation could have been exploited by an ambitious officer like Pacatianus when the soldiers (and possibly also Pacatianus himself) did not know that Philip had used germ warfare against the Goths.

The usurper Pacatianus is primarily known from Zosimus and Zonaras (both quoted below) and from his extant coins. It is thanks to the coins that we have his complete name: T. Claudius Marinus Pacatianus. See the attached illustrations and plates. He was a Roman commander on the Danube frontier and most modern historians think it is probable that he held senatorial rank even though Zonaras considered him unworthy of this position. On the basis of Zonaras's terminology it is likelier that he was a relatively low ranking officer. He was supported by the forces posted in Moesia (Zosimus, Zonaras) and in Pannonia (Zosimus). Pacatianus appears to have captured the mint of Viminacium because it did not strike any coins for Philip in 248/9.[43]

7.6 The Usurpation of Decius in about April/May 249 and the Death of Philip in about August/September 249

What follows next is uncertain. As noted above, we do not know how, when or where Jotapianus was killed, and the same with Pacatianus. All that we know is that both were killed by their own soldiers. Furthermore, the exact circumstances and places of the usurpation of Decius and the place of the death of the two Philippi are hopelessly confused in the sources. As Pat Southern (2001, p.74) and Yasmine Zahran (124–9) correctly note, there are two main versions. Firstly, the sources that claim that Decius usurped power in Moesia/Balkans and then advanced to Italy where he fought a decisive battle against Philip at Verona where at least Philip Sr. died in combat. Secondly, there are sources which claim that Decius usurped power in Rome and that Philip Sr. was killed by assassins at Beroea. It is therefore worthwhile to present the evidence for both alternatives. The principal sources which claim that Decius usurped power in the Balkans consist of Zosimus, Aurelius Victor and Zonaras.

Zosimus describes the events as follows:
'As there were at that time [*in 248*] many disturbances in the empire, in the eastern provinces, which were uneasy, partly owing to the exactions of exorbitant tributes, and partly to their dislike of Priscus [*Priscus needed money to support the joint war*

effort of Khosrov the Great of Armenia and the Romans against the Persians and also for the building of Philippopolis (modern Shabba) and for other projects in the East. If the war effort against the Persians is to be dated to have taken place in about 245/6–49 then it is clear that the extraordinary taxation required to support the Armenians was the reason for the revolts], their governor, who was a man of intolerably evil disposition, wished for innovation, and set up Iotapianus [*M. F. Ru. Iotapianus, who according to Aurelius Victor claimed to be a descendant of Alexander*] for emperor, while the inhabitants of Moesia and Pannonia were more inclined to Marinus [*usurper Ti. Claudius Marinus Pacatianus⁴⁴*]. Philip, being disturbed by these events, desired the senate either to assist him against such imminent dangers [*There are two possible reasons for this. Firstly, if Philip had converted only in 248, he had by then confessed his sins publicly so he did not want to commit any further acts of sin requiring public repentance. Secondly, he appears to have been in poor health, see below*], or if they were displeased with his government, to suffer him to lay it down and dismiss him quietly. No person making a reply to this, Decius, a person of illustrious birth and rank [*and at that time the praefectus urbi*], and moreover gifted with every virtue [*This is the pagan view of Decius who was in truth a horrible failure as Emperor and person. Zosimus was a pagan himself and his writings reflect this*], observed that he was unwise in being so much concerned at those events, for they would vanish of themselves, and could not possibly subsist. [*It is possible that Decius's answer was planned in advance with Philip so that the whole event was orchestrated to test the senators while also calming them*] And… the event corresponded with the conjecture of Decius, which long experience… had enabled him to make, Iotapianus and Marinus being taken off with little trouble, yet Philip was still in fear [*this suggests that both usurpations ended by April 249*], knowing how obnoxious the officers in that country were to the army. He therefore desired Decius to assume the command of the *tagmata* [*usually translated as legions, but actually means just large military units*] in Moesia and Pannonia. As he refused… Philip… compelled him to go to Pannonia to punish the accomplices of Marinus. [*This was a vast ranging command uniting all of the Roman forces in the Balkans with the title dux Moesiae et Pannoniae. The reason why the Balkans needed a commander with such wide ranging powers was probably that there was a risk that the Goths could exploit or had exploited the Roman civil war depending on how one interprets the sources. Philip could not take the command in person possibly because of his Christian convinctions and/or his poor health or simply because Decius and Philip had planned this all along. It is possible that the references to Decius's actions in Jordanes' Getica, namely the dismissal of soldiers from service, should be placed here, but as noted the year 245/6 is likelier*] The army in that country, finding that Decius punished all that had offended, thought it most politic to avoid the present danger and to set up a sovereign who would better consult the good of the state, and who, being more expert in both civil and military affairs, might without difficulty conquer Philip. For this purpose they clothed Decius in purple,… Philip therefore, on hearing that Decius was thus made emperor, collected all his forces to overpower him. The supporters of Decius, though they knew that the enemy had greatly the advantage in numbers, still retained their confidence, trusting to the general skill and prudence of Decius in affairs. [*It is possible that this laudatory account of Decius's performance is falsified as regards the relative sizes of the two armies. It is inherently likelier that if Decius had been dispatched to the Balkans that he had taken some reinforcements with him. If he then revolted in the Balkans, he had access to the armies located there plus the reinforcements that he had taken with him. In contrast, Philip would have had access only to those forces that he had in the immediate vicinity of the capital which were certainly fewer than the armies posted in the Balkans. On the other hand, it is clear that both had time to collect reinforcements because Decius usurped in about May and the decisive battle took place only in August/September. If the revolt of Decius took place in Rome so that the two men exchanged places after Decius had dismissed the supporters of Pacatianus from the ranks and Philip had taken over command of operations against the Goths as the accounts of John of Antioch (see below) and Jordanes' Getica may suggest, then it is clear that Decius had fewer men than Philip because he had access only to those still in the vicinity of Rome. If Decius had fewer men than Philip then it is probable that he conducted a similar feigned flight with an ambush as he did later against the Goths, and that Philip foolishly swallowed the bait and died in the front ranks as Zonaras states (see below). But even in this case there is the problem that John of Antioch claims that Philip died at Beroea at the hands of men sent by Decius. One possible solution would be that Philip lost at Verona and then fled to Beroea where he was then killed]* And when the two armies engaged, although the one was superior in number, yet the other so excelled it in discipline and conduct that a great number of Philip's partisans were slain, and he himself amongst them, together with his son, on whom he had conferred the title of Caesar. *[This account suggests that Philip was losing the battle and lost his life because of that, but this is not conclusive because the source is overtly hostile]* Decius thus acquired the empire. The Scythians, taking advantage of the disorder which everywhere prevailed through the negligence of Philip, crossed the Tanais, and pillaged the countries in the vicinity of Thrace [*This is an obvious distortion of the facts. It had been the revolt of Decius that had opened the route for invasion in 250*]. But Decius, marching against them… [*The rest is told in my biography of Gallienus*]' Zosimus 1.20.2–22.2, tr. by anon. 1814, p.14 with changes, corrections and comments.

Aurelius Victor describes the same as follows:
'After completing these projects [*The millenium celebrations and the forbidding of male prostitution*] he [*Philip Sr.*] left his son in the city and set out in person against Decius, even though he was physically weak for his age. [*This text therefore suggests that Philip was not in good physical shape so it would been because of this that he dispatched Decius to Illyricum rather than go there in person*] He fell at Verona after the defeat and loss of his army. [*This account suggests that Philip died because he lost the battle, but is not conclusive because the source is hostile to him*] When the news of this had reached Rome his son was killed in the praetorian camp.' Aurelius Victor 28, tr. by H. W. Bird, p.30 with comments added.

Zonaras claims that the circumstances were as follows:
'When others were silent, Decius told him that he did not need to be concerned about Marinus [*Pacatianus*], as he would be killed by the soldiers themselves,… which is what happened a little later… [*Was this another special operation by Philip's*

agents like the killings of Marcus Silbannacus and Severus Sponsianus and which has been suppressed by sources hostile to Philip? I would suggest that this is quite possible, but I would still suggest that Decius had a role in these actions. As praefectus urbi Decius was certainly involved in special operations and this could have been performed officially on behalf of Philip. Furthermore, it is possible that the confidence of Decius was the result of him being a member oft the pagan cabal and that it had been this group that committed the murders] Then, on account of this, Philippus admired Decius [*This suggests that in the capacity of praefectus urbi Decius had indeed directed his special operatives to kill both usurpers. Philip clearly trusted Decius because Decius had been an enemy of the Gordiani*] and urged him to depart to Moesia and punish the instigators of the revolt [*This connects these events with the account of Jordanes*]… Though unwilling, he departed. [*It is possible that we should place here the above-mentioned quote from the Getica of Jordanes in which Decius was placed in charge of the forces in the Balkans so that Decius then dismissed Roman soldiers from service and that they then deserted to the Gothic forces, and that when the Goths and these men then invaded, Philip marched there in person and defeated the Goths and was advancing towards Byzantium when he learnt that Decius had usurped power in Rome. This, however, is likely to be one of the anti-Philip lies in which the sacking of rebels caused the enemy invasion, while in truth it was the usurpation of Decius that opened the borders*] After he had departed the soldiers immediately hailed him sovereign. [*This piece of information states that Decius usurped power in Moesia*]… from there he wrote to Philippus not to be troubled, for if he advanced on Rome, he would set aside the trappings of sovereignty. But distrusting this, Philippus took the field against him. When he had attacked Decius's men, he fell fighting in the front ranks. [*This account does not state whether Philip was winning or losing when he died*] With him too was killed his son Philippus. [*It is probable that he was killed in Rome, see below*] With them dead, all went over to Decius. [*The fact that the soldiers surrendered after the death of the Emperor suggests that Philip's army had not been defeated at the time of his death*]' Zonaras 12.19, tr. by Banchich/Lane (47) with comments added.

The above sources therefore claim that when Philip learned of the revolts of Pacatianus and Jotapianus, he offered to resign if the Senate wished him to. The most likely reasons for the claimed 'panic' of Philip was that he was in poor physical condition (or possibly because he had recently confessed his Christianity) and was therefore in no position to lead a military campaign. But there is a likelier alternative – Philip wanted to show the senators that he was irreplaceable. If true, then it was probably a ploy to test the loyalty of the senators in a situation in which there were usurpations. However, in consideration of what followed next, it is very possible that Philip's health was not what it used to be. It is said that Decius consoled him by stating that the revolts would soon be crushed with ease. And so it seems to have happened. Pacatianus was killed by his soldiers. Undoubtedly the secret service agents had had some role in it – the 'consoling words' imply that. The same fate awaited Jotapianus. It was Decius who received his head. This also appears to have been a special operation because he too was killed by his own men. It is uncertain who the man was who directed the special operatives in these cases. Both Philip and Decius certainly knew how to perform such operations and so did Priscus in the east; but if Decius directed the operations, then he did it as Philip's subordinate in the capacity of *praefectus urbi*.

After this, Philip appointed Decius to take charge of the Balkan army to purge the remaining pockets of resistance. Decius seemed perfect for the job for many reasons. He had shown the right spirit, he was a pagan and native of the Balkans, and as a former enemy of the Gordiani he was most likely loyal and trustworthy. He knew the theatre of operations well for he had been born in the Pannonian village (*vicus*) of Budalia near Sirmium in ca. 190 AD, and had also served as governor of Moesia in 234 and he may also have served in the area in 245, so he had local contacts that he could be expected to exploit. In addition, he was acceptable to the Senate and soldiers because he was a senator and former consul. It was then that Decius purged the Roman army, as stated by Jordanes and Zonaras. It is also possible that Decius and Philip used a stratagem to spread germs to the Gothic population when they sacked Pacatianus's supporters if they included Goths likely to return to their native lands. However, as stated, on the basis of *Eis Basilea* it is far likelier that Jordanes has misplaced the different parts of his account and that Decius merely purged the army (possibly for the first time in 245–6 and then again in 249 which could easily have caused the confusion) and that there were no Gothic invasions in about 248–9 even if most historians think there were,[45] unless it took place very late in 249. Jordanes clearly places the invasion of Cniva to the year 250–1.

According to this version of events, Philip and his son were both in Rome when Decius usurped power in the Balkans, and Philip then advanced against the usurper from Rome. The problematic part in this version is the claim of Zosimus that Philip would have had superior numbers, because it is clear that in normal circumstances there were more men in the Balkans than there were in Rome. However, this could be explained by the time it took for the two sides to fight the decisive battle, which would have allowed Philip to bring mainly cavalry reinforcements from Gaul and Raetia before the engagement. This is quite plausible in light of the information provided by Zosimus, Zonaras and Aurelius Victor. The sources clearly state that it was Philip who attacked and that he died fighting in the front ranks. The side which attacks is usually the stronger one. Furthermore, the location of the decisive battle, the area close to Verona, may suggest that Philip had brought reinforcements through the Brenner Pass; the other alternative being that Decius had marched through the pass after he had collected reinforcements from Raetia.

Unfortunately none of these descriptions give any details of the actual combat. All that is stated is that Philip died while fighting in the front ranks; we do not even know whether he was winning or losing the battle before he died. If the latter is the case, then it is probable that Decius would have used the same feigned flight cavalry tactic against Philip as he later used against the Goths and that Philip swallowed the bait because he had superior numbers. The location (see the maps section) certainly has many valleys on the east side of the Athesis/Adige River that would have enabled the placing of an ambush, but since the area was well-known to both sides the existence of these valleys was not a secret. Furthermore, it is possible that the battle was fought on the plain west of the Athesis/Adige River.

If Philip was winning the battle at the time of his death, then it is probable that this was just a regular cavalry battle, with the infantry left behind, in which Philip had decided to follow the example set by Caracalla and Maximinus Thrax in that he lead his men from the front in a heroic manner hoping to encourage his numerically superior forces to crush the upstart. It would then have been the poor physical shape of the man and sheer bad luck that decided the battle, Philip dying in the midst of his attack. This alternative is probably likelier in light of Philip's successful career as a military leader and because the sources are favourable towards Decius, but not conclusively so because Decius had also demonstrated his military skills earlier in Spain when his surrender was obtained only through negotiations. It is easy to think that in anger the brave Philip could have easily been carried and spearheaded the pursuit of the forces of the treacherous usurper only to be ambushed and killed. Whatever the truth, it is clear that the seventh *schola* created by Philip was not able to save his life.

It is probable that Philip's son did not die on the battlefield as claimed by these sources, but in Rome as claimed by several other sources. The *Epitome* (28.2–3) claims that Philip the father was killed by the army at Verona, his head split from the top down to his teeth, while his 12-year-old son was killed in Rome. The details given of the cut (likely to be a sword cut) means that the man who delivered it had pretty good technique. Eutropius (9.3) also states that Philip and the son were killed by the soldiers, Philip in Verona and his son in Rome. This piece of evidence could be interpreted so that Philip was killed by his own men or that he was killed by the enemy army, the latter being likelier on the basis of the other texts. Philip certainly died a hero's death at close quarters fighting with swords. The heroic bent of Philip is confirmed by the *Eis Basilea* (29), which refers to his personal bravery – it was this bravery that caused his death.

John of Antioch (frg 226, Roberto ed. p. 408 = frg. 1.48 Müller FHG 4, p.598) provides still another version of the events, the important point being that this text claims that Philip Sr. and Philip Jr. died in different places and that Philip Sr. was killed at Beroea rather than near Verona. Orosius (7.20) also claims that the father and son died in different places and that one of them died as a result of a mutiny of soldiers while the other as a result of the treachery of Decius. In light of this it would seem safest to assume that at least Philip Jr. died in Rome, while Philip Sr. died in Beroea, but obviously one cannot be certain.

'Philippus, after he had become sovereign and conquered the Scythians, began to advance against Byzantium. [*This would imply that it was Philip who was fighting against the Goths in 249 and that the Goths had exploited the usurpation of Pacatianus by invading and that Decius was then unable to crush them. The problem with this is that it would leave very little time for the war between the Gepidae and Goths and for the peaceful remaining rule of Ostrogotha, and it is also contradicted by Eis Basilea. It is therefore probable that this is just a general statement referring to the victory of Philip over the Goths at some point in time during his reign*] And when he arrived at Perinthus, as it was announced to him that there had occurred in Rome civil disturbances, which Decius one of the consuls and prefect of the city had fomented, he sent capable men to check what was being done and to frustrate Decius's uprising. And… (Decius), with his sons, began to make offers to comply. As soon as the men whom Philippus dispatched to Rome had been won over by both gifts and flatteries of the people and the senate, they both renounced Philippus and, with the Romans, declared Decius emperor… When these things had been announced to Philippus, [who was] fleeing to Beroe… and they killed him with daggers hidden under robes, after he had directed affairs for five years. And in Rome the soldiers of the city killed his son.' John of Antioch frg. 226, tr. Banchich/Lane, 93.

On the basis of John of Antioch and Jordanes, it would be possible to think that Decius purged the army in the Balkans but was then unable to defeat the Goths, or alternatively, as suggested by York, he did not even attempt to do that because his only aim was to foment support for himself in the army. In other words, he punished the soldiers unreasonably and claimed that all this was done in the name of Philip against his own will. It was then because of this that the armies of Pannonia and Moesia were unable to do anything against the invading Goths so it required the presence of Philip who duly marched to the Balkans and defeated them. When this then took place, Decius exploited the absence of Philip from Rome and obtained the support of those in the capital. In the meantime, after having defeated the Goths Philip marched towards Byzantium with the idea of crossing the straits to crush the revolt of Jotapianus, if it had not yet ended, but then he learnt that Decius had usurped power in Rome. At first Philip tried to win over the Senate and people through his representatives, but Decius managed to bribe them to join his cause. Philip could do nothing else but march against the usurper. John does not mention the battle of Verona, but since Philip was fleeing to Beroea it is possible to think that he lost a battle there, or alternatively that there was no battle at all so that Philip was assassinated when he retreated to Beroea to assemble his forces. This would mean that the battle at Verona resulted from the confusion of Beroea and Verona in the sources. It was then at Beroea in September 249 that he was killed by the assassins carrying hidden daggers.[46]

It is impossible to know with certainty which of the versions is correct, but in light of the problems with Jordanes's account, namely his references to the fighting between Gepidae and Goths and the peaceful remaining rule of Ostrogotha and the clear reference to the use of intellect against the barbarian invaders by Philip in *Eis Basilea*, it is in my opinion preferable to think that the accounts of Zosimus, Zonaras and Aurelius Victor are correct in claiming that there was a battle near Verona where Philip the Elder died, except that it is likely that Philip the Younger was not killed at Verona but in Rome after the death of his father. This version also receives support from the results of the probable use of germ warfare by Philip the Arab against the Goths in about 246/7. The payments made to the Goths besieging Marcianopolis in about 246/7 would explain why Pacatianus was able to usurp power in the Balkans in 248 after a very successful military campaign of Philip the Arab which earned him the titles of *Germanicus Maximus* and *Carpicus Maximus*. Philip was hated by the common soldiers and by a low ranking officer like Pacatianus because they did not know the facts. The closure of brothels may also have had a role.

And why is there this other version of events presented by John of Antioch which may get support also from Jordanes? There is no conclusive answer for this, but it is possible that the mix-up could have resulted from the purge of the rebels possibly conducted by Decius in 244 and/or 245/6 and 249, and that the usurpation of Decius at Rome in 249 was actually the usurpation Marcus Silbannacus in 244, and that the murder of Severus Sponsianus was committed by the murderers dispatched by Silbannacus at Beroea, or that John's source has just confused the assassination places of these usurpers, Silbannacus at Rome and Sponsianus at Beroea, at the hands of Philip's operatives with those of the two

Philippi (Philip Sr. killed at Beroea and Philip Jr. at Rome) and connected these with the usurpation of Decius. It would be easy to see how Decius could have been promoted by Philip in the aftermath of the murder of Gordian III, because Decius was known as the enemy of the Gordiani and might well have been put in charge of the purge of the rebels also in 244, but none of the sources mention it. All of this is just speculation and there are innumerable other alternatives.

The death of the two Philippi naturally led to a purge of all Philip's supporters, some of whom chose to kill themselves rather than await the inevitable. These included the nine co-conspirators of Philip who all killed themselves to avoid being handed over to the merciless Decius (*HA Gord.* 33.4–5). The new Emperor Decius had an intense hatred of Christians and Christianity, which manifested itself soon enough in the launching of the first great persecution of Christians since the reign of Nero – the persecutions that preceded this were small-scale in comparison. The Edict of Decius which began the persecution dates probably from December 249 or January 250. It is claimed that one of the victims of this persecution was Martyr Eugenia. The actual text, *Martyrdom of Eugenia*, and some other sources claim that Eugenia was the daughter of Philip the Arab and died because of her faith. However, other sources claim that this identification is

A coin of Emperor Decius celebrating the Illyrian Army. When this is taken together with the fact that he fought his wars against the Goths with cavalry, this may imply that he celebrated the Pannonian cavalry recruits that had been trained by Maximinus Thrax. There is obviously no definite evidence for this conclusion, except the fact that Decius had been one of the last men who remained loyal to the cause of Maximinus Thrax even after his death by maintaining the fiction that Maximinus was still alive. This is the likeliest reason for the minting of this coin. It was now Decius who led the army of Maximinus Thrax. Source of the image: Cohen.

A coin of Decius depicting a hoplite on the reverse. This may imply the survival of Alexander's hoplites until the reign of Decius, but not conclusively so thanks to the medium with its artistic conventions. Source of image: Beger 1696.

false and that Eugenia's father was not the Emperor, who had been Praetorian Prefect, but another Philip who had been Prefect in Egypt. These sources claim that the father of Eugenia was Cn. Domitius Philippus who was appointed as *dux/stratelates* of Egypt in 242. It is impossible to know for certain which of the sources is correct. All that is known for certain is that this Eugenia suffered martyrdom for her faith during the persecution launched by Decius. There also exists a tradition that Philip had another son called St. Cyrinus/Quirinus the Deacon who was martyred during the reign of Claudius II, but it is impossible to say how much truth there is behind these claims.[47] For the events of the reign of Decius, see my biography of Gallienus.

7.7 Philip the Arab: one of the best Roman Emperors

Philip the Arab belongs to the category of underappreciated emperors largely thanks to the fact that we do not possess good sources of his reign.[48] Furthermore, the accounts that we have suffer from the prejudices of the upper class pagans towards Arabs and Christians, and from the Constantinian era falsifications. It is also probable that the sad end of Philip's reign has adversely affected our view of him. It is entirely possible that he died in his last battle only because of bad luck or that he was just assassinated.

Funnily enough, the fact that historians know that the sources are biased against Philip the Arab has also resulted in the misrepresentation of him as Emperor and ruler because historians assume that he cannot have committed the treacherous acts described by the sources because these sources are hostile to him. This fails to fully appreciate the beauty of the means that he employed to achieve his position and what means he then used to secure his throne. He was not a nice guy, but he was certainly very effective in achieving what he aimed at, and from the point of view of military history any man capable of fooling his enemies is always to be considered at least competent as a military leader; but this is also an understatement of the capabilities of Philip. Philip the Arab was a true master of devious methods – a bona fide plotter and user of unorthodox warfare. He had managed to murder both Timesitheus and Gordian III and this while the Persian war was still going on and without causing the defeat of the Roman armies.[49] Considering the two disastrous cavalry charges conducted by Gordian III, it could even be claimed that Philip the Arab saved the Romans by killing him. Philip then fooled Sapor I with promises that he did not keep while he assassinated the usurpers in Rome and Balkans. The fooling of Sapor enabled Philip to inflict a series of defeats on the Persians while he himself fought wars against the Germans, Carpi and Goths in the Balkans. In other words, he fought two major wars at the same time and was victorious in both. The Goths had invaded with 300,000 men and the Persian army was certainly not any weaker. This was a great achievement. The best way to gauge the scale is to compare the situation prevailing when the brothers Philip and Priscus were in power with the situation after them. While they were in charge the Roman armies were victorious against enemies in Africa, Europe and in Asia, but when they were removed from the picture the Goths and their allies ravaged the Balkans and killed the Emperor Decius while the Persians crushed the Romans and advanced as far as Antioch. The two Arabic brothers were clearly irreplaceable at this time as military leaders.

A coin of the underappreciated emperor Philip the Arab. Note that the elephant depicted on this coin appears to be African with the implication that the Romans transported elephants both from Africa and India. It was elephants like these that prepared the Roman soldiers against the elephants used by the Persians. Sourse of image: Cohen

However, it is probable that Philip was too ingenious for his own good in the way in which he fought against the Goths. He appears to have incited them to fight a war by refusing to pay their subsidies so that he could then infect them with germs during their invasion of Roman territory. The fact that Philip then paid the Goths to leave Roman territory enabled an unscrupulous officer named Pacatianus to usurp power. In the East the heavy taxation and favouritism of Arabia and Christians also led to troubles and the usurpation of Jotapianus. Both usurpers, however, were easily dispatched as Decius promised and it is probable that Decius led this special effort on behalf of Philip. They were killed by their own men. Then Philip made the fatal mistake of trusting Decius and gave him the command of the Roman armies in the Balkans with the result that Decius usurped. The exact circumstances why Philip fell in the front ranks during the decisive battle of Verona are shrouded in mystery, but it is probable that he died because of bad luck leading his cavalry from the front while in poor health.

In the field of internal politics Philip acted like a dutiful relaxed ruler who showed tolerance towards both pagans and Christians. However, there is evidence that he favoured Christians, and this was detested by the staunchest pagans like Macrianus, Valerian and Decius. It appears probable that these men formed a cabal to overthrow Philip and Priscus, and that the most successful of these men was Decius who unfortunately managed to convince Philip that he was a man of honour. It is also clear that Philip's legislative work that ensured the flow of taxes produced such harsh taxation, at least in the Roman East, that it led to trouble. There were also plenty of people who detested his prudish attitude to sex.

The legacy that Philip left for his successor was actually a good one, even if the ultra-pagan Decius failed to appreciate the improved position of the Christians. The economy was relatively stable despite the problems the Romans faced from the revolts and usurpations of 247–9. The Roman army was also in tip top shape and became used to winning its wars – it had defeated both the barbarian invaders in the Balkans and the Persians repeatedly. It is likely that it was basically the same army as had originally been created by Alexander Severus, but with the difference that its cavalry arm had became used to fighting alone without infantry support if the use of cavalry by Decius in 250–51 and the encounter between the Carpi and Philip can be used as evidence for this.

The only blot in his legacy was that the invading Goths of the year 250 in all probability carried with them a more virulent version of the plague than Philip's special operatives had spread to them. However, the effectivess of his germ warfare is still evident because when the Goths and their allies invaded in about 245–246/7 they had 300,000 men, but in 250 under the Gothic king Cniva they had only 70,000 and a shielding force which would have had fewer men than this main army. If we estimate the overall size of the force fielded by Cniva to have been at most about 120,000 men, we are probably not far from the mark. It is clear that the germ warfare had worked like a dream and it should have been relatively easy for Decius to defeat this much smaller army now that its numbers had been dimished.

In sum, Philip was a treacherous master of unorthodox warfare, but in spite of this he fell victim to another treacherous fellow, Decius. That was the sad fate of Marcus Iulius Verus Philippus, Imperator Caesar, Pius Felix, Invictus Augustus, Persicus Maximus, Parthicus Maximus, Carpicus Maximus, and Germanicus Maximus better known as Philippus I Arabs. However, it was an apt end for a Christian sinner: 'for everyone who uses the sword will die by the sword' Matthew 26:52.

Select Sources

Primary sources:
Ammianus, Anonymous Continuator of Cassius Dio/Peter the Patrician, Arrian, Cedrenus, *Chronicon Paschale*, Dio, *Epitome de Caesaribus* (Pseudo-Aurelius Victor), Eusebius (*Church History*), Dexippus, Eutropius (*Breviarum*), Rufus Festus (*Breviarum*), Herodian, *Historia Augusta*, Jerome/Eusebius, Jordanes (*Getica, De summa temporum/Romana*), Julius Africanus, Philostorgius, Malalas, Orosius, Petrus Patricius, *Strategikon* (Maurice), Syncellus, *Synopsis Chronike/Sathas*, Aurelius Victor, Vegetius, Zonaras, Zosimus.
All these sources are available on the Internet. The sources for Rome's eastern wars have been conveniently collected in translation in Dodgeon and Lieu (=REF1), and most of the rest have now been conveniently collected and translated by Banchich and Lane 2009, and Banchich 2015.

Select Sources:
Agathangelos, *History of the Armenians*, Tr. R.W. Thomson, Albany (1976).
Anonymous, Eis Basilea, Greek text by B. Keil, *Aelii Aristidis Smyrnaei quae supersunt omnia II* (Berlin 1898), 253–64, which is also available online at Internet Archive; English translation and commentary by Louis J. Swift, 'The Anonymous Encomium of Philip the Arab, GRBS 7 1966, 268–289 (tr. and commentary on pp.272–89), which is also available online.
Banchich, Thomas M. (2015), *The Lost History of Peter the Patrician*.
Banchich, Thomas M., and Lane, Eugene N., *The History of Zonaras From Alexander Severus to the Death of Theodosius the Great*, Routledge, London and New York 2009.
Bernards, see Historia Augusta
Bird, H.W. (1994), *Aurelius Victor: De Caesaribus*. Liverpool.
Birley, A.R., (1998), 'Decius reconsidered', in L*es empereurs illyriens. Actes du colloque de Strasbourg (11–13 octobre 1990) organisé par le Centre de Recherche sur l'Europe centrale et sud-orientale*, édités par Edmond Frézouls et Hélène Jouffroy, Strasbourg 1998, 57–80.
Bohec, Yann Le, (2005), *Histoire de l'Afrique romaine*. Paris.
—— (1994/2000), *The Imperial Roman Army*. London and New York.
Bosworth, A.B. (1988/1995), *Conquest and Empire. The reign of Alexander the Great*. Cambridge.
Bowersock, G.W. (1983/1994), *Roman Arabia*. Harvard.
Brauer, George C. Jr., *The age of the soldier emperors: Imperial Rome, A.D. 244–284*, New Jersey 1975.
Cambridge Ancient History, Vol. XII. The Imperial Crisis and Recovery A.D. 193–324, (1939), eds. S.A. Cook, F.E. Adcock, M.P. Charlesworth, N.H. Baynes. Cambridge.
Cambridge Ancient History, 2nd ed. Vol. XII. The Crisis of Empire, A.D. 193–337, (2005) eds. A.K. Bowman, P. Garnsey, and A. Cameron. Cambridge.
Campbell, Brian (2005), 'The Severan Dynasty', in *CAH 12, 2nd edition*, 1–27.
Cascio, Elio Lo (2005), 'The Emperor and his Administration, 6C,' in *CAH 2nd*. ed., 156–9.
Christol, Michel, (2006) *L'empire romain du IIIe siècle 192–325 apr. J-C*. Paris.
Continuator of Dio, see Banchich 2015.
Corbier, Mireille (2005), 'Coinage and Taxation: The State's Point of View, AD 193–337,' in *CAH*, 327–91.

Dexippus, Dexipp von Athen, ed., tr. and commentary by Gunther Martin. Tübingen 2006. The references to the fragments follow the numbering found in this edition. The earlier editions can be accessed online, these include Dindorf (*Historici Graeci Minores* 190ff.) and Müller (*FHG* 682ff.).

Dio, Dio's Roman History, in Nine Volumes, English translation by Earnest Cary, Loeb (Vols. 8–9, 1925–7); H.B Foster.

Dodgeon & Lieu, see REF1

Ensslin W. (1939), 'Chapter II. The Senate and the Army,' in *CAH 12*, 57–95.

Estiot, S. (1996),'L'empereur Silbannacus, un second antonien', in *Revue numismatique 151*, pp.105–17.

Eusebius, *The History of the Church*, tr. by G.A. Williamson revised and edited with a new introduction A. Louth. London 1989.

Foster, see Dio

Goodman, Martin (2008), *Rome and Jerusalem. The Clash of Ancient Civilizations*. New York.

Hamdoune, Christine (1999), *Les auxilia externa africains des armées romaines*. Montpellier.

Hermann, Katrin (2013), *Gordian III. Kaiser einer Umbruchszeit*. Speyer.

Herodian, Herodian in Two Volumes, tr. by C.R. Whittaker. Loeb 1969; *Herodian's History*, tr. by Hart, London 1749.

Historia Augusta, Scriptores Historiae Augustae, 3 vols., tr. by D. Magie. Loeb 1921–32; *The Lives of the Roman Emperors*, 2 vols. tr. by John Bernard. London 1693.

James, Simon (2004), *Excavations at Dura Europos 1928–1937. Final Report VII. Arms and Armour and other Military Equipment*. Oxbow Books.

John of Antioch, *Ioannis Antiocheni Fragmenta ex Historia chronica*, ed. and Italian tr. by U. Roberto. Berlin and New York (2005). Excerpts also in Banchich-Lane, 2009.

Julius Africanus, *Kestoi: Cesti, The Extant Fragments*, edition and translation by Christophe Jean-Daniel Guignard, Laura Mecella, Carlo Scardino and Martin Wallraff, Gruyter 2012.

Kettenhofen, E. (1982), Die römisch-persischen Kriege des 3. Jahrhunderts. n. Chr. Nach der Inschrift Sāhpuhrs I an der Ka'be-ye Zartošt (ŠKZ). Wiesbaden.

Körner, Christian (2002), *Philippus Arabs. Ein Soldatenkaiser in der Tradition des antoninisch-severischen Prinzipats*. Walter de Gruyter Berlina dn New York.

—— (1999), 'Rebellions During the reign of Philip the Arab (244–249 A.D.): Iotapianus, Pacatianus, Silbannacus, and Sponsianus', in *De Imperatoribus Romani www.roman-emperors. org/decius/htm*.

—— and Meckler, see Meckler

Loriot, Xavier (1975a), 'Les premières années de la grande crise fu IIIe siècle. De l'avenement de Maximin le Thrace (235) à la mort de Gordian III (244), *ANRW II* (1975), 657–787.

—— (1975b), 'Chronologie du règne de Philippe l'Arabe (244–9 après J.C.)', *ANRW II* (1975), 788–97.

—— (1998) 'Trajan Dèce', in *Les empereurs illyriens. Actes du colloque de Strasbourg (11–13 octobre 1990) organisé par le Centre de Recherche sur l'Europe centrale et su-orientale*, édités par Edmond Frézouls et Hélène Jouffroy, Strasbourg 1998, 43–55.

Maksymiuk, Katarzyna (2015), *Geography of Roman-Iranian wars. Military operations of Rome and Sasanian Iran*. Siedlce.

Malalas, *The Chronicle of John Malalas*, tr. by E. Jeffreys, M. Jeffreys and R. Scott with others. Melbourne (1986) Contains both the Greek and Slavic versions in English.

Mattingly D.J.(2003), 'Historical Summary', in *The Archaeology of Fazzān. Vol. 1, Synthesis*, ed. D.J. Mattingly. London (2003), 75–106.

McMahon Robin (2001), Pupienus (238 A.D.) and Balbinus (238 A.D.), in De Imperatoribus Romanis website.

Meckler Michael L. (2001c), Gordian III (238–244 A.D.), in *De Imperatoribus Romanis website*.

—— (2001b), Gordian II (238 A.D.), in *De Imperatoribus Romanis website*.

—— (2001a), Gordian I (238 A.D.), in *De Imperatoribus Romanis website.*

—— (1997), Maximinus Thrax (235–238 A.D.), in *De Imperatoribus Romanis website.*

Meckler Michael L. and Körner C., (1999), Philip the Arab (244–249 A.D.) in *De Imperatoribus Romanis website.*

Mielczarek Mariusz (1993), *Cataphracti and Clibanarii. Studies on the Heavy Armoured Cavalry of the Ancient World.* Lódź.

Minchev, Alexander, (2007) 'Funerary practices and grave types of 2nd–3rd C. AD in the Roman cemeteries of Marcianopolis,' in *Acta Terrae Septemcastrensis 6.1.*

Moses Khorenats'i, *Moses Khorenats'i: History of the Armenians* [HATS 4] (Cambridge, MA, 1978). English tr. also by Robert Bedrosian (rbedrosian.com).

Pearson, Paul N. (2016), *Maximinus Thrax.* Barnsley.

Peter the Patrician, see Banchich 2015.

Philostorgius, *Church History*, tr. by P.R. Amidon. Atlanta (2007).

Pöppelmann, see Roms

Potter, David S., *The Roman Empire at Bay AD 180–395*, Routledge, London and New York (2004).

REF1 = *The Roman Eastern Frontier and the Persian Wars* (AD 226–363). A Documentary History compiled and edited by Michael H. Dodgeon and Samuel N.C. Lieu, London and New York 1991.

Roms Vergessener Feldzug. Die Schlacht am Harzhorn (2013), eds. Heike Pöppelmann, Korana Deppmayer and Wolf-Dieter Steinmetz, Darmstad.

– Geschwinde, Michael and Lönne, Petra (2013), 'Die Entdeckung eines Schlachtfeldes, das es eigentlich gar nich geben konnte', in Roms, 58–64.

– Hose, Martin (2013), 'Ausgelöschte Geschichte. Der Feldzug des Maximinus Thrax in das Innere Germaniens 235/236 n. Chr. in der historischen Überlieferung', in Roms, 111–15.

– Wolters, Reinhard (2013), 'Wiedergewonnene Geschichte. Der Feldzug des Maximinus Thrax in das Innere Germaniens 235/6 n. Chr. in der numismatischen Überlieferung', in Roms, 116–23.

– Fuhrmann Jens and Steinmetz, Wolf-Dieter (2013), ,Nach seiner Ankunft ließ er das ganze Land verheeren…' Germanische Besiedlung entland des römischen Marschweges, in Roms, 135–41.

– Rau, Andreas (2013), 'Die germanischen Krieger und ihre Bewaffnung im 3. Jh. n. Chr.', in Roms, 172–9.

– Fischer, Thomas (2013), 'Die Soldaten des Maximinus Thrax. Die Einheiten und ihre Bewaffnung', in Roms, 198–206.

– Fischer, Thomas (2013), 'Ein bemerkenswerter Kavalleriehelm aus dem 3. Jh. n. Chr. Der Adlerhelm aus dem Museum in Mougins', in Roms, 207.

– Hund, Ragnar (2013), '*Maximiana* – zu einem ehrenden Beinamen militärischer Formationen im frühen 3. Jh. n. Chr.', in Roms, 208–16.

– Meyer, Michael and Moosbauer, Günther (2013), 'Schlachtreihe gegen Einzelkämpfer. Die Wurf- und Hiebwaffen der Römer und Germanen', in Roms, 218–21.

– Meyer, Michael and Moosbauer, Günther (2013), 'Osrhoener, Mauren und Germanen Bogenschützen und Speerschleuderer', in Roms, 223–6.

– Amrhein, Carsten (2013), 'Die lorica segmentata (Schienenpanzer)', in Roms, 227.

– Fischer, Thomas (2013), 'Zur Bewaffnung und Ausrüstung der Kavallerieformationen Roms in der Zeit des Maximinus Thrax', in Roms, 228–34.

– Wiegels, Rainer (2013), 'Reiter Roms an Germaniens Grenzen im frühen 3. Jh. n. Chr.', in Roms, 235–41.

– Moosbauer, Günther (2013), 'Torsiongeschütze', in Roms, 242–8.

– Erklenz, Christina (2013), 'Die Logistik eines Feldzuges und die medizinische Versorgung', in Roms, 249–55.

– Geschwinde Michael, Lönne Petra, and Meyer Michael with Michael Brangs, Torben Schatte and Thorsten Schwarz, 'Das Harzhorn-Ereignis. Die Archäologie einer römisch-germanischen Konfrontation im 3. Jh. n. Chr.', in Roms, 294–348

Shahid, Irfan (1984), *Rome and the Arabs*. Washington DC.

Southern, Pat, (2001) *The Roman Empire from Severus to Constantine*. London and New York.

—— (1989) 'The Numeri of the Roman Imperial Army', *Britannia 20, 81–140*.

Strategikon, *Maurice's Strategikon*, English tr. by George T. Dennis. Philadelphia (1984). This treatise is usually attributed to the emperor Maurice. For a full analysis of this treatise, see Syvänne, 2004.

Swift, see Anonymous

Syvänne, Ilkka, *A Military History of Late Rome vols, 3 (395–425) 4 (425–457), 5 (457–518), 6 (518–565), 7 (565–641)* Pen & Sword forthcoming in 2020/1.

—— (2019), *The Reign of Gallienus*. Barnsley.

—— (2018b) *A Military History of Late Rome Vol.2 (361–395)*, Barnsley.

—— (2018a) 'Nation and Empire Building the Iranian Way. The Case of the Sasanian Empire in the Third Century', *Historia i Swiat 2018*, 71–86. The article is based on *The 10th ASMEA Conference*, Washington DC, 2017. The writing of this was generously supported by the ASMEA Research Grant.

—— (2017) *Caracalla: A Military Biography*, Barnsley.

—— (2016) 'The Eyes and Ears: The Sasanian and Roman Spies AD 224–450', *Historia i Swiat 2016*, Based on research paper of *The 8th ASMEA Conference*, Washington DC, 2015. Written with the generous support of the ASMEA Research Grant.

—— (2015b) *A Military History of Late Rome 284–361*. Barnsley.

—— (2015a), 'La campaña de Juliano en Persia (363 d.C.). Un análisis crítico', *Desperta Ferro 2015*.

—— (2013) A research paper 'Caesar's Use of Unorthodox Warfare against Pompey in 49–48 BC', *The 10th ICMG Conference* in Aviemore, Scotland, UK on 18 June, 2013. I will make this available online at academia.edu later, but much is already available online at academia.edu (see 2011a below)

—— (2012) A research paper 'Julius Caesar vs. Cnaeus Pompeius, 45 BC: Caesar's Last Campaign', *Historicon 2012*, July 20, 2012 (available online at academia.edu)

—— (2011d) An enlarged version of the research paper 'Campaigns of Germanicus, 13–16 AD', *Historicon 2011*.

—— (2011c) A research paper 'Campaigns of Germanicus, 14–16 AD', *6th International Fields of Conflict Conference, 15th–18th April 2011 in Osnabrück and Kalkriese*.

—— (2011b), 'The Reign of Decius 249–251', in *Slingshot* May 2011, 2–8 (available online at academia.edu).

—— (2011a) A research paper 'Duel for Power. Caesar vs. Pompey 49–48 BC', *Historicon 2011*. (available online at academia.edu).

—— (2010) 'El sistema militar Godo,' in *Desperta Ferro Nº1, 2010*.

—— (2006)'Water Supply in the Late Roman Army', in *Environmental History of Water*, Eds. Petri S. Juuti, Tapio S. Katko and Heikki S. Vuorinen, IWA Publishing. London 2006, Chapter 6 (pp.69–91).

—— (2004) *The Age of Hippotoxotai. Art of War in Roman Military Revival and Disaster (491–636)*, Tampere UP 2004

See also academia.edu for these and other studies.

Syvänne Ilkka, and Maksymiuk Katarzyna, (2018), *Military History of the Third Century Iran*. Siedlce.

York, John Marvin, *Philip the Arab: The First Christian Emperor of Rome*. Ph.D. Diss. University of Southern California 1964.

Zahran Yasmine (2001), *Philip the Arab. A Study in Prejudice.* London.

Zonaras, see Banchich & Lane.

Zosimus, *Nea Historia*: *Zosime, Histoire Nouvelle*, tr. and ed. Paschoud. Budé Paris. 1971–1989 4 Vols.; A dated and out of copyright English translation by unknown hand (possibly J. Davis) *The History of Count Zosimus Sometime Advocate and Chancellor of the Roman Empire*, (London 1814); The latest English translation is *Zosimus. New History.* tr. by R.T. Ridley. (Melbourne 1990).

Notes

Chapter 1

1. As in my biography of Gallienus, in some rare cases I have left some of these sources unmentioned in the footnotes because their information (with a reference to the source) has been included in a secondary source that I mention in the note. There is also a good discussion of the sources and their biases in York, 1–11.
2. See the perceptive comments of York (1–11), especially his comments regarding Licinius on p.11. The statement that Licinius claimed descent from Licinius comes from the *Historia Augusta* (*Gordiani* 34.5), which many historians would discount, but I agree with York that there is every reason to accept it as valid.

Chapter 2

1. The following text closely follows the text of my biography of Gallienus. For those interested in Roman society and military organization, my biography of Caracalla and *MHLR* Vol.1 deal with these matters in greater detail. In fact, some of the sentences here have been taken from the former.
2. This chapter is based on my biographies of Caracalla and Gallienus and follows their text closely, sometimes word for word.
3. The 'national' before the *numeri* is meant to separate the ethnic tribal *numeri* from the regular units which could also be called *numeri* for a number of reasons. For details of the term *numerus/numeri*, see Southern 1989. I will call the national *numeri* henceforth just '*numeri*'.
4. See the Appendix 1 in Syvänne, *Aurelian and Probus*, for further details.
5. These lists are included in *MHLR Vol.1*, *Caracalla*, *Gallienus*, and *Aurelian and Probus*.
6. A fuller discussion can be found in the text and also in my biography of Caracalla.
7. Discussed in greater length in my biography of Caracalla.
8. Discussed in greater length in my biography of Caracalla.
9. This chapter is borrowed from my biography of Gallienus and follows it sometimes word for word.
10. Follows closely the text of my double biography of Aurelian and Probus.
11. This chapter is borrowed from my biography of Gallienus and follows it sometimes word for word.
12. This chapter is once again borrowed from my biography of Gallienus.
13. See my article dealing with spies on *Historia i Świat 2016*.

Chapter 3

1. The following account of the reign of Alexander Severus is primarily based on Dio 80.1ff.; Herodian 6.1ff. and Aelius Lampridus *Historia Augusta, Antoninus Heliogabalus/Elagabalus, Alexander Severus*. I will refer to specific parts of these only when it is necessary for the argument. References to secondary literature will be included when they add information missing from the previous or complement them, as is the case with the material in Syvänne and Maksymiuk.
2. For an analysis, see Syvänne, *Caracalla*, Appendix 2, 311ff. According to several rabbinic texts, a prominent Jewish leader of the early third century called Judah haNasi (Judah the Patriarch)

had a very close relationship with a Roman Emperor called Antoninus, so close in fact that the tradition claimed that Antoninus converted to Judaism, but this was not accepted by all Jews, with good reason. This Antoninus merely visited a synagogue, which did not make him a Jew. For an analysis of these texts, see Goodman (482–4). In my opinion this Antoninus was none other than Antoninus Magnus, better known as Caracalla.

3. The new taxes introduced for prostitutes, catamites, makers of trousers, weavers of linen, glass-workers, furriers, locksmiths, silversmiths, goldsmiths and other artisans and workers were used for the upkeep of the public baths, theatre, circus, and stadium. See *HA Alex. 24*. They were not used for the upkeep of the army.

4. Ardashir had defeated the last Parthian monarch in 224. Caracalla had struck a mortal blow to the Parthian realm with his superb diplomatic and military manoeuvres. His meddling in Parthian affairs had made it possible for Ardashir to begin his own revolution in Persis/Fars. For details, see Syvänne, *Caracalla*.

5. Sources collected in Dodgeon & Lieu, 17ff. (e.g. Moses 2.73 mentions that Khosrov continued his campaign against the Persians without any help from the Romans); Syvänne and Maksymiuk, 68–9; Syvänne, 2018a.

6. For a fuller analysis of the Persian military, see: Syvänne, 2004 and *MHLR Vol.1* , 113–29; Syvänne and Maksymiuk, 53–66.

7. Dio 80.3.2ff.; Herodian 6.2.1ff. with Whittaker's comments; Zonaras 12.15 and Syncellus AM5710–11; Syvänne, *Caracalla*, 195–6; Syvänne and Maksymiuk, 68–9.

8. McHugh, 183–6.

9. Dio 80.3.2ff.; Herodian 6.2.1ff. with Whittaker's comments; Syvänne, *Caracalla*, 195–6; Syvänne and Maksymiuk, 68–9.

10. For a longer discussion of where roads were built, who was appointed to which position etc. see McHugh (176ff.) and Pearson (49ff.). Note, however, that I reconstruct differently the actual Persian war and the career patterns of Pupienus and Maximinus Thrax. My own reconstruction of this war is based on the sources quoted and on Syvänne and Maksymiuk (68–74), though I make some modifications and changes to its conclusions and add some new information missing from the former e.g. to the battle tactics and units of Alexander Severus and Maximinus's role.

11. Julius Capitolinus (HA Max. 5.3–7.2) states that after Elagabalus had died, Maximinus hastened to Rome where Alexander received him with joy and made him tribune of the *legio IV* immediately, which Alexander had raised and which Maximinus then formed and trained as a legion. This sequence is clearly false because the evidence suggests that Alexander raised new units only just before his eastern campaign. Capitolinus also places the promotion of Maximinus as general immediately after this. Therefore it is clear that this incident refers to the raising of new legions on that occasion.

12. For this, see Syvänne, *Caracalla*, 169.

13. For the names of some of these units, see McHugh, 182ff. and Pearson 51ff.

14. McHugh (193–9) discusses the personnel left behind or chosen for the campaign. However, I have one major disagreement with him. He suggests that Pupienus was left as Prefect of the City in 231. I consider this very unlikely. I agree with the majority view among historians that he was appointed as *Praefectus Urbi* only in 234 for the reasons that will be made clear later in the text. It is notable that Caracalla had a great eye for talent. These two men were not the only instances of Caracalla's promotion of talent over birthright.

15. Strength of the *argyroaspides/argyraspides* in Bosworth, 270.

16. This and the following discussion is based on the *Kestoi* of Julius Africanus. The newest edition and translation of this key text is by Guignard et al. It divides the military material in the *Kestoi* in a new way (p.33ff.) as follows: D11 Contents of the Seventh Cestus F12.1–20. For an analysis of the contents of this material on the basis of earlier editions by Viellefond, see Syvänne, Caracalla, Appendix 2.

17. This is the same tactic as was adopted by Julian the Apostate against the Sassanians at the battle of Ctesiphon on 7 June 363. It was a sound tactic and Julian certainly did the right thing when he used it against the Persian cavalry. For additional details, see Syvänne, *MHLR Vol.2*, 95–7.
18. For example by Magie, 200–201.
19. This attitude is in general agreement with his other actions: He forbade mixed baths used by both sexes; he introduced new taxes on prostitutes and catamites; women of ill repute were forced to become public prostitutes; catamites who had had intercourse with the women were drowned in shipwrecks; he forbade the attendance of women of bad reputation in the levees of his mother and wife; he was temperate in his love life and had nothing to do with the catamites (*HA Alex.* 24.2–25.11, 29.2). There was clearly a conservative undertone in all of his actions, and it is clear that his mother Julia Mamaea had a role in this.
20. See my biographies of both for examples.
21. Syvänne and Maksymiuk, 70.
22. The fact that Alexander was victorious is confirmed by the following: Aurelius Victor (24.2), Festus (22), Europius (8.23), Jerome (a.232), Orosius (7.18.7), and Syncellus (AM5715) all of which are translated in the REF1 (26–8). Cedrenus (p.450) and Zonaras (12.15), however, follow Herodian. Modern historians have all too often chosen to follow Herodian in this because of their distrust of the *Augustan Histories*. However, as this account makes clear Herodian was indeed guilty of being hostile towards Alexander as claimed by the *Augustan Histories*.
23. See e.g. Syvänne, *Caracalla*, 32 and *Gallienus*, 74.
24. The presence of Alexander is attested at Palmyra (REF 1, 23) and I connect this with the invasion route. The concentration of the forces at Palmyra would have hidden them from the enemy scouts close to the border.
25. For a discussion of the likely size of this cavalry army, see Syvänne, *Gallienus*.
26. For a discussion of the likely size of this cavalry army, see Syvänne, *Gallienus*.
27. For this, see Syvänne, *Caracalla*, 283ff.
28. On the basis of the reference to the chariots in the context of elephants and their existence in fourth century military manuals it is also possible that the Romans employed special chariots against the elephants and cavalry. For this, see Syvänne, *Caracalla*, 323.
29. The other possibility is that the cavalry wings and the units equipped in Greek gear charged forward at the same time as the Persians launched their attack with elephants and scythed chariots so that the Roman wings surrounded them at the same time. However, I consider this less likely, firstly because it is difficult to think that the Persians would not have covered the entire length of their battleline with the scythed chariots and elephants, and secondly because Julius Africanus refers to the use of light infantry against the elephants. The light infantry would have been typically placed in front of the heavy infantry to receive the enemy attack, but not in front when the infantry attacked on the run. Therefore it is likelier that the battle consisted of two stages: 1) the receiving of the enemy attack spearheaded by scythed chariots and elephants; 2) Roman counterattack after this had failed.
30. If the attack was conducted in crescent array the wings were in contact with the centre, but if the attack formation was the *epikampios emprostia* then the wings separated from the centre by advancing forward in the same manner as was described in the late fourth century by Vegetius (his fourth and fifth combat formations). There were two variants of this attack formation: 1) the wings advanced forward while the centre remained in place; 2) the wings advanced forward while the light infantry of the centre moved forward to protect the flanks of the advancing wings. The latter alternative is likelier in this case if the *epikampios emprosthia* array was used. For an illustration of the Vegetian tactics, see e.g. my biography of Gallienus.
31. Maximinus was a man of very humble origins. According to Jordanes' *Getica* 15 (83–8, esp. 87–8) and *Augustan Histories* (*HA Maximi Duo* 2.1ff.), Maximinus's father was a Goth and his mother an Alan. Unlike most modern historians claim, there is no reason to doubt this.

Maximinus had been enrolled into the cavalry bodyguards by Septimius Severus and he served loyally until the murder of Caracalla, after which he deserted the army so that he would not have to serve under Macrinus. He returned to service under Elagabalus because he thought that Elagabalus was the legitimate son of Caracalla. When he realized the nature of Elagabalus he did his best to avoid being in his presence. When Alexander then took power, Maximinus eagerly returned to service and was promoted by the new regime to the position of *Dux Ripae* headquartered at Dura Europos during the Persian war. Maximinus was now in his fifties, but he was still a man of action and led by personal example, which was very impressive: due to his acromegaly, he was a colossal man who towered over his comrades.

32. Inscription quoted in McHugh, 206.
33. The Romans typically operated in these areas whenever they were at war with Parthia or Persia. See Syvänne, *Caracalla* with the Military History of Late Rome series.
34. See Syvänne, Germanicus at academia.edu.
35. Julius Africanus D11/F12 2.2.14 (p.43.14) with the comment on p.44; Syvänne, *Caracalla*, 316
36. Pearson (241 n17) lists those who have suggested this.
37. See in particular my double biography *Aurelian and Probus* together with *Military History of Late Rome* vols.5–6 for examples of fighting in this area.
38. This and the following is mainly based on Herodian 6.7.5ff.; Aelius Lampridius *HA Alexander* 59.5ff.; Zosimus 1.13.2; Festus 22.1. Brian Campbell's view is in *CAH XII 2nd ed.*, p.26.
39. Ibid. with Europius 8.23.
40. In other words, in contrast to Whittaker (Herodian, p.287) I accept Herodian's reference to barbarians (presumably mainly of Gothic and Alan descent like Maximinus) as valid even though I agree with Whittaker that these Thracians were at the time Roman citizens thanks to Caracalla.
41. The following is based on Herodian 6.8.1ff., Aelius Lampridius *HA Alexander* 59.5ff.
42. Location in Ensslin, 71.
43. Whittaker/Herodian (p.143) notes that the language makes it impossible to know if the military prefect meant praetorian prefect. If it did, the names of the later prefects are not known, but one possible candidate is M. Attius Cornelianus.

Chapter 4
1. This is based primarily on Herodian 7.1ff. and Julius Capitolinus, *HA Maximini* 1.1.ff., but I have found Pearson (85ff.) also very useful. In fact, for a fuller analysis of the reign of Maximinus, I recommend Pearson, 85ff. However, note that there are differences in our interpretations because I put more trust in the sources than is usually the case and I analyze the composition of the period bodyguards and armed forces differently.
2. Loriot (1975a, 714–5), (1998, 49–53); Birley, 1998, 64–7.
3. Ensslin, 75.
4. Whittaker (156–7) suggests that it is possible that this revolt is placed in the wrong place, because the Oshroenian archers were used during the German campaign so the revolt would have occurred only later in 236. This is possible, but I have here followed the sequence in Herodian.
5. The following account is based on the sources quoted and Pearson (85–109). The sources for the battle of Harzhorn will be listed separately below.
6. This and the following account of the battle of Harzhorn are based on: a field trip to the site under the guidance of Michael Geschwinde in 2011; the book *Roms Vergessener Feldzug. Die Schlacht am Harzhorn*, which summarises the evidence (all of its articles are must-read for this battle, but I have listed separately under its title those chapters that I found particularly useful for this book); and Pearson (100–105).

7. For an earlier instance of the Romans using mobile artillery and concentrated artillery fire, see my article dealing with Germanicus's German war in AD 13–16 available online at academia. edu.
8. This is still based on the sources already mentioned plus Loriot (1975a, 677–81). Additional information can be gathered from the PIR regarding the individuals mentioned.
9. Based on Loriot (1975a, 674–6) and Pearson (96–9).
10. Based on Loriot (1975a, 673–86).

Chapter 5

1. If one counts the son of Maximinus Thrax as emperor, there were actually seven emperors in 238, but he is usually not considered an emperor despite being *Caesar*.
2. The dating of events for the year 238 is very uncertain. The different versions are collected in the following studies: Loriot 1975a, 720–2; Herrmann, 71, 173–4; Pearson, 228–9. The dates given for this year are my educated guesses based on these studies. I need to make one correction to my biography of Gallienus, p.188.n.27, where I state that *Epitome 34.2* claims that Claudius would have been sired by Decius and a woman of pleasure. This is false. I remember noting it when I read the manuscript, but I have left it uncorrected for some unknown reason. The *Epitome* actually implies that the father was the womanizer Gordian II or his father Gordian I and some woman of pleasure. The reference in the note is therefore a mistake. This only confirms what I state at the end of the note. The claim is very uncertain because Decius opposed the Gordiani vehemently. Although it is possible that this could have resulted from having been sired by one of them out of wedlock, none of this is comparable with the claimed illustrious descent of Decius nor with the results of modern research in Loriot (1998) or Birley (1998).
3. This and the following is based on Herodian 7.4.1ff; Julius Capitolinus (*HA Max*. 13.5ff and *Gord*. 1.1ff.); John of Antioch frg. 224. If other sources have been used they will be mentioned in separate endnotes like this one.
4. Ibid with Loriot (1975a, 689ff.) and Meckler *Gordian II* provides comments regarding the background and ancestry of Gordian I and Gordian II, but they do not accept the names of the parents or the ancestry given by Julius Capitolinus. I see no compelling reasons to doubt it. The fact that the cognomen Gordianus suggests a connection with Asia Minor does not preclude the existence of another connection. The Gordiani certainly had many ancestors from many different areas so that there is no reason to doubt the names of so few of those mentioned by Capitolinus. Gordian I as a friend and member of Caracalla's council: Syvänne, *Caracalla*, 215.
5. The problems concerning the age of Gordian III in 238 are discussed later. However, there is another problem that needs to be discussed. According to Julius Capitolinus (*HA Gord*. 22.4, 23.1), one or two sources claimed that Gordian III was the son of Gordian II, and then states that Dexippus was the source who claimed it. Notably, Victor (27.1) and Eutropius (9.2) both confuse Gordian II and Gordian III with each other so it is clear that there was some confusion in the sources. The extant inscriptions confirm Gordian III as son of the daughter of Gordian the Elder. However, it is possible to reconcile Dexippus with the other sources if one assumes that Gordian II had had an incestuous relationship with his sister, or that Gordian II's sister had adopted one of the illegitimate sons of Gordian II. In either case it would have been expedient to cover this up. The reason for these speculations is that Dexippus of Athens is known as a reliable period source and could have been in a position to know the rumours of his day. However, it is still probably safest to accept the generally accepted version in this case.
6. ibid.
7. This and following is based on: Herodian 7.4.1ff.; HA *Max*. 14.1ff.; *Gord*. 7.2ff.; Victor 26; John of Antioch frg. 224.16ff.; Zonaras 2.16–7.
8. *HA Max*. 14.3ff., *Gord*. 9.6ff.

9. For a list of different dating suggestions, see Herrmann (173) who collects the different theories.
10. Potter (169) also suggests that Valerian was Gordian's messenger.
11. *HA Gord.* 9.6ff.; John of Antioch frg. 224.38ff.; Loriot 1975a, 707–10; McMahon. Loriot discusses the different theories concerning the *vigintiviri*. Some historians place their creation to the period when Gordian I and II lived, while others think it existed during the interval after the death of the Gordiani to govern the Empire before the nomination of the new emperors. Some historians think it was a permanent independent body meant to advise the emperors while others think on the basis of Julius Capitolinus that Italy was divided between them for defensive purposes. I have here adopted Julius Capitolinus's version as the likeliest alternative because the Senate needed to organize the defence of Italy against Maximinus immediately after joining the revolt.
12. Loriot 1975a, 707–10.
13. Gordian I or Gordian II as possible dedicatees of Philostratus's *Lives* in Loriot (1975a, 695) and Meckler (Gordian I).
14. Herodian 7.6.4–9; *HA Gord.* 10.5–8.
15. The different theories listed in Herrmann p.173.
16. Herodian 7.7.8ff. *HA Max.14.4ff., 17.1ff.; HA Gord.* 13.1ff.
17. I do not accept Whittaker's (Herodian, p.289) suggestion that these German *symmachoi* consisted of the regular auxiliaries of the Army of the Rhine. These were clearly German allies across the Rhine.
18. Herodian 7.6.3ff.; *HA Max.14.4ff.; HA Gord.* 9.6ff. ,13.1ff.
19. Names in Loriot 1975a, 697–8.
20. The dating of events for the year 238 is very uncertain. The different versions are collected in the following studies: Loriot 1975a, 720–2; Herrmann, 71, 173–4; Pearson, 228–9. The suggested dates vary from late February up to late April and early May. I prefer earlier dates.
21. This and the following are based on: Herodian 7.9.1ff.; *HA Max.* 19.1ff.; *HA Gord.* 15.1ff., 22.1ff.; John of Antioch frg. 224.44ff. Summary also in Hamdoune, 201–2.
22. The use of wormwood in wine was recommended by Julius Africanus. Wormwood improves the appetite and helps to digest food. For this, see Syvänne, 2006.
23. One wonders if some of the busts and statues that are claimed to represent the equally fat Balbinus would actually be busts and statues of Gordian II the Younger?
24. The dating of events for the year 238 is very uncertain. The different versions are collected in the following studies: Loriot 1975a, 720–2; Herrmann, 71, 173–4; Pearson, 228–9. The dates given for this year are my educated guesses based on these earlier studies.
25. Whittaker (Herodian 224–5) is definitely correct in noting that the HA is incorrect when it states that the meeting took place on 9 July. This date is far too late for the melting snows of Maximinus's campaign.
26. Whittaker (Herodian 226–7) suggests that Herodian means the *vigintiviri*, a committee of the twenty consulars.
27. This and the following are based on: Herodian 7.10.1ff; *HA Max* 20.1ff.; *HA MB* 1.1ff.; *HA Gord.* 22.1ff.; John of Antioch frg. 224.67ff.
28. Loriot 1975a, 710–11, 718–9. For the friendship of Sabinus with Caracalla, see Syvänne (*Caracalla*, 172, 188, 215–6, 219).
29. Loriot (1955a, 717–8); Drinkwater *CAH*, 33; Corbier *CAH*, 334. The diluting of silver content was the ancient equivalent of printing money (or conjuring it up from thin air as Yannis Varoufakis would call it).
30. Loriot 1975a, 702ff.
31. All of this has naturally been suspected by modern historians, because the source is *Historia Augusta* and because there is no confirmation of such a career and positions. However I am inclined to accept the text as it is. See also Loriot (1975a, 704–5) who notes that Pupienus was clearly a *homo novus*.

32. The translator Magie (*HA*, pp.460–1) notes that Julius Capitolinus has probably confused two different men, Cornelius Balbus of Cadiz (a trusted subordinate of Julius Caesar) and Theophanes of Mitylene, but notes that the confusion is understandable because Theophanes adopted Balbus – perhaps this means that Julius Capitolinus is accurate after all in uniting the names? For the remarkable career of Balbus under Julius Caesar, see Syvänne 2011a, 2012, 2013. For a discussion of Balbinus's career and family, see: Loriot (1975a, 705–6); and Syvänne (Caracalla, 214–5), Balbinus as a friend and councillor of Caracalla.
33. This is described in some detail by Julius Capitolinus (*HA Max. 20.6ff., MB 9.1ff., Gord.* 22.7–9) and Herodian (7.11.1ff.).
34. The dating of events for 238 is very uncertain. The different versions are collected in the following studies: Loriot 1975a, 720–2; Herrmann, 71, 173–4; Pearson, 228–9. The dates given for this year are my educated guesses based on these studies.
35. The siege of Aquileia is also described by John of Antioch frg. 224.72ff.
36. Historians have suggested various different dates and durations for the beginning and end of their joint reign after the death of Maximinus Thrax. The shortest of the estimates is from 24 June until 29 July. Others have suggested from June or July until August, but most think that their rule lasted from May until June or July. The different versions are collected in the following studies: Loriot 1975a, 720–2; Herrmann, 71, 173–4; Pearson, 228–9. I have here accepted arguments of Loriot (p.722) that Pupienus and Balbinus were murdered in about 7 June 238 because the *Justinian Codex* names only one Augustus for 22 June 238 and one inscription from Virunum does the same for 23 June 238.
37. Whittaker (Herodian, 289) considers this a mistake because he thinks that the German *symmachoi* consisted of regular German auxiliaries of the German provinces which would therefore have remained with Pupienus. In my opinion, this is a mistake. We are here dealing with real allied forces, which is also clear from the statement of Herodian (8.6.8). These Germans had been sent by their own states.
38. This and following is primarily based on Herodian 8.7.1ff. with *HA MB* 11.1ff.
39. Herodian 8.7.7ff.; *HA MB* 11.1ff.
40. Loriot 1975a, 713–4.
41. Loriot (1975a, 714–5), (1998, 52–3); Birley, 1998, 65–7; with references to Townsend's suggestions in both.
42. HA *MB 16.3* = Dexippus of Athens which in the latest edition and translation of all fragments of Dexippus by Gunther Martin is included in the 'Spuria et Incerta' pp.146–7; Peter the Patrician, Banchich ed. F 170 (p.111) = Müller FHG 4, pp.186–7.
43. This sentence means that if the Carpi wanted to show obedience to the Emperor (i.e. become clients of the Roman Empire), the Emperor could hammer the joint/welding to unite them.
44. Loriot 1975a, 713–7; Drinkwater after Loriot and others in *CAH*, 33.
45. For this, see Syvänne, *Gallienus*, 29–36.
46. Zonaras 12.17 and Syncellus (AM5731) are incorrect in stating that Nisibis and Carrhae were lost under Maximinus because Herodian (7.8.4) states in no uncertain terms that the Persians 'feared' the Romans when Maximinus was in power and did nothing. REF1, 32–3 collects the evidence for the Persian attack. The only solid dates are the graffito that mentions the Persian attack against Dura Europos on 20 April 239 and the capture of Hatra in 240. This means that the Persians probably started to prepare the invasion very soon after they had learnt of the Roman civil war and that it was launched only in 239 after the preparations were complete.
47. This and the following is based on: Herodian 8.8.1ff.; *HA MB* 12.1ff.

Chapter 6
1. The principal source for the reign of Gordian III is Julius Capitolinus (*HA Gord.* 22.1ff.).
2. The number of Gordian's edicts in the *CJ* varies according to the researcher. E.g. Hermann (p.96) gives 271, but other researchers suggest 222 or 275. See later.

3. Drinkwater, CAH, 33–4; Loriot 1975a, 726–8.
4. Drinkwater, CAH, 33–4; Loriot 1975a, 729–34.
5. Loriot 1975a, 729–34; Herrmann, 120ff.
6. Corrected from 500⁰/00.
7. Loriot 1975a, 733–5.
8. Notably he appears to have been related to Egnatia Mariniana, the wife of P. Licinius Valerianus, the future emperor Valerian, who was a member of the senatorial block and Gordian Faction within it. See Loriot 1975a, 743.
9. Loriot 1975a, 726ff., 743–4; Drinkwater, *CAH*, 33–4. For the legislative work, see in particular Hermann, 96ff. Note, however, that Herrmann (96) and Loriot (1975a, 742) have calculated the number of Gordian's laws/edicts preserved in the Codex Iustinianus differently. On the basis of modern studies Herrmann claims that there 271 laws while Loriot calculates only 222. The difference is significant, but it is beyond the scope of this study to discuss this problem.
10. *HA MB* 23.4–5; Loriot 1975a, 734–5. According to Loriot, Restitutianus is attested at Mauretania Caesariensis in 239–40 and he became Prefect of the Vigiles in ca. 243–4. Loriot also notes that J. R. Rea suggests that he was active in in Egypt in 250.
11. This and the following discussion of the North African troubles is based on Loriot 1975a, 745–53. The analysis of the Moors as a military threat is based on Syvänne, *MHLR Vol.1* (146–56) and Syvänne, *The Age of Hippotoxotai* (398–403). *MHLR Vol.1* lists the differences between the tribes and confederacies.
12. This has led some to speculate that the late Roman *limitanei* farmer-soldiers were created either under Alexander Severus (the *HA* refers to these under him) or by Gordian III. This is wrong. Firstly, it is a misunderstanding of the sources that the *limitanei* were farmer-soldiers. They were soldiers who were supported by local farms. Secondly, the army had been posted along the frontiers from the first century onwards and were therefore frontier soldiers (*limitanei*) from that date onwards even if they were not called with this title yet. Thirdly, the army had always been supported from the local sources whenever this was possible.
13. Loriot 1975a, 747–51; Mattingly, 83–5.
14. Loriot 1975a, 751–3.
15. Loriot 1975a, 753–4.
16. E.g. Loriot 1975a, 716–7, 759–60; Kettenhofen, 21–2; Syvänne and Maksymiuk, 74–5.
17. The sources of the Persian war collected and translated in REF1, 32–45. For the dating of the siege of Hatra, see Syvänne and Maksymiuk (74–5) and Loriot 1975a (761–2) and Kettenhofen, 20.
18. Loriot 1975a, 760–1.
19. The principal source for the reign of Gordian III is Julius Capitolinus (*HA Gord.* 22.1ff.).
20. There were at least two praetorian prefects simultaneously in office. In the beginning of Gordian's reign one Aedinius Julianus held the prefecture, while in 240 the sources mention one Domitius holding the office. See Ensslin, CAH, 82. It is not entirely certain who was Julianus's partner in office or Domitius's partner, but it appears probable that Felicio was only appointed to the post as a result of Macia Faustina's machinations.
21. This list is based on Ensslin and Herrmann (p.175) whose list is based on Johne (2008) and *Codex Iustinianus*.
22. Loriot 1975a, 742–3 has 222 laws while Loriot claims on p.776 that there were 275 laws. The discrepancy is probably an accidental mistake that Loriot just failed to note.
23. Tabari i.828–30 with the REF1 283–5. Even with the 'romantic' undertones, the story of al-Tabari is plausible, not least because it explains why an almost impregnable city was taken in so short a time by Sapor when so many Roman emperors had been frustrated in their attempts to take Hatra. It is entirely plausible that an inexperienced and foolish young virgin could fall madly in love with a handsome king. Syvänne and Maksymiuk (74–5) provide an alternative account of this war.

24. See Syvänne and Maksymiuk, 75–7.
25. Listed in Loriot (1975a, 763–5) who also belongs to the doubters like Kettenhofen (22) and York (22–3). York and Loriot both maintain that Antioch remained in Roman hands throughout the war so we should discard the evidence presented by Julius Capitolinus. Funnily enough both note that the minting of coins can be used as evidence of either continued Roman occupation or of its loss. Loriot notes that Fink and others claim there was a cessation in the minting of coins in Antioch in 240–42, while York argues for continued occupation by basing this on the studies of Bellinger and Welles that claim that there was no cessation in minting. As can be seen, the same material can be used to argue opposite claims. Neither, however, is conclusive because even if the mint of Antioch had continued to mint coins through 240–42, and specifically 242, this proves nothing because the mint could have minted its first series for 242 in early 242 before the Persians captured the city and the second after the Romans had recaptured it in late 242. In short, it is safest to accept the claim of Julius Capitolinus that the Persians captured Antioch.
26. Loriot (1975a, 762) also suggests that the Persians captured the legionary camps of Resaina and Singara.
27. Tabari i.826.
28. Date in Loriot 1975a, 728.
29. Ensslin, *CAH*, 85–6; Loriot 1975a, 736–8; York, 12–7.
30. Loriot 1975a, 738–40; Potter, 230–1.
31. *Eis Basilea 11–2, 20*; Ensslin, *CAH*, 87; Loriot 1975a, 740–2; Potter, 230–1; York, 16–9 (confuses the Philippi); Körner, 2002, 49ff., 71ff., 366.
32. Loriot 1975a, 742; Potter, 230–1.
33. Based on Loriot (1975a, 765–6) so that his information is expanded with additional conclusions based on the material provided by him.
34. Eutropius 9..2; Loriot 1975a, 766; Christol, 98.
35. Loriot 1975a, 766.
36. Loriot 1975a, 754–5.
37. Loriot 1975a, 755.
38. The nations mentioned by Julius Capitolinus are quoted below. The name of the Carpi is added to this list on the basis of Peter the Patrician who notes that the Carpi remained at peace until 241 with the implication that in 242 they joined the others in invading Roman territory.
39. Loriot 1975a, 766–7.
40. For a discussion of similar Roman responses during the first century AD, see Syvänne (2011c-d), available online at academia.edu.
41. Loriot 1975a, 767–70; Kettenhofen, 23–7.
42. Loriot 1975a, 769; Christol 99 agrees with Loriot's view.
43. For a discussion of these events, see: Syvänne, Gallienus, 70, 85; Syvänne and Maksymiuk, 85–95.
44. Christol, 99.
45. For a discussion of the oppressive Zoroastrian police state customs, see Syvänne 2016.
46. For Roman uses of the hollow oblong and square arrays, see Syvänne (2011c-d, the latter available online at academia.edu), *Caracalla* (179, 284ff.) and *MHLR Vol.2* (17–20).
47. Sources collected in REF1, 35–45.
48. Ibid.
49. The relevant texts have also been translated by Banchich/Zonaras (p.90 after Cedrenus p.441, Scutariotes/Synopsis Sathas 33.10–2).
50. The question of whether Philip murdered Timesitheus or not has divided historians. Some accept it, as do I and York (25–7), (Zahran lists the historians who accept the claim that Philip murdered Timesitheus), while others oppose this view like Zahran (54ff.), Loriot (1975a, 769–70) and Körner (2002, 72). In my opinion, in light of the evidence, the case for the murdering

is stronger than the case against it even if one cannot ultimately know. Philip certainly had good reasons to kill Timesitheus. However, I do not accept York's claim that Philip/Priscus and Timesitheus belonged to opposing factions within the court and Senate, because it is clear that Timesitheus actually promoted the careers of both, as stated by Loriot. Philip was an ambitious man who had his own reasons to fear Timesitheus.

51. Eusebius (*Ecclesiastical History* 6.34) and most sources after him call Philip Christian and in light of the evidence this is likely. It is probable that the brothers owed their careers mostly to the religious tolerance prevailing under Alexander Severus.

52. Various views are collected in Swift, who also provides a translation and commentary of the text.

53. Translation (13) by Louis J. Swift p.275.

54. In this context it should be noted that many historians are much too ready to accept Sapor's propaganda at its face value. The fact that it is period evidence does not make it definitely true. The Sassanians were entirely capable of fabricating stories. Sapor did not have any real opposition to his claims inside the Persian Empire. He controlled the 'media'. In contrast, the Roman sources portray a great variety of different views. Like the Sassanian *shahanshahs*, the Roman emperors did try to control the media (historians and public announcements), but the fact that the Romans didn't have one single dynasty in power but a succession of individuals or dynasties that were at odds with each other ensured better survival of contrasting views. In short, the Roman emperors were not as successful as the Sassanians in their attempts to limit the spread of news.

55. The story can be found in Malalas, Zonaras and Georgius Monachus (sources collected in REF 43–44). See the quotes included here. The story of the death resulting from the fall is likely to have been borrowed from the false report of Philip to the Senate (See REF1, p.357 n.23).

56. This and the following account is based on the sources collected in REF1, 34–45, excepting the anonymous Encomium of Philip the Arab (13–15) which adds very important material, and Jordanes (*Romana* 282–3), and Orosius (7.19). The account of Syvänne and Maksymiuk of the Persian War of Gordian (79–82) is essentially the same in its main conclusions, but I add here some additional comments and material which are not included in it. This especially concerns the details of combat and material derived from the Encomium (esp. 13–15). The question of whether Philip the Arab murdered Gordian or whether he died as a result of falling from the horse or whether he was killed in battle has divided opinion among the historians. Some like Zahran (55f.) and York (27–51) see in the claim of murder a bias against Philip because he was an Arab, or that there is no way of knowing if Philip had any role in the murder of Gordian committed by the Roman army as Potter (236) and Southern (2001, 70) think. As will be shown, and contrary to the popular view among modern historians, the account of Julius Capitolinus in particular is not confused but has actually preserved for us an accurate report of the events when those are put on the map.

57. For the location of Zaitha vis-à-vis Dura Europos, see James (12) and Kettehofen (maps). Drinkwater (*CAH*, 36) and all the modern historians who claim that Philip was deep inside the Persian territory at the time of Gordian's murder are entirely mistaken. Their view rests solely on the assumption that Gordian died at Mesikhe or very close to it, but this is not supported by the extant Roman sources. Sapor's propaganda is not to be trusted as we shall see. In practical terms the Romans had already reached Roman territory as the opposite shore belonged to Rome. There is therefore every reason to believe that Philip had cleverly machinated the lack of provisions, as claimed by the Roman sources.

58. Körner (2002, 329ff.) lists all the senators and procurators under Philip. The list includes obvious candidates for other officers, generals and governors that supported Philip on this occasion. The list with the careers and sources for this information is too long to include here, but it is probable that Philip's supporters from it included Agilius/Attilius Cosmianus/

Cominius/Cosminus (legate in Coele Syria under Philip); Antonius Memmius Hiero (legate in Cappadocia 244–7, probably given this post when Philip marched to Rome in 244); Coresnius Marcellus (legate in Thrace 244–9, probably left in Thrace when Philip marched through it); Q. Caecilius Pudens legate in Germania Superior 244–7, probably participated in the eastern campaign because he was rewarded with this); Claudius Capitolinus (Bassus?) (legate in Arabia 245/6); Claudius Herennianus (legate in Dalmatia in 247, may have been rewarded with this for services redendered); L. Egnatius Victor Lollianus (*proconsul Asiae* 244–7, possibly left there when Philip marched to Rome, and possibly *praefectus urbi* under Philip), Sex. Furnius Publianus (legate in Thrace 247–9), C. Ulpius Prastina Messalinus (governor of Moesia Inferior 244–7), …sulan(us) (legate in Syria 244–7); Flavius Antiochus (governor of Syria 244–9) D. Simonius Proculus Iulianus (legate in Syria Coele in 245, and possibly *praefectus urbi* under Philip); Aelius Aemilianus (*praefectus classis praetoria Misenensis* in 28.12.247); Licinnius Pacatianus (*dux ripae* in 245) and so forth.
59. Körner (2002, 32ff. 63–4); Bowersock (1983, 123); York (17); Meckler and Körner; Zahran, 72–3. It is not known with certainty whether Priscus was really the older brother. This is an assumption based on the fact that he became Praetorian Prefect before his brother Philip.
60. The dating is based on Loriot (1975a, 774; 1975b, 789).
61. Loriot 1975a, 775–7.

Chapter 7
1. Dating is based on Loriot (1975a, 774; 1975b, 789).
2. Christol. 100; Körner, 2002, 123–4.
3. Sources collected in REF1, 45–50.
4. See REF 48 *(alae novae firmae miliariae catafractiae Philipianae)*.
5. York, 52–3; Körner, 2002, 391–3. Körner lists the progressive confusion in the name of Hostilianus into Severus Stilianus, Oustilianos, Ioustillianos, Ioustilianos and then finally into Ioustinianos in the 'Byzantine' sources.
6. The following discussion is based on Estiot, Meckler and Körner, Körner (2002, 386–91) and Syvänne (Gallienus, 41–2; Aurelian and Probus) and sources mentioned therein, but I suggest new alternative solutions to the problems of identity missing from these.
7. Loriot 1975b,
8. Christol, 100; Körner, 2002, 131.
9. Christol, 103–4; Körner, 211ff.; York, 53–4; Zahran, 70–1.
10. Unknown Arian historian in Philostorgius, *Appendix 7* (p.205) in Amidon edition and translation = *Chronicon Paschale* anno 253. The question of Christianity is discussed by: York, 89ff. (accepts Philip as Christian); Zahran, 105ff. (accepts Christianity); Shahid, 65ff. (accepts); Körner (2002, 260–73) does not accept Philip as Christian. York includes other examples of historians, besides myself, who think that the conversion of Philip might have taken place only later in 248. However, in this study I have tentatively accepted that the conversion took place before Easter 244 and the Easter visit took place in 244. All of the arguments for and against Philip's Christianity are presented in these studies. My personal opinion is that the argument for Philip being Christian is far stronger than the case against it. His performance of the duties as a pagan ruler does not prove him to have been a pagan. As aptly noted by Yasmine Zahran, had this been the case then Constantine the Great and his sons should not be considered Christians either because they were pagan priests too while being Christians.
11. York (54–5), Christol (104–5) and Körner (2002, 63–4) with the sources quoted.
12. For the date, see Körner (2002, 95–7) who reverses the earlier dating based on extant inscriptions which suggested that Philip returned to Rome before 23 July. The fact that Pomponius Iulianus was still in charge of the reserves of the *legio II Parthica* left behind in Rome on 23 July means that Philip had not yet returned. This Pomponius may have had an important role in the killing of Marcus Silbannacus.

210   Gordian III and Philip the Arab

13. Christol, 104–5; York, 55, Körner, 2002, 95–7.
14. For a fuller discussion of the careers, see Körner, 2002, 190ff., 329ff.. For a list of known influential persons under Philip the Arab, see Körner, 2002, Appendix I: Senatoren und Procuratoren unter Philipp, pp. 329–85.
15. See e.g. Frontinus (*Stratagems* 1.9.13); Suetonius (Caesar, 59); Syvänne, *Aurelian and Probus*.
16. Brauer, 11ff. (Despite what Eusebius and other Christian sources and the later 'Byzantine' sources state, Brauer does not consider Philip as Christian, but only open-minded towards it. I disagree with this view and rather follow what the sources state); York, 35–6, 122ff.; Christol, 106–8; Potter, 238–9; Ensslin, 89–90; Cascio,161; Körner, 238ff..
17. Zahran, 90–2; Potter, 238–40. Potter does not consider the debasing of silver coinage as dramatic, but I do.
18. For a fuller discussion, see Ensslin (89–90) and especially York (122ff.), Körner (2002, 158–89) and Zahran (90ff.). The number of laws credited to the reign of Gordian III is disputed and Loriot (1975a, 742–3,.776) even includes two different figures in the same study – what is certain, however, is that Gordian's administration was one of the busiest as far as legislative work is concerned. Modern research therefore seems to confirm the laudatory remarks of *Eis Basilea* (17–10) which praises Philip as a judge, which was the result of his own education.
19. Loriot 1975b, 792–3; Körner, 2002, 146ff.; York, 57–8. Note, however, that Korner reconstructs the dates of the adoption of the titles and wars differently.
20. Dating of the title in York, 57.
21. For an alternative reconstruction of the Danubian wars, see Körner (2002, 134–57).
22. For a discussion of the war between Cniva/Kniva and Decius, see Syvänne, *Gallienus*, 31–6.
23. See Syvänne, *Gallienus*, 36.
24. See Syvänne, *Caracalla*, 317–8. In the latest edition of Julius Africanus' *Kestoi* by Guignard et al the relevant part is in D11/F12.2.43ff. (p.45.43ff.).
25. Date in Loriot 1975b, 793.
26. See Syvänne, *Gallienus*, 33–6, 70–5.
27. See Syvänne, 2011c-d, and *Gallienus*.
28. York, 58; Loriot 1976b, 792; Christol, 106.
29. Bohec, 2005, 83; Körner, 2002, 243ff.
30. Ensslin, 90; Brauer, 12; Zahran, 120.
31. Ensslin, 90–1, York, 59–60.
32. Julius Capitolinus *HA Gord.* 33.1–2; Jerome (Eusebius-Hieronymus, *Chronica* anno 249); Bird/Victor, 126; York, 58–62; Ensslin 91.
33. For a discussion of Caracalla's reaction, see Syvänne, *Caracalla*, 226. For the outrageous behaviour of Elagabalus, see e.g. Herodian 5.5.7ff.; *HA Elagabalus* 5.3ff. Dio 80.11.1ff.. Elagabalus was a bisexual person who practised the submissive 'female' version of the homosexual relationship, which was not acceptable even to those who accepted homosexual behaviour; he chose praetorian prefects and city prefects on the basis of the size of their penis; Elagabalus wanted to cut off his genitals to get a vagina, and so forth.
34. York, 122ff.; Zahran, 90 after York.
35. *Eis Basilea*, 1, 21, 29–36.
36. Eusebius, *Ecclesiastical History* 6.41; York, 73–5; Syvänne, Gallienus, 43, 89–91, 106–9.
37. Zahran, 123.
38. Körner, 1999 and 2002, 277–82; York, 68ff.
39. York, 68–73.
40. For the actions of Valerian, Macrianus, Ballista, and Odaenathus, see Syvänne, *Gallienus*, 37, 43, 46, 65, 67, 88–91.
41. Syvänne and Maksymiuk, 108.
42. See e.g. Ensslin, 93; Southern, 2001, 73–4; Bird/Victor, p.127; Christol, 119.

43. Körner, 1999, and 2002, 282–8. Körner lists the various theories regarding Pacatianus's career on the basis of inscriptions, which I have not included here because the important point here is that Pacatianus was supported by the troops of Moesia and Pannonia.
44. For further information, see Körner (1999) and (2002, 283–8).
45. See e.g. Ensslin, 93; Southern, 2001, 73–4; Bird/Victor, p.127; Christol, 119.
46. Zahran, 126–7; York, 75–88.
47. For a discussion of Eugenia, see Zonaras/Banchich, 47, 91–2. And, for a discussion of St. Cyrinus/Quirinus, see York, 106ff.
48. I.e. he is not to be classed among the bad emperors as he is in *HA Aur.* 42.6.
49. In fact, *Eis Basileia* (7) praises Philip precisely because his rise to power had not caused harm and bloodshed to the Romans even if the text funnily calls his rise to power just and proper and without bloodshed (5–8).

Index